Dynamics of Regulatory Change

Dynamics of Regulatory Change

How Globalization Affects National Regulatory Policies

Edited by David Vogel and Robert A. Kagan

UNIVERSITY OF CALIFORNIA PRESS
Berkeley • Los Angeles • London

UCIAS is a partnership of the University of California Press, the California Digital Library (CDL), and internationally oriented research units on eight UC campuses. The Digital Collection publishes articles, monographs, and edited volumes that are peer-reviewed according to standards set by an interdisciplinary UCIAS Editorial Board and approved by the University of California Press. UCIAS makes digital versions of these works available free of charge to a global network of scholars and encourages international intellectual exchange and research collaboration.

University of California Press
Berkeley and Los Angeles, California

University of California Press, Ltd.
London, England

© 2004 by the Regents of the University of California

Library of Congress Cataloging-in-Publication Data available upon request

ISBN 0-520-24535-0

Manufactured in the United States of America

This book is a print-on-demand volume. It is manufactured using toner in place of ink. Type and images may be less sharp than the same material seen in traditionally printed University of California Press editions.

Contents

Introduction

Dynamics of Regulatory Change
How Globalization Affects National Regulatory Policies

David Vogel and Robert A. Kagan

I. INTRODUCTION

The intellectual impetus for this volume emerged from the issues addressed in *Trading Up: Consumer and Environmental Regulation in a Global Economy* written by David Vogel (1995), one of the volume's editors. In *Trading Up*, Vogel explicitly challenged the claim made by globalization critics, especially those from the environmental community, that economic liberalization leads to a lowering of regulatory standards. Vogel argues that, on the contrary, under certain circumstances, global economic integration can actually lead to the strengthening of consumer and environmental standards. The result is thus more akin to a "race to the top" than to a "race to the bottom."

Trading Up primarily dealt with one category of national policies—those that governed the safety and environmental impact of traded products. The aim of this volume is to extend the focus of *Trading Up* by focusing on a broader array of issue areas. Since the impacts of globalization are likely to vary by policy area, we solicited essays on the impact of globalization on labor rights, women's rights and capital market regulations, in addition to environmental standards.

This volume both draws upon and contributes to an ongoing body of scholarship on the impact of globalization. In 1996, two edited volumes were published on the domestic impact of economic interdependence: *National Diversity and Global Capitalism*, edited by Suzanne Berger and Ronald Dore, and *Internationalization and Domestic Politics*, edited by Helen Milner and Robert Keohane. This volume expands the focus of these collaborative research projects in a number of ways.

Nearly all the essays in the Milner and Keohane volume deal with the impact of globalization on macro-economic and sectoral policies. One essay, by Haggard and Maxfeld, deals with financial regulations in developing countries, but only on one aspect, namely the impact of these regulations on international capital flows. The essays in the Berger and Dore volume are more diverse. Several deal with the impact of globalization on the nature of capitalism. Thus they examine the dynamics of convergence and divergence with respect to industrial policy, corporate governance and competition policy.

The focus of this volume is distinctive in that it addresses the impact of globalization on government regulation. We are interested in exploring not only the extent to which globalization impacts national policies, which is the central concern of the Milner/Keohane and Berger/Dore volumes, but the direction of this impact. To the extent that globalization affects national regulatory policies, to what extent and under what circumstances does it strengthen or weaken them? Thus this volume represents one of the first efforts to systematically investigate the existence and dynamics of the possible "race to the top," or "race to the bottom."

This introductory essay consists of three parts. The first provides an overview of the scholarly literature on the impact of globalization on regulatory policies. The second explores the scholarly debate on the "California effect," introduced in *Trading Up*. The third presents an analytical overview of the ten essays published in this volume.

We would like to express our appreciation for the generous financial support provided by the Center for German and European Studies at the University of California, Berkeley and as well as to the Center for the Study of Law and Society for hosting our seminars and workshop. This project would never have come to fruition without the dedicated assistance of Diahanna Post who worked with us closely from its inception to completion.

II. RACE TO THE BOTTOM?

The impact of globalization on the regulatory policies of governments has been the focus of considerable public debate and scholarly research. The public debate has been largely shaped by critics of globalization, who claim that the integration of national economies has undermined national autonomy and forced nations to relax their regulatory standards. According to this perspective, as capital and corporations move more freely across national boundaries, governments are forced to engage in regulatory competition. In order to either retain current investments or attract new ones, they must lower the costs of doing business. One way of doing so is to weaken labor and environmental standards. The result is a "race to the bottom" as political jurisdictions compete with one another by progressively reducing the protections they provide to their citizens.

The political influence of the "race to the bottom" (RTB) imagery has been considerable. It informs much of the recent opposition to globalization in general and trade liberalization in particular, most notably in the United States, but also in Europe. In the United States, trade unions, along with environmentalists and citizen groups such as Ralph Nader's Public Citizen, have blamed globalization for undermining worker rights and working conditions and for impairing environmental quality and consumer protection. Much of their ire, as revealed by the demonstrations in Seattle against the ministerial meeting of the World Trade Organization in 2000 and at the World Economic Forum in Davos in January 2000 and 2001, has been directed at institutions and agreements that seek to facilitate international flows of trade, finance and investment (Wallach and Sforza 1999). Thus Donahue (1994: 47) writes: "The world has become a huge bazaar with nations peddling their workforces in competition against one another, offering the lowest price." According to Daley (1993: 27), whose critique of globalization has focused on its impact on environmental regulation, "unrestricted trade imposes lower standards."

Among scholars, the notion of a regulatory race to the bottom derives from the study of competition within federal systems, most notably the United States. Students of corporate law have employed it to explain the weakness of state corporate chartering laws in the United States. Because corporations could be chartered in any state, and this charter allowed them to conduct business in all the others, states competed to relax their chartering requirements in order to attract the revenues from chartering. The "winner" in this competition is Delaware, whose chartering rules are considered most favorable to management. In effect, Delaware's floor became a ceiling for other states. The concept of the "Delaware effect" was subsequently employed to denote other examples of devolution within federal systems, such as the existence of pollution havens that attract runaway factories. As trade liberalization made competition among countries more similar to that among American states, the Delaware effect became a model for a hypothesized international race to the bottom.

Over the last decade, an extensive scholarly literature has emerged on the impact of globalization on national policies. Most scholars have found little support for the claim that increased economic integration has undermined either the autonomy of governments or their ability to protect their citizens.[1] Geoffrey Garrett (1998) argues that globalization has been far less constraining than many of its critics have alleged. In fact, he observes that increased market integration has commonly been associated with more interventionist government policies and greater policy divergence among nations. Among OECD countries, government spending and effective rates of corporate taxation have tended to increase even as their economies have become more integrated—without resulting in capital flight. Nor has the autonomy of governments over their fiscal policies been reduced, although their ability to run substantial deficits has been constrained.

In seeking to explain why governments have not reduced either the size or scope of their welfare states in order to become more "competitive," Garrett argues that more conservative social policies do not necessarily improve international competitiveness. On the contrary, a more generous social safety net may actually strengthen the ability of governments to adjust to rapidly changing international market conditions. Thus, even to the extent that concerns about competitiveness do affect national policy-making, these concerns do not dictate either any particular mix of policies or less progressive ones. Globalization has produced neither policy convergence nor a race to the bottom.

The contributors to *National Diversity and Global Capitalism* also find limited evidence of policy convergence with respect to either macroeconomic policies or micro-policies. National differences in interest rates, as well as corporate governance and the organization of production, remain substantial. They do find evidence of convergence in some policy areas, such as competition policy, but these they attribute to a gradual process of institutional adoption rather than to global economic constraints.[2]

Miles Kahler (1998) notes the difficulty of measuring and explaining possible gaps between popular preferences and national policies—a gap whose existence is asserted by RTB. He claims that the best indirect evidence of regulatory laxity as an instrument of international competition would be national policy convergence. "If policy convergence is absent, the case for a RTB is undermined" (Kahler 1998: 15). Yet he observes little evidence of increased convergence even in areas such as taxation where presumably differences in national policies would be expected to have important competitive consequences. He concludes: "If a RTB had been completed, no tax havens, offshore banking or Delaware effect would remain: the 'bottom' would have been reached" (Kahler 1998: 19).

While policy convergence may be a necessary sign of the existence of a RTB, factors other than economic pressures may lead countries to adopt similar policies. Bennett (1991) identifies four mechanisms of policy convergence. These are emulation, when state officials copy action taken elsewhere; elite networking, characterized by the role of transnational policy communities; harmonization though international regimes; and penetration by external actors and interests. According to Bennett, all but the lattermost are compatible with the maintenance of state autonomy. But even penetration is not necessarily associated with RTB, as transnational actors can use their influence to pressure countries to raise standards as well as lower them.

Much of the literature on the impact of globalization has focused on environmental regulation. One such study examines trends in urban air quality in China, Brazil, Mexico and the United States. David Wheeler, who works with the World Bank, reasons that if the RTB model were valid, then "after decades of increasing capital mobility and economic liberalization . . . pollution should be increasing everywhere. It should be rising in poor countries because they are pollution havens, and in high-income economies because they are relaxing standards to remain cost-competitive" (Wheeler 2000: 3). Yet Wheeler's data reveals that contrary to the predictions of RTB, major urban areas in China, Brazil, Mexico and the US have all experienced significant improvements in air quality.

According to Wheeler, empirical research has undermined each of the assumptions that underlie RTB. First, while the RTB model assumes that pollution control is a critical cost for most firms—hence their incentive to relocate to pollution havens—in fact compliance costs are relatively modest. Second, low-income communities do not passively accept polluting firms; they often mobilize to pressure such companies to improve their environmental performance, even in the absence of effective government regulation. Third, as countries become richer, environmental regulations invariably become more effective. Finally, large multinational firms generally adhere to OECD standards in their developing country operations.

This last point is documented in David Sonnenfeld's (2002) study of the impact of social movements in rich countries on pulp and paper manufacturing in developing countries. Sonnenfeld finds that these social movements, based primarily in northern Europe, along with government agencies, have played a critical role in transforming pulp and paper production in Southeast Asia. Thus foreign investment has served as a vehicle to improve environmental performance in developing countries. Ronie Garcia-Johnson makes a similar argument in *Exporting Environmentalism* (2000), which documents the role of American based multinationals in promoting a voluntary code of environmental responsibility among foreign and domestic chemical firms in Mexico and Brazil.

That is not to say that rich-world multinational corporations invariably impose identical pollution controls on their third-world factories. A Tufts University study found that in many cases American corporations' operations in developing countries were less protective of the environment (partly due to inadequate local infrastructure and a less experienced workforce) than their U.S. facilities. Yet others found cases where environmental measures in overseas operations "were more innovative than the comparable U.S. facility" (Rappaport and Flaherty 1992: 138; see also Fowler 1995).

Other cross-national studies of environmental standards and performance, primarily among relatively developed countries, demonstrate the extent to which globalization has proven compatible with improved environmental performance in many areas.[3] Note however, that such studies do not by themselves refute the claim that globalization has created a "political drag effect."[4] For even if environmental conditions have improved along with globalization, governments may still be reluctant to mandate the still higher levels of environmental protection preferred by their citizens because they fear a loss of competitiveness—even if such fears are in fact unwarranted. It is, of course, difficult to specify how much stricter some national environmental standards might be if the global economy was less integrated. Alternatively, factors other than concerns about international competitiveness may temper the level of national regulatory standards and the vigor with which they are enforced.

The claim that political jurisdictions are not forced to lower regulatory standards to attract investment is supported by the extensive empirical literature on both the interstate and international effects of environmental regulation. These studies all come to a similar conclusion, namely that environmental regulations have had little impact on firm location decisions. Thus there is no evidence that either those American states or countries that have relatively strict environmental standards have experienced greater difficulty in attracting or retaining investments than political jurisdictions with laxer standards (Jaffee 1995; Levinson 1996; and Stewart 1993).

In this context, it is worth recalling that most international investment, as well as international trade, takes place among relatively rich countries, whose environmental standards are roughly comparable. While some studies point to large growth of direct overseas investment in high-pollution industries in lesser developed nations (Low and Yeats, 1992: 98), Anderson and Kagan (2000) found that US overseas investment in dirty industries" has grown more rapidly in *OECD* countries than in lesser-developed countries. Because OECD countries feature more strict regulations and more effective enforcement than lesser-developed countries, this investment trend tends to undercut the "pollution haven" hypothesis.

Of course, the environmental policies of all countries may not be equally unaffected by the constraints of international competition. Porter (1999) argues that the problem is not the existence of a RTB in relatively rich countries. As he notes: "no empirical evidence has been found that any OECD country has settled for suboptimal environmental standards in response to international competitiveness concerns" (Porter 1999: 138). Rather, he opines that the negative impacts of competitiveness concerns are to be found in rapidly industrializing countries, many of whom have been reluctant to enforce their environmental standards out of fear that their economies will suffer a competitive disadvantage vis-à-vis other relatively poor nations. The regulatory standards of these countries, he claims, are "stuck at the bottom." Thus, they are "dragging down" the regulatory standards not of rich countries but of other poor ones. Porter, however, does not offer any systematic evidence to support this contention.

Spar and Yoffie advance a theoretical explanation for why increased capital mobility has not invariably created a "downward spiral or rivalry that works to lower standards among all affected parties" (Spar and Yoffie 2000: 1). They argue that multinational firms are most likely to have a negative impact on national regulations when four circumstances hold: the products or key inputs for the firms are homogeneous, cross-border differentials are significant, and both sunk and transaction costs are minimal. Since all four circumstances rarely hold, firms in most international industries have neither the capacity nor the incentive to freely move their facilities around the world, thus pressuring governments into lowering their standards.

In addition to suggesting how races to the bottom are forestalled by the internal dynamics of various industries, Spar and Yoffie show how the establishment of common standards can curtail "races," even after they begin. These can either by imposed by agreements among governments, as in the case of international environmental treaties, or through private initiatives. The latter are playing an increasingly important role in the areas of human rights and labor standards, as well as in the environmental policies of some international industries. Their analysis points to an important dimension of globalization, namely that it involves more than the exchange of economic inputs and outputs. It also is associated with the spread of values and norms across national boundaries.

Bernstein and Cashore (2000) make a useful distinction between globalization, by which they refer to structural economic factors associated with rising levels of trade, finance and direct foreign investment, and internationalization, which involves the influence of transnational actors and institutions, and the rules and norms they embody, on domestic policy. They argue that "global economic factors alone generally do not determine the direction of domestic policy responses" to international pressures (Bernstein and Cashore 2000: 73). The four paths of internationalization they identify—market dependence, international rules, international normative discourse and infiltration of the domestic policy process—also have a major effect on domestic policy and may either complement or challenge the effects of economic globalization.

These latter two analyses point to an important insight: to understand the dynamics of globalization as well as the extent and direction of its impact on national policies, we need to examine not only its economic dimensions, but its legal and social ones as well. Globalization is associated not only with increased economic interdependence but with an expansion of international political and social interaction. The latter includes the adoption of common regulatory policies though international agreements, as well as the spread of international norms and advocacy networks.[5]

III. THE CALIFORNIA EFFECT

The "California effect" offers a model of firm behavior that is the mirror image of the Delaware effect and its "race to the bottom." The California effect is predicated on the existence of relatively large, highly regulated markets in the world's richest countries. Firms seeking to export to these markets must meet the latter's relatively strict environmental and consumer standards. Having been forced to adjust their exports to meet these standards, it is then in their interest to have their home country adopt similar regulatory standards, since this enables them to achieve better economies of scale by producing more similar products. Higher regulatory standards may also give them some advantage vis-à-vis domestic competitors who have not geared up to meet the standards of "stringent regulation" countries. To the extent that it is easier for domestic firms to comply with relatively strict regulatory standards than it is for rival firms from less regulated jurisdictions, the former will advocate stricter standards, often in alliance with non-governmental organizations (NGOs). Without global markets, there would be fewer such coalitions between Baptists (environmentalists) and bootleggers (certain regulated firms), since bootleggers would have less incentive to support stricter regulatory standards in order to disadvantage foreign competitors.

Thus trade liberalization can strengthen regulatory standards in two ways: it facilitates the "export" of stricter standards and it encourages firms to support stricter domestic standards than they otherwise might prefer. In short, stricter regulatory standards can be a source of competitive advantage. Kahler writes, "Essentially, Vogel argues that the scale of home country market in firm calculations forces transaction cost considerations to the fore, rather than production cost burdens" (Kahler 1998: 22). Yet at the same time, as Kahler notes, Vogel's model suggests conditions under which the export of regulatory standards might weaken or fail.

First, the model assumes that nations with larger markets prefer more stringent regulations. While this may be true in the case of environmental and consumer standards, since affluence and social regulation are strongly correlated, it does not necessarily hold for other areas of regulation, such as financial and telecommunications. In the latter areas, rich countries such as the United States may prefer less stringent standards—due in part to the political influence of domestic firms—which are then "exported." In addition, "the contribution of home country regulation to production costs must not outweigh the transaction costs benefits of operating with similar standards abroad, and forcing competitors to meet host country standards at home" (Kahler 1998: 23). Kahler suggests that while environmental regulation in rich countries may pass this cost/benefit calculation, taxation probably does not.

Vogel (1995) acknowledges that the California effect does not even apply to all aspects of environmental regulation. Its effectiveness may be largely limited to product regulation, since these regulations directly affect environmental quality and health and safety in the consuming country. But much environmental regulation is geared toward production processes. Scharpf (1995) observes that there is no incentive for producers to adopt stricter foreign process standards since "such regulations do not affect the usability, the safety or quality of products so produced." He adds: "Steel from furnaces with high sulfur dioxide emissions is indistinguishable from steel produced with the most expensive emission controls—and the same is true for automobiles produced by workers with or without paid sick leave in firms with or without codetermination."

According to Swire, "Vogel's analysis . . . shows the central role that public choice plays in driving competition among jurisdictions" (Swire 1996: 81). In addition to the two mechanisms of "trading up" that Vogel cites, namely that international-oriented producers will support the stricter standards once they are already complying with that standard in the greener market," (81) and that "domestic producers can hope to gain market share by helping craft environmental or safety standards to their own advantage" (82), Swire offers a third mechanism: "the demonstration effect of the strict standard—the ability of producers to meet the strict standard in one jurisdiction proves that the standard is technologically achievable at reasonable cost" (82). Yet, like Scharpf, Swire argues that Vogel's "Race to Strictness" analysis applies to only a highly limited subset of environmental laws, namely those that govern product standards. But "a large fraction of environmental protection laws do not fit Vogel's model" (85). There is no "race to the top" for air, water or ground pollution from stationary sources such as factories, nor for ambient air, water or groundwater quality standards. Moreover, "the entire and important realm of natural resources protection . . . also fall(s) completely outside the California effect."(85). Thus "other jurisdictions can . . . kill dolphins, cut down rain forests, or destroy wetlands, without any sign of the California effect" (85). While Swire's analysis of the limitations of the California effect is intended to demonstrate the need for federal environmental standards within the United States, his analysis applies with even greater cogency to the global economy.

On the other hand, another strand of Vogel's thesis—the idea that political coalitions between Baptists (environmentalists) and Bootleggers (certain regulated firms) can drive domestic regulatory standards up—can apply not only to product regulations but to production or process regulations. Multinational firms that have learned to meet demanding anti-pollution controls in stringent-regulation nations sometimes can achieve reputational gains and an advantage over less-experienced competitors by allying with environmentalists and pressing for tougher regulations in less-stringent nations where they have operations. Similarly, in federal systems such as the United States, companies with installations in strict regulation states often have pressed for nationwide federal anti-pollution regulations that impose higher standards on their competitors who operate in states where laxer standards prevail. The extent to which this Baptist-Bootlegger dynamic offsets business incentives to push for *weaker* process standards remains an open question.

There have been a number of empirical studies of the existence, or non-existence of the California effect. Golub (2000) finds a California effect operating within the European Union. A number of environmental product standards enacted by the EU's "greener" Member States, most notably Germany, the Netherlands and Denmark, have served as unilateral trade barriers, making it difficult for products from less green Member States to enter their markets. In many such cases, notably automobile emission standards or standards for energy efficiency, the EU has responded by harmonizing product standards at levels approximating those of its greener member states.

Thus there has been a "California effect" in Europe: green country preferences for stricter product standards have been exported to the EU's less green Member States. But the mechanism by which this upward harmonization has occurred is not exclusively a market phenomenon. Rather it has also required the involvement of a set of institutions that have the authority to establish uniform product standards among countries with diverse regulatory standards. In other words, in the case of the EU, while the California effect originates in the greener preferences of the EU's largest market (Germany), and in use of regulations as trade barriers (as the theory predicts) the "export" of stricter standards to other EU Member States has taken place not through market mechanisms but through political ones. It is a supranational body, namely the EU, which has harmonized European standards upwards.

At the same time, Golub observes that *process* standards within the EU have followed a rather different dynamic. Not only do stricter production standards place firms in the EU's greener member states at a comparative disadvantage, the standards cannot be used to exclude products produced by less green Member States. Since such standards do not affect the single market, the leverage of nations such as Germany, the Netherlands and Denmark over the terms of harmonized standards is limited. Not surprisingly, the EU's harmonized production standards have often tended to reflect lowest-common-denominator bargains, often codifying existing standards in most Member States, rather than raising them to the level of the EU's greener members. "Examples of such minimal ratcheting include EU standards covering sulfur dioxide and nitrogen dioxide emissions, ambient lead levels, gas and fuel oil content, large industrial plants, detergents, aquatic mercury levels, PCBs, shellfish and freshwater fish, and waste disposal." (Golub 2000: 187) Golub's analysis provides empirical support for the lack of application of the California effect to production standards, as predicted by Swire and Scharpf.

Genschel and Plumper (1997), like Golub, expand the definition of the "California effect" to include the role of international cooperation in driving regulatory standards upwards. They present two case studies. One is the successful standardization of capital adequacy requirements in international banking, demonstrating that "multilateral cooperation among nation states can stop a deregulatory downward spiral and turn it into a *race to the top*" (Genschel and Plumper 1997: 627, italics in original). Their second case—the failure of the EC to counter tax competition by agreeing on a common withholding tax on interest payments—suggests the circumstances when such co-operative turnarounds are likely to fail.

Genschel and Plumper conclude that the likelihood of a negotiated "California effect" depends on two structural factors: the size of the smallest possible coalition that can gain from cooperation all by itself (the k-group) and the external effect of cooperation on non-cooperators. Thus a California effect is more likely to take place if the minimum number of countries that would benefit unilaterally from adopting a strict standard is relatively small, since under these conditions those countries will more easily agree on adopting such a standard even if they have to bear a disproportional part of the associated costs. Secondly, strict standards are more likely to spread if a network effect exists, whereby the benefits relative to the costs of adopting them increase as more countries adopt them. This dynamic held for strict banking standards, in which a few countries derived benefits from the adoption of a common set of strict standards and the benefits increased as more countries adopted the strict standards. It did not hold for tax policies, for in this case harmonization only made sense if a relatively large number of countries agreed to adopt common policies. Moreover, non-cooperators were not disadvantaged if a relatively large number of countries agreed to adopt common tax policies.

Sebastian Princen's (1999) research tests one dynamic of the California effect by examining the impact of the EU's environmental policies on its trading partners. He presents a two-step process by which the California effect shifts standards for traded goods. Initially, a country has to decide to require other countries to comply with certain standards if they want to retain access to its markets. Subsequently, the exporting country has to decide to adopt these stricter standards. He argues that the successful completion of these steps depends on three groups of factors. First, the implementation of the California effect must be consistent with the trade rules under which the two countries are operating. If trade rules prohibit a country from excluding products, which do not meet its domestic standards, there can be no California effect.

Second, the California effect depends on the relative size of the two countries' markets. The larger the market size of the stricter country relative to that of the less strict country, the more likely there will be a California effect. Third, the willingness of a country to pressure a trading partner to adopt its higher standard depends upon the preferences and political strengths of public interest groups in the two countries. The more these groups have similar preferences for stricter regulatory standards, the more likely such standards will be adopted in the laggard country.

Princen compares two trade disputes which involved the EC, the US and Canada. The first case he examines is the EC's leg-trap ban, (a "process standard" for fur-bearing animal products). Here the EC was able to use its economic leverage to strengthen the regulatory policies of its trading partners, though its influence was greater on Canada than on the US. In his second case, the EC's beef hormone ban, there was no California effect: the US did not adjust its regulatory policies upward to reflect those of the EC, even though the latter's policies denied the US an important export market. While Princen is not able to isolate the relative importance of the three factors in explaining these different outcomes, his analysis points to the importance of incorporating the economics of "trading up" in any systematic theory of the California effect.

In a subsequent essay, which explores the differences in European and American regulations of genetically modified foods, Princen adds another dimension to this variable—namely the relative costs of target country regulatory adjustment. Thus, in the case of the EU's leg-trap ban, the costs of strengthening American regulatory policies to maintain its access to the European market were relatively modest, while in the case of the EU's beef hormone ban, the costs to the United States of meeting stricter European standards were substantial, as in the case of EU regulations for genetically modified foods. Hence a California effect occurred in the former case, but not the latter two.

The importance of the preferences of trading partners on whom one is dependent also underlies the work of Hoberg, Banting and Simeon (1997). According to this study, Canada has progressively tightened its automobile emissions standards as a response to changes in regulatory policy by both the state of California and the United States, while economic integration between the United States and Canada has also pulled Canadian newspaper recycling requirements upward. In addition "demands from European governments and consumers for chlorine-free paper products and more environmentally sensitive forest practices have encouraged the industry to adopt expensive controls to reduce emissions of dioxins and furans and the province of British Columbia to [strengthen] overall its regulatory regime" (Hoberg et al., 1997:19). Hoberg concludes that Canada is fortunate in that its largest trading partner tends to have relatively stringent standards. "If the balance of trade flows within NAFTA changed, and 80% of Canada's exports were to Mexico rather than the current level of 3%, the balance of pressures would obviously be quite different" (Hoberg et al., 1997:19).

In sum, the California effect focuses on the role of market forces in leading to the adoption of stricter regulatory standards by producers in a nation's trading partners. It is most likely to occur when four conditions apply. The first condition has to do with the nature of the regulation: product standards are more likely to produce a race to the top than production or process standards (Swire 1996, Scharpf 1995, Golub 2000). The second condition has to do with the relative size of the market of the two countries: the larger the market size of the stricter country relative to that of the less strict country the more likely is the latter to adopt the former's standards (Princen 1999). The third condition requires that the costs of the regulatory change be low relative to the benefits of market access (Princen 1999). The fourth condition has to do with regulatory policy of a nation's trading partners. The California effect is more likely to occur when a country's major export market has significantly stricter regulatory standards. (Hoberg et al, 1999)

However, it is important to note that these market mechanisms do not exhaust the vehicles through which nations may "export" stricter regulatory standards. Genchel and Plumper (1997) and Golub (2000), note that international agreements or institutions constitute an alternative mechanism though which stricter standards may be globalized. In addition, Swire (1996) argues that the California effect can work through more informal mechanisms. These include the demonstration effect of stricter standards, the decisions of MNCs to adopt uniform regulatory practices and the scrutiny of NGOs. While in the remainder of this essay, we use the term "California effect" to refer only to market mechanisms, all three mechanisms have played an important role in strengthening regulatory standards. Equally importantly, the latter two mechanisms, namely informational agreements or institutions and informal mechanisms can apply to production or process standards as well as product standards.

IV. THE RESEARCH IN THIS COLLECTION

The ten essays in this volume attempt to contribute to the understanding of both the impact of globalization in general and the role of the California effect in particular. As is the case with much of the literature in this area, the majority of these essays address various aspects of environmental regulation. Carr and Scheiber explore regulatory regimes for marine conservation, Delmas examines the globalization of environmental management standards, Kelemen looks at federalism and environmental regulation, Post discusses environmental standards in East Central Europe, Murphy investigates the regulation of ozone depletion and marine mammal protection, and O'Neill focuses on hazardous waste management. The remaining four essays explore other areas of regulatory policy: Victor addresses food, plant and animal safety standards, Gelb looks at women's rights, Gitterman examines labor market regulation and Simmons explores capital market regulation. In addition, one of Murphy's case studies deals with shipping regulation, which entails labor and environmental standards.

These essays demonstrate that there are three primary ways in which globalization can affect national regulatory policies. One mechanism has to do with *the dynamics of market or competitive forces.* Murphy and Simmons posit a world in which both firms and governments seek to maximize their economic interests vis-a-vis the global economy and then explore how these interests affect regulatory outcomes. Murphy, like Vogel, emphasizes the ways in which market forces directly trigger changes in national regulations, as national governments, often pushed by domestic business interests, strive to gain competitive advantages.

Simmons, however, emphasizes the ways in which some configurations of competitive pressures trigger action through *transnational or international institutions.* Her focus is on international competitive dynamics, as when politically and economically powerful nations use transnational bodies, such as the European Union or push for international treaties that impose their own standards on other countries. Kelemen, Victor, Gitterman and Post also focus on regional and international institutions. Victor examines the role of the World Trade Organization, specifically its Sanitary and Phytosanitary Agreement on food safety standards, while both Post and Gitterman explore the regulatory impact of the European Union, the former on environmental conditions in East and Central Europe and the latter on Member States' labor regulations. Kelemen's essay is broader in focus, exploring the impact of a number of different trade agreements, primarily on environmental standards, in federal systems.

Of course, the intermediation of international or transnational institutions does not always cancel out the continuing influence of market pressures. Thus Carr and Scheiber's and O'Neill's contributions explore the interplay between institutions and market forces. Carr and Scheiber examine the relationship between various international agreements to promote fisheries conservation and market pressures while O'Neill looks at similar dynamics to understand trends in the shipment and treatment of hazardous wastes. Delmas' essay presents a variation of this theme: it examines the interaction among market forces, domestic regulations, and the adoption of a voluntary environmental standard, namely ISO 14,000.

The third mechanism of globalization described in this volume is the *internationalization of norms and international advocacy networks*. This is the subject of Gelb's contribution, which explores the impact of these mechanisms on the treatment of women (although she notes that transnational institutions, particularly the European Union, can enhance the effects of new normative developments).

In principle, these three mechanisms of globalization, acting either alone or with one another, may produce one of three outcomes. First, globalization may have little or no impact on protective regulations. Second, globalization may strengthen these regulations, resulting in a race toward the top (RTT). Third, globalization may weaken protective regulations, resulting in a race toward the bottom (RTB). It is important to note that these three outcomes are related to, though logically distinct from, the issue of policy convergence/divergence. Thus both a RTB and a RTT can produce either increased convergence or divergence, depending on the intensity of international pressures. That is, some countries may sprint ahead in the general direction of greater stringency or greater laxity, while others move only somewhat or not at all in that direction. Even if a race exists, not all countries may be contestants.

The essays by Simmons and Murphy each suggest a simple general model for understanding globalization's likely effect on national regulations, and then test or illustrate the efficacy of their models through several case studies of different spheres of regulatory policy. As we shall see, both models help explain the dynamics explored in many of the other chapters.

As noted above, Beth Simmons's essay, "The International Politics of Harmonization: The Case of Capital Market Regulation," makes nation-states and their perceived interests the keys to changes in national regulatory policy. Simmons focuses on regulations concerning capital adequacy standards, anti-money laundering, public offering accounting standards, and information sharing. In none of the four cases is there evidence of a race toward the bottom. Rather Simmons is interested in explaining when there is a race toward the top, rather than continued regulatory divergence.

When a dominant financial center initiates a stricter regulation, other countries may or may not have an incentive to emulate it. In the cases of both capital adequacy requirements and accounting standards for public offerings, Simmons observes that it is in the interest of other countries to adopt these stricter regulations since doing so maintains or enhances their ability to attract capital. Accordingly, as in Vogel's "California effect," we have a race toward the top based on market mechanisms.

In the case of both anti-money-laundering regulations and capital adequacy standards, Simmons points out a *second* dynamic that comes into play. In both cases, the heterogeneity of national policies generates strong negative externalities for the dominant financial centers since the latter are negatively affected if other countries do not adopt equally stringent standards. In the case of anti-money laundering regulations, however, other jurisdictions have no incentive to adopt similar restrictions; indeed, it might well be in their interest not to do so. Yet since there are negative externalities for the dominant financial centers, they have an incentive to pressure international institutions to force other countries to adopt similar policies against money laundering. The result is movement towards the top, but not in the form of a market driven "California effect," but rather due to the political control of international institutions by polities that favor stricter standards.

In Simmons's fourth case, information sharing among securities regulators, there are neither negative externalities experienced by the dominant financial centers nor an incentive to emulation on the part of other countries. Hence the outcome is continued divergence.

Simmons suggests that her framework can be useful in accounting for other issue areas in which there is a strong imbalance, or asymmetry, of standards and of economic or political power among countries. Implicitly challenging the RTB model, she posits that large, powerful jurisdictions which enact regulations that they believe are in their interest are not likely to retract them simply because other jurisdictions have not chosen to emulate them. The question then becomes, first, whether the choices made by a major jurisdiction give other countries incentives to emulate, to diverge, or make no difference to them; and second, whether the major jurisdiction suffers from the failure of others to emulate it. In the area of environmental policy, for example, the lure of access to rich greener markets might provide an important incentive for producers in laxer regulation states to emulate strict-nation product standards (e.g., for motor vehicle emissions), an incentive that would be lacking in the case of the green market's *production* standards. Hence "trading up" is more likely to occur in the former case than the latter.

This brings us to the second question. If the other jurisdictions do not have an incentive to emulate, what difference does this make to the country with higher standards? For example, if important political constituencies in rich greener countries believe the weak production standards of less-green nations impose negative externalities on their populations, then the green states, in Simmons's model, have an incentive to use international organizations or economic muscle to pressure the less-green states to make their production standards stricter. This might occur, for example, if competitive pressures from industry in non-green states threaten the jobs of rich green-nation workers, or if the non-green state's standards are seriously damaging particular environmental resources that are treasured by rich-nation environmentalists, such as an endangered species or the ozone layer.

Alternatively, if divergence in national regulations generates no negative externalities for the first jurisdiction, then there will be continued divergence. This analysis is useful in accounting for when greener countries seek to impose their higher standards on other jurisdictions through international environmental agreements, such as the Montreal Protocol analyzed in Murphy's essay, and when they simply maintain stricter standards unilaterally, as in the case of virtually all domestic production standards in rich countries.

Simmons, however, posits the impossibility of a race toward the bottom, since she assumes the dominant power or powers have the ability to impose their preferences on other countries if they need to do so in order to maintain the effectiveness of their own standards. This may well be the case with respect to financial regulations in which there are marked international power asymmetries. But what if the political jurisdiction or jurisdictions with a preference for stricter standards is unable to impose them on other countries? In other words, suppose there are no significant international power asymmetries?

In such a case, one could well imagine that if a strict-regulation country suffered significant enough negative externalities from its imposing higher standards than other countries, then it might be forced to lower its standards. In this context, it is worth recalling that the RTB model assumes that some nations experience significant competitive disadvantages as a result of maintaining adequate wages, a strong social safety net and stringent consumer and environmental standards, and jurisdictions that prefer more progressive policies are incapable of imposing them on other countries. Under these two circumstances, there would be, according to this analysis, a RTB. In none of the case studies in this volume, however, does that scenario unfold.

Dale Murphy's essay, "The Business Dynamics of Global Regulatory Competition," looks more closely at the kinds of market structures and international competitive dynamics that induce nations to change their regulations. He argues that variations in regulations among jurisdictions may generate three trajectories: convergence toward a lower common denominator (RTB), convergence toward a higher common denominator (RTT), and no impact, i.e. continual heterogeneity. He presents a three-part model to account for these outcomes. The first part refers to the asset specificity of investments and transactions. Firms whose investments are mobile, he hypothesizes, are likely to relocate to less restrictive regulatory environments, thus encouraging a RTB, while investments with high asset-specificity deter firms from moving to lax regulation countries. High asset-specificity in turn creates incentives for firms to push for common regulations across borders, which may encourage a RTT or at least harmonization at a higher level of stringency.

The second part of Murphy's analysis distinguishes between (a) process or production regulations, which he hypothesizes may spawn competition in laxity, and (b) product or market-access regulations, which may lead producers to favor stricter domestic regulations which can function as trade barriers and produce a RTT. The third part addresses market structure: Murphy hypothesizes that changes in regulatory policies are more likely to be achieved by dominant, established firms in large, concentrated markets.

Murphy employs his model to explain three cases. The first involves shipping registration, which exhibits competition in laxity toward a lowest common denominator, especially among less developed nations that establish ship registries. In this case, process regulations (concerning ship safety, environmental, and labor standards), low asset specificity (ships are movable), and competitive pressures combine to produce a segmented race toward the bottom, as standards in rich nations remain unchanged but become less relevant because many shippers have re-registered their vessels in poorer countries which have laxer standards. There is no RTT because stringent-regulation nations have not pushed hard, either by a "California effect" restriction on market access or an international treaty, to compel flag-of-convenience states to upgrade their standards—partly because stringent-nation corporate customers, and presumably consumers as well, benefit from lower shipping costs. For their part, the shipping firms in strict regulation countries have no incentive to either encourage their governments to lower their standards or to protect them from international competition, since they can simply reflag their easily moveable assets in lax regulation countries. The result is a de facto RTB among nations seeking to attract ship registration.

Murphy's second case examines the successful negotiation of the Montreal Protocol, which raised production standards in twenty-four countries to restrict the production and use of CFCs, thereby reducing the depletion of atmospheric ozone. Why did this RTT occur? According to Murphy, the chemical industry was characterized by high market concentration and its dominant producers favored a ban on CFCs in order to capture the benefits from selling CFC substitutes. The US was sufficiently powerful to pressure for the adoption of an international treaty that effectively made American standards international ones. The result was an international agreement that both protected the interests of American domestic producers and enhanced environmental protection.

Murphy's third case is one in which American tuna producers supported applying the strict American dolphin-protection standard not only to tuna caught by American vessels sold in the US but to tuna imported from Mexican tuna boats. Notwithstanding successful challenges from the GATT—which prohibited the exclusion of products based on their method of production—this ban lasted more than a decade, thus enabling American tuna fishers to maintain their domestic market share, while maintaining stringent dolphin protection and thus appeasing American environmentalists. It eventually led to the strengthening of Mexican dolphin protection standards and an international dolphin protection treaty, thus producing a RTT, in the former case by "California effect" market mechanisms and in the latter through international institutions.

In both the CFC and the tuna-dolphin RTT cases, pressures for stricter regulations emerged from a Baptist-Bootlegger coalition, i.e. an alliance of business and environmentalists. By contrast, according to Murphy, "Baptists" have not played an active role in pressuring for more effective international shipping regulation—the RTB case. In strict-regulation countries, neither seamen's unions nor NGOs have been able to deny port access to reflagged foreign ships that fail to meet domestic labor or safety standards. Conversely, as Murphy notes, stringent-regulation countries *have* banned access by any oil tankers that do not meet stringent spill-prevention standards largely because both domestic NGOs and large petroleum companies—especially in the wake of the Exxon Valdez disaster—have a common stake in preventing oil spills within their territorial waters and globally. Not incidentally, such regulations helped reduce industry over-capacity.

Christopher Carr and Harry Scheiber's essay, "Dealing with a Resource Crisis: Regulatory Regimes for Managing the World's Marine Fisheries," addresses another kind of failure of regulatory governance: even if international institutions can bring about more stringent worldwide regulatory restrictions, they are not always able to assure their effective implementation and enforcement. Carr and Scheiber describe the inability of nations to develop an adequate regime to manage the world's marine fisheries, which are becoming depleted due to over-fishing. As Simmons's model would predict, there have been a large number of international efforts, many led by the United States, an important fishing nation, to promote the sustainable use of this critical global resource. Treaty has followed upon treaty. But in contrast to Simmons's model, these efforts have repeatedly faltered at the level of implementation and enforcement. The question is why.

As Carr and Scheiber demonstrate, many governments find it in their short-term political interest to continue to subsidize fishing fleets and encourage their domestic producers to harvest as many fish as they can. Meanwhile, countries that have tried to manage their fishing stocks in a more sustainable manner lack the capacity to force other countries to adopt similar policies. Complicating the efforts of all countries to more responsibly manage this resource are the difficulties of policing fishing catches by thousands of highly mobile individual fishing boats, a lack of scientific consensus regarding the size of worldwide and regional fishing stocks, and the ability of fishing vessels to shift their registration to countries whose conservation standards, as actually enforced, are less demanding.

Note however that as in the case of flag-of-convenience countries, Carr and Scheiber do not describe a universal race toward the bottom, in which "greener" countries have been forced to relax their own conservation efforts, but rather demonstrate how stringent-regulation countries' efforts have often failed as more boats from lax-regulation countries ply the seas, confounding schemes to enforce quotas and other restrictions. Even when stringent regulation countries are able to deny market access to fish caught in unsustainable ways, as permitted by a number of international treaties, such efforts often have failed because foreign fishing vessels can sell their catch in other international markets. In short, there is no "California effect" because stringent regulation countries lack sufficient market power. This reminds us that effectively enforced international standards are the exception rather than the rule: in all but a handful of cases, greener countries have been unable to force or persuade other countries to enforce common standards for marine conservation.

The fisheries example therefore shows the limits of Simmons's assumption that if powerful countries experience externalities from others' weak standards, they can force them, through international organizations or economic pressure, not only to adopt but also to enforce stricter standards. Her response might be that these particular negative externalities—declining high-seas fisheries—have not been so great as to be politically or economically intolerable to powerful polities. Americans and Western Europeans have been more concerned about the fate of whales than about the disappearance of cod from the Georges Bank. Alternatively, monitoring and enforcement may present more serious problems in the case of fisheries than in the case of capital market regulations.

A somewhat more hopeful scenario is described in "Globalization and Hazardous Waste Management: From Brown to Green," by Kate O'Neill. Her focus is on the problem of hazardous waste management, a problem that has been exacerbated by the fact that a significant share of these wastes is exported for disposal. A number of countries, most notably in northern Europe, have implemented policies to reduce the amount of wastes they produce and improve their treatment. Since these regulatory "steps toward the top" increase domestic disposal costs for domestic producers, there have been a number of efforts, as Simmons's model would predict, to export stricter standards for the disposal of hazardous wastes, both within Europe through the European Union and internationally through such agreements as the Basel Convention. The EU has attempted to improve waste management practices in Central Europe, and a number of developing nations have established state of the art facilities for the disposal of such wastes, yielding at least some further steps toward the top.

While noting some improvement in national practices in this area, O'Neill observes that the overall strengthening of waste management policies around the world is uneven. The illegal transfer and disposal of hazardous wastes remains common, especially to and within poorer nations. What she describes is not so much a race to the bottom, but rather a hydraulic effect, whereby stricter regulations in country A, by increasing costs, provoke increased efforts to evade them by seeking cheaper options abroad. Thus, the more comprehensively a country regulates waste disposal within its borders, the more likely it is that some of its waste will be exported to countries with laxer or more poorly enforced standards. In terms of Murphy's typology industrial wastes—like ships, but unlike an industrial furnace that produces air pollution—are moveable. In terms of Simmons's typology, poor disposal practices elsewhere impose only relatively small environmental and economic costs on greener countries, and green countries' power to impose higher standards on some lax regulation countries is limited.

Due to pressures from environmentalists, especially in Europe, the Basel Convention has been negotiated, seeking to limit exports of hazardous wastes to developing countries. Yet, as in the case of international fisheries agreements, the impact of this international treaty has been limited, O'Neill tells us, largely due to a lack of international consensus as to what constitutes a hazardous waste as well as the fact that the ban on hazardous waste exports is not yet in force. Moreover rich country producers continue to benefit from laxer standards in developing countries because this lowers their waste disposal costs, while, as in the case of fisheries, many poorer countries benefit financially from less stringent standards. The result is slow progress toward a RTT.

The difficulties powerful jurisdictions experience in exporting their standards also is an important theme in Diahanna Post's essay, "Closing the Deception Gap: Accession to the European Union and Environmental Standards in East Central Europe." Post examines the EU's efforts to impose its environmental standards on Poland, Hungary and the Czech Republic, three countries that are in the process of negotiating membership in the EU. In principle, the leverage of the EU over the environmental policies of the countries of east central Europe (ECE) is considerable: the latter eagerly want to join the EU and the EU is in a position to determine the conditions of their accession. In addition, reflecting an important factor in Simmons's model, the EU has incentives to require the ECE countries to adopt its environmental standards. For one thing, it faces the problem of negative externalities: its producers will be at a competitive disadvantage if they are forced to compete with imported products produced according to the much weaker standards currently prevailing in the ECE. In addition, European environmentalists very much favor an improvement in environmental conditions in the ECE, which are widely regarded as deplorable, if not catastrophic. Western manufacturers investing in the ECE already have environmental technologies and managerial know-how, and hence seem likely to support tougher standards. All the preconditions for the California effect appear to be in place. The stage is set for a race toward the top.

Post reports that such a convergence is happening on paper, but not in practice. She describes a phenomenon that might be labeled a "Potemkin harmonization." There appears to be an unspoken consensus to accept the ECE's promises to improve environmental quality and adopt EU standards, although in fact, there is an enormous gap between official policies of the ECE and their actual practices. Her essay depicts the enormous obstacles that can stand in the way of "exporting" stricter environmental practices. These include the lack of an adequate enforcement capacity, the weakness of domestic NGOs, modest public interest in environmental issues, and a lack of technical and financial resources on the part of many domestic industries.

The extent to which the EU is willing to overlook the shortcomings of the ECE's compliance with its standards may suggest that the negative externalities EU countries experience from ECE's relatively weak environmental performance may not be all that significant. For the same reason, the ECE's failure to strengthen its environmental standards is unlikely to pressure the EU to lower theirs. ("Deception" is not only an external phenomenon: there is substantial non-compliance with EU directives among the fifteen Member States.) In the long run, as in the case of developing country standards for the treatment of hazardous wastes, the environmental performance of the ECE is likely to improve. The primary problem is not a RTB; rather it is the slow rate at which national standards are converging upward.

The continued divergence of many environmental norms is the theme of Magali Delmas' essay, "Globalization of Environmental Management Standards: Barriers and Incentives in Europe and in the United States." Delmas traces the international dissemination of ISO 14001, a voluntary standard calling for formal corporate environmental management and mechanisms for continuous improvement, developed by the International Organization for Standardization in Geneva. ISO 14001 can be viewed as a market-based mechanism for pressuring firms in lax-regulation countries to upgrade their corporate environmental management standards: while governments of greener countries cannot, under WTO rules, exclude imported products made in countries with less stringent environmental production methods, companies in greener countries can (and often do) refuse to do business with firms that are not "ISO 14001 certified." This standard has been widely adopted by Western European firms and by firms in other countries (particularly Japan and Canada) that sell to those European firms. However, relatively few American firms have sought ISO 14001 certification.

Delmas attributes this contrast to differences in the nature of interaction between business and government. In Europe, government regulators have embraced ISO 14001 and provided companies with important incentives to adopt it. The more legalistic and adversarial nature of the business-government relationship in the US means that there are few advantages for American based firms to adopt ISO 14001. Indeed, its adoption may even make them more vulnerable to lawsuits. Since the US does not experience any competitive disadvantage from the adoption of formalized environmental management in EU firms, American government has not promoted its adoption in the US. And since production costs are escalated in the US by the legalistic American approach to regulation (Kagan & Axelrad, 2000; Anderson & Kagan, 2000), the EU does not suffer any negative externalities from the widespread adoption of ISO certification in Europe and has therefore not pressured the American government to mandate or encourage ISO 14000 certification in the U.S. The result is continued policy divergence.

The persistence of national policy divergence in an increasingly globalized economy is also the theme of David Victor's essay, "The WTO's Effort to Manage Differences in Sanitary and Phytosanitary Policies." A Sanitary and Phytosanitary Agreement (SPS) was incorporated into the Uruguay Round trade agreement. In order to prevent nations from using human, animal and plant safety standards as non-tariff barriers, it seeks to promote the harmonization of national standards. The agreement specifically urges countries to adopt the SPS standards set by various international bodies, the most important of which is the Codex Alimentarius Commission established in 1962 under the auspices of the UN and the World Health Organization.

This agreement can be seen as an effort, led by major agricultural exporters including the United States, to develop an international legal mechanism to cope with the negative externalities of diverse national

SPS standards. In contrast to the case of capital requirements regulation, in which NGOs displayed little interest, or the Montreal Protocol, where NGOs were highly supportive, this international agreement was opposed by many NGOs based on fears that it would undermine the stricter national standards of Europe and the United States. On the other hand, many developing countries feared that they would be required to adopt the generally stricter standards of the industrialized nations.

Victor's essay represents the first systematic effort to assess the impact of the SPS Agreement, now approximately six years old. His central conclusion is that the agreement has had little impact on national regulatory standards for food and related agricultural products: there has been no increase in convergence around international standards. Ironically, one of the results of investing the Codex with more authority over trade law has been to make it more difficult for this body to establish new standards. The standards it is now setting are increasingly broad, often providing nations with little guidance even if they wanted to adopt them.

Equally importantly, in none of the three disputes that have been adjudicated under the SPS agreement by the WTO were nations required to adopt international standards. In the case of two of the disputes, such standards did not even exist, while in the third case—the beef hormone dispute between the US and the EU—the appeals panel explicitly held that the EU was not required to adopt them. Nor does the fact that all three cases were decided in favor of the plaintiff suggest that the WTO's implementation of the SPS Agreement is undermining the ability of nations to protect humans, animal and plants. For in each case, the dispute panel was able to identify alternative SPS measures that would lead to the same level of protection with less distortion of trade.

Victor does suggest that the SPS Agreement is having an impact, although not the one anticipated by the nations that initiated it. While it is having little impact on either the level of food safety or the convergence of national standards, it is affecting the way countries go about establishing SPS standards. Specifically it is encouraging the use of risk assessments and the aligning of risks at "comparable levels," since such measures will enable national regulations to withstand challenges under WTO rules. Forcing nations to base their SPS regulations on scientific risk assessments is likely to encourage them to strengthen rather than weaken their standards—especially when such assessments are accompanied by the increased use of the precautionary principle—and ironically may lead to the increased diversity of SPS levels.

R. Daniel Kelemen's essay, "Globalization, Federalism and Regulation," addresses a related issue, the impact of international legal integration on national standards. Kelemen defines such integration broadly. His analysis encompasses trade organizations like NAFTA and the WTO as well as international environmental agreements and the treaties that define the European Union. His specific focus is on the impact of international legal integration on the centralization of power within federal systems as well as on the stringency of regulatory standards. This is a central issue because, as noted above, concerns about RTB originated in the study of federal systems, where it was claimed that the concerns about attracting investments limited the ability of sub-national jurisdictions to establish standards as strict as they would like.

Kelemen notes that while there have been cases in which economic integration has impeded the establishment of social regulations, most notably in the case of US child labor laws early in the 20th Century, he finds little empirical evidence in support of the RTB hypothesis in the area of environmental regulation. Thus he notes that within both the US and the EU, greener political jurisdictions continue to maintain stricter standards. In view of the fact that the competitive pressures added by globalization are minimal compared to those that already exist in federal systems, he finds no reason to believe that globalization will push states within federal polities into a RTB competition.

Globalization, however, has encouraged the centralization of regulatory policy in federal systems. Since federal governments are accountable for violation of international trade or environmental agreements by sub-national jurisdictions, the former have an incentive to restrict the latter's autonomy. At the same time, there is a growing trend within the EU and the US to devolve more regulatory responsibilities onto local jurisdictions and the EU has in fact upheld the legality of a number of *more stringent* Member State regulations, even though they interfere with the single market.

Kelemen finds a similar mixed picture with respect to the impact of international legal institutions on the stringency of standards. On one hand, dispute resolution bodies have successfully challenged a few stringent social regulations. While the immediate impact of such challenges has been limited, there is evidence that they may have had a "chilling effect." But on the other hand, international environmental agreements and the EU have had a much more substantial impact in precisely the opposite direction, that is, pushing them incrementally towards "the top".

Joyce Gelb's essay, "Globalization and Feminism: The Impact of the New Transnationalities" covers a diversity of international institutions. Gelb's focus is on the globalization of norms surrounding the treatment of women, encompassing such policies as maternity leave, child-care, equal pay, non-discrimination and sexual harassment. She explores the impact of international institutions, structures and agreements ranging from the UN Commission on the Status of Women and the Division of the Advancement of Women, to the Convention on the Elimination of Discrimination Against Women, the International Labor Organization and the European Union.

What makes the focus of Gelb's analysis distinctive is the absence of any role for business or indeed of market forces. Whatever negative externalities a country with weak gender equality laws may impose on those with stronger regulation, they seem to be modest. They do not compel nations whose policies toward women are relatively progressive to pressure countries with which they compete to adopt similar policies. Nor can progressive policies toward women function as trade barriers; in short, there are no bootleggers.

There are, however, Baptists. Indeed, the vehicle for the international dissemination of feminist policies is the international women's movement, working with international organizations to create high-visibility events such as the International Women's Year (1975) and the Decade of Women (1975–85). The vast number of NGOs who operate in more than one country—more than 15000 of them—has played a critical role in placing human rights issues affecting women on the international political agenda.

Gelb examines the impact of new international norms related to gender equality on the domestic policies of Japan, an industrialized nation in which women's interests have been relatively unprotected. She notes that Japan found itself under international pressure to ratify a number of important international agreements regarding gender equality, and their ratification required Japan to review and revise a number of domestic policies. In many cases the resulting policy changes were cosmetic, but at the same time, the ability of Japanese feminists to draw on international gender equality norms has raised awareness and produced new legislation. Thus "Baptists alone" have played a role in pressuring a laggard nation to bring its policies into closer alignment with new international norms.

Not surprisingly, the EU, a much more powerful institution than the UN and other international bodies, has had a more substantial policy impact. The EU's willingness to steadily expand the scope of its policies aimed at ensuring greater gender equality has provided domestic NGOs with greater political and legal leverage, especially in those countries in which such groups have historically enjoyed little influence. An important example of this dynamic can be seen in the case of Great Britain. EU directives and court decisions have had a considerable impact on British policies in areas such as equal pay, equity with respect to retirement pensions, maternity leave, sex discrimination and sexual harassment.

Gelb does not discern any RTB: nations with relatively progressive gender equality policies do not appear under any competitive pressure to modify them. But she notes that some gender equality policies—most notably equal pay, child care and maternity leave—can impose considerable costs on employers, making it in the latter's interest to oppose them. In such cases, international pressures, legal as well as extra-legal, still have a critical role to play.

In two important respects Daniel Gitterman's essay, "A Race to the Bottom, a Race to the Top or the March to a Minimum Floor? Economic Integration and Labor Standards in Comparative Perspective," offers the most formidable test of the impact of economic integration on regulatory policies. Gitterman focuses on public policies affecting labor—an area in which the impact of pro-labor regulations on firm costs is substantial. His geographic focus is the EU—the region in which economic globalization has proceeded further than anywhere in the world. According to the RTB model, we should expect some "social dumping," expressed through the displacement of producers in high-cost labor policy regimes by those from Member States characterized by labor policies that impose lower costs, thus leading the former to lower their wages and standards and the latter to keep them low in order to remain competitive. A diametrically opposed prediction, based on Simmons's model, would be political pressure by strong labor-regulation states for the harmonization of labor policies by the EU, thus creating a level playing field.

Yet Gitterman finds that neither outcome has materialized, with the exception of some "harmonization up" with respect to regulation of working conditions. The core aspects of labor market regimes of the

Member States show little evidence of convergence: the nature and character of labor market protection continues to be primarily set by national governments and the political systems in which they are embedded. Harmonization by the EU has attempted to reduce potential conflicts between the free movement of labor and national employment rules. In addition, the EU has harmonized regulations governing equal opportunity, health and safety and living and working conditions and these policies have had an important and progressive impact on national labor market regulatory systems—a movement toward the top in this realm of regulation. But the core features of labor market regimes, namely collective bargaining and pay determination, remain nationally specific. In sum, there is relatively little evidence of either policy convergence through legal mechanisms, or of a RTB through economic pressures.

Gitterman suggests that one solution to this puzzle may be that progressive or more generous labor market policies are not necessarily a source of competitive disadvantage, partly because compensation costs are not the only determinant of competitiveness. Indeed, high-wage countries often have compensating advantages over low-wage ones, such as a more skilled workforce, better infrastructure and higher productivity.   Other international trade agreements, namely NAFTA, MERCOSUR, ASEAN and the WTO, have been even less effective in harmonizing labor standards; indeed most have not even attempted to do so. While the adoption of some core labor standards has been supported by governments from some high-wage countries, as well as their unions, such effort have had little impact. This is in part due to opposition from many developing countries who worry that unions and domestic producers would use such standards to exclude their exports on the grounds that they are produced "unfairly." In principle, international labor standards do exist: the International Labor Organization has adopted fundamental principles of labor rights. But it lacks any mechanism for enforcement. In short, while high-wage countries have not been pressured into lowering their labor standards, they have been either unable or unwilling to pressure their trading partners into raising theirs. The result is continued policy divergence.

V. CONCLUSION

The evidence presented in this volume weighs heavily against the notion that globalization induces a general regulatory race to the bottom, compelling nations to relax their regulatory standards in order to become or remain economically competitive. In most of the several regulatory policy fields discussed in these chapters, the direction of national regulatory policy has been toward greater stringency, toward the standards of the regulatory leaders. Even when divergence prevails, stringent regulation countries have not weakened their standards, and with some notable exceptions—shipping regulations, fisheries conservation, labor standards, and waste disposal—lax regulation states generally have taken significant steps toward greater stringency. Indeed, the primary reason for continued divergence noted in many of the case studies has been due less to the failure of more lenient-regulation states to enact tougher laws and regulations than to their inability to create effective on-the-ground enforcement systems—a failure that often reflect reflects weaknesses in governmental capacity that is still common in many developing countries.

The European Union, where the international economic integration characteristic of globalization has been especially pervasive, has been one major mechanism driving all Member States, as well as states that want to be members, toward higher regulatory standards, partly because of the EU's strength as a transnational governance institution, and partly because of its importance as an economic market. Thus EU regulators have pushed the environmental policies of member states both toward greater convergence and greater stringency. (Keleman) The EU has drawn regulatory laggards toward the stricter workplace safety standards of the EU's regulatory leaders (Gitterman), has pressured member states to adopt more uniform and more stringent rules concerning women's rights in employment (Gelb), and has induced the Czech Republic, Poland and Hungary to at least formally adopt stricter environmental standards (Post).

Even in the absence of the institutional leverage provided by the EU, globalization has facilitated international pressures for tougher national regulations. Gelb points out that globalization in the realm of communications and culture has abetted linkages between national and international non-governmental organizations dedicated to women's rights, generating new international norms and pressuring reluctant countries such as Japan to adopt more stringent regulations. In the realm of bank regulation, globalization has encouraged a race to the top in national regulatory standards concerning capital reserves and in corporate accounting standards (Simmons). Through the Montreal Protocol, twenty-four industrial nations agreed on a coordinated and rapid increase in the stringency of standards restricting the manufacture and use of CFCs, which have been eroding the earth's atmospheric ozone layer (Murphy).

Yet in the majority of the regulatory areas examined in this volume, policy convergence among the nations studied has been quite incomplete. Instead, the modal outcome is continued heterogeneity. Globalization has not been a juggernaut driving regulatory policy inexorably either to the top or to the bottom.

Businesses in the US, in contrast to their European colleagues, are wary of adopting ISO 14001 standards for corporate environmental management (Delmas). When national regulatory standards do converge on paper toward more stringent ends, actual practice often continues to diverge. Thus the SPS agreement on food safety, David Victor found, has had only a weak effect on countries' regulatory policies. East European countries, while adopting more stringent Western European environmental regulations, often have failed to implement them in practice (Post). In many countries, hazardous waste management regulations, driven by treaty commitments, have become more stringent, moving toward the top, but collection, transportation and disposal practices around the world remain uneven (O'Neill). The actual impact of Japan's laws concerning equal employment of women has been disappointingly limited (Gelb, 2000). Even within the European Union, where the removal of trade barriers has exposed all Member States to more intense competition, core labor policies, Gitterman tells us, continue to be set primarily by national governments and diverge considerably.

On balance, most case studies of continued regulatory divergence portray a heterogeneity that has moved in the direction of more stringent rather than more lax national regulatory standards. The regulatory course triggered by globalization has been toward the top, although the laggards remain sufficiently behind the leaders that it seems not so much a "race" as the movement of a migrating herd.

On the other hand, parts of some herds have drifted off in the opposite direction, toward lax regulatory standards. Years of international regulatory efforts have not arrested the depletion of many oceanic fisheries, as some national fishing fleets continue to fight against demanding regulatory standards or their strict implementation (Carr and Scheiber). Similarly, Murphy describes the ongoing competition among certain countries, from Liberia to Belize to Malta, to invite reflagging of commercial vessels by means of the implicit promise of weaker enforcement of international labor and environmental standards. In both of these cases, to use Murphy's helpful typology, the reasons for RTB lie in the fragmented character of the regulated industries and the ease with which the regulated facilities (ships) can be relocated or escape detection.

In neither case, however, is there significant evidence that the countries with more stringent standards have felt compelled to relax them; the race to the bottom has been selective. Rather, in these instances the stringent-standard countries have not been willing or able to use either political might, economic leverage, or import restrictions to impose and enforce more stringent rules on the lax-standard countries—partly due to WTO rules, and partly because in these regulatory arenas, the "negative externalities" that the lax-regulation states impose on the stringent-rule states (Simmons) have not been politically or economically intolerable.

The central shortcoming of global regulatory governance, these studies suggest, lies in the inability and/or unwillingness of strict regulation countries to impose their standards on countries with laxer standards, either through market or political mechanisms. In some cases, producers in the former countries may benefit from the continued disparity of standards, such as in the areas of labor rights, flags of convenience, and waste disposal. In principle, these economic interests could be challenged by NGOs, but the latter's political influence is limited in these policy areas. In other cases, most notably fisheries and national environmental standards in central Europe, what is lacking is not so much the desire of strict regulation countries to export their standards but their inability to make other countries actually implement and enforce stricter standards—an inability compounded by the fact that many lax regulation countries either have no interest in investing in enforcement systems or lack the administrative capacity to do so.

Simply changing the values of the causal variables that Murphy and Simmons emphasize helps account for the cases in which national regulatory policies have converged on greater stringency. When the regulated markets are highly concentrated or production is location specific (that is, not easily moved to lax-regulation countries), "upward convergence" seems more likely, as in the case of the ban on CFCs. That is one reason why countries with relatively strict environmental regulations have not been forced to relax their policies due to competition from lax regulation countries.

When politically and economically dominant nations suffer substantial negative externalities, economic or perceived, as a result of lax regulation elsewhere, they face incentives, as Simmons points out, to use their economic and political power to find ways of imposing those standards on those other countries. They can't always do so completely, partly because World Trade Organization rules prevent them from excluding imports from lax regulation countries—as in the case of fisheries regulation. But sometimes, dominant nations can find a way, as when the U.S. ultimately pressured Mexico to agree to regulate fishing to protect dolphins.

Finally, as Simmons points out, sometimes it is the lax regulation countries that suffer economically from being in that position, as when capital flows not to them but to countries that have the most reliable bank regulation. This gives the lax bank regulation countries a strong incentive to emulate the strict regulation countries. Here, too, is where aspects of the "California effect" become relevant. In the lax regulation country, banks that already have high standards (perhaps because they also do business in the strict regulation countries) may lobby their government to make such standards mandatory. Simmons's model helps explain why governments in areas other than bank regulation too may have an incentive to respond to domestic advocates of strict regulation, whether those advocates are businesses or NGOs. Still, as noted earlier, although lenient regulation countries not infrequently have incentives to strengthen their regulations, that is not always sufficient to bring about international regulatory convergence in practice (rather than merely on paper), since they may lack the resources, administrative capacity, and social support to adequately monitor compliance by regulated enterprises.

The upshot is that the manifold strands of globalization generate a variety of economic and political incentives and lead to a variety of regulatory patterns. Every important regulatory policy leads to benefits for some nations, industries and political constituencies while imposing costs and disadvantages on others. In some cases, the studies show, international institutions *impede* efforts by stricter-regulation nations to export their standards to other countries (as in the GATT decision in the tuna-dolphin case) while in other cases, such as the Montreal Protocol on CFCs and the European Union's environmental, workplace safety, and gender discrimination policies, transnational institutions have been the key to "upward convergence" in national regulatory standards. In some cases, the drive to push regulatory laggards toward the standards of stricter-regulation countries is driven by dominant governments (with the support of business and labor interests as well as NGOs), as in the case of EU pressures on central European countries (Post) and the Basel accord on hazardous waste trade (O'Neill). But sometimes the pressures for diffusion of regulatory standards comes solely through NGOs, using international forums to generate normative expectations that regulatory laggards feel politically obligated to meet.

The general movement toward more stringent regulatory standards that these case studies reveal does not imply that globalization tends to produce optimal regulatory policies, for it simultaneously generates competitive pressures that lead to political resistance to tougher regulations. Everywhere, powerful business interests argue against costly increases in national regulatory stringency. Virtually no national government supports regulatory enforcement agencies well enough to ensure reliable monitoring and enforcement, and that shortfall is far greater in less developed nations. Harmonization on paper thus does not preclude considerable differences in methods and effectiveness of implementation.

Nevertheless, it is worth reiterating that the overall tendency of globalization, as indicated by these varied studies, is toward greater rather than less regulatory stringency. Although not explicated in the problem-focused case studies themselves, the overriding background factor, accelerated by globalization, may be a steadily if unevenly increasing political demand—in all democratic nations and in many others as well—for greater protection against risks to human safety and health, environmental destruction, and economic security. This political demand for what Lawrence Friedman (1985) has called "total justice" accelerated in the richer democracies in the latter third of the 20th century. Globalization, with its instantaneous communication of information about risks and solutions, helps enhance that demand around the world. Its vectors are multinational corporations and international NGOs, scientific journals, news media, and governmental reports. In stimulating the flow of news around the world, globalization increases the visibility of poorly governed, heedless business activity wherever it occurs. Multinational corporations know that their behavior in Indonesia and Nigeria, if severely violative of home nation standards, will not remain a secret from its customers and NGOs in rich nations.

This background political pressure for adequate regulation does not always prevail of course. The studies in this volume indicate the particular circumstances in which particular interests are most motivated and able to exploit it or to resist it. But it rarely fades away entirely, or rather is always available to be invoked. That, combined with the "California effect" political and economic mechanisms discussed in these chapters, suggests that most regulatory races are likely to continue to move, however haltingly, in the direction of greater stringency.

In conclusion, our understanding of the dynamics of regulatory convergence can be briefly summarized as follows. The first element has to do with the interests of strict regulation countries in having their standards adopted by their trading partners. Such interests may stem from a variety of causes, such as producers who suffer a competitive disadvantage from the lack of a level playing field, the existence of negative externalities, and pressures from NGOs. Alternatively, strict regulatory countries, or to be more precise, those interests which define national preferences, may benefit from the continued disparity of regulatory standards, in which case there is likely to be less pressure for convergence. If policy-makers in strict regulatory countries do support international regulatory convergence, the outcome then turns on their ability to create an effective international regulatory regime.

If such regulatory convergence is also in the interests of their trading partners, then the likelihood of regulatory convergence is considerably enhanced. However, if laxer regulatory countries do not benefit from the adoption of the standards of strict regulatory countries, then the issue turns on mechanisms of "enforcement." There are three primary mechanisms by which regulatory standards can spread across national boundaries. One has to do with market access, which the California effect specifically addresses. A second involves international institutions or agreements. The third involves pressures from international NGOs either directly or on multinational corporations. Each of these mechanisms, however, has both strengths and shortcomings.

This suggests that an important research agenda for scholarship on regulatory policy is to focus on the dynamics of regulatory implementation and enforcement—particularly the mechanisms through which stringent-regulation countries, acting through restrictions on market assess, international institutions and NGOs can induce weak-enforcement states to improve compliance with international or harmonized regulatory standards by domestic firms.

David Vogel is the George Quist Chair of Business Ethics at the Haas School of Business and a Professor of Political Science at the University of Caifornia, Berkeley. His recent publications include *Trading Up: Consumer and Environmental Regulation in a Global Economy* (Harvard) and *Benefits of Barriers? Regulation in Transatlantic Trade* (Brookings). Robert A. Kagan is a Professor of Political Science and Law at the University of California, Berkeley. His most recent books are *Adversarial Legalism: The American Way of Law* (Harvard) and *Shades of Green: Business, Regulation, and Environment* (Stanford).

Notes
1. For an excellent summary and critical analysis of the "myth" of a race to the bottom, see Drezner 2000. For a dissenting view, see Rodrik 1997.
2. See also Pauly and Reich 1997.
3. See, for example, the evidence cited in Vogel 2000.
4. See, for example, Esty and Geradin 2000.
5. For the latter, see for example Keck and Sikkink 1998.

References
Anderson, C. Leigh, and Robert A. Kagan. 2000. Adversarial Legalism and Transaction Costs: The Industrial Flight Hypothesis Revisited. *International Review of Law and Economics* 20:1–19.

Bennett, Colin J. 1991. What is Policy Convergence and What Causes It? *British Journal of Political Science* 21 (2):215–234.

Berger, Suzanne, and Ronald Dore, eds. 1996. *National Diversity and Global Capitalism*. Ithaca, NY: Cornell University Press.

Bernstein, Steven, and Benjamin Cashore. 2000. Globalization, Four Paths of Internationalization, and Domestic Policy Change: The Case of Ecoforestry in British Columbia, Canada. *Canadian Journal of Political Science* 33 (March):67–99.

Daley, Herman. 1993. The Perils of Free Trade. *Scientific American*, November.

Donahue, T. 1994. International Labor Standards: The Perspective of Labor. Paper read at International Labor Standards and Global Economic Integration: Proceedings of a Symposium, at Washington, DC.

Drezner, Daniel. 2000. Bottom Feeders. *Foreign Policy*

(November/December):64–70.

Esty, Daniel C., and D. Geradin. 2000. Regulatory Competition. *Journal of International Economic Law* 3 (2):235–255.

Fowler, Robert. 1995. International Environmental Standards for Transnational Corporations. *Environmental Law* 25:1–30.

Friedman, Lawrence M. 1985. *Total Justice*. New York: Russell Sage Foundation.

Garcia-Johnson, Ronie. 2000. *Exporting Environmentalism: US Multinational Chemical Corporations in Brazil and Mexico.* Cambridge, MA: MIT Press.

Garrett, Geoffrey. 1998. Global Markets and National Politics: Collision Course or Virtuous Circle? *International Organization* 52 (4):787–824.

Gelb, Joyce. 2000. The Equal Employment Opportunity Law: A Decade of Change for Japanese Women. *Law and Policy* 22:385–407.

Genschel, Philipp, and Thomas Plümper. 1997. Regulatory Competition and International Cooperation. *Journal of European Public Policy* 4 (4 (December)):626–42.

Golub, Jonathan. 2000. Globalization, Sovereignty and Policy-making: Insights from European Integration. In *Global Democracy: Key Debates*, edited by B. Holden. London: Routledge.

Hoberg, George; Keith Banting, and Richard Simeon, eds. 1997. *Degrees of Freedom: Canada and the United States in a Changing Global Context*, Kingston and Montreal: McGill-Queen's University Press.

Jaffe, Adam B., Steven R. Peterson, Paul R. Portney, and Robert N. Stavins. 1995. Environmental Regulation and the Competitiveness of US Manufacturing: What Does the Evidence Tell Us? *Journal of Economic Literature* 33 (March):132–163.

Kagan, Robert A. and Lee Axelrad, eds. (2000) *Regulatory Encounters: Multinational Corporations and Adversarial Legalism.* Berkeley, CA: University of California Press

Kahler, Miles. 1998. Modeling Races to the Bottom. Paper read at American Political Science Association, September 3–6, at Boston.

Keck, Margaret E., and Kathryn Sikkink. 1998. *Activists Beyond Borders: Advocacy Networks in International Politics.* Ithaca, NY: Cornell University Press.

Levinson, Arik. 1996. Environmental Regulations and Industry Location: International and Domestic Evidence. In *Fair Trade and*

Harmonization: Prerequisites for Free Trade? Volume I: Economic Analysis, edited by J. Bhagwati and R. E. Hudec. Cambridge, MA: MIT Press.

Low, Patrick, and Alexander Yeats. 1992. Do 'Dirty Industries' Migrate? In *International Trade and the Environment. World Bank Discussion Papers.*

Milner, Helen V., and Robert O. Keohane. 1996. Internationalization and Domestic Politics: An Introduction. In *Internationalization and Domestic Politics,* edited by R. O. Keohane and H. V. Milner. Cambridge: Cambridge University Press.

Pauly, Louis W., and Simon Reich. 1997. National Structures and Multinational Corporate Behavior: Enduring Differences in the Age of Globalization. *International Organization* 51 (1):1–30.Rappaport, Ann, and Margaret F. Flaherty. *Corporate Responses to Environmental Challenges: Initiatives by Multinational Management.* New York: Quorum Books, 1992.

Porter, Gareth. 1999. Trade Competition and Pollution Standards: 'Race to the Bottom' or 'Stuck at the Bottom'? *Journal of Environment and Development* 8 (2):133–151.

Princen, Sebastian. 1999. A Comparison of the Leghold Trap and the Beef Hormone Issues between the EC and the US and Canada. Paper read at European Community Studies Association Sixth Biennial International Conference, June 2–5, at Pittsburgh, PA.

Rappaport, Ann, and Margaret F. Flaherty. 1992. *Corporate Responses to Environmental Challenges: Initiatives by Multinational Management.* New York: Quorum Books.

Rodrik, Dani. 1997. *Has Globalization Gone Too Far?* Washington, DC: Institute for International Economics.

Scharpf, Fritz. 1995. Negative and Positive Integration in the Political Economy of European Welfare States: European University Institute. Jean Monnet Chair Papers 28.

Sonnenfeld, David A. (2002). "Social Movements and Ecological Modernization: the Transformation of Pulp and Paper Manufacturing," *Development and Change* 33(1): 1–27.

Spar, Debora, and David B. Yoffie. 2000. A Race to the Bottom or Governance from the Top? In *Coping with Globalization,* edited by A. Prakash and J. A. Hart. London: Routledge.

Stewart, Richard B. 1993. Environmental Regulation and International Competitiveness. *Yale Law Journal* 102 (8):2039–2106.

Swire, Peter P. 1996. The Race to Laxity and the Race to Undesirability: Explaining Failures in Competition Among Jurisdictions in Environmental Law. *Yale Law and Policy Review* 14 (2):67–110.

Vogel, David. 1995. *Trading Up: Consumer and Environmental Regulation in a Global Economy.* Cambridge, MA: Harvard University Press.

———. 2000. Environmental Regulation and Economic Integration. *Journal of International Economic Law* 3 (2):265–279.

Wallach, Lori, and Michelle Sforza. 1999. *Whose Trade Organization? Corporate Globalization and the Erosion of Democracy.* Washington, DC: Public Citizen.

Wheeler, David. 2000. Racing to the Bottom? Foreign Investment and Air Quality in Developing Countries. Washington, DC: Development Research Group, World Bank.

Chapter 1

The International Politics of Harmonization
The Case of Capital Market Regulation

Beth Simmons

The explosion of international financial activity over the last decade has been a central fact of international economic life. Balance of payments statistics indicate that cross-border transactions in bonds and equities for the G-7 rose from less than 10% of gross domestic product in those countries in 1980 to over 140% in 1995.[1] International bond and equity markets have reached staggering proportions: by the end of 1997, portfolio holdings of equity and long-term debt securities reached nearly $5.2 trillion.[2] Capital flows to developing countries and countries in transition grew from $57 billion in 1990 to over $286 billion in 1997 before plummeting to $148 billion in 1998.[3] Foreign exchange transactions reached an estimated average *daily* turnover of nearly $1.5 trillion in 1998 compared to $590 billion daily turnover in 1989.[4] The annual turnover in derivatives contracts—financial agreements that derive their value from the performance of other assets, interest or currency exchange rates, or indexes—was valued at $3.4 trillion in 1990.[5] In 1998 trading and derivatives activities of 71 of the world's leading banks and securities firms totaled more than $130 trillion.[6]

Global capital markets pose dilemmas for national financial regulators. On the one hand, financial liberalization and the removal of capital controls calls for the sophisticated "re-regulation" of capital markets.[7] Liberalization has increased competition in banking, which in turn has encouraged some firms to take on more risk. Innovative financial instruments and strategies and accounting and reporting standards that are difficult to compare across jurisdictions have compromised transparency. As capital controls have been lifted, the opportunity to use international markets for illicit activities has increased.[8] On the other hand, national regulatory authorities are finding it more difficult than ever to achieve their purposes unilaterally.[9] The speed with which international transactions take place, the complex structure of many financial contracts, and the multi-country network of branches and affiliates through which these transactions pass often makes it difficult for national authorities to properly supervise and regulate financial markets. Competitive concerns are also important. As in other areas of economic activity, national regulators typically want to avoid rules that raise costs for national firms or that encourage capital or financial activity to migrate to under-regulated jurisdictions.

Efforts to coordinate national policies to regulate specific aspects of international capital markets have cropped up repeatedly since the mid-1980s. They have varied in their degree of politicization and mode of institutionalization. This article provides a framework to explain such variation. It focuses on the *mechanisms* that encourage convergence across various sub-issue areas of financial regulation. Many of our traditional theories are not especially well suited to explaining this variance. Theories of "races to the bottom," for example, are of little help. They suggest that mobile capital will lead to competition in regulatory laxity across national jurisdictions, as governments vie for footloose capital, try to attract financial business, and attempt to grant competitive advantages to national firms. The predicted result is market-induced downward pressures on regulatory standards. It is difficult, however, to reconcile this simple competitive mechanism with the general *tightening* of regulatory standards in a number of areas. A capital adequacy requirement for banks provides one example.

Nor are prevalent theories of cooperation very useful in explaining the variance we see in the role and strength of international institutions in this area. If international institutions are created to reduce uncertainty and transactions costs,[10] it is surprising that they are much less developed in the regulation of financial markets than in trade. Volatility and volume of transactions should make financial regulation a good candidate for institutionalization, according to this argument. But cooperative arrangements to create common capital markets regulations are far less formal, comprehensive, and inclusive than those for trade.

Finally, contra arguments that underlie neo-liberal institutionalism, the international arrangements that have developed are not uniformly Pareto-superior to uncoordinated national policies. Some governments have resisted "harmonized" regulations precisely because they exact higher costs than they confer benefits within their jurisdiction. In some cases, harmonization has been coerced; in others it has taken place as the best available response to a changed regulatory environment over which smaller jurisdictions typically have little control. Theories that rest on joint gains will seriously mis-specify the mechanisms at work in these cases.

There are many aspects of international regulatory harmonization worthy of explanation. One could ask whether or not harmonization is likely at all, or ask whether harmonization is likely be "up" toward more rigorous standards, or "down" toward greater laxity. This article addresses these issues only indirectly. Its primary focus is on the *mechanisms* that account for the harmonization that we do observe across sub-issue areas of international finance. Just as we would like to know whether firms have arrived at similar prices for a good through collusion or through competition, it is important to distinguish *political* pressures to harmonize from *market* pressures to do so. The arguments developed here also inform a discussion about whether international institutions will play a roll in the process of harmonization, and if so, what that role will be. In short, the dependent variable of this study is primarily on harmonization *processes*.[11] This focus on process mechanisms provides a theoretical and practical understanding of the role of market incentives, political pressure, and multilateral institutions in the coordination of regulatory policies.

I propose a simple framework that focuses on strategic interactions between a dominant "regulatory innovator" and the rest of the financial world. Regulatory innovation in the dominant financial power is taken as exogenous. The dominant regulator does have to think strategically, however, about how foreign regulators react to its innovation. I argue that the two key explanations for how harmonization unfolds are (1) the incentives other regulators face to emulate or diverge from the regulatory innovation of the dominant financial power, and (2) the nature of the externalities produced by this reaction, as experienced in or anticipated by the dominant jurisdiction. These features help explain outcomes that vary across financial issue areas, specifically, whether harmonization will be economically or politically induced, as well as the role (if any) of international institutions in this process.

This model implies that most of the regulatory harmonization that has taken place in the 1980s and 1990s has not been "cooperative"; it has had much more to do with the unilateral imposition of decisions by the dominant financial center(s), than with mutual adjustment. The decisions of regulators in dominant financial centers can change the choice set for other countries drastically; they create a gestalt shift compared to which negotiations that follow may be little more than detailed hairsplitting. This does not mean that the United States, the United Kingdom, or even the G-10 always easily get their preferred regulatory outcome worldwide, for as I argue below, foreign regulators may have negative reaction functions that cause them to choose *divergent* regulatory trajectories. In these cases, harmonization is unlikely without political pressure from the dominant financial centers. Under certain conditions developed below, multilateral institutions are created to enhance political pressure.

The article is organized as follows. The first section outlines the basic argument of the paper. Section two provides evidence to show that in four issue areas illustrative of the variance in the two key explanatory variables—incentives to emulate and nature of externalities—the mechanisms of harmonization broadly accord with the expectations of the framework. The final section concludes.

I. HARMONIZING INTERNATIONAL CAPITAL MARKET REGULATIONS: THE ARGUMENT

The nature of international finance
Efforts over the past decade to coordinate the regulation of internationally active financial entities have been diverse and ad hoc. There is neither a single venue nor a unitary process for hammering out a regime for the regulation of international capital markets. No "World Capital Organization" parallels the World Trade Organization, nor have international rules been approached comprehensively, as was the case with the Law of the Seas during the 1970s. In fact, legally binding conventions for the international financial sector are rare (outside of Europe). Rule development has tended to involve small numbers of national regulators or supervisors, working briefly but intensively on relatively narrow issues, and producing nonbinding agreements. Arguably, the very nature of international finance has necessitated such an approach. Formal, protracted negotiations would be rapidly overtaken by technological change, financial innovation,

and other market developments. Rapid changes in financial markets undercut the value of detailed, legally binding agreements that take time to ratify and implement legislatively. Overall, financial markets are swiftly moving targets whose supervision and regulation requires streamlined decision making and a tremendous amount of technical expertise.

Finance is distinct in another way as well: in few other issue areas is the dominance of one or two countries so profound. The United States and the United Kingdom dominate international financial issues by virtue of the size, efficiency, and internationalization of their markets as well as the sophistication of their regulatory structures. This in turn has to do with the special role of the dollar and sterling in international trade, as well as the extent to which firms from the United States and United Kingdom engage in trade and foreign direct investment. Some 85% per cent of world foreign exchange transactions involve the US dollar, a preeminence that does not yet seem to be challenged by the Euro. Moreover, firms headquartered in the United States and the United Kingdom accounted for 45% of total OECD foreign direct investment inflows and 38% of outflows in the 1990s.[12]

Finance is big business in both of these countries. The financial sector accounts for about 14 per cent of United States GDP, or to about 1.3 trillion dollars in 1998.[13] The private banking sector in the United States provided domestic credit equal to 162% of GDP in 1998. Only Switzerland's banking sector provided a higher ratio (177%) but for a much smaller GDP base (the average figure for high income countries was 140% of GDP).[14] Institutional investors mobilize more assets in the United States and the United Kingdom than anywhere else on the globe: In the United States, the ratio of these assets to GDP is 170 per cent, while in the United Kingdom the ratio is 162 per cent. These figures compare with 77, 75, and 46 percent for Japan, France, and Germany respectively.[15] A spate of bank mergers in the late 1990s left the United States with three of the six largest internationally active banks in the world by market capitalization.[16] More importantly, however, these are the prime centers in which foreign financial institutions conduct business. The biggest foreign banks in the world keep more assets in the United States and the United Kingdom than anywhere else.[17] London is the most highly internationalized financial center in the world, with over 550 international banks and 170 global securities houses in the city.

The United States and the United Kingdom are also heavyweights in the financial component of international trade. Together, these two countries exported on average during the 1990s $12.6 billion of financial services,[18] only slightly less than the total for the rest of the OECD combined. The United States was the second largest importer of financial services in the OECD as well (with average imports of $2.74 billion), second only to Italy (with $3.9 billion) and far ahead of third place Japan ($1.57 billion).[19] Banks from the United States and the United Kingdom are also at the center of the interbank payments system: together they account for nearly half of all intra-G-10 message flows between financial institutions for purposes of facilitating international payments.[20] As a result, regulators in the United States and the United Kingdom exercise jurisdiction over financial institutions and networks that are strategically important to the global financial system as a whole.

The dominance of these two countries' banking sectors is matched, and perhaps exceeded, by their dominance in equity markets. The world's largest stock markets are located in New York and London.[21] The American stock market alone accounts for nearly 50% of the world's stock market valuation.[22] The global market value of firms listed on the New York Stock Exchange (NYSE) and NASDAQ (the American over-the-counter equities market) in 1999 was $11.4 and $5.2 trillion respectively, while the corresponding figure for the London Stock Exchange is $3.0 trillion and Tokyo is $4.5 trillion.[23] U.S. stock markets raised $14.5 trillion dollars for firms in the United States over the course of the 1990s.[24]

Exchanges in the United States and London are highly internationalized and becoming even more so. The London Stock Exchange lists companies from 60 countries,[25] while the comparable figure for the New York Stock Exchange (NYSE) is 49. The number of foreign companies listed on the NYSE quadrupled between 1992 and 2000, for a current total of 400 firms.[26] Meanwhile, the volume of trade in non-U.S. shares on the New York Stock Exchange reached $687 billion in 1999.[27] The United States also dominates the $22 billion international market for depositary receipts,[28] accounting for three-quarters of the world total.[29] With the most active exchanges in the world, the North America accounts for nearly as much turnover in exchange-traded options and futures as do Europe and Asia combined.[30]

Finally, though difficult to quantify, much of the world's regulatory expertise with respect to finance is concentrated in the United States and United Kingdom. What come to be known globally as "best practices" with respect to supervision and regulation usually emanate from these centers (from the public regulatory apparatus, but also from the self-regulatory practices of private entities).[31] While only an indirect measure of regulatory capacity, it may also be significant that the Federal Reserve System produces and analyzes much more quickly the data that is relevant to understanding market trends than do central banks elsewhere.[32] Since the Basel Committee for Bank Supervision came into existence in 1974, either an American or an Englishman has chaired it for 19 years, by a Dutchman for four years, and by an Italian for four years.[33] It is interesting, given the strong norm of rotating power in many euro-centric institutions, that a central banker from Germany, Switzerland, France or Japan has never chaired this committee. An American with extensive supervisory and regulatory experience was recently chosen to chair the new Financial Stability Institute, whose purpose it is to assist bank supervisors around the world in improving and strengthening their financial systems.[34]

The argument

This concentration of financial power has profound implications for regulatory harmonization. The size of the internal United States market gives regulators there an incentive to take unilateral regulatory decisions, even if foreign regulators do not follow suit. The United States is "hegemonic" in finance in the sense that it is costlier to alter its preferred regulatory innovation than it is to try to change the policies of the rest of the world. US regulators can be thought of as *unconditional* first movers: financial regulatory innovation will be motivated by and respond to internal regulatory needs and politics (such as the soundness of the national financial system, the protection of domestic investors, improved transparency or efficiency or other social or political goals). Certainly regulatory decisions are taken subject to competitive constraints, but the size and efficiency of US financial markets and institutions often render such constraints non-binding. The framework developed here therefore takes US regulatory innovation itself as an exogenous expression of the domestic political economy. Virtually every political account of financial regulation in the secondary literature supports this assumption.[35] *International* policies of the dominant power, however, are formulated in response to or in anticipation of the reactions of the rest of the world to a particular regulatory change.

Whatever the content of the United States' regulatory innovation, enhancement, or deregulation, *it has the potential to change significantly the context for financial markets and hence regulators in the rest of the world.* Such a change does one of three things. It may (1) provide incentives for other regulators to *emulate* (implying a positive reaction function), (2) provide incentives for other regulators to *diverge* (a negative reaction function), or (3) have *no effects* on others.[36] One can think of this reaction function forming a continuum ranging from strong incentives to defect (resembling a collaboration game) to strong incentives to emulate (resembling a coordination game). In the middle of this range, strategic incentives are undefined, as the regulatory innovation of United States regulators does not change the conditions facing the rest of the world significantly.

We can summarize the impact of regulatory change in the dominant financial center by its effect on the profitability of firms operating in foreign jurisdictions. Emulation will be reinforced if the innovation renders non-conforming jurisdictions relatively costly or risky sites to conduct business. In this case, emulation would be a logical competitive move in order to maintain or attract business to the national jurisdiction. Access to the markets of the dominant financial center also provides a powerful market incentive to conform to their regulatory environment. In both of these cases, market pressures and opportunities that follow directly from the regulatory change in the United States encourage harmonization. When this is the case, the dominant power can afford to take a politically passive approach to international harmonization.

On the other hand, some regulatory changes can prompt divergent policy choices in foreign jurisdictions. This is most clearly the case when a regulatory policy taken elsewhere creates an economic premium for taking the opposite response. Economic sanctions provide a well-known example: a rule against providing goods or credit to a particular country in effect increases the (market) returns to those willing to defy the sanctioning coalition. Or imagine the effect on the price of a therapeutic drug in Mexico that has not been approved by the American Food and Drug Administration. Assuming Mexican authorities have reached an independent conclusion regarding safety and efficacy, they have powerful incentives to make such a drug available, *especially* in light of its non-availability in the United States.

In these cases, the market does not reinforce the regulation of the dominant jurisdiction. On the contrary it may raise the (opportunity) costs of harmonization.

The second dimension—the nature and extent of externalities—is essential to understanding the dominant financial center's international policies relating to a particular innovation. The key question is whether the rest of the world's aggregate equilibrium reaction creates a significant negative externality for the first mover. Because the dominant power has already determined that the regulatory innovation is in its own domestic interest, no combination of responses on the part of the rest of the world's regulators will cause it to alter its own internal regulatory stance. It will, however, anticipate costly foreign resistance to its regulations. If negative externalities are significant, the question the dominant financial center faces in formulating its international policies is how it can change the choices of other financial regulators at reasonable cost.

Suppose the world's reaction to the initial move causes a high negative externality for the first mover. Rather than meekly retract its regulatory innovation, regulators in the dominant financial center anticipate costly foreign resistance, and will mobilize political pressure to try and change the reactions of important foreign regulators. In fact, it would be reasonable to expend political resources up to the cost of the negative externality it is importing. If the negative externality is very costly, we should see the exertion of a good deal of political pressure on the part of the dominant financial power. We should also expect to observe efforts to minimize the costs of addressing these externalities. For example, if the sources of the externalities are distinct or if the externality is divisible we could expect the United States to target its pressure accordingly. Where the source of the externality is uncertain or constantly shifting, or where the externality is not easy to target, multilateral institutions might be a more efficient way to press for regulatory change in foreign jurisdictions. On the other hand, if the negative externalities experienced or anticipated by the dominant power as a result of the reactions of the rest of the world are small, there is no reason to expect a very active international component to the regulatory change. The United States should not care in this case whether the rest of the world adopts the policy innovation or not.

The role for multilateral institutions flow from the hegemon's anticipation of externalities. These institutions can be created and used strategically by the dominant financial center to achieve its desired regulatory outcome—the mitigation of negative externalities—in an economical fashion. Their strength and role should reflect the strategic problems of the dominant center. After all, collective action problems and disagreements over distributive issues render institutions built by opposing regulatory coalitions highly unlikely. Where multilateral approaches are unnecessary to avoid externalities in the center, this framework expects multilateral institutions to be weak, or at most facilitative rather than active enforcers of regulatory harmonization.

By combining these two dimensions—the extent to which foreign regulators have an incentive to emulate, along with the extent and nature of the externalities anticipated by the dominant financial center—it is possible to lay out the mechanisms by which harmonization is expected to come about, and the role for international institutions in this process (see Figure 1).

INSTITUTIONAL IMPLICATIONS

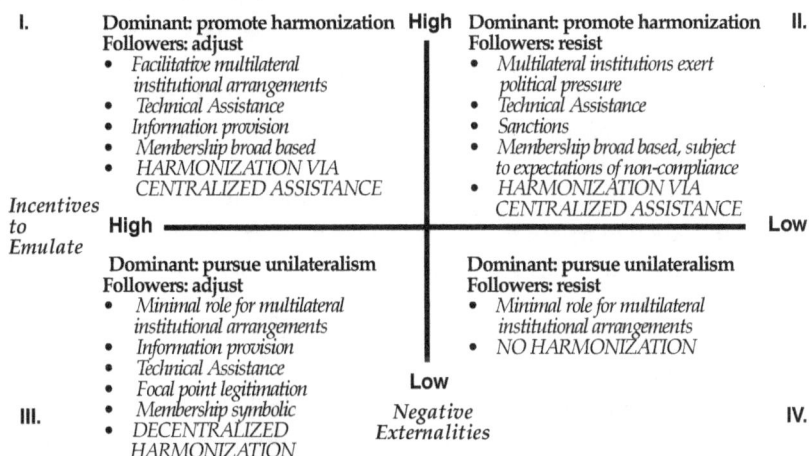

Figure 1. Expectations: Incentives for Regulatory Harmonization
(dominant power, followers)

In Figure 1, quadrant I, regulators in smaller jurisdictions have an incentive to emulate in a policy area in which the potential negative externalities for the dominant power are high. The dominant center supports these adjustments, due to the potential for negative externalities in the absence of harmonization. It is in the dominant center's interest to support the creation and activities of an international institution with broad-based membership encompassing the range of the sources of anticipated externalities. This institution need only play an informational role regarding the nature of the dominant financial center's standards, and may provide technical assistance to jurisdictions wishing to implement them. While these standards may not have been preferred in the absence of the dominant center's innovation, smaller financial centers have incentives to respond by adjusting their own regulations. In this quadrant, we should expect harmonization to take place primarily through market incentives and to be facilitated by the dominant financial center through an institution designed to bolster the technical ability of smaller jurisdictions to adhere.

Quadrant 2 has very different expectations. The key difference here is that smaller jurisdictions have an incentive to resist the financial center's regulatory innovation. Moreover, their reaction creates negative externalities within the jurisdiction of the dominant financial center. The dominant center, concerned to limit the impact on its national firms or at home, pressures smaller jurisdictions to match its financial regulations. One way to do this is through unilateral pressure, which is a reasonable response as long as the sources of the externality are stable and distinct. In some cases, the dominant financial center may be able to target or divert negative externalities at minimal cost; for example, bilateral agreements can be reached or unilateral action taken that mitigate the transmission of the negative externality from one jurisdiction to another.[37] However, in some issue areas, buying off one producer of a negative externality may only encourage the private entity that is the source of the externality to migrate to another jurisdiction. This is especially problematic when jurisdictions are highly substitutable for the kind of activity under consideration, and when curtailing the activity in some jurisdictions actually *raises* the payoffs to its few remaining (unregulated) practitioners. If these externalities cannot be targeted or diverted at reasonable cost, it is more rational for the dominant financial center to press for regulatory harmonization through the creation and backing of multilateral institutions that not only provide technical assistance (which would not be sufficient to convince smaller jurisdictions to harmonize their rules in this case) but also that exert overt political pressure on jurisdictions that do not comply.

Since defection problems often create incentives to misrepresent behavior, multilateral institutions under these conditions will often be essential in gathering "objective" information through surveillance protocols. International institutions will also be important to the dominant financial center for coordinating potentially costly punishments that might be subject to problems of free-ridership in their absence.[38] If externalities are not divertible, or if their source is uncertain or constantly shifting, (that is, if they approximate a "public bad") we would expect membership in such an institution to be broad (with a caveat that it may be limited by a desire to include only those who can be persuaded through institutional mechanisms to comply).[39] If harmonization takes place, it will be through overtly political pressure from the financial center, most likely exercised through a multilateral institution.

Quadrant 3 predicts just the opposite. Smaller jurisdictions have market incentives to adjust to the regulatory change in the center, and the negative externalities anticipated by the financial center are minimal. Smaller jurisdictions have market motives to adjust, and the financial center has little incentive to respond at all. There is little reason to create an international institution in this case; harmonization is likely to proceed in a very decentralized fashion. Multilateral institutional arrangements that do develop are likely to do little more than provide technical assistance, or legitimate a "focal point"[40] that provides a multilateral veneer to an essentially unilateral decision taken in the dominant financial center. Market forces rather than overt political pressure will foster decentralized harmonization in this case.

Finally, consider the case in which smaller jurisdictions have no incentive to adjust their regulations in response to the center, yet the center experiences no externalities as a result of such resistance (quadrant 4). Smaller jurisdictions do not want to emulate, but the dominant center does not care. There is no reason to expect the dominant center to invest in multilateral institutions; nor should we expect harmonization to take place under these conditions. But if it does, the mechanisms will be political rather than market based.

It is worth pointing out how this framework differs from institutionalist theories that rest on more liberal functionalist formulations. There is nothing particularly "cooperative" or even Pareto-improving to this situation. Regulators elsewhere may not even have been consulted or have participated in any meaningful way in decisions that fundamentally alter their regulatory landscape. Smaller financial centers may have had to adjust to decisions taken by the United States to avoid worse outcomes, but may have preferred no innovation at the center to begin with.[41] Indeed, this framework predicts an important role for coercion and persuasion when incentives to diverge are strong and negative externalities are severe. Financial dominance of the United States precludes a return to the status quo as an option, even if that is what many smaller centers would prefer.

Furthermore, by taking both incentives to emulate as well as externalities into account, this framework is able to provide nuanced expectations based on the strategic context that can differ notably across sub-issue areas of finance. Much of the literature on international institutions has been inspired by the analysis of cooperation games versus coordination games. [42] Most of these analyses assume rough parity among the players and ignore the role that power and persuasion play in arriving at a stable equilibrium. The anticipation of externalities in this model provides the motivation for the dominant power to use political pressure to counter uncooperative behavior and to provide technical or other assistance to emulate (if necessary). The nature of externalities also allows for more nuanced predictions with respect to institutional form, with shifting, uncertain, or worldwide sources encouraging the dominant center to invest in multilateralism.

This framework also differs from theories that expect regulatory races to the bottom.[43] There are good reasons to expect dominant financial jurisdictions to function as "regulatory anchors" in the sense that they do not respond in kind to what may seem to be competitive regulations by foreign jurisdictions. Indeed, if the dominant financial center is large and competitive enough, it seems utterly arbitrary to assume that it will sacrifice its national regulatory preferences to engage in a downward competitive spiral with foreign jurisdictions. In this framework, I make the more reasonable assumption that a financial center as large and competitive as the United States is unlikely to reverse its domestically preferred regulatory course. This would not of course prevent races to the bottom among smaller or less efficient jurisdictions,[44] but does provide a backstop to the generalized regulatory deterioration sometimes alluded to in the literature.

III. ISSUE AREAS

This section provides some evidence for the argument developed above. The research design is simple: I examine four sub-issue areas of international finance that are illustrative of the four different combinations of values on the key independent variables (incentives to emulate and the nature and extent of externalities). "Financial dominance" is constant throughout these cases. The central question is whether the mechanisms of harmonization (the relative role of market incentives versus political pressures) and the role of international institutions (whether they are unimportant or central to the harmonization process; whether they are designed to facilitate, legitimate, or enforce) fit the expectations I have set out above.

Quadrant I: High negative externalities, high incentives to emulate: the case of capital adequacy rules

The globalization of banking increases the possibility that any weak bank involved in the increasingly dense network of interbank relations potentially can transmit its weaknesses via the interbank market throughout the international banking system. One can gain an appreciation of these linkages by looking at the size of the interbank market: for banks in countries reporting to the Bank for International Settlements, between 1983 and 1997 interbank claims averaged about 58 per cent of total assets and interbank liabilities averaged about 62 per cent of total liabilities.[45] Furthermore, banks that are linked through the interbank market are highly leveraged, which raises "the possibility that failure of one bank to settle net transactions with other banks will trigger a chain reaction, depriving other banks of funds and preventing them from closing their positions in turn."[46] Capital adequacy standards are explicitly intended to "protect the safety and stability of the system as a whole"[47] from risky activities of weakly capitalized firms. Highly leveraged loans linked through a transnational interbank market make for an issue area in which the American banking system is potentially subject to the negative externalities of poor capital adequacy regulation in other parts of the world.

On the other hand, there are strong incentives to emulate an American regulatory innovation with respect to capital adequacy standards. The fundamental reason is that international banking is characterized by information asymmetries that provide an opening for opportunistic behavior. Rules regulating capital adequacy may convey important information on the quality of a firm as a counterpart to an agreement. In this environment, appropriate prudential regulations are a competitive advantage that other jurisdictions have an incentive to copy. In the words of the Chairman of the Federal Reserve Bank of Australia, once capital adequacy requirements are adopted by the Central Banks in G-10 countries, ". . .there is considerable [market] pressure on others to follow—otherwise their banks risk being perceived as somewhat inferior institutions in competitive situations."[48] A regulatory race to the bottom is conceivable in the absence of any obvious focal point,[49] but once the dominant financial center has adopted a clear standard, there is very little incentive to reduce standards and risk developing a reputation as "poorly regulated." Most banks are simply in no position to forego concerns about reputation and compete for international business on price alone. For this reason, strong incentives exist to emulate the standards adopted in the leading financial center. Capital adequacy standards are thus illustrative of the kinds of cases that fall into the upper left hand quadrant of Figure 2.

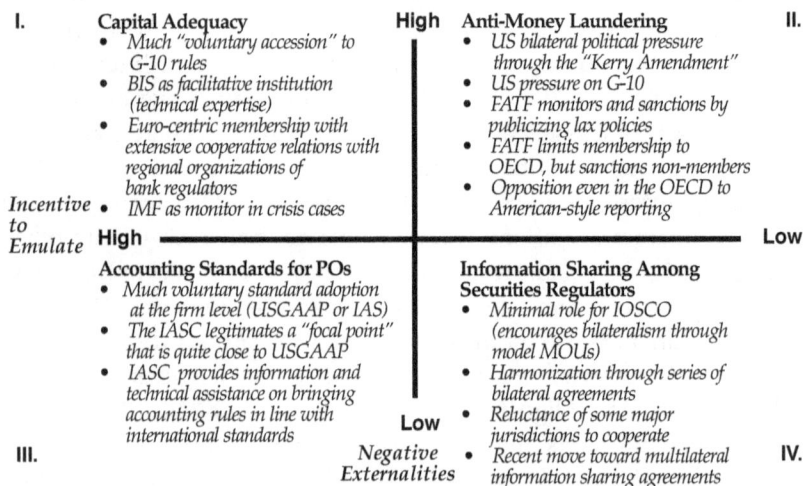

I.	Capital Adequacy	High	Anti-Money Laundering	II.
	• *Much "voluntary accession" to G-10 rules*		• *US bilateral political pressure through the "Kerry Amendment"*	
	• *BIS as facilitative institution (technical expertise)*		• *US pressure on G-10*	
	• *Euro-centric membership with extensive cooperative relations with regional organizations of bank regulators*		• *FATF monitors and sanctions by publicizing lax policies*	
Incentive to Emulate	• *IMF as monitor in crisis cases*		• *FATF limits membership to OECD, but sanctions non-members*	
	High		• *Opposition even in the OECD to American-style reporting*	**Low**
	Accounting Standards for POs		**Information Sharing Among Securities Regulators**	
	• *Much voluntary standard adoption at the firm level (USGAAP or IAS)*		• *Minimal role for IOSCO (encourages bilateralism through model MOUs)*	
	• *The IASC legitimates a "focal point" that is quite close to USGAAP*		• *Harmonization through series of bilateral agreements*	
	• *IASC provides information and technical assistance on bringing accounting rules in line with international standards*	**Low**	• *Reluctance of some major jurisdictions to cooperate*	
III.		*Negative Externalities*	• *Recent move toward multilateral information sharing agreements*	IV.

Figure 2. Harmonization and Institutional Outcomes

IV. INSTITUTIONAL IMPLICATIONS

Regulatory innovation in this area began in the United States in response to the savings and loans crisis of the 1980s. Worried by a trend toward capital deterioration despite growing financial risks associated with internationalization and liberalization—and the initial serious concern that differential approaches to capital requirements would constitute a competitive disadvantage for banks chartered in countries with more stringent requirements—the Federal Reserve and the Bank of England struck a bilateral agreement that provided for a common definition of capital. They agreed to adopt of a risk-weighting system for each class of assets, to include "off-balance sheet" items in risk determination, and adopted a formula for calculating specific capital requirements for individual banks, based on their weighted-asset risk profile.[50]

The case of capital adequacy standards fits the expectations of the proposed framework reasonably well. Strong market-based incentives have encouraged convergence in this area. The bilateral accord between the two largest players immediately sparked intense negotiations among the G-10 to adopt a common approach to capital adequacy. By some accounts, Japan, Germany, and France accepted the US/UK framework (with minor changes) because they were concerned that, without adjustment, their banks might not meet standards prevailing in the United States and United Kingdom.[51] In December 1987, central bankers from the G-10 countries adopted guidelines for evaluating the adequacy of capital in their international banks and agreed to reach an established minimum level by 1992. By the end of 1993, internationally active G-10 banks had capital ratios that *exceeded* the prescribed minimum, often significantly. [52]

By the mid-1990s the European Union had followed suit in their decision to use the G-10 guidelines as a basis for the Capital Adequacy Directive (CAD), which came into effect in January 1996.[53] Even more significant, a number of countries that did not participate in the G-10 process and have *n o obligation whatsoever* to follow guidelines originating in Basel have voluntarily done so. Many developing countries have, for example, adopted the Basel Committee's 8 per cent capital adequacy rule for international banks. Others have decided unilaterally to match Basel rules regarding disclosure requirements for derivatives activities, citing G-10 rules as "global standards."[54] By 1994, every country out of the 129 surveyed by the BIS had capital requirements of some description, and in 92% of cases, a Basel-like risk weighted approach was reportedly followed. Capital charges for market risk exposure—a relatively new development—were imposed by 23% of the sample, and fully 85% of non-G-10 countries declared their intention to implement the 1995 Amendment to the original 1988 Capital Accord.[55] Even if these figures are exaggerated, they reflect an apparent desire to emulate the G-10's rules.

The process of rule development and dissemination has largely been market driven, though the Bank for International Settlements and more recently the IMF have played a facilitative role. Through meetings, informational conferences and technical training courses with regional central banking organizations, the BIS has actively supported the dissemination of G-10 prudential banking regulations

and standards among emerging financial markets.[56] In the wake of the
Asian financial crisis, banking supervisors in Indonesia have moved to
phase in Basel's 8% capital adequacy ratio[57], despite the estimated
price of recapitalization at this ratio of nearly 15 per cent of GDP.[58]
Korea has also declared its intent to upgrade its prudential standards
to meet Basel core principles, and mobilized trillions of won for
purposes of recapitalization with the Basel ratios in mind.[59] Thailand
adopted 8.5% recapitalization ratios for all surviving banks.[60] The
explicit adoption of these targets has been essential for establishing the
credibility of national bank reforms. To assist in the promulgation of its
standards in the region, the BIS opened its first Representative Office
outside of its headquarters in Basel in July of 1998.

No banking supervisor in the world has been able to speak of
prudential regulations without reference to "international standards"
which have spread from the initial US-UK agreement to the G-10 to the
EU to a number of emerging markets. The BIS has provided technical
assistance and promoted its rules as a focal point against which to
judge the adequacy of banks' capital ratios in jurisdictions around the
world. Despite some effort by the IMF to subject adoption of these
rules to some form of conditionality,[61] the market pressure to meet
international standards has been far more important than has
organized political pressure to harmonize these rules. Capital
adequacy standards have become more rigorous and more widespread
than a model of competitive regulatory laxity would suggest. It
remains to be seen just how well these rules will be implemented,
especially in the Asian financial centers whose restructuring is
currently underway. But generally speaking, market pressures to
match international standards have been far more important than
political pressure, in sharp contrast to the case of anti-money
laundering efforts, discussed below.

Quadrant II: High negative externalities, low incentives to emulate: the case of anti-money laundering

Money laundering supports a negative externality in the United
States—criminal activity—that is extraordinarily difficult to eliminate,
to target, or to divert. Estimates of the amount of money laundered
provides an upper limit to the range of this externality: by some
estimates, one billion dollars of criminal profits finds its way into the
world's financial markets *every day*.[62] Estimates of the annual amount
of drug profits moving through the United States financial system have

been as high as $100 billion.[63] Michel Camdessus, former director of the International Monetary Fund, estimated that in 2000 the yearly global value of illicit money laundered was equal to between 2 and 5 per cent of world production.[64] Even if only a fraction of this total results from crimes affecting the United States, the potential negative effects are considerable. And as the recent case of the laundering of stolen aid to Russia indicates, the precedent crime does not have to be committed *in* the United States to frustrate broader American interests. Moreover, the situation will likely deteriorate as capital controls around the world continue to loosen and the scrutiny given international transactions continues to ease.[65] As evidence that the United States views money laundering as a serious threat, the Treasury Department operates the largest currency transaction reporting system in the world[66] at an estimated cost to the banking industry as high as $136 million annually.[67]

For a number of reasons, foreign jurisdictions tend not to want to emulate tighter anti-money laundering regulations. Indeed, stringent reporting requirements in the United States may make the banking secrecy offered by the legitimate private banking industry in such countries as Switzerland, Liechtenstein, and Luxembourg even more lucrative. Certainly, adopting tough reporting requirements could push funds offshore.[68] Swiss officials have long recognized that bank secrecy has contributed significantly to the high standard of living and thus "at least indirectly concerns substantial economic interests of the state."[69] In Liechtenstein, even mild rules regarding "due diligence " that require bankers to report suspicious activities to authorities "pose a direct threat to Liechtenstein's basic competitiveness," according to Bankers in Vaduz.[70] Developing economies may be even more resistant. Banking secrecy combined with loose supervision may be an attractive development policy for a large number of smaller resource-poor countries and territories. In an effort to jump-start an international financial services sector, some jurisdictions have instituted easy rules of incorporation, no recording requirements for large cash transactions, and a limited asset seizure capability. The fewer the jurisdictions willing to provide such services with minimal scrutiny, the better the terms these jurisdictions are likely to be able to extract from "investors." The conclusion in this case is quite different from that of capital adequacy regulation. Unlike the interest financial institutions may have in developing a reputation for safety, " . . . it is not necessarily in the direct financial interest of financial institutions to adopt anti-laundering behavior."[71] Anti-money laundering efforts provide no clear economic payoff, and may in fact exact immediate and unrecoverable costs to financial intermediaries.

As in the capital adequacy case, international initiatives to control money laundering have come primarily from the United States, in alliance with the United Kingdom, but also with France, and increasingly Australia.[72] By 1986, the United States was the only country to have criminalized money laundering, and it remains by far the leader in prosecutions.[73] Because most countries do not wish to emulate American policies, and because the externalities to the United States have been high, what harmonization has taken place has been driven by hardball political pressure. The US Congress began with the "Kerry Amendment,"[74] which required the US Treasury to negotiate with foreign countries with the objective of having foreign banks record all cash deposits over US $10,000 and to provide information to US authorities in the event of a narcotics related investigation. Should a bank fail to agree, the amendment gave the President the power to deny that bank access to the U.S.'s clearinghouse system. But for a number of reasons—including the universal nature of the problem, opposition from Treasury,[75] the fear of stimulating foreign alternatives to US clearing facilities, and the fear of retaliation against US banks—this unilateral approach fizzled with few tangible results.

It has been difficult for the United States to drum up support for its anti-money laundering crusade, but with Europe's eventual support the Financial Action Task Force (FATF) was created by the OECD countries in 1989. This is an institution that uses the only instrument at its disposal—peer pressure—to embarrass governments into adopting stricter controls over money laundering. The FATF uses a graduated set of sanctions to review and influence the policies of its own members and those of non-members to follow the spirit of its "Forty Recommendations" promulgated in 1990 (updated in September 1995). These recommendations call for states to ratify the 1988 Vienna Convention Against Illicit Traffic in Narcotic Drugs and Psychotropic Substances, which specifies "intentionally" laundering drug profits as a criminal activity.[76] They also call on governments to adopt effective seizure and forfeiture laws, and to prohibit anonymous accounts. The FATF employs a system of mutual review in which each member's laws and efforts are scrutinized by a FATF team and then assessed by the full membership. The mildest sanction is a letter from the president indicating shortcomings in a particular country; the harshest sanction is expulsion. Turkey has been sanctioned—for several years it was the only country in the FATF that had failed to date to make money laundering a crime—and significantly changed its laws as a result.[77] The FATF's "Recommendation 21" also calls for sanctions against non-cooperative *non-members*. The Seychelles was one of the first countries to be on the receiving end of such a sanction.[78] The FATF routinely urges financial institutions to avoid doing business in countries with seriously wanting money laundering law, and posts the list of such jurisdictions on its website.[79] Meanwhile, the United States and United Kingdom often coordinate their bilateral pressure on uncooperative jurisdictions, and recently have denounced Antigua as unfit to conduct business with their national firms.[80]

The convergence across national jurisdictions since 1986 has been detectable but hard fought and far from complete. Almost all industrialized countries now agree that money laundering should be considered a crime, but few countries have embraced the American approach of comprehensive reporting of all cash transactions above $10,000 (most banks have lobbied their governments hard to reject US-style record keeping and reporting).[81] Tightening money-laundering rules continues to meet with significant resistance in much of the financially influential world. Outside of Japan, Singapore, and Hong Kong, money laundering is not a crime in much of Asia. Cooperation in the Western Hemisphere provides an interesting contrast: here sustained US leadership in such forums as the "Summit of the Americas" keeps laggards in the international spotlight. Many more Central and South American countries have made money laundering a crime, and have even agreed to "self-assessment" (though not mutual assessment, as in the FATF) in their own regional grouping, the Caribbean Financial Action Task Force (CFATF).

In short, harmonization with respect to money laundering depends on political pressure from the dominant financial centers. This follows from the nature of the issue area, in which emulation has its costs, and the negative externalities are high. Nor are these externalities easily controlled through unilateral efforts or by targeting individual juris-dictions. This provides incentives to create multilateral organizations with surveillance and enforcement powers. A multilateral institution, exerting strong peer pressure coordinated by the dominant centers, has been crucial to rule harmonization in this area.

Quadrant III: Low negative externalities, high incentives to emulate: the case of accounting standards for public offerings

National securities regulators formulate the conditions under which companies can offer their shares to the public on stock exchanges within their jurisdiction. Yet the accounting rules used to evaluate the worth of companies so offered can vary greatly from country to country. For example, when Daimler Benz first reconciled its accounts based on "United States Generally Accepted Accounting Principles" (USGAAP) as a condition of listing on the new York Stock Exchange, potential investors were stunned to learn that Daimler's *DM615 million profit* in 1993 under German accounting rules dissolved into a *DM1.8 billion loss* using USGAAP for the same period.[82]

Accounting standards for public equity offerings illustrate the conditions denoted in the lower left-hand quadrant of Figure 2. In common with capital adequacy standards, but in contrast to anti-money laundering regulations, there are significant incentives for regulators and firms to adopt the accounting rules of the major financial center. Because stock trading was originally influenced by time zones, this pattern is clear at the regional level.[83] Thus, Canada's standards tend to resemble those of the United States,[84] New Zealand's those of Australia, the Scandinavian countries those of Germany. Such coordination is useful in the absence of global, or even G-10 agreement. Disagreements emerge over which rules should be the international standard, but no national regulator has the incentive to differ radically from a major market, and once accepted, there are virtually no incentives to defect.[85] For internationally active firms, the transactions costs of keeping up to speed on multiple standards are likely to exceed the one-time adjustment costs to a single widely used standard no matter what its "nationality". Stock exchanges themselves want to attract as much high quality foreign business as possible, making them strong proponents of international standards.[86] As is the case with prudential regulations regarding bank capital, market pressures reinforce harmonization: once the adjustment costs are paid, there is no reason to buck the regulatory trend.

On the other hand, there are few if any negative externalities to the United States if other jurisdictions continue to use their own national standards for public offerings. In contrast to capital adequacy and anti-money laundering regulations, inadequate accounting rules may result in allocative inefficiency but are not discussed in terms of generating significant streams of negative externalities or serious systemic risks for the United States.[87] Widely varying accounting rules can add to transactions costs for firms that want to offer shares on foreign exchanges, potentially deter cross border listings (relatively few American firms list on the London and Tokyo exchanges, for example)[88], and confuse investors.[89] Negative externalities, however, have not been central to the definition of the problem for the dominant center.

Market dominance in equities is central to how harmonization takes place. Key is the fact that the Securities and Exchange Commission (SEC) insists that any firm listing in the US must use USGAAP. Market power alone has led to harmonization in this area: if companies want to list on American stock exchanges, they must be willing to pay the one-time adjustment cost. Many firms have prepared their statements voluntarily in order to maximize their access to international capital. Thus, in the last few years, there has been a trend by Swiss, French, and Belgian companies to adopt USGAAP or the somewhat less stringent International Accounting Standards (IAS) currently under development by the International Accounting Standards Committee (IASC).[90] In April 1996 Germany's fourth largest company, Veba, an energy and industrial conglomerate now moving into telecoms, adopted USGAAP, its CEO explaining, "It is a global capital market, and we all have to play by the same rules."[91] A raft of European multinationals, and most of corporate Germany, including Bayer, BASF, and Hoechst, and many companies awaiting privatization, including Deutsche Telekom, may seek New York listings and may have to opt for USGAAP standards before IASC standards are complete.[92] Interestingly, the newly established Easdaq—a pan European over the counter equities market established at the initiative of the European Commission—has opted to use USGAAP.[93] Harmonization in accounting standards for public offerings has been decentralized and market driven toward conformity with the rules of the dominant equities market.

Because the SEC knows firms that want to list on American exchanges are likely to be willing to pay the adjustment cost of reconciling their accounts to USGAAP, it has little incentive to foster international institutions to harmonize accounting rules. Thus, the International Accounting Standards Committee (IASC) has enjoyed little support from American standard setters, and in many respects has had to reconcile its "multilateral" rules to the demands of the SEC.

After all, the IASC knows its standards have little credibility unless the SEC accepts them, and as one might expect, those rules that the SEC has accepted have been quite close to US practices.[94] All the while, tighter regional coordination among the Anglo-Americans outside of the IASC remains a live, indeed a thriving option.[95] Meanwhile, Britain has opposed standardizing accounting rules at the European level. The EU has instead pursued a policy of mutual recognition, and the European Commission has formally given up any effort to create a European Accounting Standards body.[96] Their strategy has been to try to influence the work of the IASC,[97] which is politically more palatable than accepting USGAAP without any pretense of multilateralism.

Harmonization has been driven in this case by decentralized market forces, primarily the desire to access the world's most established equities markets. Firms adjust their accounts based on calculations of how much they would benefit from a foreign listing. Simple market power is moving harmonization toward the dominant center's preferred accounting approach. A multilateral accounting institution does exist, it does not explain harmonization in this area. Without much active American support, the IASC has provided the cover of multilateral legitimacy to mostly American standards. In doing so, they have provided a focal point that bears a close resemblance to SEC rules.

Quadrant IV: Low negative externalities; low incentives to emulate: information sharing among securities regulators

Internationalization of securities and related derivatives markets has made it nearly routine for advisers in one country to propose a trading strategy to a money manager in a second country which involves taking a position in a market in a third country, while offsetting it in a derivatives market in yet a fourth. When trading networks cross multiple jurisdictions, regulators' efforts to access information that would expose fraudulent or highly risky trading activities are greatly complicated. Information available only to foreign regulators is often essential for a national authority to perform its functions.

In order to prosecute fraudulent or risky securities trading behavior, regulators often need to harmonize their rules about the release of information that may be useful for that purpose. It is clear, however, that national regulators have reasons to resist making and honoring such agreements.[98] Often, concerns about confidentiality are important. In order to assess systemic risks, national regulators need to know foreign firms' market exposure and positions. Foreign regulators, under pressure from national firms, are typically very cautious in providing such sensitive information. When a request relates to illegal activities, there may also be concerns about attempts to exercise extraterritorial jurisdiction, especially if cooperation is sought to prosecute a foreign national trading from a computer screen in his or her own country. Agreements on the conditions under which information is to be shared among regulators do not provide market incentives for emulation.

Whether or not the United States is likely to experience serious negative externalities in this issue area depends on the reasons the information is sought. If it is for purposes of prosecuting securities fraud, negative externalities may exist, but are likely to be limited. In that case, the externality does not exhibit the same potentially global character as does money laundering, nor are there the same systemic risks posed by inadequate bank capital. When information is sought to prosecute fraud, this issue area belongs in the lower right-hand quadrant of Figure 2.

Increasingly, however, information sharing among securities regulators is viewed as crucial to detecting *systemic risks*. The collapse of Barings in 1995 did much to bolster this perception, even though no systemic consequences were in fact felt. Information that would have exposed Barings' dangerous aggregate position was compartmentalized in the Singapore and Osaka exchanges, and not readily available to any single regulatory body.[99] Revelations of how little anyone knew about Barings' total trading position is the reason that regulators have begun to view information sharing as essential to establishing the actual risk position of securities firms.[100] Thus, information sharing may be necessary to avert negative externalities of a more systemic nature. If so, this issue area may be migrating north toward quadrant II.

In the simple fraud case, there are no incentives to emulate, but neither is the dominant financial center likely to experience extensive negative externalities. The framework suggests little harmonization and a minimal role for multilateral institutions. The first part of this expectation is not quite met here: the issue area is in fact characterized by a series of bilateral agreements that represent a segmented form of harmonization. The prediction for the role of multilateral institutions does hold up. The relevant institution in this case is the International Organization of Securities Regulators (IOSCO), a relatively passive organization that has primarily encouraged regulators to negotiate and file their bilateral information sharing agreements. It provides technical advice where necessary and offers "model agreements" to interested parties.

The dominant financial center has proceeded bilaterally to secure understandings on information sharing for quite some time. U.S. regulators have negotiated a series of explicit bilateral information sharing agreements, modified somewhat depending on the circumstances, across an expanding set of dyadic regulatory relationships. Pioneered by the SEC in 1986, these agreements typically take the form of bilateral Memoranda of Understanding (MOUs). MOUs state the intentions of the parties to make information available under certain conditions, but are not legally binding. A typical MOU calls on each regulator to pass on information that gives rise to a suspicion of a breach of the laws of the other party. A few grant mutual authority for on-site inspections of fund managers in each other's jurisdictions.[101] By the end of 1997, United States regulators had on record with IOSCO more than 90 bilateral memoranda of understanding and similar agreements; British regulators had 45; French, 28; Spanish, 17; Italian, 14; Japanese, 4.[102] For reasons arising from its federal structure, German securities regulators have only entered into such agreements since 1995.[103] Out of 49 countries whose regulatory entities have entered into information sharing agreements, 21 made their first agreement with their counterpart in the United States. By the early 1990s, a number of securities regulators in emerging markets began to develop bilateral information sharing agreements as well. Securities regulators in China and Russia have now entered into such arrangements—first and foremost with the SEC.[104]

Clearly, there are some moderate externalities associated with the prosecutorial practices in other jurisdictions, but in this case, externalities are easy to target on a bilateral basis and prior to the Barings case were perceived to have no important systemic consequences. This explains the institutional response: bilateral agreements are easier to negotiate than multilateral accords, and minimize defection via specific reciprocity. As securities markets globalize, the incentive to replicate information sharing agreements increases, while the transactions costs of doing so declines (there are numerous tested "models" from which to select). Particular bilateral arrangements are invoked repeatedly between jurisdictions that transact a high volume of business, as is the case for example between the United States and the United Kingdom.[105] The key point here is that negative externalities are easily targeted; it makes sense in this case to negotiate agreements that constitute bilateral "club goods" that provide benefits (mutual access to information) for members only. Particularly in the prosecution of illegal practices, broad multilateral cooperation is not as important to the dominant financial center as having clear agreements with a few key regulators or exchanges.

Only recently have *multilateral* information sharing agreements been made, and as the framework presented here would suggest, these aim primarily to facilitate the detection of *systemic risks* that pose potentially far greater negative externalities for the dominant financial center. In March 1996, some 49 exchanges and clearing houses (14 of which are situated within the United States), as well as 14 regulatory agencies, signed international information sharing agreements which informally commit signatories to share market and financial information about members.[106] The expressed purpose is to allow a more comprehensive assessment of the inter-market risks. Thus, systemic concerns are beginning to make cooperation among securities regulators more closely resemble that among banking regulators. Arguably, this case has migrated from the lower to the upper region of Quadrant IV after 1995, indicating that harmonization of information sharing arrangements among securities regulators depends on the purposes to which the information will be put. Increasingly, these purposes have to do with averting potential systemic risks.

The framework offered here predicted little role for a multilateral institution in this issue area. After all, the segmented and targetable nature of the externalities arising from illegal trades makes bilateral arrangements more cost effective than broad multilateral approaches. As expected, IOSCO has been passive. They are not in the business of enforcing MOUs or even publicizing the extent of their use or patterns of compliance. Its innocuous role is reflected in its membership, which is ridiculously broad and practically little more than symbolic: about 95% of the world's exchanges belong.[107] In this issue area, enforcement is enhanced by bilateralism, which has the capacity to customize obligations and make expectations explicit, thus reducing defection, yet allows for face-saving ways to exit an agreement. As systemic concerns and the potential for negative externalities have increased, however, the SEC and major US exchanges have been willing to engage in multilateral commitments to share information on firms' trading positions.

III. CONCLUSIONS

Capital markets have developed so rapidly over the past decade that regulators have had to struggle to keep up with the changing markets they are charged to supervise. All across the regulatory spectrum, from bank supervision to securities regulation, from accounting requirements to anti-money laundering efforts, national authorities are finding that the ability to achieve their objectives at a reasonable cost is influenced by the action (or inaction) of their counterparts in foreign jurisdictions.

Power and influence in international finance is so asymmetric that we can understand the mechanisms of rule harmonization and the role of international institutions in this process with a fairly simple model. Essentially, once the dominant financial center initiates a regulatory innovation (which is exogenous to this model and is assumed to be determined by the domestic political economy), it is important to know two things. First, it is crucial to assess whether the rest of the world faces incentives to emulate or to resist regulatory change. Second, it is important to assess whether the negative externalities affecting the dominant financial center flowing from these choices are significant, and if so, whether they are easily targeted or diverted. The first condition explicitly acknowledges that foreign regulators' utilities can be either positively or negatively correlated with a particular regulatory innovation. If the former is the case, there will be market incentives to harmonize rules with those in the financial center. If the latter is the case, foreign jurisdictions may have incentives to implement regulations that run counter to those in the dominant financial center in order to collect a premium that the market is offering for services foreclosed by the regulatory innovation in question. Harmonization, if it is to occur, will require mechanisms that involve the use of political pressure, coordinated by the major financial center.

Externalities are central to this framework because they have much to do with whether regulators in the dominant jurisdiction have an incentive to pressure other regulators to conform. Thus they are central to a determination of whether the mechanism that accounts for harmonization flows from the market or from overt political pressure on the part of the dominant financial center. Moreover, we expected weak or merely symbolic international institutions where the dominant center experiences few negative externalities as a result of the rest of the world to its innovation. In this case, there is little reason for the dominant center to invest heavily in institutional infrastructure, and in the absence of such investments international institutions are not likely to be central to the harmonization process. As the application of the model developed, it became clear that it is also important to know whether or not negative externalities imported by the financial center are easily targeted or diverted. If not there may be an important role for broad multilateral institutions (subject to concerns about non-compliance if there are no market incentives to harmonize). But if so, bilateral arrangements can be effective without the dominant center expending resources to achieve compliance among a broad heterogeneous membership. When there is no market incentive for other jurisdictions to match the regulatory change in the dominant financial market, and this incentive leads to choices that impart negative externalities to the dominant center, international institutions are not only likely to be multilateral. They are expected to perform important surveillance and sanctioning functions as well.

This simple model is reasonably successful at explaining the mechanisms through which harmonization is achieved, and the role (if any) that international institutions play in this process. It helps to understand why a surprising number of national banking supervisors have been willing to adopt the Basel Accord's approach to capital adequacy standards: markets virtually demand it as an indicator of a "well-regulated" jurisdiction in an uncertain and asymmetrical informational environment. The major financial centers support the dissemination of these standards through the technical help and informational role of the Bank for International Settlements. The framework is also useful in understanding why harmonization has been a slow, partial, painful, and highly politicized process in the area of anti-money laundering rules. Emulation in that area is costly yet the United States is determined to address crime at home by enlisting often reluctant foreign jurisdictions to help ensure that crime does not pay. The United States has been central to the creation of an institution—the Financial Action Task Force—that can pass judgment on and sanction both members and non-members. Accounting standards for public offerings provides a good example of incentives to emulate combined with low negative externalities for the United States. Predictably, market forces have fueled harmonization and the efforts of the International Accounting Standards Committee have largely served to provide international legitimation for standards very close to those upon which the SEC has insisted. The most uncomfortable fit was found in explaining the outcome with respect to rules on information sharing among securities regulators. In retrospect, I have probably underestimated the externalities associated with the unwillingness of foreign regulators to cooperate in prosecutions by of fraud by providing needed information to the SEC. While limited, the externalities are not likely to be zero. Moreover, American regulators have found a relatively low-cost way to address what is essentially a private negative externality: strike a series of informal bilateral deals with the most significant jurisdictions and rely on specific reciprocity for enforcement. Increasingly, as information sharing has been needed to assess systemic risks with broader indivisible negative externalities, as the framework would predict, agreements have become more multilateral in their scope and more institutionalized in their provisions.

The attractiveness of this model in understanding regulatory harmonization generally will depend on its ability to "travel" convincingly to other issue areas. The strong asymmetry among financial jurisdictions may seem at first somewhat inappropriate for other issues such as environmental or labor regulations. Yet on closer examination it may not be inappropriate. The dominance of the financial center in this model serves to remind us that large jurisdictions take actions that correspond to their nationally determined preferences, and that these regulatory choices are not likely to be retracted simply because other jurisdictions have not chosen to emulate. It seems reasonable to assume that asymmetries are significant enough in a number of other areas to warrant such an assumption. Across a range of regulatory cases it should be possible, in principle, to ask whether the choices made by a major jurisdiction provide incentives to emulate, to diverge, or make no difference to other countries. Furthermore, whether or not the externalities are strongly negative enough for the dominant jurisdiction to respond with political pressure seems to transfer readily to other regulatory domains. The real difficulty in applying this approach is the inherent difficulty one has in specifying in advance just how costly a negative externality is likely to be in any given issue area. How, for example, can one rigorously quantify the (potential) externality imposed on the United States if other jurisdictions do not follow Basel standards of prudential banking supervision? Economists might be able to offer a theoretical response having to do with the cost of returning to the status quo, but actually measuring externalities will often be extremely complex.

Nonetheless, the framework offered here suggests two crucial dimensions that help explain the mechanisms behind observed regulatory harmonization. The first is incentives that smaller jurisdictions have to emulate changes taken by regulators in major markets. These incentives these incentives vary by issue area, as the research presented here reveals. This is one reason why competitive races to the bottom occur with less frequency than some analysts expect. The second important dimension is the nature and extent of externalities that affect an actor large enough to shape the role and strength of international institutions (if any). Neoliberal institutionalism to date has not provided a convincing explanation for the kinds of institutional variations this framework addresses. Moreover, analyses inspired by liberal functionalist approaches have played down important differences between market pressures and political pressures to harmonize policies, and have emphasized joint gains while submerging the more coercive aspects of "cooperative" arrangements. This framework brings these issues to the fore, and helps to make sense of a bewildering array of agreements, institutional arrangements, and unilateral practices designed to address the problems posed by rapidly changing international capital markets.

Beth Simmons is a Professor of Government at Harvard University.

Notes
Beth A. Simmons, "The International Politics of Harmonization: The Case of Capital Market Regulation," *International Organization*, 55:3 (Summer, 2001), pp. 589-620. © 2001 by the IO Foundation and the Massachusetts Institute of Technology. This article previously appeared in 21 *Stanford Environmental Law Journal* 1, January 2002..

I would like to thank Vinod Aggarwal, David Andrews, Michaela Dabringhausen, Jeffry Frieden, Robert Kagan, Miles Kahler, Robert Keohane, Robert Pahre, Louis Pauly, Robert Powell, David Vogel, Steven Weber, Nicholas Ziegler and two anonymous reviewers for useful comments on significantly different earlier versions of this paper. Research was accomplished primarily while on an International Affairs Fellowship sponsored by the Council on Foreign Relations, during which time the author worked in the Capital Markets and Financial Studies Division of the International Monetary Fund. Final research was completed with financial support from the Abigail Reynolds Hodgen Publication Fund Award, University of California. Support from these institutions is gratefully acknowledged. Thanks to Aaron Staines for excellent research assistance.

1. Figures exclude the United Kingdom.

2. IMF Global Portfolio Investment Survey, http://www.imf.org/external/np/sec/nb/2000/NB0008.HTM

3. IMF1999, Ch. 2 Box 2.2.

5. BIS 1998.

6. BIS, *International Banking and Financial Market Development*, various issues, and ISDA statistics.

7. BIS 1999.

8. Cerny 1993.

9. Strange 1996.

10. For a summary of the basic purposes of financial regulation, see Herring and Litan 1995: 50.

11. Keohane 1984.

12. The focus here is not to explain the specific content of regulatory regimes.

13. Thomsen 2000, p. 6.

14. The most specific disaggregation of the service sector conventionally available includes finance, insurance and real estate (FIRE). See United States Department of Commerce 1998. (NIPA, table 601c, "National income without capital consumption by industry", line 16). http://www.lib.virginia.edu/socsci/nipa/nipa.html

15. World Bank 2000, 260–261.

16. OECD1997, as cited by OECD1998: 131.

17. As of April 2000. The three American banks are Citigroup, Bank of America, and Chase Manhattan. *Economist,* April 18, 2000, p. 82.

18. The 25 biggest foreign banks in the world keep roughly 5.6% ($536 billion) of their assets in the United States. *International Banking Regulator,* July 29, 1996, p. 4.

19. Financial intermediation services and auxiliary services between residents and non-residents, including: commissions and fees for letters of credit, lines of credit, financial leasing services, foreign exchange transactions, consumer and business credit services, brokerage services, and underwriting services.

20. OECD2000.

21. BIS 1997(?) Table 13, p. 136. The United States and United Kingdom accounted for 240 thousand settlements messages through the Society for Worldwide Interbank Financial Telecommunications (S.W.I.F.T.) while the rest of the G-10 *together* accounted for 290 thousand such messages.

22. In May 2000, the London Stock Exchange and Deutsche Börse announced plans to merge to create "iX"—international exchanges. US based Nasdaq has signed a memorandum of understanding with iX—international exchanges to create a pan-European high-growth market. According to the announcement, iX will be headquartered in London, with major operations in Frankfurt. London Stock Exchange Press Release, http://www.londonstockexchange.com/press/story.asp?id = 1

23. *Economist,* July 8, 2000, p. 77.

24. New York Stock Exchange, 1999, p. 3.

25. New York Stock Exchange, 1999, p. 6.

26. London Stock Exchange website, http://www.london stockexchange.com/international/default.asp

27. Economist, June 17, 2000.

28. New York Stock Exchange, 1999, p. 4.

29. Negotiable certificates issued by a US bank for shares of stock issued by a foreign corporation. The securities are held in a custodial account, usually in a foreign bank, while the depositary receipt itself is registered with the Securities and Exchange Commission, and give the holder the same benefits of ownership as a shareholder.

30. Economist, January 15, 2000, p. 77.

31. Futures Industry Association Data; Bank for International Settlements.

32. As a "self-regulatory organization" the NYSE has a sophisticated computerized program for detecting suspicious trading activities, and has been active in investigating activities that break its own regulations. This task is performed using the Automated Search and Match (ASAM), which contains the names of 800,000 executives, lawyers, bankers, and accountants, plus public profile data on officers and directors of approximately 80,000 public corporations and 30,000 corporate subsidiaries. Between 1992 and 1999, 176 cases on an annual average basis were referred to hearings panels for disciplinary action. NYSE website.

33. According the to the Economist, the Federal Reserve System is much faster at collecting and analyzing data than is the European Central Bank or the Bank of Japan. Economist, April 22, 2000, p. 74.

34. The Basel Committee on Banking Supervision has been chaired as follows: 1974–1977: Sir George Blunden (Executive Director of the Bank of England); 1977–1988: W.P. Cooke (Associate Director of the Bank of England); 1988–1991: H.J. Muller (Executive Director of de Nederlandische Bank); 1991–1993: E. Gerald Corrigan (President of the Federal Reserve Bank of New York); 1993–1997: T. Padoa-Schioppa (Deputy Director General of the Bank of Italy); 1977–1978: T. deSwaan (Executive Director of de Nederlandische Bank); and 1998-present: William J. McDonough (President and Chief Executive Officer of the Federal Reserve Bank of New York). A history of the Committee can be found at http://www.bis.org/publ/bcbsc101.pdf.

35. The FSI was formed in 1998 by the Bank for International Settlements and the Basel Committee on Banking Supervision. Its chair is John Heiman, whose resume includes a Directorship at Merrill Lynch, US comptroller of the Currency, the Federal Deposit Insurance Corporation, and the New York Federal Reserve.

36. Sobel 1994 a and b, Reinecke 1995, Oatley 1998.

37. Pahre 1999.

38. However, as Ken Oye (1992, 26) has noted, every diversionary agreement increases the expected negative impact that the externality will have on other jurisdictions, creating a strong incentive to strike bilateral deals with a number of foreign regulators.

39. Martin 1992b.

40. Downs and Rocke, 1995. They argue that since enforcement of

agreements can be costly, there are informational conditions under which exclusion of some "relevant" players from international agreements is reasonable, even though they may be producers of negative externalities. Uncertainty over compliance conditions any expectation of a direct relationship between the extent of externalities and the scope of participation in formal harmonization.

41. This is the function that Garrett and Weingast (1993) emphasize in the case of the European Court of Justice.

42. See for example Gruber 2000.

43. Stein 1983, Snidal 1985, Martin 1992a. Krasner (1991: 364) notes, however, that there has been little effort to classify existing international regimes by the nature of the problem, reinforcing a tendency to emphasize prisoners' dilemmas over coordination games.

44. The "race to the bottom" thesis is usually intended to convey the idea that in a competitive situation regulatory standards tend to fall below an optimal level, and not that they literally crash to the level of the lowest existing national standard. The thesis is propounded in a number of issue areas, including environmental standards (Porter 1999), corporate law (Daniels 1991), and capital adequacy standards (Bradley 1991 and Worth 1992). However for critical analysis and contrary findings in the areas of trade and finance respectively, see D. Vogel 1995 and S. Vogel 1996.

45. See for example Porter 1999.

46. Bank for International Settlements website, www.bis.org

47. Fitch 1993: 600.

48. E. Gerald Corrigan, President of the Federal Reserve Bank of New York, 1990.

49. B.W. Fraser, Governor of the Reserve Bank of Australia, 1995. Note that this does not imply a linear relationship between higher capital adequacy standards a reputation for safety. At some point (which even large banks and regulators would find it difficult to specify) the costs of holding capital in reserve exceeds the value of the added safety, and no longer contributes in any meaningful way to a safe reputation. Thus, there is little danger of a "race to the top": banks' competitive attempts to top one another's capital adequacy ratios indefinitely.

50. Kapstein 1989: 324.

51. Kapstein 1989: 323–347, Reinicke 1995.

52. Kapstein 1989: 340–341.

53. Tommaso Padoa-Schioppa, "Banking Supervision in a Global Market," Vienna, October 1994.

54. John Tattersall, "CAD—Implementation," *Foreign Exchange and Money Market,* May/June, 1995, p. 28. This has not been without some complications for the EU, since they are in the business of creating binding directives with which national legislation must be brought into conformity, a process that can barely keep up with the changes in regulatory recommendations coming out the group of G-10 central bankers (and in fact may not be optimal given the high degree of technical uncertainty and the value of incomplete contracting in this area). Harmonization has also been complicated by the fact that the G-10

focuses its attention on large money center banks, while the EU necessarily crafts directives for large and small banks that comprise national banking systems.

55. White 1996, p. 22

56. Survey results are cited by Padoa-Schioppa 1996.

57. White, p. 22; Padoa-Schioppa, 1994.

58. All banks were to achieve a minimal capital adequacy ratio of 4% by the end of 1998, rising to 8% by the end of 1999 and 10% by the end of 2000. Banks that did not meet these ratios were subject to sanction by the Bank of Indonesia. IMF website, www.imf.org

59. Part of this figure includes repaying the Bank of Indonesia for provision of liquidity, and much is expected to be recovered as recapitalized banks are sold. Memorandum of Economic and Financial Policies, Indonesia, 10 April 1998, IMF website, www.imf.org

60. Korea Memorandum of Economic Policy, November 1998. IMF website, www.imf.org

61. Thailand, memorandum of Economic Policy 25 August 1998. IMF website, www.imf.org

62. Meeting Basel standards is included in every discussion of financial and economic plans among the Asian countries seeking IMF assistance, but the IMF does not consider prudential banking standards to be among its "core responsibilities", and thus collaborates with the BIS on dissemination of these principles. The Fund has however, intensified efforts to use Article IV consultations to promote these rules. IMF 1998.

63. Estimate given by Eduardo Vetere, head of the Crime Prevention and Criminal Justice Branch at the opening sitting of the European Regional Preparatory Meeting for the 9th UN Congress on Crime Prevention and the Treatment of Offenders (1995); 28 February 1994, Vienna.

64. www.ustreas.gov/fincen/border.html

65. *Economist*, July 1 2000, p. 70.

66. See testimony in April 1989 the Governor of the Bank of Italy, quoted in Gurwin 1990. See also Tanzi 1996.

67. www.ustreas.gov/fincen/follow1.html

68. This is an industry estimate. Powis 1992.

69. Troshinsky 1996, p. 1 and 6. On the size of the private banking industry in Switzerland see Rodger 1995.

70. This statement is a translation of official Swiss Federal Government policy, quoted in Aubert, Kernen and Schoenle 1978:59. (Translation from a summary generously supplied by an official of the International Monetary Fund.)

71. *Euromoney*, July 1996, p. 151.

72. Quirk 1996: 24.

73. With one of the most technologically sophisticated methods for detecting financial patterns associated with illicit activities, Australian authorities have used their own forfeiture funds to establish a secretariat for the Financial Action Task Force (FATF) in Asia. Discussion with officials from the US Treasury and FINCEN, 5 and 8 August 1996.

74. Between 1991 and 1993 the number of cases filed and tried under Title 18 USC 1956 or 1957 approximately quintupled. In 1993, 822 cases were filed and 106 tried. Justice Department figures, reported in Courtney 1994.

75. Section 4702 of the 1988 Omnibus Drug Bill. See also Crocker 19xx.

76. United States Congress 1990, p. 28. This opposition was also confirmed in an interview with a Treasury official, 7 August 1996, Washington DC.

77. The Vienna Convention (20 December 1988), Article 3, section 1, (b) (i) and (ii).

78. Interview with a Treasury Official, August 5 1996, Washington DC.

79. In February 1996, the FATF vigorously and publicly opposed provisions of that country's "Economic Development Act" which guaranteed anonymity, immunity from criminal prosecution, and protection of all assets to anyone who invests more than $10 million in approved investment schemes in the Seychelles. The (American) FATF president publicly termed the Act "an incitement to criminals throughout the world to use the Seychelles as a clearing bank for their illegally acquired gains with full immunity." Quotations reported by AP, Worldstream, International News, dateline Paris, 1 February 1996; and in "We love the EDA," *The Indian Ocean Newsletter*, No. 705, 10 February 1996. Seychelles' defense of the law is reported by Litchen 1996, p. 17.

80. Countries currently so listed include nine island countries as well as Israel, Lebanon, Liechtenstein, Panama, Philippines, and Russia. http://www.oecd.org/fatf/pdf/NCCT2000-en.pdf, p. 12.

81. *Economist*, July 1 2000, p. 70.

82. R. D. Fullerton, Chairman and CEO, Canadian Imperial Bank of Commerce, Toronto, 1990.

83. *The Economist Intelligence Unit*, 5/13/96. *New York Times*, 16 December 1993; *New York Times*, 31 March 1993, Section D, p. 8.

84. Jean-Francois Theodore, Chairman and Chief Executive, SBF-Paris Bourse, 1995.

85. Associate Chief Accountant, Securities and Exchange Commission, interview by telephone, Washington DC, 13 August 1996. American and Canadian accounting boards routinely coordinate their standard setting, often jointly publishing drafts and reports. See also *Financial Times*, 30 May 1996, London Edition p. 28.

86. One might object that there are incentives to diverge from foreign standards that are patently inferior to those currently promulgated nationally, but this is very unlikely to be the case. Major markets are only likely to develop in the presence of reasonable regulatory regimes (Sobel 1999), minimizing the theoretical possibility that small markets might have objectively justifiable reasons to prefer their accounting rules over those prevailing in a major market.

87. Interview, Official of the New York Stock Exchange, New York City, 8 November 1995.

88. See for example the discussion in the introduction to Bloomer 1996.

89. Sobel 1994.

90. Michael Sharpie, Chair of the International Accounting Standards Committee (IASC). 1995. There continues to be a divide between the "Anglo-American" versus the "Continental" approaches to accounting, which in turn

have histories rooted in the way firms have traditionally been financed. The former stresses the shareholders' need for information about earnings and profitability, and is common where capital markets have traditionally provided the major source of external financing for firms. Countries using in this school include the United States, United Kingdom, Australia, New Zealand, and the Netherlands. On the other hand, a number of countries, especially in continental Europe, use their tax books as the basis for financial reporting, which tends to mingle signals about a firm's profitability with its tax accounts, and focuses on the long run source of income rather than profitability per se. Countries with accounting standards that fit this description include Germany, the Scandinavian countries, France, Belgium, Italy, and Spain. Cummins, Harris, and Haste 1994: 27.

91. Sharpie 1995.

92. *Economist Intelligence Unit,* 15 April 1996.

93. *Economist Intelligence Unit,* 13 May 1996.

94. See the EASDAQ's rulebook which is found at http://www. easdaq.com/pdf/rulebook.pdf.

95. Official at the NYSE, Interview, 8 November 1995, New York.

96. American standard setters, notably the Financial Accounting Standards Board (FASB) remain deeply skeptical of the IASC, and continue to nurture the Anglo-American accounting alliance through the "Group of 4+1" countries—the US, UK, Australia, and Canada, plus an IASC representative. In the view of American standard setters, it is crucial to continue a dialog with this group of "like minded" standard setters, and not to count on progress at the IASC, which is viewed as far more likely to promulgate stretchy rules unacceptable to the US. The strategy of US standard setters has been to make as much progress as possible in the Group of 4+1 so that the Europeans are persuaded to participate essentially on Anglo-American terms. Interview by telephone with Vice Chairman of the Board, FASB, Norwalk, CT. 15 August 1996.

97. *Economist Intelligence Unit,* 13 May 1996; *The Financial Times,* 6 June 1996, London Edition, p. 29.

98. See the comments of Mario Monti, Commissioner, European Commission, 1995.

99. Interview with Special Counsel for International and Regulatory Affairs, Trading and Markets Division, Commodities and Futures Trading Commission, by telephone, Washington DC, 22 August 1996.

100. See *Financial Times,* July 19, 1995 p. 7.

101. *International Securities Regulation Report,* 28 March 1996, p. 3, 13–14, for an interview of Simona Locatelli, Derivatives Division of the Italian Stock Exchange Council.

102. SEC and the UK's Investment Management Regulatory Organization (IMRO) signed such an agreement in May 1995. *International Securities Regulation Report,* 25 May 1995, p. 9.

103. Website of the International Organization of Securities Regulators (IOSCO), www.iosco.org

104. Prior to 1995, this was due to the fact that supervision of Germany's eight exchanges was a responsibility of the federal states. The

Bundesaugsichtsamt fur den Wertpapierhandel (BAWe) now has the authority, but prefers to cooperate on a project by project basis. Georg Wittich, President, Bundesagusichtsamt fur den Wertpapierhandel, 1995.

105. Russian regulators' first and Chinese regulators' second such agreement (after one with Hong Kong authorities) is with the United States Securities and Exchange Commission. Both concern technical cooperation, mutual assistance and consultation between the SEC and the Russian and Chinese counterparts. IOSCO website, www.iosco.org.

106. Interview with Special Counsel for International and Regulatory Affairs, Trading and Markets Division, Commodities and Futures Trading Commission, by telephone, Washington DC, 22 August 1996.

107. Due to national regulatory structures, Japanese authorities were not able to sign the agreement, triggering criticisms that country's national laws were hampering international cooperation among regulatory authorities. Italian regulators signed, but the Italian Stock Exchanges could not because they are not allowed to engage in surveillance of their members. The MOU does, however, allow signatories to join the agreement at a later date, and Japan is expected to do so. See *International Securities Regulation Report*, 28 March 1996, 9:8, p. 1 and 8.

108. Eduard Canadell, Secretary General of IOSCO, 1995.

References

Aubert, M., P.J. Kernen and H. Schoenle. 1978. *Das Schweizerische Bankgeheimnis* Bern.

Bank for International Settlements. *International Banking and Financial Market Development*, various issues.

——. 1996. *Central Bank Survey of Foreign Exchange and Derivative Market Activity*, Monetary and Economic Department: Basle Switzerland. May.

——. 1997. Statistics on Payments Systems in the Group of Ten Countries: Figures for 1997. Table 13, p. 136. http://www.bis.org/wnew.htm.

——. 1998. *Central Bank Survey of Foreign Exchange and Derivative Market Activity*, Monetary and Economic Department, Basle Switzerland, May.

1999. *Trading in Derivatives Disclosures of Banks and Securities Firms: Results of the Survey of Public Disclosure in 1998 Annual Reports.* Joint Report of the Basel Committee of Banking Supervisors and the Technical Committee of the IOSCO. December.

Bloomer, Carrie (ed.) 1996. *The IASC-US Comparison Project: A Report on the Similarities and differences between IASC Standards and USGAAP* (Based on a study undertaken by the FASB Staff).

Cerny, Philip G. 1993. The deregulation and re-regulation of financial markets in a more open world. Ch. 3 in Philip G. Cerny (ed.), *Finance and World Politics: Markets, Regimes, and States in the Post-hegemonic Era.* Brookfield E. Elgar.

Courtney, Adam . 1994. The Buck Never Stops. *The Banker,* 144:825, November. 88–89.

Crocker, Thomas. Bankers, Police Yourselves. *International Financial Law Review,* 9:6. 10–11.

Cummins, Jason G., Trevor S. Harris, and Kevin A. Hassett. 1994. Accounting Standards, Information Flow, and Firm Investment Behavior. NBER Working Paper No 4685. March NBER: Cambridge MA.

Daniels, R. J. 1991. Shall provinces compete? The case for a competitive corporate law market. *McGill Law Journal.* 36. 130–190.

Downs, George W., David M. Rocke. 1995. Optimal Imperfection? Domestic Uncertainty and Institutions in International Relations. Princeton, NJ: Princeton University Press.

Fitch, Thomas. 1993 *Dictionary of Banking Terms,* 2nd edition. New York: Barrons.

Garrett, Geoffrey and Barry Weingast. 1993. Ideas interests and institutions: Constructing the European Community's internal market. In *Ideas and Foreign Policy,* edited by Judith Goldstein and Robert Keohane, 176–206. Ithaca New York: Cornell University Press.

Gruber, Lloyd Gerard. 2000. *Ruling the World: Power Politics and the Rise of Supranational Institutions.* Princeton: Princeton University Press.

Gurwin, Larry. 1990. 1992 Means a Single Market for Crime, Too. *Global Finance.* 4:1, January. 48.

Herring, Richard J. and Robert E. Litan. 1995. *Financial Regulation in the Global Economy* Washington DC: Brookings Institution.

International Monetary Fund. 1998. Report of the Managing Director to the Interim Committee on Strengthening the Architecture of the International Monetary System. October 1. www.imf.org/external/np/omd/100198.htm

———. 1999. *World Economic Outlook Database;* IMF, World Economic Outlook: International Financial Contagion. October 1999.

Kapstein, Ethan B. 1989. Resolving the regulators' dilemma: international coordination of banking regulations. *International Organization,* 43:2, Spring 1989. 323–47.

Keohane, Robert O. 1984. *After Hegemony: Discord and Cooperation in the World Political Economy.* Princeton NJ: Princeton University Press.

Krasner, Stephen. 1991. Global communications and national power: Life on the Pareto frontier. *World Politics*. 43. (April): 336–66.

Litchen, Mark. 1996. Storm Rages over Proposed Seychelles Investor Legislation. *International Money Marketing*, 16 February, p. 17.

Martin, Lisa L. 1992a. Interests, power, and multilateralism. *International Organization*, 46:4, (autumn): 765–792.

———. 1992b. *Coercive cooperation: Explaining multilateral economic sanctions*. Princeton: Princeton University Press.

New York Stock Exchange. 1999. Year in Review. http://www.NYSE.com/pdfs/intro99.pdf.

Oatley, Thomas and Robert Nabors. 1998. Redistributive cooperation: Market failure, wealth transfers, and the Basle Accord. *International Organization*. 52:1, winter. 35–54.

OECD. 1997. *Institutional Investors Statistical Yearbook 1997*. (Paris: OECD).

———. 1998. *OECD Economic Survey: United Kingdom*. (Paris: OECD).

———. 2000. *Financial Market Trends*, No. 5, March. p. 28. http://www.oecd.org/daf/financial-affairs/markets/FMT75Cross-Border.pdf.

Oye, Kenneth A. 1992. *Economic discrimination and political exchange: World political economy in the 1930s and 1980s*. Princeton NJ: Princeton University Press.

Pahre, Robert. 1999. *L eading Questions: How Hegemony affects the International Political Economy*. Ann Arbor : University of Michigan Press.

Porter, Gareth. 1999. Trade competition and pollution standards: "race to the bottom" or "stuck at the bottom"? *Journal of Environment and Development*. 8:2. June. 133–151.

Powis, Robert. 1992. Money Laundering: Problems and Solutions. *The Banker Magazine*, 175:6, November/December. 52–56.

Quirk, Peter J. 1996. Macroeconomic Implications of Money Laundering. Working Paper 96/66: June. Monetary and Exchange Affairs Department. Washington DC: International Monetary Fund.

Reinicke, Wolfgang H. 1995. Banking, politics, and global finance: American commercial banks and regulatory change, 1980–1990. Edward Elgar.

Rodger, Ian. 1995. Survey of Swiss Banking. Financial Times, 26 October, London, p. III.

Snidal, Duncan . 1985. Coordination versus prisoners' dilemma: Implications for international cooperation and regimes. American

Political Science Review. 79 (December) 923–42.

Sobel, Andrew C. 1994a. *Domestic choices, international markets: Dismantling national barriers and liberalizing securities markets.* Ann Arbor: University of Michigan Press.

———. 1994b. Breaching the levee, waiting for the flood: Testing beliefs about the internationalization of securities markets. *International Interactions,* 19:4. 311–338.

———. 1999. *State Institutions, Private Incentives, Global Capital.* Ann Arbor: University of Michigan Press.

Stein, Arthur. 1983. Coordination and collaboration: Regimes in an anarchic world. In Stephen Krasner, *International Regimes* 115–40. Ithaca: Cornell University Press.

Strange, Susan. 1996. *The Retreat of the State.* London: Cambridge University Press.

Tanzi, Vito. 1996. Money laundering and the international financial system. Working Paper 96/55, May. International Monetary Fund, Fiscal Affairs Department: Washington DC.

Thomsen, Steven. 2000. *Investment Patterns in a Longer Term Perspective.* OECD Directorate for Financial, Fiscal, and Enterprise Affairs, Working Papers on International Investment, No. 2000/2, April. http//www.oecd.org/daf/investment/fdi/wp20002.pdf

Troshinsky, Lisa. 1996. Ex-Nat West Lawyer Fears 'Know Your Customer' Fallout. *International Banking Regulator,* 96:31, 5 August, p. 1 and 6

United States Congress. 1990. Drug money laundering, banks, and foreign policy: A report to the Committee on Foreign Relations, United States Senate. 101th Congress 2d session, February. Subcommittee on Narcotics, Terrorism, and International Operations, USGPO: Washington DC.

United States Department of Commerce. 1998. *National Income and Product Accounts of the United States,* (Bureau of Economic Analysis). United States Government Printing Office: Washington DC (April) http://www.lib.virginia.edu/socsci/nipa/nipa.html.

Vogel, David. 1995. Trading Up: Consumer and Environmental Regulation in a Global Economy. Cambridge MA: Harvard University Press.

Vogel, Steven Kent. 1996. Freer markets, more rules: regulatory reform in advanced industrial countries. Ithaca, N.Y. : Cornell University Press.

White, William. 1996. International agreements in the area of banking and finance. Paper presented at the conference "Monetary and

Financial Integration in an Expanding (N)AFTA: Organization and Consequences," Toronto, 15–17 May.

World Bank. 2000. Entering the 21st Century: World Development Report 1999/2000. http://www.worldbank.org/wdr/2000/pdfs/engtable16.pd

Officials quoted or cited in public settings

Canadell, Eduard. 1995. Secretary General of IOSCO, *International Securities Regulation Report*, 8:22, October 26, pp. 1, 10–11.

Corrigan, E. Gerald. May 3, 1990. Statement before the United States Senate Committee on Banking, Housing, and Urban Affairs (as quoted by Yasushro Maehara, "Comments," in Herring and Litan. 154).Fraser, Bernard W. September 25, 1995. Governor of the Reserve Bank of Australia, to the 24th Conference of Economists, Adelaide. (Reprinted in the *Reserve Bank of Australia Bulletin*, October 1995.)

Fullerton, R.D. 1990. Chairman and CEO, Canadien Imperial Bank of Commerce, Toronto, Canada. "Clearing out the Money Launderers," Portions of a speech made before the Bankers Association for Foreign Trade Conference. (Reprinted in *The World of Banking*, 9:5, September-October 1990, pp. 5–7.)

Monti, Mario. 1995. Commissioner, European Commission. "The Establishment of Regional Financial Areas and Perspectives on Regulatory Harmonization," presentation at the 20th Annual Meeting of IOSCO, Paris. July 13.

Padoa-Schioppa, Tommaso. Chairman of the Basle Committee on Banking Supervision, "Banking Supervision in a Global Market," Vienna, October 1994.

———. June 12–14 , 1996. Address to the 9th International Conference of Banking Supervisors, Stockholm.

Sharpe, Michael. 1995. Chair of the International Accounting Standards Committee (IASC). *International Securities Regulation Report*, 8:22, 26 October. p. 1, 4.

Theodore, Jean-Francois. 1995. Chairman and Chief Executive, SBF-Paris Bourse, "The Emergence of Transnational Financial Zones and Prospects for Harmonization," presentation at the 20th ISOCO Conference, Paris. July 11–13,

Vetere, Eduardo. February 28, 1994. Head of the Crime Prevention and Criminal Justice Branch at the opening sitting of the European Regional Preparatory Meeting for the 9th UN Congress on Crime Prevention and the Treatment of Offenders (1995); Vienna.

Wittich, Georg. July 13, 1995. President, Bundesagusichtsamt fur den Wertpapierhandel, Germany. Presentation, "International Cooperation: the Exchange of Information between Regulators and its Development," IOSCO's 20th Annual Conference, Paris.

Chapter 2

The Business Dynamics of Global Regulatory Competition

Dale D. Murphy

I. DEFINING THE PROBLEM

Regulatory differences among jurisdictions can open the door to opportunistic competition among states, and between states and firms. Firms and states differ in their estimates of the risks of economic activity, and differ in their preferences for those risks and activities. Within any given jurisdiction, regulations on economic activity can create a credible commitment among firms to restrict or enable certain prohibited or prescribed behavior. Growth in cross-border trade and investments, and reactions to them, have pushed these issues "above the fold" in headlines around the world and on top decision-makers' agendas.

A pattern emerges from this dynamic, which begs for explanation. Over time, variations in regulations among jurisdictions may generate any of the following three analytical trajectories for a given policy issue:

- convergence toward a lower common denominator (LCD)
- convergence toward a higher common denominator (HCD)
- persistence of national differences (heterogeneity)

These three analytical trajectories are mapped in Figure 1. The first two are akin to the terms used in this volume of "races to the bottom" (RTB) and "races to the top" (RTT). "Heterogeneity" is similar to "no race," although it includes active protectionist responses to cross-border competitive pressures. The goal of this chapter is concept formation and to explore a plausible explanation for these divergent outcomes, as a step toward building a causal model.[1] On the horizontal axis is the *commonality* of regulations among states: that is, do states adopt homogenous regulations (common among some group of states with competing industries), or heterogenous regulations (in which national differences persist)? On the vertical axis is the *stringency* of regulations: most simply, do they become more stringent or lax? The focus here is on *de facto* implemented standards, not *de jure* laws on the books.

Figure 1. The Dependent Variable: Trajectories of
Interjurisdictional Regulatory Competition Among
Competing States

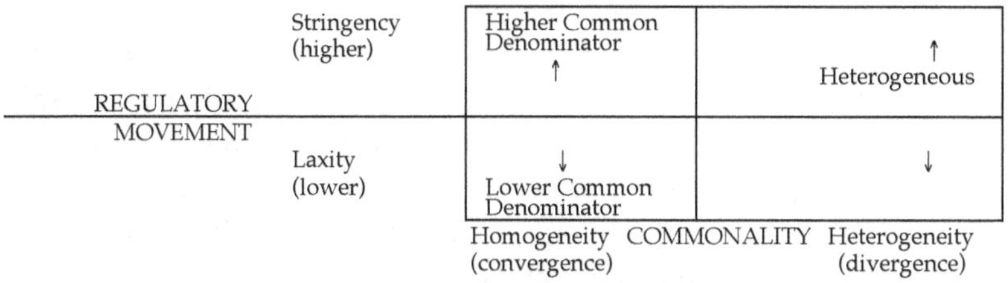

	Stringency (higher)	Higher Common Denominator ↑	↑ Heterogeneous
REGULATORY MOVEMENT			
	Laxity (lower)	↓ Lower Common Denominator	↓
		Homogeneity (convergence)	COMMONALITY	Heterogeneity (divergence)

The dichotomy is for conceptual clarity. Stringent is defined as: "marked by rigor, strictness or severity, with regard to a rule or standard," from the Latin *stringere*, to bind tight. "Homogeneity" or "commonality" are similar but preferable here to "harmonization" or "convergence." "Harmonization" has benign normative overtones (as opposed to "disharmony"), and "convergence" has teleological overtones and references to broader sociological studies on modernization.[2] Some cross-border regulatory arrangements such as mutual recognition agreements (MRAs) fall in between; these are discussed in the conclusion. "Regulations" here are defined broadly, as "direction from a competent authority." This includes a wide variety of policies, including laws, administrative guidelines, bureaucratic regulations, standards, etc.

Competition among jurisdictions may lead to increasing government intervention, as states and firms "trade up," as described by David Vogel.[3] Conversely, competition may lead to a "competition-in-laxity" downward to more lax or liberalized outcomes as states compete to attract or maintain economic activity.[4] Finally, competition may lead to divergent outcomes, as states use regulations as a barrier-to-entry.[5] The consequences of "globalization" on domestic regulations are thus varied.

These trajectories constitute the "dependent variable" of this research; that is, the puzzle to be explained. What causes each outcome? This chapter focuses on three cases with a substantial environmental or labor component. All three also have a broad international component, and involve firms and regulations primarily in the US, Europe, and Central America.

No normative content is imputed here to laxity or stringency; homogeneity or heterogeneity. Laxity does not mean undesirable. Liberalized or lower common denominator (LCD) trajectories may be desirable, e.g., if the stringent regulations had protected vested interests over the general welfare, hampered innovation, created gross inefficiencies, and so on. In other instances, LCD regulations may result in negative externalities such as environmental damage, systemic risk, financial instability or degradation of labor standards that outweigh gains from efficiency. Similarly, higher regulations may be protective, or protectionist, or both. This chapter steps back from the rhetorical heat over so-called "antiglobalization" debates and focuses instead on the determinants of regulatory preferences.

As Vogel (1995) and other authors in this volume point out, "races to the bottom" are less frequent than critics suggest.[6] Yet some instances do occur. There are four forms of such races, or competitions-in-laxity: (1) "De jure competition-in-laxity" is when countries actually lower their regulatory standards, in response to competitive pressures. (2) De facto competition-in-laxity occurs in two variations. It is most striking in its "de facto relocation" form, when domestic firms relocate production or registration into countries with lax regulations. (3) But it can also occur in a "de facto market-share" form, if foreign firms operating in countries with certain lax regulations increase their market-share of world production. This competition could well be desirable, if it improved sustainable net welfare. (4) A fourth form of competition-in-laxity is "regulatory chill," or a "political drag effect" when countries stay anchored to the bottom," not raising their regulatory standards, for example even in the face of scientific evidence (climate change, say), or in the face of rising standards in other countries.[7] In the interest of analytic clarity, this chapter focuses on the first two, starkest forms of competition-in-laxity: de jure changes and de facto relocation.

Anecdotal evidence suggests that the more common outcomes are higher common denominator and heterogeneity. The second and third case studies analyze these, and explain why.

II. A PLAUSIBLE ANSWER

In laying out an explanation for the observed trajectories, this chapter follows George Stigler's emphasis on market pressures as a source of regulatory change, as a heuristic. Part of the answer to the puzzle lies in differentiating private sector interests, and identifying government responses to them. Over time, producer preferences are likely to influence state regulations.[8] Producers may seek policies that restrict rivals' entry, restrict substitute products (e.g., highways versus mass-transit), raise prices, offer direct subsidies, or weaken buyers or suppliers. In other cases they may seek deregulation, to lower production costs.

The explanation—of which trajectory occurs when—has three parts. The first part, asset specificity, explains movement toward commonality among states. The second part, the locus of regulations (on production processes versus products' market-access), explains movement toward stringency or laxity. The third part, industrial structure, explains the degree of change.

Changes in domestic regulations typically depend on the incentives and strategies of private sector firms and governments. Firms seek a regulatory environment to maximize their value. They face three options: relocating production to a new location (exit); lobbying, educating, and litigating to shape regulations to reflect the firm's interests (voice); or accepting whatever regulations come their way (loyalty).[9] Each firm calculates its interest, with bounded rationality and opportunistic behavior.

Governments respond to firm behavior, as they balance the interests of their constituencies, as well as their own interests. Government regulatory options are also threefold: they may do away with unilateral regulations that increase production costs to domestic firms (deregulation), they may exert pressure on foreign countries to remove or erect regulations (extraterritorial influence), or they may erect regulations that protect domestic firms (protection). Both influence abroad and protection may depend on governments' ability to use access to their domestic markets as a "club" to bring about the desired regulatory outcome.

This approach follows Stigler's inductive method: "The truly intended effects should be deduced from the actual effects." Whereas nonprofit organizations deliberately place issues on the public agenda via the mass media, and governments must publicly legitimate their decisions, firms are usually more discreet in publicizing their regulatory agendas and successes. The choice of environmental or labor cases helps bolster the plausibility of my proposed explanations, as these issues have been cited (Wilson 1980) as "least likely" to comply with Stigler's approach.[10] It must be emphasized that the goal of this approach is a necessary but not sufficient explanation. Firms do not (usually) write their own legal code, and they are obviously not the only interest group affecting regulatory outcomes. Various non-governmental organizations (NGOs) play a role as detailed in other chapters in this volume, as do governments themselves, and firms may face rivalry over regulations from other firms. However, it is remarkable how much of regulatory outcomes one can explain with a simple emphasis on firms' preferences.

A. Multinational Asset Specificity (MAS)

The first part of the explanation is that the asset specificity of investments and transactions affects the degree of regulatory homogeneity across countries. The more specific a firm's assets, the greater its stake in regulations of that asset. Following Oliver Williamson, asset specificity means "durable investments that are undertaken in support of particular transactions, and that would lose considerable value if the transaction were prematurely terminated." The investments may include human, dedicated, physical, site, and brand specificity.[11] Site specificity is of particular importance in international cases. Williamson's assumptions apply here: uncertainty is present, transactions are recurrent, and parties to an agreement are opportunistic.

Assets are specific to the extent they cannot easily be deployed elsewhere (without losing considerable value). *Low* asset specificity means that assets can easily be re-deployed; they are not specific to their current use. *High* asset specificity means alternative asset uses are much less valuable to a firm. *Domestic* asset specificity means that assets are specific to transactions in one country (or site). *Multinational* asset specificity (MAS) means that a firm's assets are specific to transactions in more than one country. MAS therefore means: durable investments that are undertaken in support of cross-border transactions, and that would lose considerable value if the cross-border transaction were prematurely terminated. This includes assets dedicated to particular export markets, or dedicated to greater production than the domestic economy can absorb; as well foreign direct investments and other cross-border transactions.[12]

These different investment patterns affect firms' incentives to respond to regulations in the following ways:

- Firms with investments with *low* asset specificity, i.e., assets that are mobile or have valuable alternative uses, may relocate to less-restrictive regulatory environments or uses. The result is movement toward "self-help" governance structures and less regulation. Low asset specificity facilitates a *competition-in-laxity*, in which moves by one state to attract (or keep) industry through lax heterogeneous regulations are matched by other states. Movement is toward more lax regulations, among competing states.

- Investments with *high multinational* asset specificity create incentives for firms to push for common regulations across borders. Firms with assets devoted to multinational transactions will seek regulatory homogeneity on issues that affect their asset-specific investments. They seek to reduce transaction costs.[13] They will oppose divergent regulations that inhibit effective use of those assets, and that increase transaction costs.[14] *Ceteris paribus,* firms with high MAS therefore seek regulatory homogeneity for two reasons: a) most simply, to operate those assets under one set of rules worldwide reduces transaction costs; and, b) as asset specificity increases, "exit" would become more costly to firms than "voice." The more a firm has invested in specific assets across borders, the more likely it is to support regulatory homogeneity across those borders. Firms seek credible commitments from governments in the form of regulations to uphold those rules.[15]

- Firms with investments specific to transactions only in a given *domestic* market will fight against regulatory homogeneity that threatens their investment. They will support heterogeneous regulations that protect the investment. When a firm has sunk assets into transactions particular to a given domestic regulatory environment, it cannot redeploy those assets elsewhere without losing considerable value.

These effects on regulations of the asset specificity of investments are summarized in Figure 2. The first author to make this connection between asset specificity and firms' different inter-jurisdictional regulatory preferences was Murphy (1993). That paper, my dissertation (Murphy 1995) and several similar conference papers (Murphy 1994, 1996, 1998) were provided to a variety of authors (e.g., Spar 1999),[16] and my explanation has received additional confirmation in their work. Other empirical work backs up these hypotheses (Alt 1999).[17] Large investments that are specific to cross-border transactions created incentives for firms to seek a common regulatory framework for their transactions.[18]

Figure 2. Multinational Asset Specificity Favors "Higher Common Denominator" Outcomes

		Multinational		Domestic
Asset Specificity	High	HCD		Heterogenous Regulations
	Low	← Competition-	in-Laxity →	

Nature of Transactions

Research on asset specificity stems from the study of contract structures. Williamson (1985) distinguishes four types of structures for arranging contracts: market structure, third-party, two-party, and unified. Movement from lax or heterogeneous regulations toward stringent or homogenous regulations is a public sector analogy of movement away from free-market (self-help) structures and toward more unified structures. In private-sector unified structures, "the transaction is removed from the market and organized within the firm subject to an authority relation."[19] In government regulations, conversely, part of the contracting structure is removed from the market, and organized within society; the authority relation is the coercive power of the state.

When asset specificity is high, firms need more complex contracting structures to ensure credible commitments and continuity. Otherwise, the parties are reluctant to enter into or sustain a transaction involving assets that would lose considerable value if the transaction were prematurely terminated.

Regulations are a form of contracting. The contract is both between firms and governments (two-party or "bilateral"), and among firms with the government acting as a third-party ("trilateral") enforcement mechanism. Homogenous regulations act to harmonize contracts involving the prohibited or prescribed behavior. Firms with high multinational asset specificity support those regulations.

Asset specificity creates incentives and constraints for firms and governments, but it is not deterministic. Over the long term, asset specificity may change as firms change their investment strategies, or as demand for products (and substitutes) changes. These firm-level decisions and others are noted in the case studies and the conclusion.

Transaction costs and asset specificity are difficult to measure. The economists who developed these concepts concede this challenge, and defend the qualitative research approach as adopted here:

> [Both ex ante and ex post transaction costs] are often difficult to quantify. The difficulty, however, is mitigated by the fact that transaction costs are always assessed in a comparative institutional way, in which one mode of contracting is compared with another. Accordingly, it is the difference between rather than the absolute magnitude of transaction costs that matters. . . . Empirical research on transaction cost matters almost never attempts to measure such costs directly. Instead, the question is whether organizational relations (contracting practices; governance structures) line up with the attributes of transactions as predicted by transaction cost reasoning or not. (Williamson, op. cit. 21–22)

> Measurement tasks [of asset specificity] are not trivial . . . data can be very difficult to obtain . . . we are certainly not going to find these numbers written down neatly in a book of industry statistics. The best that we can hope for is more qualitative information. . . . Schmalensee and I would have been much happier with our analysis if there had been more (any!) empirical support available for the transactions cost perspective that we found so intuitively appealing and so consistent with the historical evolution of the electric power industry. (Joskow, 1988) [20]

For this chapter I rely on discrete comparative categories of "domestic or multinational," and "high or low." This qualitative approach follows the received literature.

B. National Process versus Market-Access Regulations

The second part of the explanation concerns the locus of regulations. Nations may limit or prohibit manufacturing or service-industry *processes* within their jurisdiction (national process restrictions). Or, they may restrict the *market-access* of particular services or products (market-access restrictions).[21]

The process versus market-access distinction emphasizes the

different interests of export-oriented and import-competing industries and the different political resources available to producers and consumers. Firms seek regulations that add to their value; they will seek to capitalize on the differential effect of a regulation on itself versus its competitors.

Heterogenous national restrictions on manufacturing or service-industry *processes* **may spawn competitions in laxity.** Process restrictions increase the cost of manufacturing. Domestic business and labor in a nation with costly restrictions on manufacturing processes tend to operate at a disadvantage with respect to competitors in less-regulated nations. In the absence of common international action for a common higher standard, both export-oriented and import-competing sectoral interests will fight for lax national restrictions on manufacturing processes to improve their competitive position. In cases of costly regulation or inexpensive relocation, firms may move manufacturing to less-regulated states. The threat of industrial relocation and the resultant loss of jobs and tax revenues may convince governments to keep process standards lax.

Heterogenous national restrictions on the market-access of services or products (sale, consumption or disposal) may spawn increased protectionism. Domestic business (and labor) in a nation will push for a market-access restriction if it reflects their parochial interests. Unilateral market-access regulations are likely to give firms an advantage with respect to foreign competitors in less-regulated nations. In the absence of common international action against market-access restrictions as *de facto* trade barriers, firms may seek to impose domestic market-access regulations that improve their competitive position.

This concept of "market-access regulations" is broader than the GATT's concept of "product regulations." Market-access regulations by definition include all restrictions on imports, regardless of the rationale for them. By contrast, the GATT restricts its definition of product regulations to include only those justified by the nature of the product itself. This is because the GATT sought to limit *de facto* trade barriers. The GATT permits product restrictions if they do not discriminate against imports. Hence, the narrower the definition of product restrictions, the fewer constraints on trade. The GATT prohibits all restrictions on imports if the rational of the restriction is the process or production method (PPMs) by which a good is made. Internationally, of course, no country has the jurisdiction to impose process regulations on economic activities inside another country. The GATT is thus forced to assess the motivation for regulations. The GATT's product-process distinction can be contentious. In the Mexican tuna-dolphin case discussed below, the distinction was at the center of debate. The broader "market-access" concept used here offers greater analytical clarity for understanding the sources of regulatory change.

A country's market-size may determine the extent to which it can effectively use market-access regulations. Governments of states with large internal markets may use market-access regulations not only to protect domestic industry, but also as a "club" to influence regulations in other countries. If those foreign countries do not move toward a common (higher) process regulation, or toward fewer discriminatory market-access regulations, their exports may be denied market access. Although the GATT/WTO prohibits such activity, states with very large markets such as the U.S., Europe, or Japan may contravene their GATT agreements. Small states may have little economic incentive to pursue the WTO's only remedy of authorized trade sanctions or countervailing duties, because they might fear retaliation in other arenas. *Ceteris paribus,* the outcome here is a pattern of market-access regulations moving toward higher (heterogenous) standards that reflect producer interests in dominant states. The concept of market-access regulations helps explain the "California effect," if countries are able to exclude products or services which do not meet domestic standards.

Process and market-access restrictions are likely to have markedly different international consequences and yield markedly different results. Especially if a firm is threatened by imports, it is likely to push for lower domestic process standards, and to push for market-access restrictions on imports if it can't get lower domestic process standards.[22] Among open economies, this part of the explanation predicts movement toward more lax regulations in the case of process restrictions, and toward more stringent regulations in the case of market-access restrictions.

C. Industrial Structure

The third part of the explanation, industrial structure, addresses the extent of regulatory change. *Regulatory movement is more likely to be achieved by dominant, established firms in large, concentrated markets.* These findings are well-established in political economy studies. These studies range from free trade and tariffs at the turn of the last century, to New Deal regulatory bodies, to "voluntary" export restraints in the 1970s, to nontariff barriers in the 1990s.[23] Firms calculate their interest in regulatory change, and the resources available to them to achieve that change. In order to achieve regulations that reflect their particular interests, firms must significantly influence governments. That influence can be direct or implicit, or even imputed by governments. Governments are more likely to respond to dominant firms both as a result of lobbying pressures and to improve their own political survival by boosting employment and economic growth.

Concentrated markets facilitate collective action and the ability to shape regulations. Oligopolies have greater resources to absorb regulatory costs and to achieve their regulatory goals through lobbying, funding of research, litigation, and education or advertising.[24] They also have asymmetrical access to information; indeed, they are often the only source of information available to the regulatory agencies. They have incentives to erect barriers to entry, to maintain market share and prices, and to impede (or dominate) substitute goods. Organized firms with concentrated interests are more likely to affect outcomes than small firms with diffuse benefits or costs, or inchoate consumers and voters.

However, industrial structure is dynamic, not deterministic (particularly at the product-line level), as firms make strategic production decisions. The decision by a dominant firm to invest in a new product (e.g., chlorofluorocarbon substitutes) or a new production technology (e.g., totally chlorine-free pulp) may alter the structure of a particular market. These investment decisions will also affect regulatory preferences.[25]

Firms may form lobbying coalitions with each other or in alliance with public interest groups. One expects firms to take advantage of so-called "Baptists and bootleggers" coalitions in a synergistic alliance of "the good and the greedy." Regulations are legitimated in terms of the public interest. Public interest groups can play a valuable legitimizing role for firms, if common ground can be found between them. Likewise, politicians who support regulations commonly favored by both firms and interest groups can expect support from them both.[26]

III. EMPIRICAL EVIDENCE, FROM CASE STUDIES

The explanations proposed above were applied to a number of case studies.[27] The criteria for selecting cases are they must involve the movement of goods, capital or services across borders; the regulations must impose significant costs on some firms; and, initially, no single jurisdiction has regulatory authority over the issue.

Three cases are summarized here, for purposes of illustration, one for each of the three basic trajectories. The first is the case of shipping flags of convenience, a case of LCD. The second is the Montreal Protocol on chlorofluorcarbons (CFCs), a case of HCD. The third is U.S. regulations on tuna imports, a case of heterogeneous regulations.

A. Competition-in-laxity toward a Lower Common Denominator

Lower common denominator outcomes exhibit movement downward, the result of either a competition-in-laxity between competing states, or negotiated deregulation. Shipping is among the clearest examples of the former. Shipping registration (and certain financial services) may be particularly amenable to competition-in-laxity, because of the extreme ease and low cost of relocation. The flag-of-convenience (FOC) system is an example of location decisions based on comparative regulatory advantage.

Overall, the case illustrates the adoption or lower standards in common among competing flag-of-convenience states. There are elements of heterogeneity within the shipping case, as first one nation seeks to attract registration through lax regulations. As other nations join in that laxity, one sees a competition-in-laxity among states competing for the same industry. There are also elements of protectionism, e.g., on domestic shipping (*cabotage*). For clarity and to avoid the critique that "laxity" cases are merely anecdotal exceptions, the shipping industry is treated as one case study, here. International shipping offers an archetypical case of competition-in-laxity circumventing national tax and labor laws (thereby lowering the cost of transported goods), and also circumventing national safety and environmental regulations (with less desirable effects). These are the result of location decisions based on comparative regulatory advantage.

What difference does a ship's flag make? It determines most of the regulations that ship must abide by and it allies the ship with the diplomacy of its flag-country. Registration is a process regulation. Generally, only flag states may enforce compliance by vessels of their flag. A ship operated with no flag could be confiscated on the high seas as a "ship without nationality"; in effect, a pirate.

"Flags-of-convenience" (FOCs) are ship registration systems

outside the beneficial owners' country. The *raisons d'etre* of FOCs are low taxes, lax domestic regulations and little enforcement of international regulations. The term is often used derogatorily, although there are some "excellent flags-of-convenience and appalling national registers."[28] FOCs save ship-owners costs in the "process" of shipping, by reducing the number of conventions, regulations and taxes they must comply with. These include various regulations on issues such as pollution and environmental concerns, vessel safety and navigational standards, crew requirements, worker safety, and unions and collective bargaining. Internationally, these included three International Maritime Organization's [IMO] International Conventions: Prevention of Pollution from Ships [MARPOL] adopted in 1973, Safety of Life at Sea [SOLAS] adopted in 1974, and Standards of Training, Certification and Watchkeeping for Seafarers [STCW] adopted in 1978. Environmental issues go well beyond the most visible instances of oil spills: much more oil pollution occurs as a result of routine and intentional discharges.[29] Even if a FOC has formal regulations in place, however, enforcement of them is often lacking. Data on such *de facto* laxity are often nonexistent. In some FOCs the relevant question is which–if any–standards are being met, not which standards are being avoided.

The transaction of registering a ship is very non-specific. It involves discrete, autonomous, recurrent, "market contracting," in Williamson's parlance. Ship-owners have no compelling reason to embed contracts in a protective governance structures to promote continuity, ensure credible commitments, or compliance. They have no interest in the particular identity of registry agents (and vice versa). They can move registration easily from one registry to another. The fact that there are no durable, firm-specific assets in ship-registration means that "hit-and-run entry and exit" is feasible. Williamson (1985) noted that in deregulation of the trucking and airlines industries the "investments in question here really are 'assets on wheels,' hence lack specificity." Likewise, one can label ships 'assets that float.'

The structure of the world shipping market contains both thousands of independent ship-owners with only a few ships to their name, and oligopoly competition between cartels. Regulatory movement in this case tended to be driven by the more powerful large owners. Within the shipping industry, a distinction is made between bulk (or tanker) and cargo (or liner) ships. The bulk sector transports grains, ores, raw materials, and, most importantly, oil. Shipping in this sector is dominated by multinational corporations. Within the oil-tanker sub-sector, the "Seven Sister" oil companies (now the "Fraternal Four") controlled roughly twenty percent of world tanker tonnage. Exxon was the largest, with 168 tankers in 1977, Shell was the second largest with 163, followed by British Petroleum with 107. Other oil companies controlled another twenty percent of the oil subsector. Independent owners controlled sixty percent.[30] Liner shipping carries manufactured goods. A number of shipping conferences or cartels were influential, particularly those from the US, Norway, Greece, and Japan, although the number of independents is also large.

The FOC case shows a pattern of domestic regulation, followed by significant industrial-flight to countries where taxes are lower and regulations are often nonexistent or poorly enforced. The outcome shifts from lax heterogeneity, to lower common denominator (among competing states), in a classic competition-in-laxity. That trajectory is fairly constant over a forty-year period.[31]

To review, ship-owners relocated in droves to flags-of-convenience following World War II, seeking lower costs. There was a steady increase in market share by these FOCs, over a fifty-year period. By 1992, one fourth of the entire world's major tonnage sailed under a convenience flag. In general, ships in convenience-flag states sank more often, polluted more, and lost more lives. Every year from 1948 through the early 1990s more FOC ships were lost as a percentage of the number in their fleet, and also as a percentage of tonnage in their fleet. On average, FOC fleets lost nearly three times as many ships as national fleets (1.20 percent versus 0.45 percent). The losses resulted in greater pollution and loss of life. In 1990, for example, 471 seafarers died in shipping accidents, and 303 of these deaths (64 percent) were on FOC ships. Insurance rates are calculated on a per-ship basis, not per-flag, but on average are somewhat higher among FOC fleets. Consumers of shipping services benefited from the cheaper market prices, but these did not reflect the cost of negative environmental externalities or labor abuses. However, there are also many beneficial aspects of FOCs: by lowering transportation costs, they also lowered prices on traded goods, facilitated gains from trade, and provided employment for seamen in emerging markets.

An exception to these general trends was the "sub-case" of oil tankers owned by major companies. Here, one saw industry support of selected stringent regulations. Large ship-owners supported these regulations not from their love of pristine nature nor their fears of ever-more costly regulations (although these may have played a role); large ship-owners stood to gain from the reduction in surplus capacity, which antitrust laws prevented them from doing on their own. With their enormous investments and revenues elsewhere, the costs of regulation were relatively insignificant for the large oil companies, compared to independent tanker-owners. (The infant formula case, discussed elsewhere, illustrates the risks to industry when collusive behavior in the market is not sanctioned by formal government regulation.) Even within this sub-case, the logic of my explanation is evident. For example, Shell Oil, Exxon and British Petroleum all pushed the load-on-top (LOT) system in the 1960s, over the head of their governments.

> An important point about the development of LOT is that it was done completely independently of governments and in a very short time. In fact, the oil companies had adopted a system which by their own admission violated both the 1954 Convention (then in force) and the 1962 Amendments then being ratified by many governments. "Thus, their actions . . . [forced] the hands of governments by presenting them with a *fait accompli*. It was . . . because governmental enforcement of the existing regulations was so poor . . . that the industry was able to implement its own alternative. (Note: The preemption by industry of government was so successful that [an expert] did not think that there was a tanker over 20,000dwt in the world complying with the 1962 Amendments despite the fact that they had been law for seven years.)"[32]

A more recent example followed the Exxon Valdez oil spill, when the U.S.–with its enormous markets–passed the Oil Pollution Act of 1990 that would phase out market-access to U.S. harbors for oil tankers that did not have double-hulls. Despite the magnitude of the spill of the public outcry over it, the full ban would not take effect until 2010, twenty years after its passage, giving U.S. industry enough time to amortize its old fleet.[33]

Heterogeneity continued to exist in standards between industrialized countries and convenience flag states (the *status quo ante*), but there was movement toward a lower common–albeit unstable–denominator among the FOCs. Many U.S.-owned ships were re-flagged in Panama or Liberia, in a clear example of *de facto* relocation. (The U.S. did not drop standards for cabotage among its domestically-flagged fleet, so the case is not one of the uttermost possible lowest common denominator, but the overall trend is clearly one of competitive pressures and lax regulations–including taxes–enticing ship-owners to relocate.) Liberian and Panamanian standards converged through the 1970s, at which point Liberia's standards improved under the pressures from large tanker owners identified in the text. Exit from Liberia is also noted at this point, as an even lower set of standards emerged in Cyprus, Malta, and other new registries in the 1980s. Simultaneously, in response to the exit of their fleets, several European states (including the United Kingdom, Norway, France, Germany, Belgium and Denmark) deliberately created "international registries" with lower taxation and manning requirements. The latter permitted the hiring of crews under conditions that would violate domestic labor laws.

The driving force behind the creation of flag-of-convenience havens in Panama and Liberia was American ship-owners, with the strong support of prominent government officials. Process regulations, a fragmented market, low asset specificity and competitive pressures combined to yield laxity. One sees the creation of new centers of laxity, and responses that combine protection with deregulation.

The shipping case is worth studying not only for its theoretical insights, but also for its policy insights. It offers some support to critics' fears of regulatory collapse; though the benefits from cheaper transportation and gains from trade must also be considered, as must the role of dominant firms seeking barriers-to-entry. The extreme ease of relocation facilitated this competitive deregulation. Other examples of competition-in-laxity, with varying normative outcomes, include offshore banking centers (which account for a substantial proportion of all international finance), the relocation of California's furniture refinishing industry to the *maquiladora,* US state regulations on savings and loan institutions, and incorporation in Delaware. Some production standards in Europe have coalesced around lower standards, as noted in the introduction to this volume, in limits on air and water effluents, lead and PCBs, etc.[34] Some critics argue that the spread of genetically-modified foods reflects the spread of laissez-faire U.S. GMO regulations. Despite these examples, increased cross-border commerce has not resulted in the overall race to the bottom that some critics feared. The next two sections illustrate other outcomes, and help explain why.

B. Higher Common Denominator
On September 16, 1987, delegates from 24 major countries to the Montreal convention reached agreement on the Protocol on Substances

that Deplete the Ozone Layer.[35] As revised, the Protocol phased out production of chlorofluorocarbons (CFCs) by 1995, and reduced production of halons, carbon tetrachloride, and methyl chloroform.[36] The sale and distribution of new CFCs would be foreclosed. Trade sanctions would be imposed against countries not complying with the Protocol. The effect of the Protocol was widespread: 70 percent of the US food supply depends on refrigeration at some point, and CFCs were the best coolants available. The global market for CFCs in 1990 totaled nearly two billion dollars. However, far from fighting the restrictions tooth-and-nail, as one might expect if one assumed industry opposed all regulations, dominant producers ended up supporting the Protocol. Indeed, by 1994, DuPont was poised to phase out CFC production early; and, in an ironic twist, the EPA requested DuPont to continue production for another year.

It is necessary to understand the role of dominant multinational producers in order to understand this movement toward homogenous, stringent market-access restrictions. Just over a dozen firms worldwide produced CFCs. The three largest were E.I. DuPont de Nemours Company (DuPont) in the U.S., Imperial Chemicals Industries (ICI) in the UK, and Elf-Atochem in France. Each had large multinational investments. DuPont accounted for 25 percent of the world market. It had factories in the U.S, Canada, the Netherlands, Japan, and Latin America. In the US, DuPont controlled nearly 50 percent of the market.[37]

But the major producers' hold on the market was slipping. As CFCs became an undifferentiated commodity and new competitors entered the market, prices fell and alternative uses of industry assets became more valuable. Even before the Montreal Protocol took effect, ICI and others sunk large specific investments into substitutes for CFCs. Asset specificity in CFCs was declining; but was high in substitute goods. The asset value of CFC investments was declining, and CFC producers faced increased competition and thinning profit margins. The cost of prematurely terminating these CFC contracts was declining. The asset specificity of substitute goods was high, but without government intervention to restrict CFCs, the demand for substitutes would be low. Unlike in the shipping case, ICI and DuPont could not simply move production offshore, as the existent supporting business infrastructure would be too expensive to replace, and the cost of transporting CFCs too high. In effect, ICI and DuPont *et alia* contracted with governments, to retire CFCs and force consumers to buy more expensive substitutes–to preserve the ozone layer, in a Baptist and Bootlegger alliance. (Unlike in Stigler's work, there is no presumption here that this acquisition of regulations by industry was not in the societal interest.) The Montreal Protocol was a transaction-specific regime. It created a *de facto* cartel for CFC producers, giving them hope for windfall profits to fund continued investments in CFC substitutes.

This case fits the initial explanation well. Two dominant firms had high market concentration. Asset specificity in CFCs was declining; as profit margins fell, investments in alternatives became more profitable. Initially, US heterogeneous market-access regulations on use of CFCs in aerosols hurt DuPont and Allied Signal. These US producers objected to the unilateral measures, and seized the opportunity presented by scientific evidence to help achieve homogenous restrictions that covered competitors worldwide. They devoted assets to the development of substitutes, and stringent market-access regulations were adopted in common with all major producing countries. Industry at first sought direct subsidy of research on substitutes. As CFCs production was squeezed, industry benefited from oligopoly profits.[38] Later, industry pushed to have those profits guaranteed to existing producers, through the EPA quota system. When the market for alternatives to CFCs seemed certain, CFCs themselves became the restricted "substitute," in Stiglerian fashion.

DuPont had initially opposed controls on CFCs, and vehemently resisted unilateral US regulations. A year before the Montreal Protocol was signed, DuPont changed its position and indicated its support for limits on worldwide emissions of CFCs. According to the chief US negotiator there, private sector interests backed the UNEP proposals, sometimes against the wishes of Reagan Administration officials. According to the Executive Director of UNEP himself, Mustafa Tolba, industry was vital in shaping the final Protocol: "The difficulties in negotiating the Montreal Protocol had nothing to do with whether the environment was damaged or not. It was all who was going to gain an edge over who; whether DuPont would have an advantage over the European companies or not." This role is consistent with the primary emphasis here on producer preferences.

C. Heterogeneity

The US-Mexican dispute over tuna-dolphin is a well-known case of heterogeneity and a focal point for trade-and-the-environment disputes within the GATT/WTO system. The case involves the imposition of market-access regulations on the importation and sale of certain tuna caught with methods lethal to dolphins. In brief, the dominant American tuna processor hoped to capitalize on consumer sympathy for dolphins to boost its market share against low-cost competitors. Its assets were largely specific to the US domestic market. It was assisted by Federal legislation, which two GATT panels later ruled to be inconsistent with international law. The US unilaterally flouted the GATT ruling for over four years, but Mexico chose not to pursue the matter, for fear of upsetting other trade ties with the U.S.

Between 1975 and 1990, the US embargoed tuna imports on 23 different occasions. Mexican yellowfin tuna was banned from 1980 to 1986, in retaliation for the seizure of American tuna-boats fishing within Mexico's 200-mile coastline. After that ban was lifted in 1986, Mexican tuna exports tripled in three years, despite a long-standing US tariff of 12%-35%. (The tariff on canned tuna was higher than on lower value-added unprocessed tuna). On August 28, 1990, a U.S. federal judge again banned imports of Mexican tuna, this time on the grounds that Mexican tuna purse-seiners exceeded US standards for dolphin mortality in the Eastern Tropical Pacific (ETP). Only in the ETP do dolphins school with tuna.

The largest tuna canner, StarKist (owned by the H.J. Heinz Company), not only did not fight the US regulations; it pre-empted them by four months. On April 12, 1990, one week before Earth Day (and two days before the "International Dolphin Week"), Heinz announced a unilateral suspension of tuna purchases that were not dolphin-safe. The other major canners followed suit.

Heinz deliberately adopted a strategy of green marketing. In October 1989 (six months before its April announcement, and ten months before the US ban on Mexican tuna), J.W. Connolly, the president of Heinz-USA, wrote to top management, encouraging a dolphin-safe strategy: "I am interested in the possibility of seizing the environmental high ground by offering the only tuna guaranteed not caught off dolphins . . . I know about the potential cost impact on the procurement of raw tuna . . . However . . . If I am right in this, and we can solve the procurement problems, we could have a very substantial volume opportunity." If Connolly were correct, his plan would contrast sharply with the characterization by some activists that corporate greed is antithetical to protecting the environment.

The US Marine Mammal Protection Act (MMPA) and its embargo on ETP tuna was supported on aesthetic and moral grounds. Dolphins in the ETP were never endangered species, and by 1990 their population was growing 2%-6% annually. A National Academy of Sciences study, conducted under Congressional mandate, recommended that dolphin-setting techniques be improved through international education, monitoring, and incentives, but not stopped.[39] Mexican tuna posed no human health threat.

The US tuna processing industry was an oligopoly. Three large companies dominated 71% of the US canned tuna market in 1989: Heinz (StarKist) with a 36% market share, Van Camp (Chicken of the Sea) with 21%, and Unicord (Bumble Bee) with 14%.[40] The parent companies of the big three tuna labels were major producers of packaged foods: H.J. Heinz, Inc., for example, had assets of $4.9 billion, annual net sales of $6.6 billion, and an annual gross profit of $2.5 billion in 1991. (By contrast, the tuna-fishing industry was fragmented, had tiny revenues in comparison to the canners, and little national political influence. Their regulatory preferences would be swamped by those of the much larger canners.)

StarKist's MAS in the ETP was low. StarKist's assets devoted to the purchase of raw tuna were non-specific, they bought tuna from around the world, not just from the ETP. International transactions involving the purchase of raw tuna were on the spot market and were not asset specific. The US canning industry dissolved its ties to the tuna fishing fleet by 1979, as many Asian and Latin countries invested in their fishing sectors. The major US canners turned to the international spot market for raw tuna. They moved some canning operations to American Samoa and Puerto Rico, taking advantage of special US tax provisions there.[41]

StarKist's domestic US asset specificity in canning and marketing, by contrast was high. Most of its assets were deployed domestically in the US (and US territories). Most of its tuna sales were in the US. Overseas in the UK, for example, StarKist's market share was only 5%, or one-seventh its share of the US market. Despite Chicken of the Sea's and Bumble Bee's transfer to Asian ownership in 1989, their canned tuna sales were also largely specific to the US. Asset specificity in marketing for the big three was high. They relied on brand-name recognition to boost sales and retail prices.

The brand-name recognition bought higher prices—but low-cost producers threatened the price-margins. For the smaller private label firms, by contrast, assets were more specifically invested in the ETP. Their market share depended on low-costs and narrow profit margins. They relied on fishermen and canneries near the ETP to reduce transportation costs. Mexico had invested in its tuna industry with the expectation of access to the US market.

Rather than reach a multilateral agreement on dolphin protection, or let consumer preferences determine the demand for "dolphin-safe" tuna, the US Congress and courts unilaterally banned the importation or domestic sale of tuna that was caught using methods lethal to dolphins. The effective ban lasted for over ten years. The ban on the sale or importation of a product or service is a "market-access regulation," as defined here, whatever the motivation for the ban. (The GATT ruled that the U.S. laws contravened the GATT's definition of "process" regulations. However, the U.S. International Dolphin Conservation Act prohibited the importation of sale of products within the U.S., but it would technically have permitted a U.S. fisher to use the process of dolphin-setting and sell that tuna catch overseas. As defined in this chapter, the U.S. regulations were market-access, not process.) This denial of market-access followed shifts in consumer demand, a retail price war, and the voluntary end of dolphin-set tuna purchases by market-leader StarKist and the other two dominant firms. The regulations met with StarKist's enthusiastic support and assistance. The U.S. Human Society had called for a boycott of dolphin-set tuna since 1972, nearly twenty years earlier, with little noticeable change in consumer preferences. When StarKist finally agreed to boycott dolphin-set tuna, the change was immediate and dramatic: with regulations in place banning dolphin-set imports, consumers had no choice.

StarKist's CEO, Richard Wamhoff, wrote to Senator John Kerry in October 1992:

> Dear Senator Kerry: ... StarKist enthusiastically supported the enactment of the Dolphin Protection Consumer Information Act in 1990 and ... continues its firm commitment to its dolphin safe policy. With respect to the International Dolphin Conservation Act [1992], we would like to make clear that StarKist generally supports the Bill ... Again, we want to make clear that StarKist and Heinz support the aims of the International Dolphin Conservation Act and remain firmly committed to a dolphin-safe policy. ... We stand ready to assist you and members of your staff to address in detail means to provide solid legislation which meets the cause of marine mammal protection.
>
> Very truly yours,
> Richard H. Wamhoff

StarKist supported the dolphin-safe legislation, and registered concern only about regulations outside the ETP. In response, Senator Kerry reassured StarKist: "I would like to assure Mr. Wamhoff that it is my expectation that the Secretary of Commerce will only exercise his or her authority . . . after consulting with the appropriate segments of the tuna industry, with scientific and regional fishery management organizations, and with conservation or environmental organizations." The record here suggests cooperation between industry, environmentalists and politicians; each one sensitive (but not beholden) to US consumer preferences.[42] (As with the CFC and other cases, no Stiglerian normative judgment is implied here. Many would argue that StarKist should have undertaken this step many years earlier for normative reasons; others argue it should have pushed for a homogenous international agreement rather than a unilateral U.S. policy. These are not exclusive.)

The U.S. stood by its heterogeneous ban, even after the GATT ruled against it twice. Nearly a decade later–only after consumer preferences had changed to support the major companies in their "dolphin-safe" campaign, only after consumers had reestablished strong brand-loyalty to the three big U.S. producers, only after dolphin-deaths had fallen by 97% to less than 2,000/year from 150,000/year a decade earlier (and from over 500,000/year when U.S. cannery-boats pioneered dolphin-setting in the 1960s), only after producers were no longer threatened by low-cost imports, and only after the U.S. environmental community had split and Greenpeace recognized that dolphin-setting was less ecologically disruptive than the alternative of log-setting—only then did the U.S. technically legalize the importation of dolphin-set tuna, provided that scientific studies determined the imports were ecologically safe. Even then, the U.S. retained the right to block tuna imports anytime it deemed they had an "adverse effect" on dolphins. Further, NGOs created a "Flipper Safe" label, which a tuna canner could use only if it did not use dolphin-set tuna at all (and–incidentally–only if it paid an annual licensing fee to the "Flipper Program"). By 2001, even with the vastly improved safety record, little if any Mexican dolphin-set tuna had entered the U.S. market. In short, the GATT/WTO did not overturn U.S. environmental law. In fact, to the extent Mexican fishing practices were improved to protect dolphins, there was something of a movement toward a higher common denominator, as Mexico moved closer to U.S. practices. The U.S. use of market-access (or threats to close it) may help explain why the worst fears of some environmental activists have not been born out, and one finds convergence in a number of regulations.[43]

IV. CONCLUSION

There is a pattern in these cases: private sector interests shaped the outcome of inter-jurisdictional regulatory competition, be it downward or upward, in common with other states or in isolation. These interests are often legitimated in terms of the public good and with the assistance of public interest groups. They were certainly not the only actors involved, and this chapter's aim was limited to a plausible, necessary-but-not-sufficient explanation. These findings are supported not only by the cases summarized above, and others, but also by the sub-cases and details within them.

First, the specificity of firms' investments shapes the firm preferences for the regulatory harmonization. Investments with low asset specificity lead to a competition-in-laxity (ship flags, offshore banks) as firms seek less restrictive (market governance) regulatory environments. They increase the "exit" option of firms, thereby reducing the corresponding options of governments. To the extent Internet-based commerce reduces the specificity of assets (by reducing certain transaction costs and facilitating market governance), it may also encourage the circumvention of taxes and other national regulations. Conversely, investments specific to transactions across borders induce firms to support multinational regulatory convergence (unified governance, as in CFCs or BIS capital requirements). Investments specific to domestic transactions lead to heterogeneity in regulations among countries (tuna-dolphin, US advertising collusion, Danish bottle bill, Asian tobacco monopolies). In these cases, firms' exit options are limited and "voice" options become more attractive. Governments are more likely to "listen" to their own producers than to foreign firms.

Second, the locus of regulatory policy affects the direction of regulatory change, toward laxity or stringency, reflecting producer preferences. Process regulations are associated with laxity (general ship flags case, offshore banking centers, Delaware incorporation). In the shipping case, by 1994 more of the world's shipping fleet flew a flag-of-convenience than a flag from the seven largest OECD fleets combined; these FOC fleets also sank three times as often and were more prone to labor abuses and pollution and inspection violations. All labor laws, from union organizing to minimum wages to occupational safety laws, are process regulations, and in general one finds large firms opposing stringent labor laws. Process regulations may by collinear with low asset-specific investments, future research should evaluate the relative weight and interaction of these two variables. Conversely, one finds market-access regulations generally associated with stringent regulations (CFCs, tuna-dolphin, Danish bottle recycling). Market-access regulations included the actual or threatened use by large economies of market regulations on products and services as a "club" to raise process standards overseas (BIS capital requirements, regulation of oil tankers). In certain cases, one finds large firms supporting these barriers-to-entry.

Third, industrial structure affects the strength of the process-market access distinction. Governments are more likely to respond to demands for regulatory change from dominant, established firms in concentrated markets. The evidence shows a pattern of powerful firms using stringent regulations as a barrier to entry to competitors (Heinz-StarKist, DuPont, ICI, Abbott-Ross, Bristol-Myers, monopolies on tobacco in Asia, Shell on LOT). DuPont even lobbied to save the Vienna Convention and Montreal Protocol against Reagan administration critics. Powerful actors also acted to create or seek havens with lower taxes or more favorable regulations in order reduce production costs (Harriman and Dulles in Panama, Stettinius in Liberia, DuPont in Delaware); smaller firms took advantage of these once created.

So-called "Baptist and Bootlegger" coalitions are clearly identifiable and influential in several of these cases, notably the tuna-dolphin controversy, and the Montreal Protocol. They did not emerge in the overall ship flagging case, a case overall of laxity, but did in the subcase of higher oil-tanker pollution regulations. While not exhaustive, these cases all lend credence to the importance of Baptist-Bootlegger coalitions.

Mutual recognition agreements (MRAs) are a "middle ground" between laxity and stringency, and between commonality and heterogeneity. In MRAs, products "approved once"(in any member county) are "accepted everywhere" for the purpose of trade. These helped facilitate integration of the single European market, and since 1995 have been a major goal of the Trans-Atlantic Business Dialogue (TABD). As a less-distinct dependent variable MRAs are less useful analytically for theory-building, but they are important from a policy perspective. Consistent with this chapter's emphasis, the clear driver for MRAs has been major producers' preferences.[44] The TABD consists of major corporations from the U.S. and Europe, paired with their government officials. Xerox Corporation and Goldman Sachs stepped up and began the preparations for the first TABD meeting in Seville in November 1995, and BASF and Ford assumed the TABD chairmanship in 1996. They were followed in subsequent years by Phillips and Tenneco, DaimlerChrysler and Warner-Lambert, Suez Lyonnais and Xerox (again), Lafarge and United Technologies, and Electrolux and PricewaterhouseCoopers. The host companies pay for the TABD Director's office, staff, and travel budget. U.S. and EU governments are fully supportive of this effort. As U.S. Under Secretary of Commerce Timothy J. Hauser noted, "We should put the business 'horse' before the government 'cart'."[45] To date, seven MRAs have reached the implementation stage, within telecommunications, medical devices, electromagnetic compatibility, electrical safety, recreational craft, pharmaceuticals, and capital markets. TABD Director Jeff Werner notes that because U.S. and EU standards are often quite high to begin with, "it is less frequent that the TABD would look to raise them," with exceptions such as intellectual property.[46] NGOs have played only a very minor role in this process. The Trans-Atlantic Environmental Dialogue" has died on the vine. Its website (www.taed.org), notes acerbically that, "TAED suspends its activities due to the failure of US government to stick to its commitments." And the Trans-Atlantic Consumer Dialogue (www.tacd.org) has had only limited success. Other consumer groups are more critical of MRAs.[47]

The logic of capitalism arguably may lead to the continued growth of large corporations that seek to capture economies of scale and scope.[48] To the extent this is true, and these findings of this research are correct, one can expect an increasing reflection of corporate interests in regulations. The rapidly growing number of cases before the WTO and the rapidly growing public reactions against them are only the most visible sign of the amount of economic activity affected by the juncture of national regulations and cross-border commerce. World trade doubled from 1980 to 2000, and foreign direct investments (FDI) grew even faster. To the extent that selling these FDI assets prematurely would involve greater losses than with comparable domestic investments, due to the greater transaction costs and risks of FDI, this helps explain why FDI might be associated with increasingly homogenous regulations.

These outcomes of competition among jurisdictions reflect

producers' constrained preferences. Constraints are imposed by a variety of other factors not examined in this chapter. These include technology, science, economic conditions, competition among firms; INGOs, NGOs, interest groups, media coverage, norms, ideologies, and other non-market institutions; domestic and international institutions, labor unions, domestic party politics, and changes in consumer preferences. These are exogenous to the focus of this research, which aims for a necessary (if not sufficient) explanation of regulatory outcomes. Obviously, not every firm can write its own legal code. To the contrary, firms compete with each other in the regulatory arena as well as in the market, and regulatory strategies carry a significant cost to firms. Acting under conditions of uncertainty, it is not surprising that firms and governments both make mistakes and are affected by forces beyond their control. Nevertheless, it is striking that across such a diverse set of cases one finds a pattern of behavior that can be reasonably well explained by a few simple propositions.

This chapter offers a cut at concept formation and confirmation; additional studies support these findings (Murphy 1993, 1995, 1996, 1998, and forthcoming; Alt 1999, Spar 1999). These include detailed case studies of the origin of offshore banking, the Basle Accord on capital adequacy, and infant-formula marketing. Further research must refine, operationalize, and test these propositions in light of other cases. Low asset-specificity interacts with the process variable, and future research should distinguish which is more important under specified circumstances. Some public policies, such as US restrictions on tobacco, may (or may not) have disadvantaged domestic firms. These cases need to be reexamined, to ascertain why, for example, the Liggett Group broke ranks with other US cigarette manufacturers, or to properly conceptualize the role of state attorney-led lawsuits. The role of trade unions poses another conceptual challenge. There are other outlying cases. Many large US firms complained that the unilateral 1974 Foreign Corrupt Practices Act put them at a competitive disadvantage, although the first conviction did not take place for a decade and resulted in a relatively minor fine; these same groups have since supported multilateral adoption of US rules.[49] In other cases, such as gender equality in the workforce (see Gelb chapter), policies may not put domestic firms at a competitive disadvantage, and might well benefit them. These would not then be subject to the competitive pressures of globalization analyzed here. As shown in the other chapters in this book, to fully explain any one case a wide variety of factors must be examined, including both formal institutions and informal pressures.

Although producer preferences can be forecasted, these forecasts are not completely determinate–preferences involve business strategy and human choice, and regulatory outcomes are affected by other groups and variables. The conclusion of this chapter is not one of nihilistic acceptance that narrow material interests are the sole driver of outcomes. There is still room for leadership and creativity in both business and regulatory politics. The creation of new coalitions, new alliances, new business and political strategies, and so on, all depend on human agency. Consumer demand is the ultimate driving force for most producers, and consumers' preferences may themselves by subject to suasion, sometimes by NGO efforts, e.g., in a shift to "green" products. Governments are likely to have greater autonomy in devising policy solutions, especially when a split in policy preference occurs between evenly matched major producers or industries, or in times of crisis. Policy managers and activists can and have taken advantage of this, by deliberately identifying and assisting those firms or business-associations whose policy preferences align with their own, or by developing compromise policies such as labeling requirements or MRAs. Identifying the implications of large firms' asset-specific investments is as useful for non-governmental organizations and governments as it is for corporations.

The underlying logic of this chapter is that producer preferences shape outcomes that affect their interests, and that producers will seek the regulations that benefit them. The chapter goes beyond this, to examine under what conditions different producers will prefer different outcomes. Previous debates on "globalization" and "convergence" have tended to assume unidirectional movement. The explanation given here opens up the "black box" of firm-state relations in the global economy. It shows why simultaneous movements toward regulatory homogeneity and heterogeneity (convergence and divergence) may occur, as a reflection of differentiated producer preferences. The pressures identified here must be considered by firms, governments, and policy activists alike, in order to devise effective strategies for enduring regulations, whatever the desired outcome.

Dale D. Murphy is an Assistant Professor at the Robert Emmett McDonough School of Business at Georgetown University.

Notes
This chapter draws on several earlier research papers, notably Dale D. Murphy, "Open Economies' Competition For Comparative Regulatory Advantage," MIT Center for International Studies IEIRS working paper November 1993. (This paper laid out the core concepts, arguments and cases, and was widely circulated among MIT, Harvard, Berkeley and other international relations research centers. The original text is available upon request via permanent email: dale@alum.mit.edu.) Dale D. Murphy and Kenneth A. Oye, Interjurisdictional Harmonization and Divergence Across Open Economies," American Political Science Association annual conference paper, August 1994. Dale D. Murphy, *Open Economies and Regulations: Convergence and Competition among Jurisdictions*, PhD. diss., MIT Department of Political Science, 1995, Kenneth A. Oye adviser. Dale D. Murphy, paper for panel on "Asset Specificity and International Cooperation: Lessons from Transaction Cost Economics," International Studies Association, San Diego, CA, April 1996, David Lake discussant. Dale D. Murphy, "Comparative (Regulatory) Advantage: Firm-State Relations in the Global Economy," International Studies Association conference paper, Minneapolis, MN 1998, Daniel Verdier discussant Thanks to Kenneth Oye and David Vogel for many years of encouragement of this line of research, and to Robert Kagan for very helpful detailed comments here. Any errors in this paper, which emphasizes transaction costs, are the responsibility of the author.

1. On the value of concept formation and its priority over premature quantification, see Giovanni Sartori, "Concept Misinformation in Comparative Politics," *American Political Science Review* 64 (1970) pp.1033–1053. On the value of intentionally selecting on the dependent variable in a qualitative case-study methodology see Gary King, Robert O. Keohane, and Sidney Verba, *Designing Social Inquiry*, (Princeton Univ. Press, 1994) pp.128–149. This approach permits causal inferences, although not descriptive inferences such as the number of cases falling into each category. This research design "may help us to gain some valuable information about the empirical plausibility of a causal inference ... [I]f this design is to lead to meaningful—albeit necessarily limited—causal inferences, it is crucial to select observations without regard to values of the explanatory variables." (original emphasis) p.141. The latter is the case here, in which case studies were chosen to reflect a clear distribution in the dependent variable. Thanks to Keohane for a discussion of these issues at an MIT-Harvard Seminar, December 2, 1993, and for furthering my understanding of international relations on too many other occasions to list. Thanks to Thomas Homer-Dixon for additional discussion of the value of intentionally selecting on the dependent variable in a necessary-but-not-sufficient theoretical argument.

2. See Suzanne Berger and Ronald Dore, eds., *Convergence or Diversity? National Models of Production and Distribution in a Global Economy* (Cornell

University Press, 1996).

3. See David Vogel, *Trading Up* (Harvard Univ. Press 1995).

4. US Federal Reserve Board Chairman Arthur Burns (1974) described the US federalist financial system as a "competition in laxity." Thanks to Ethan Kapstein for this reference, and much useful discussion. Similar terms are "race of laxity," used by Supreme Court Justice Brandeis (1933); "race to the bottom" picked up in the Cary v. Winter debate over Delaware (see below); "degenerative competition" used by David Moss in describing the phossy-jaw case; and the more neutral "interjurisdictional competition" and "competitive deregulation" preferred in law and policy journals. The general subject falls under legal "conflict of laws" studies. This competition can be beneficial, as competition among states leads to a more optimal allocation of capital. E.g., see Theodore H. Moran, *Foreign Direct Investment and Development*, IIE 1998. Critics suggest it can also be detrimental. E.g., see Noreena Hertz, *The Silent Takeover* (London: Heineman 2001; Lori Wallach and Michelle Sforza, *Whose Trade Organization*, 1999; Dani Rodrik, *Has Globalization Gone Too Far?*, IIE 1997.

5. Martin Khor, "How the South is getting a Raw Deal at the WTO," in *Views from the South*, 1999.

6. See also Daniel Drezner, "Bottom Feeders," *Foreign Policy* (November/ December 2000). Ronie Garcia-Johnson, *Exporting Environmentalism* (MIT Press, 2000). Adam B. Jaffee et al., "Environmental Regulation and the Competitiveness of US Manufacturing," *J. of Economic Literature* (March 1995) 33: 132–163. Arik Levinson, "Environmental Regulations and Industry Location," in *Fair Trade and Harmonization*, Vol. I., ed. J. Bhagwati and R.E. Hudec (MIT Press 1996). Leigh C. Anderson and Robert Kagan, "Adversarial Legalism and Transaction Costs," *International Review of Law and Economics* (2000), 20:1–19. Thanks to Vogel and Kagan for drawing my attention to several of these sources.

7. See Kyle Bagwell and Robert W. Staiger, "The WTO as a Mechanism for Securing Market Access Property Rights: Implications for Global Labor and Environmental Issues" (mimeo May 2001). Thanks to J.P. Singh for calling my attention to this work. See also Daniel Esty and D. Geradin, Regulatory Co-opetition," *J. of International Economic Law* (2000), 3:2, 235–255.

8. This does *not* imply that the state government apparatus is irrelevant. As Stigler (1971) notes: "The state . . . is a potential resource or threat to every industry in the society . . . [It] can and does selectively help or hurt a vast number of industries." The state has the power to coerce, tax, seize assets, control the movement of resources, and constrain economic decisions. Nor does Stigler deny that public interest groups may influence regulations. Nonetheless, over the long run, concentrated producer preferences are reflected in state regulations.

9. "Loyalty" in this context might be in the expectation of future political "goods." Hirschman 1970.

10. James Q. Wilson, ed., *The Politics of Regulation*, (1980).

11. Oliver Williamson, *The Economic Institutions of Capitalism* (New York: Free Press, 1985). Williamson distinguishes the four types of asset specificity as follows. *Site specific:* the buyer and seller are located in a "cheek-by-jowl"

relation to each other. *Human asset specific:* investments in relationship-specific human capital, such as skills that are imperfectly transferable across employers. These often arise in a learning-by-doing fashion, or from team configurations. *Dedicated assets:* involve expanding existing plant on behalf of a particular buyer. *Physical asset specificity:* when one or both parties to a transaction invest in specialized equipment designed specifically for that transaction; and the equipment would have lower value in alternative uses. On *brand specificity,* see Oliver Williamson, The New Institutional Economics: Taking Stock, Looking Ahead," *Journal of Economic Literature,* 38 (September), 2000, pp. 595–613.

12. For simplicity, "higher" asset specificity here refers to investments that involve both qualitatively more-specific transactions, and larger sums of money. "Lower" asset specificity similarly refers here to both qualitatively less-specific transactions, and smaller sums of money. Obviously, small investments that are very specific, or large investments that are not so specific, fall somewhere between these extremes. Both dimensions are important, future research might delineate their differences.

13. Transaction costs are the "costs of running the economic system." They are the economic equivalent of friction. *Ex ante* transaction costs are the costs of drafting, negotiating, and safeguarding an agreement. *Ex post* transaction costs include maladaption costs when transactions go awry; haggling costs if efforts are needed to correct misalignments; the setup and running costs associated with the governance structures to which disputes are referred; and the cost of effecting secure commitments. Williamson (1985)

14. "Most American multinational companies adopt worldwide environmental standards at their facilities regardless of where they are located ... It is simply more efficient to use the same environmental standards in Mexico as in the United States." USTR interagency task force study, October 15, 1991. The UN Centre on Transnational Corporations similarly found that "although parent company policies and standards were not fully adopted by TNCs operating in host developing countries, their policies and practices were generally superior to standards contained in local environmental regulations. Standards of TNCs in pollution-intensive industries have exceeded local standards as indicated by all the country studies ... [Eighty-three percent of all parent companies] directed subsidiaries to operate within the standards adopted in the home country of the parent company," (emphases added) ESCAP/UNCTC Publication Series B, 1990) Thanks to co-author Tyn Myint-U for lending me this book, and other discussions.

15. Exceptions are rare, in which heterogenous rules discriminate in favor of a particular foreign firm.

16. See Debora Spar and David Yoffie, "Multinational Enterprises and the Prospects for Justice," *J. Int'l Affairs* 52:2, Spring 1999, 557–581, reprinted in Prakash and Hart, *Responding to Globalization* (Routledge: 2000). Thanks to an anonymous reviewer for making me aware of the need to clarify this intellectual lineage.

17. Alt et al. make major contributions to this literature, in developing quantitative indices of sectoral asset specificity and lobbying preferences. See

JE Alt, F Carlsen, P Heum, K Johansen, "Asset Specificity and the Political Behavior of Firms: Lobbying for Subsidies in Norway," *International Organization* 53:1 (Winter 1999) 99–116. Broader aspects of factor specificity and trade policy are addressed in Alt and Gilligan (1994) and Alt, Frieden, Gilligan, Rodrik, and Rogowski (1996). David Lake was a reader and discussant of the Murphy (1996) paper, at the April 1996 ISA conference in La Jolla, CA.

18. Colin J. Bennett, "Review Article: What is Policy Convergence and What Causes It?," *British Journal of Political Science* v21 n2 (April 1991) pp.215–234; Ronald Brickman, Shelia Jasanoff and Thomas Ilgen, *Controlling Chemicals: The Politics of Regulation in Europe and the United States* (Ithaca, NY: Cornell University Press, 1985), pp.302–3; in a broader sense Helen Milner, *Resisting Protectionism: Global Industries and the Politics of International Trade* (Princeton University Press, 1988).

19. In the context of private sector contracts, Williamson uses the terms "bilateral" and "trilateral" in place of two-party and third-party, respectively. The diplomatic overtones of these terms would be confusing here, hence cognates are used. Unified means "vertical integration" within a firm. Williamson uses the terms "governance structure" and "contracting structure" interchangeably. "Market governance" is most clear in spot-market purchases. More important in this study is multinational "idiosyncracy," or highly specific investments. Williamson maps the governance structures onto a two-by-three table, not a one-dimensional hierarchy. Thanks to Lael Brainard for a key discussion of this literature; this adaptation is not her fault. Thanks also to James Rosberg for a discussion of this and other issues.

20. Paul Joskow, "Asset Specificity and the Structure of Vertical Relationships: Empirical Evidence," *J. of Law, Economics, and Organization*, v4 n1 (Spring 1988), p.103–6. For current empirical studies on transaction cost economics, see: Scott Masten and Stephane Saussier, "Econometrics of Contracts: An Assessment of Developments in the Empirical Literature on Contracting," *Revue D'Economie Industrielle*, No. 92, 2000, pp. 215–236; and Robert Dahlstrom and Arne Nygaard, "An Empirical Investigation of Ex Post Transaction Costs in Franchised Distribution Channels," *J. of Marketing Research*, 36 (May 1999): 160–170.

21. This distinction is adapted from the product-process distinction in Vogel 1995, and Murphy and Oye 1996.

22. Thanks to Robert Kagan and David Vogel for this latter point.

23. See Robert E. Baldwin, *The Political Economy of US Import Policy* (MIT Press: 1985). J. Lawrence, Broz, *Rent-seeking and the organization of the fiscal-military state: central banking in England and the United States, 1694–1834.* (Harvard Center for International Affairs, working paper no. 94–1, 1994). Helen Milner, *Resisting Protectionism: Global Industries and the Politics of International Trade* (Princeton Univ. Press, 1988). E.E. Schattschneider, *Politics, Pressure and the Tariff* (New York: Prentice-Hall, 1935). Miles Kahler, "Modeling Races to the Bottom," mimeo c.1999. Jean-Jacques Laffont and Jean Tirole, "The Politics of Government Decision-Making: A Theory of Regulatory Capture," *Journal of Law, Economics and Organization* (1991). James Cassing, Timothy McKeown & Jack Ochs, "Political Economy of Tariff Cycle," *American Political*

Science Review, v80 n3 September 1986, pp.843–862. Jeffrey S. Banks and Barry R. Weingast, "The Political Control of Bureaucracies Under Asymmetric Information," *American Journal of Political Science* v36 n2 (May 1992), pp.509–525. Jonathan J. Pincus, *Pressure Groups and Politics in Antebellum Tariffs* (Columbia Univ. Press, 1977). Peter Gourevitch, "International Trade, Domestic Coalitions and Liberty," *Journal of Interdisciplinary History,* Autumn 1977. John A.C. Conybeare, "Voting for Protection: An Electoral Model of Tariff Policy," *International Organization* v45 n1 (Winter 1991) pp.57–81. Douglas A. Irwin, "The Political Economy of Free Trade," (mimeo, October 1992; Univ. of Chicago Graduate School of Business). Timothy McKeown, "The Politics of Corn Law Repeal and Theories of Commercial Policy," *British Journal of Political Science* 19 (July 1989), pp.353–380. Stephen Magee & Leslie Young, "Endogenous Protection in the US, 1900–1984," and "Comment" by J. Peter Neary, Chapter Four in Robert M. Stern (ed), *US Trade Policy in a Changing World Economy* (MIT Press: 1987). For critiques, see e.g., Wilson 1980 (op cit.), Alexander Wendt, *Social Theory of International Politics,* Cambridge Univ. Press 1999.

24. Full citations available upon request. Classic economic research on oligopolies includes Bain 1956, Modigliani 1958, Olson 1965, and Chandler 1988, McCraw ed.. See also Stigler's critique 1968, among others, on mechanisms to achieve collective action; Dixit 1979, 1982 on duopoly; McKeown 1984; Williamson 1985; and Aggarwal, Keohane and Yoffie 1987. P.G. Porter and Livesay (in McCraw 1988) offer a useful working definition of oligopoly as a situation in which six or fewer firms manufacture 50 per cent or more of the total product value of an industry, or twelve or fewer firms manufacture 75 percent or more of total industry product, as defined by the US *Census of Manufactures.*

25. Industrial structure points to a possible exception to the market access-process distinction during market shake-outs. This exception to the rule is subordinate to the larger pattern. As firms compete for dominance, oligopolies may temporarily seek higher process regulations (in a "bleeding game"), so long as the gains from eliminating competitors exceeds the higher cost of production. Similarly, firms forced to endure stringent process standards (for whatever reason) may seek to impose these stringent standards on their competitors, through federal or international regulations. Conversely, oligopolies may temporarily seek lower market-access regulations, to undermine a competitor's protected market. The relevant aspect in these exceptions is the differential affect of the regulation on various firms, and the governments' responses.

26. See Bruce Yandle, "Bootleggers and Baptists: the Education of a Regulatory Economist," *Regulation,* May-June 1983. The phrase refers to the American Prohibition on alcohol (1919–1933, Constitutional Amendment Eighteen), when product bans on alcohol led to windfall profits for illegal distributors ("bootleggers"). Those in the temperance movement ("Baptists") unwittingly found themselves in an "unholy" alliance with bootleggers: both wanted to keep stringent regulations on alcohol, albeit for different reasons. Politicians who voted for prohibition (or later bans on Sunday liquor sales) were supported by both groups. See also Odegard 1928/[1966].

27. See footnote 1. A book-length treatment of these cases is being published elsewhere (Murphy, forthcoming). These cases and their details offer data supporting the conclusions that can only be summarized here.

28. Lloyd's 1991. Liberia has the lowest accident rate of the FOCs, improving by 1980 to the same level as Japan, Norway and the U.S. Greece has the worst accident rate, often higher than the FOCs. Calculations by the authors, from Lloyd's data various years.

29. R. Michael M'Gonigle and Mark W. Zacher, *Pollution, Politics, and International Law: Tankers at Sea* (Berkeley: Univ. of California Press, 1979).

30. See also Alan W. Cafruny, "The Political Economy of International Shipping: Europe versus America," *International Organization* v39 n1 (Winter 1985), pp.79–119, for a discussion of power and hegemony in the context of the shipping industry. Cafruny, *op. cit.* Data are for 1977.

31. See Murphy (1993) for details.

32. M'Gonigle and Zacher, 1979.

33. In the latter case, U.S. industry may have acted to forestall even tougher regulations, or to better control their legal and political risks. See Joseph Rees, *Hostages of Each Other,* (Univ. Chicago Press 1994) and Richard O. Brooks and Thomas M. Hoban, *Green Justice* (Westview 1996). Thanks to Robert Kagan for these references.

34. Jonathan Golub, "Globalization, Sovereignty and Policy-Making," in *Global Democracy,* ed. B. Holden (Routledge 2000). Thanks to Vogel and Kagan for this reference.

35. Thanks to Sanford Weiner and James Maxwell sharing and discussing their research (1993) in this area, and to Nathan Foster and Judith Layzer for comments on these issues. On government and INGO negotiations see Richard Benedick 1991. On epistemic communities see Peter Haas 1992. See also Litfin 1994 and Solingen 1993.

36. The Montreal Protocol was made increasingly stringent in Helsinki in 1989, London in 1990, and Copenhagen in 1992. Unless otherwise specified, the entire set of agreements is referred to here loosely as the "Montreal Protocol." The London revision included a non-binding resolution to phase out HCFCs as well, by 2030.

37. Allied Signal held another 25 percent. (Elf-Atochem purchased Pennwalt in 1989; it also owned Racon.)

38. If industry had created such a cartel on its own, it might have been charged with price-fixing.

39. US, not Mexican fishermen pioneered purse-seining technology in the 1960s. By the 1970s, ETP northeastern spotted dolphin stocks had dropped by up to 70%. The US did not then embargo ETP tuna despite the hundreds of thousands of dolphins killed annually. By 1989, as fishing techniques improved, the northeastern stock increased by roughly 4% per year. (National Research Council 1992). None of the dolphin species in the ETP were listed as in danger of extinction.

40. The big three were American-owned in 1988. By 1989 only StarKist remained American-owned, as Chicken of the Sea and Bumble Bee were sold to Indonesian and Thai interests, respectively. The latter had even weaker ties to the ETP. The sale of ownership would have little impact on regulations

within the U.S., however, as the firms' assets, branding, business strategy and government ties remained solidly American.

41. StarKist closed its last California cannery in 1984, "in response to high costs and the Government's failure to provide relief from low-priced canned tuna imports" (H.J. Heinz 1985 Annual Report, 17).

42. Emphases added. Coincidentally, Kerry is married to the widow of H.J. Heinz' grandson, the late Senator John Heinz.

43. See Vogel 1995 (op. cit.), Robert Kagan and Lee Axelrad, *Regulatory Encounters* (UC Berkeley Press, 2000).

44. Maria Green Cowles argues that European integration itself was the result of preferences by dominant producers with significant asset-specific investments across European borders. "The Politics of Big Business in the European Community: Setting the Agenda for a New Europe," Ph.D. dissertation, American University, 1994. The role of the European Round Table of industrialists (ERT) was particularly influential; it's early white-papers are remarkably similar to the final Single European Act. On the TABD, see www.TABD.com. MRAs do not obviate the utility of the three analytical trajectories used here (LCD, HCD, and heterogeneous), just as warm water does not obviate the distinction between cold and hot. They do raise an interesting new question, as to what conditions lead to their implementation.

45. US Under Secretary of Commerce Timothy J. Hauser, acting Under Secretary of Commerce for International Trade, in testimony before the Subcommittee on Trade of the House Committee on Ways and Means, Hearing on New Transatlantic Agenda, 23 July 1997, 105th Congress, first session.

46. Interview with TABD Director Jeff Werner, December 2001.

47. E.g., www.publiccitizen.org/trade/harmonization/MRA .

48. Alfred DuPont, with the assistance of Takashi Hikino, *Scale and Scope: The Dynamics of Industrial Capitalism*, (Cambridge, MA: Belknap Press, 1990). This logic is not inevitable, as some factors work against increased concentration of industry. These include flexible-specificiation technologies (Piore and Sable 1984), networked forms of industrial organization (Locke), strategic alliances, and entrepreneurship.

49. The 1974 Foreign Corrupt Practices Act was adopted at the peak of other shake-ups in Washington, DC power circles, and other "Sunshine Laws." These historical anomalies may explain the Act's adoption. The first major conviction was not until 1985, when U.S.-based Crawford Enterprises was fined $3.5 million for having bribed officials of Mexico's PemEx with a total of $10 million. The movement in the late 1990s toward harmonization of corruption laws was led by US firms, notably General Electric, which helped fund and promote Transparency International.

Chapter 3

The Globalization of Conservation Standards In Marine Fisheries

Christopher J. Carr and Harry N. Scheiber

I. INTRODUCTION

The fate of marine fisheries is one of the most urgent resource problems facing the international community today. Around the world, countries have closed some of their historically most profitable commercial fisheries. Most notably, both Canada and the United States have declared a full moratorium on fishing in their respective jurisdictions of the great Northwest Atlantic cod fishery. Other fishing industries have been forced to accept severe cutbacks in their authorized harvest quotas and face additional reductions as fishing yields continue to stagnate or fall. For instance, the European Union countries now face a sixty percent or greater cut in harvest quotas, a compromise following a recommendation from European Union fishery agency scientists for cuts as high as eighty-five percent.[1] In the Pacific Northwest of the United States, the decline of salmon stocks is so severe that they qualify for protection under the Endangered Species Act. Federal protection of the salmon has enormous implications not only for river use and management, but also for the growth and zoning policies of urban and suburban centers in the area. In the Pacific Islands, dynamiting lagoons and coral reefs continues almost unabated, with destructive, irreversible effects on habitat and fish populations.[2]

The Food and Agriculture Organization (FAO) data on worldwide marine fisheries, the most authoritative statistical source on the subject, indicate that at least sixty percent of the world's top 200 commercial marine fish stocks are in fisheries classified, according to

118

catch trends, as either "mature" or "senescent."[3] These categories indicate fisheries requiring "urgent management action to halt the increase in fishing effort or rehabilitate overfished resources."[4] Fisheries in these two categories are either at or beyond full utilization: Forty-four percent were classified as "fully to heavily exploited," and sixteen percent "overexploited."[5] Those beyond full utilization are either in grave danger of depletion, or already depleted beyond hope for commercial use in the near future.[6] Indeed, if the data tracked biomass volume rather than species-specific information, the percentage of fisheries categorized as mature or endangered might well be much higher. Nor do the data account for fisheries that have already collapsed in the half-century following World War II, the most notorious example being the once-giant California sardine fishery.[7]

Many nations now recognize that overcapacity in their coastal and high seas fishing fleets has created an urgent problem and have devised domestic and international measures to address the crisis. The national fishery management programs apply to fleets operating in the offshore jurisdictional fishing zones, generally out to a marine boundary 200 miles from shore called the 200 Mile Exclusive Economic Zone (EEZ). These national programs, however, have not succeeded in reversing the parlous trends and thereby have failed to restore the health of fisheries and their habitats. Such failure extends to international management programs as well.[8]

Consequently, the last quarter century has witnessed an acceleration of new initiatives in regard to both national and international fishery management. This development, treated in Part II of this study, represents a quest to reform the basic legal ordering of fishing activity on the high seas and imposes new norms and obligations on the coastal states in their regulation of their offshore EEZs. The process of creating governing legal regimes can be seen as a "globalization" of fisheries management. The globalization process as it applies to marine fisheries management is an important attempt to define universally applicable conservation-oriented norms, formulating and implementing new rules for fishing operations based on scientific research and (in some measure) economic desiderata. The process further attempts to design and mobilize new international institutions for more effective management.

Other more conventionally defined aspects of globalization, such as those generally concerned with such phenomena as deregulation and trade liberalization, also have a causal interrelationship with the current ocean fisheries crisis. In fact, multi-national enterprise, international trade in fish products, mobility of capital in the form of vessel re-flagging and massive fleet movements have all impacted the structure of competition among fishing nations. This impact is reflected in national and international political pressures that have weakened regulatory programs and worked, in effect, to produce an international "race to the bottom."[9] In one respect, it has been a literal race to the bottom as giant trawler vessels have been depleting the bottom-fish stocks in many areas of the world's oceans by scraping the sea bottom clean![10]

Privatization, one of the globalization movement's leading features, plays a role in efforts to deal with the fisheries crisis in both the national EEZs and the resource regimes of important international and regional organizations. For instance, the assignment of private property rights in fishery resources, especially as "individual transferable quotas" (ITQs), is a technique being widely adopted. ITQs and other privatization schemes have to be distinguished, however, from examples of privatization in the communications, transport, and other international industrial sectors. In the case of fisheries, ITQs and other property rights are assigned within the framework of scientifically managed regimes with overall and national catch quotas, seasonal regulations, gear restrictions and all other aspects of conventional management except the formerly universal feature of open access. Privatization is thus a dimension of fishery management reforms that is being adopted around the world to meet the resource crisis. Property-rights and privatization schemes do not, however, represent a universalization or globalization of standards. On the contrary, these schemes vary widely, from nation to nation, in their design and administration. We mention this aspect of fishery policy issues, therefore, as part of the larger context of globalization of standards, rather than as exemplary of efforts to impose uniformity.[11]

The purpose of this study is to provide an overview of the various initiatives that seek to establish more effective global conservation norms, standards, regulations and institutions to govern the hunting of fish and cetacean stocks in ocean waters. The regulation of a natural resource—in this case, fish and cetacean stocks that were traditionally treated as common property under both national and international law—differs greatly from the regulation of trade, manufacturing, and service industries. Nonetheless, there are certain intriguing parallel and analogous issues. In addition, tensions from fishery conflicts have had major ramifications for trade policy and other legal and diplomatic issues in the global arena.[12] No less important are the ways in which emerging international norms for fisheries management reflect and interact with the dicta and specific provisions of other instruments in transnational environmental law.[13]

In Part II, we trace the development of the central principle of "sustainability"—the concept that fisheries should be exploited at a level that ensures a stable and continuous supply of fish for harvesting from one year to the next.[14] We will trace the origins of the sustainability standard in the post-World War II marine fisheries policy debates; its codification in the framework Law of the Sea conventions; and its general acceptance in multilateral fishery conservation agreements of the 1990s.

Part III explores why fishery management regimes have been almost uniformly unsuccessful in achieving their objective of achieving sustainability.[15] "Sustainability" of fish stock levels and of their marine habitats, or alternatively "sustainable development,"[16] has become the explicit normative goal of fishery management programs worldwide. The "development" goal, linked to resource conservation, remains highly salient for many national programs, and subsidies continue to play a major role in the operations of the world's fishery industries. But international and regional organizations' efforts to impose new norms have mainly emphasized conservation, and we give our attention here to that aspect of regulatory developments. Also in Part III, we assess the prospects for achieving harmonization and "race to the top" results using the new rules, policies, and institutions that are replacing the old order of "freedom of the seas."[17] We also inquire whether any important "race to the bottom" effects are internalized by existing regulatory regimes.

Part IV discusses recent efforts to implement global conservation standards for fisheries, including the use of unilateral trade sanctions; recent international "framework" agreements that are designed to strengthen conservation standards and to enhance compliance and enforcement; the movement toward multilateral trade measures to enforce conservation standards; and some uses of market forces as an enforcement mechanism through eco-labeling, boycotts, and other means.

II. GLOBAL STANDARDS FOR MARINE CAPTURE FISHERIES[18]

The effort to establish effective global, conservation-oriented management standards for marine fisheries is a relatively recent phenomenon. For centuries, the oceans were widely viewed as providing an inexhaustible supply of fish. In the 1950s, intensive industrial fishing began employing new surveying and harvesting technologies, and its scale and geographic range began growing rapidly. With this dramatic development, the international community began to more seriously consider the need for conservation standards to manage the fishing that took place on the high seas, beyond areas of national jurisdiction. The 1958 United Nations Convention on Fishing and Conservation of the Living Resources of the High Seas ("1958 Convention")[19] was the first achievement of this movement for establishing global regulatory standards. But the 1958 Convention set out (in Article 2) only very general conservation obligations aimed at achieving optimum sustainable yield from high seas fisheries.[20] The sustainability principle was carried forward in the 1982 United Nations Convention on the Law of the Sea (UNCLOS).[21] More recently, there has been an elaboration of international commitments bearing on marine resources generally and fisheries in particular. The most notable are the U.N. Fish Stocks Agreement,[22] signed in 1995, which specifically addresses the problem of high seas fishing areas outside national offshore boundaries, and the Convention on Biological Diversity,[23] which has major implications for the management of coastal area fisheries and fish habitats.[24]

From the early 1950s, many coastal states had asserted ownership and exclusive authority over fisheries located at various distances from their coasts, including, in some instances, fisheries located up to 200 miles away from shore.[25] Because the vast majority—some eighty to ninety percent—of fisheries for commercially valuable species are located in waters within 200 miles of the coast, industrialized countries whose "distant-water" fishing fleets plied coastal waters off other nations' shores opposed these claims to extended jurisdiction.[26] But the proliferation of claims to extended jurisdiction ultimately could not be resisted, and in 1982, UNCLOS completed the process of ocean enclosure, extending jurisdictional claims beyond the traditional 3 to 9 mile limits offshore. By reducing fisheries to the exclusive jurisdiction of coastal states out to 200 miles, the current EEZ, and thereby eliminating the prisoner's dilemma pathologies of open access regimes, UNCLOS in theory made it feasible for states to take effective conservation measures for most fisheries in their EEZs.

While UNCLOS formally imposed some conservation obligations on coastal states with respect to their EEZ resources it also permitted those states to continue to exercise great discretion in their adoption and enforcement of national conservation and management measures for EEZ fishery resources. Because of the special sensitivity of fisheries issues, under Article 297(3) a coastal state is not required to submit disputes relating to its management of EEZ fishery resources to binding dispute settlement.[27] Although UNCLOS does not provide for meaningful enforcement of the conservation obligations formally specified for EEZ fishery resources, high seas fishing activities are subject to compulsory, binding dispute settlement under the Convention.[28] The irony is that UNCLOS itself provides only the most general conservation obligations even for high seas fisheries.[29]

Managing for sustainability has also been the mandate of numerous international regional fishery organizations. Two prominent examples are the International Commission for the Conservation of Atlantic Tunas (ICCAT), which is responsible for establishing conservation and management measures for tuna and swordfish in the Atlantic Ocean, and the Northwest Atlantic Fisheries Organization (NAFO), which is responsible for establishing conservation and management measures for ground fish, most prominently cod, in the Northwest Atlantic Ocean. Unfortunately, both organizations' records are marked by failures—bluefin tuna stocks, for example, are severely depressed, and the sorry story of the Atlantic cod fisheries is well known. Fisheries in areas under exclusive national jurisdictions have fared little better.[30] As noted earlier, the FAO has reported that the vast majority of commercial fisheries are fully utilized or overfished.[31] Hence, even where marine fisheries are entirely under a single nation's control, the same discouraging pattern of failure has resulted, and it has been a fairly uniform pattern globally.

This brief overview of efforts to implement fishing conservation standards raises three questions. First, what accounts for this record of international and national failure? Second, what is being done to address the problem? Third, can the initiatives being taken in recent years be expected to succeed?

III. THE PROBLEMS

There are many impediments to effective conservation and management of fisheries within zones of national jurisdiction and in the high seas. These obstacles differ in certain respects because of the distinct legal regimes for EEZs and the high seas, but they are also quite similar in many ways. National laws and international conventions uniformly profess a commitment to the sustainability principle. However, overfishing has been the norm virtually everywhere. Management agencies within countries and their international counterparts have regularly set catch quotas in excess of the maximum sustainable yield for decades. The main reasons for continuing overfishing and poor management are uncertainty of scientific methods and data, the institutional structure of the fishing industry, and enforcement difficulties.

A. Scientific Uncertainty

The difficulties of methodology, and data collection, in fisheries biology and analysis of fish population dynamics are endemic to fisheries management regimes. Fisheries science is plagued by uncertainties and population projections are notoriously faulty. The simple fact that fish cannot readily be observed and counted presents tremendous problems.[32] Even in this age of remote-sensing technology, biomass is impossible to assess with a high degree of accuracy. In addition, even where basic data can be obtained, interpretation is complicated by numerous other variables, such as ocean climate conditions. Moreover, population studies have gone through changes in conceptual foundation over cycles of 10–20 years; several briefly dominant approaches have been challenged and found wanting since 1900, and new approaches are never definitive. Thus the dominant conceptual foundation of fisheries science from the 1920s to the 1940s, which involved computations of "catch per unit of effort" (CPUE), proved wanting because it failed to take account of environmental variables that interacted with fishing effort; later, theories of population biodynamics were challenged on similar grounds, giving way to attempts at ecosystem analysis that incorporated meteorological, chemical, biological, and human factors as well as inter-species fish competition for food supplies and inter-species predation.[33]

The uncertainty inherent in fisheries science exacerbates the confrontations of divergent views that typically pit scientists from industry, environmental organizations, and government against one another. This conflict is commonly found in both national and international fisheries policy decision-making. Commercial fishermen and environmental organizations frequently retain their own fisheries scientists to evaluate data, render opinions on the status of stocks, and make projections of stocks given specified fishing levels. Because scientific findings and information are used as the basis for setting a total allowable catch for a fishery, they are as critically important to regulators as they are to the industrial and environmental interests. Thus, for example, scientists for U.S. Atlantic tuna fishermen wrangle with U.S. government scientists from the National Marine Fisheries Service (NMFS) to arrive at a consensus U.S. analysis of stock conditions. The U.S. analysis is then put forward at the annual ICCAT meetings, where each country offers its own view of the condition of the stocks. Finally, these views are considered by the organization's own scientific committee in developing a position on the status of stocks.[34]

A similar process occurs for many national fisheries. In the United States, fishermen and environmental organizations have their own scientists who participate in the deliberations of the regional fishery management councils. These scientists often challenge the data and conclusions of NMFS scientists, whose findings are used as the basis for setting catch limits for U.S. EEZ fisheries. These conflicting views often neutralize the role of science in domestic and international fisheries policy decision-making and thus enable other imperatives to control and dictate policy outcomes. Ironically, such outcomes often remain cloaked in the mantle of science.[35]

But even if "better" science were available, it would not mean that a mechanistic decision-making process would produce agreement on fishing levels; in fishery management generally, biological imperatives have long been subordinated to economic imperatives. Fishing operators around the globe seize upon the slightest scientific uncertainty as a reason to push for relaxed fishing restrictions. (This is a variant of the age-old problem of fishermen who interpret any decline in productivity as evidence not of overfishing but rather that the fish have simply "migrated somewhere else.") A recent characterization of the joint Russian-Norwegian management program for the Barents Sea fisheries is applicable to most regimes around the globe: The regulations adopted may be best understood as "a compromise between what can be defended biologically, legitimized politically, and accepted on social and economic grounds."[36]

B. The Structure of the Fishing Industry

The greatest problem facing fisheries today, as most commentators will assert, is that there are simply too many vessels chasing too few fish. National governments have fostered this overcapitalization crisis by extensively subsidizing fishing vessel construction.[37] Most fishing vessel owners carry substantial debt on their vessels, and this debt can only be serviced by revenues from fishing operations. At the same time, fishing crews typically work for a "share" of the catch. So it should come as no surprise that owners and crew often feel compelled to argue for catch quotas that might exceed levels recommended by fisheries science.[38]

While government buyouts might be thought to be the answer to the over-capitalization problem, and are being used today in the Canadian Maritime Provinces, the Pacific Northwest, Alaska, and New England, they have not been widely implemented. As with the legendary family farmers who are often said to constitute the historic Jeffersonian yeomanry, there is a romanticism about the fishing industry that often serves to immunize it from reforms that would "destroy a way of life." Fishermen often profess, quite sincerely, to have no conception of alternative careers. Because so many view fishing as a way of life, and not simply a fungible job, fishermen and the coastal communities in which they live tend to focus their political energy solely on fisheries issues. In the United States, both at the national and state levels, fisheries issues have long been nonpartisan—or at least bipartisan—and have reflected local employment and industry concerns.[39] Fishermen in the United States have long enjoyed powerful political patrons. For example, currently, Alaska Senator Ted Stevens is the ranking member of the Senate Appropriations Committee and is a devoted ally of fishermen's causes. In the House, Alaska Congressman Don Young is the vice-chair of the House Committee on Resources. Massachusetts Senators Edward Kennedy and John Kerry, Chairman of the Senate Subcommittee on Oceans and Fisheries, have been reliably attentive to the needs of New England's commercial fishermen.[40]

In addition, the structure of the U.S. regional fishery management councils and many of the international management bodies is designed to give industry a direct or indirect hand in decision-making. Industry members serve on regional councils and enjoy full voting rights. They also serve on "advisory" committees that assist in formulating the U.S. positions for meetings of international management organizations, attend those meetings as members of the U.S. delegation, and often serve as U.S. commissioners to such organizations. This kind of direct interest representation in policy-making is not limited to the U.S. industry; there is a powerful "corporativist" cast to the structure and operations of many national and international fishery management bodies. The integral role of industry representatives in management structures further limits the efficacy of the "issue-linkage" technique for resolving policy conflicts in the "tightly compartmentalized" management bodies—each of which is typically devoted to only one species or a single ocean region. [41]

Finally, commercial fishing interests comprise, in the language of public choice theory, a "concentrated minority," and, as a result, they have long enjoyed certain organizational and political advantages. In contrast, the national interest in fisheries conservation is shared by a "diffuse majority," which is less motivated to act.[42] It is only within the last decade that major environmental organizations have begun to devote attention to conservation of living marine resources other than "totemic" or "charismatic" marine species, such as dolphins and whales.[43] Even so, many organizations, responding to the concerns of their constituencies, focus their energies on human health-related problems, such as water and air pollution, rather than on the question of fisheries depletion and habitat destruction.

C. Enforcement Difficulties

Fisheries regulations are difficult to enforce for many reasons. On the high seas, under the traditional "flag state jurisdiction" regime, only the country in which a vessel is registered may take enforcement action against it. Effective enforcement is very costly because of the large expanses of open water that must be covered. Furthermore, reporting of fisheries catch data is readily susceptible to falsification. What John Gulland, one of the leading fisheries management scientists of the modern era, wrote 20 years ago is still entirely valid today in many of the world's fisheries:

> Fishermen are probably no greater lawbreakers than any other group of people. However, fishing does encourage the independent view and reluctance to accept, without proper explanation, rules and regulations,

especially if they come from bureaucrats in a distant capital. Further, it is not easy for a government official to check on what the individual fisherman is doing, perhaps in a small boat in poor weather some way from land. Only in a perfect world, therefore, is it reasonable to assume that rules and regulations to manage fishing would, once adopted, be necessarily carried out correctly. In the real, but imperfect, world some types of regulation are extremely difficult to enforce.[44]

There is considerable optimism in some academic and management circles that "cooperative management," which relies more on the fishing operators' knowledge of the stock and the waters, as well as their objective interest in maintaining the health of the stocks, will produce greater respect for regulation and cooperation in enforcement (or a larger measure of self-regulation). Such systematic involvement of the fishers, it is contended, legitimates the regulatory regime and avoids the traditional problem of demonizing enforcement officers. At its heart, the theory goes, co-management also represents a way of avoiding the Hobbesian results predicted in the common-property model to which Hardin famously assigned the term "tragedy of the commons."[45] However, to other analysts who worry that this course may overestimate the potential for altruism in the minds and hearts of the typical fishing operator, the better hope lies in the electronic and communications gear that can track vessel movements and operations at sea.[46]

The problem of flag state jurisdiction is fundamental.[47] Under UNCLOS, vessels fishing on the high seas are subject to enforcement actions only by the state in which they are registered. This regime of exclusive flag state jurisdiction, in combination with the traditional high seas freedom of fishing, has severely undermined the effectiveness of regional organizations. These organizations have been powerless to act against vessels flying the flags of states not party to the organization, yet fishing on the high seas and undermining the conservation and management measures agreed to by the organization. Moreover, even where a vessel is registered in a state that is a party to the organization, that state must fulfill its responsibilities to take enforcement action against its own vessels, and often this does not happen. Where a state that is a member of such an organization does take strong enforcement action against its vessels, many vessels often "re-flag" to a country known to exercise lax regulatory authority; these vessels are then said to be flying "flags of convenience." Some regional organizations are faced with the phenomenon of "third generation" flags of convenience—vessels which change their registry from a traditional flag-of-convenience state to a state that is a member of the regional organization though not vigilant in regulating its vessels—in order to avoid being branded a flag-of-convenience vessel.[48]

The juridical fungibility of fishing vessels is matched by their physical mobility. Just as fishing vessels will move from one ocean area to another in seeking out better fishing opportunities, vessels will relocate and re-flag in order to avoid scrutiny and restrictions, sometimes traveling half way around the world to do so. Physical mobility is illustrated by an incident reported by the U.S. State Department in 1994: a vessel observed fishing outside of New Zealand's 200-mile zone was observed a short time later fishing outside of Norway's zone in the Barents Sea.[49] Entire fleets, or at least great numbers of vessels in a particular fishery, have been known to relocate. An example of such mass relocation occurred when the operators from the San Diego tuna fleet fled the United States to escape increasingly stringent restrictions imposed on them to protect dolphins under the Marine Mammal Protection Act.[50] large portion of the tuna fleet re-flagged in Costa Rica and other countries that did not require dolphin protection. Even before the re-flagging movement, many vessels formerly based in San Diego were moving to very distant Atlantic waters, unloading for processing in Puerto Rico, and rotating their crews by air flights to and from the West Coast.[51]

The size of the ocean areas to be patrolled also presents obvious problems, requiring high expenditures for effective enforcement. Even within EEZs, distances to be patrolled often pose an insuperable impediment to effective monitoring and surveillance. For instance, the longline tuna fishery around the Hawaiian Islands contains areas where fishing is altogether prohibited by regulation. These closed areas extend for a distance of some 1,500 nautical miles around the Hawaiian Islands. The Coast Guard has estimated that it would cost in excess of twenty million U.S. dollars annually to effectively patrol this area alone.[52] Moreover, many fisheries are not of sufficient value, and their regulation is not sufficiently pressing as a political issue, to command the funding needed for effective monitoring, control, and surveillance—and to justify the political backlash that may occur if enforcement is too stringent.[53]

Incomplete reporting, evasion of monitoring authorities, and the outright falsification of catch data are all troublesome aspects of

enforcement in most if not all countries.[54] Traditionally, compliance
with "closed area" restrictions has been monitored not only by at-sea
patrols, but also by dockside analysis of fishing vessel log-books that
record when and where vessels fish. However, such log books are
notoriously subject to falsification, and vessels have been known to
carry one log book for their own purposes to record favorable fishing
grounds, and another log book for review by enforcement officials.
Although at-sea transshipment of catch is widely prohibited in
order to aid enforcement of catch reporting requirements, it still takes
place. Some of these difficulties of enforcement can be addressed by
placement of neutral observers on fishing vessels to record fishing
locations and catches. But observer coverage, like at-sea patrols, is
prohibitively expensive. Finally, international organizations have
historically had to rely upon flag states to provide catch data for
their vessels operating in fisheries subject to those organizations'
conservation and management measures.[55]

IV. THE GLOBALIZATION OF CONSERVATION STANDARDS AND MECHANISMS TO ENSURE THEIR IMPLEMENTATION

Enforcement of conservation standards in both high seas fisheries and
fisheries in zones of national jurisdiction has not been wholly lacking.
A notable instance is the United States' use of unilateral trade
sanctions, throughout the 1980s, to enforce international conservation
standards for certain high seas and coastal fisheries, including
whaling.[56] Spurred on in large part by the pro-conservation position
of the United States, the international community began to negotiate
framework agreements in the 1990s designed to strengthen
conservation standards and provide mechanisms for their
enforcement. Effective implementation of these framework
agreements, however, remains subject to doubt for the reasons
discussed above. Because of impediments to effective government
regulation, private organizations in the United States are in the
process of developing eco-labeling initiatives as an alternative
mechanism to achieve the goals of the international agreements.[57]

A. Unilateral Enforcement of Standards by the United States

One of the most prominent examples of unilateral enforcement of
conservation standards involves the tuna fishery of the Eastern
Tropical Pacific Ocean, where for years tens of thousands of dolphins
were killed annually through tuna purse seine operations. From the

1950s to the 1970s, the California-based U.S. fleet dominated this fishery. In 1972, Congress passed the Marine Mammal Protection Act (MMPA).[58] Amendments to the MMPA and regulations, issued over the next 15 years,[59] gradually reduced the annual incidental take quota for dolphins for the U.S. tuna fleet, so that by 1987 many vessels had moved to new fishing grounds while others had re-flagged to different countries. As a result, foreign flag vessels came to dominate the fishery.[60]

The U.S. Congress quickly realized that the MMPA both failed to control foreign tuna fishing in the Eastern Tropical Pacific and competitively disadvantaged the remaining U.S. Pacific tuna vessels. It responded by amending the MMPA to require that foreign fleets' dolphin mortality rates be comparable to that of the U.S. fleet. Those that did not achieve comparability would face embargoes on their tuna products.[61] In 1990, the major American tuna processing companies announced they would no longer purchase tuna caught in association with dolphins and began using the "dolphin safe" label on their canned tuna. That same year, Congress codified the "dolphin safe" standard and prohibited sale of any tuna with the label that did not meet the standard.[62]

By 1990, Mexico had become the dominant player in the tuna fishery. In that year, the United States imposed an embargo on Mexico's tuna products under the MMPA's comparability requirements.[63] But in 1991, a GATT panel ruled the embargo impermissible.[64] In an effort to minimize damage to its relations with Mexico, and to "multilateralize" (make subject to multilateral, as against unilateral) dolphin conservation measures, the United States sought agreement on a "global moratorium" on dolphin fishing.[65] No nation agreed to the proposed "global moratorium." Nonetheless, the tuna processors' policy of buying only "dolphin safe" tuna effectively closed the U.S. market to tuna caught without regard to minimizing the risk of dolphin mortality.

In 1994, another GATT panel ruled on the U.S. MMPA comparability embargo in a challenge brought by intermediary nations. The U.S. ban did not fit within the exception of Article XX(b) of GATT for measures "necessary to protect human, animal, or plant life or health," the panel held, because the United States could have negotiated multilateral agreements to achieve the same ends.[66]

The United States has continued to seek a multilateral solution to the tuna-dolphin problem. In 1995, it signed an agreement (the Declaration of Panama) with most other nations fishing in the Eastern Tropical Pacific that would allow the embargo against Mexico and other nations to be lifted once those nations had put in place a separate international agreement to carefully regulate dolphin mortalities.[67] To give effect to the Declaration of Panama, Congress again amended the MMPA in 1997 to provide for the lifting of embargoes if certain conditions were met, and to authorize the Secretary of Commerce to modify the requirements for the "dolphin safe" label.[68] The following year, the United States, Mexico, and a number of other nations whose vessels fish for tuna in the Eastern Tropical Pacific signed the Agreement on the International Dolphin Conservation Program called for by the Declaration of Panama.[69] The Agreement has been ratified by the number of nations required for it to take effect, and the U.S. government is currently working to lift the embargo on those nations.[70]

In early 2000, the Secretary of Commerce relaxed the "dolphin safe" standard, to allow fisheries that catch tuna in association with dolphins, but whose practices do not lead to any dolphin deaths or serious injury, to use the "dolphin safe" label.[71] The impact this change will have is unclear, as the major U.S. tuna companies have indicated that they will continue to adhere to the previous definition of "dolphin safe."[72] Furthermore, a U.S. District Court judge has blocked implementation of the more lenient standards on the ground that the NMFS failed to adequately assess the impact of the change on dolphins.[73]

The United States has also been very active in seeking to eliminate the use of driftnets on the high seas. The United States strongly supported the 1989 United Nations resolution calling for a moratorium on large-scale high seas driftnet fishing and introduced in 1991 the United Nations resolution that terminated high seas pelagic driftnet fishing. The United Nations eventually adopted the 1991 resolution, and, as a result, Japan, Korea and Taiwan ended their high seas driftnet fisheries. In 1992, Congress amended the Magnuson-Stevens Fishery Conservation and Management Act to prohibit imports of fish and fish products from states whose vessels conduct large-scale driftnet fishing beyond their EEZs.[74] The U.S. government has used this authority to encourage countries to reach agreement on measures to end large-scale high seas driftnet fishing. Such an agreement was reached with Italy in the summer of 1999.[75]

The U.S. has also used unilateral trade sanctions to address the incidental catch of sea turtles in shrimp trawl nets.[76] In the mid-1980s, the NMFS published regulations requiring U.S. shrimp trawl vessels to carry turtle excluder devices (TEDs) in their nets to prevent sea turtles from being drowned by shrimp trawl fishing. Believing the regulations placed them at a competitive disadvantage with the shrimp fishing fleets of other countries, U.S. shrimp fishermen teamed up with environmentalists to persuade Congress in 1989 to pass a law requiring the embargo of shrimp products from countries that did not also require their vessels to carry TEDs.

To avoid a replay of the tuna/dolphin controversy, the State Department delayed implementation of the law and tried to limit its application to the wider Caribbean/Western Atlantic region. Environmentalists and fishermen brought suit, prompting the Court of International Trade to rule in 1995 that the State Department had to apply the TEDs requirement to every country in the world.[77] The State Department only reluctantly certified countries for the embargo, under compulsion of court order. At the same time, the U.S. sought to "multilateralize" the issue by seeking agreement from Caribbean and Latin American countries on a convention to address incidental sea turtle mortality in shrimp fisheries, which concluded in 1996 as the Inter-American Convention for the Protection and Conservation of Sea Turtles.[78]

As in the case of the tuna/dolphin embargo, the U.S. unilateral trade sanction on shrimp caught by fleets not carrying TEDs was declared impermissible when tested before the international trade dispute settlement forum, the Appellate Body of the WTO. The Appellate Body ruled in 1998 that although the U.S. law was a reasonable conservation measure relating to the conservation of an exhaustible natural resource, the American sanctions had not been applied in the non-discriminatory manner required by Article XX(g) of the GATT.[79] As Professor McLaughlin has noted, however, "the tribunal provided no real guidance to the U.S. indicating how it can avoid so-called 'arbitrary and unjustified discrimination' in the future." Thus only by negotiating agreements with the nations affected can the United States be certain to have complied with the GATT non-discrimination standard.[80]

The U.S. has also used unilateral trade sanctions to persuade nations to comply with the conservation and management measures of the International Whaling Commission (IWC). Between 1971 and

1979, the U.S. certified two nations as conducting fishing operations in a manner that diminished the effectiveness of the IWC, but in each instance the President declined to impose import restrictions on their fish products because the nations committed to future compliance with IWC quotas. The President's exercise of discretion and reluctance to impose sanctions prompted the enactment of the Packwood Amendment to the Magnuson Act in 1979.[81] Under the Packwood amendment, any nation certified under the Pelly Amendment for diminishing the effectiveness of the IWC must have its fishery allocation within the U.S. EEZ reduced by at least fifty percent.[82] Of course, with the complete phase-out of foreign fishing in the U.S. EEZ, this sanction is now an empty threat.[83]

In the mid-1980s, the U.S. certified the Soviet Union for exceeding the minke whale quota and threatened to impose sanctions against Japan and Norway if they did not agree to the IWC's moratorium on commercial whaling. In the late 1980s and 1990s, the United States also imposed Packwood Amendment certification and threatened to impose Pelly Amendment sanctions against Japan and Norway for their so-called "scientific whaling." The U.S. actions, along with the whaling nations' sentiment that the IWC has been converted from a whale conservation to a whale preservation organization, have prompted some of these nations to form a rival North Atlantic Marine Mammal Commission (NAMMCO).[84] This development will likely further in inhibit the United States' use of unilateral sanctions to enforce compliance with IWC measures because nations can simply threaten to leave the IWC for the NAMMCO.[85]

B. Framework Multilateral Agreements

T   framework agreements concluded in the 1990s elaborate on the conservation standards contained in UNCLOS and provide mechanisms to improve enforcement. These are the Agreement for the Implementation of the Provisions of the United Nations Convention of the Law of the Sea of 10 December 1982, Relating to the Conservation and Management of Straddling Fish Stocks and Highly Migratory Fish Stocks ("U.N. Fish Stocks Agreement"),[86] and the Food and Agriculture Organization Code of Conduct for Responsible Fisheries ("Code of Conduct").[87] While the conservation standards and enforcement mechanisms contained in the U.N. Fish Stocks Agreement have more serious implications for high seas fisheries, they also, in more limited ways, impact EEZ fisheries. The Code of

Conduct applies to both high seas and EEZ fisheries, but it is voluntary. Both agreements reflect an important, if tentative, step in the globalization of national standards for conservation and management of international and domestic fisheries.

The U.N. Fish Stocks Agreement, the better known of these framework agreements, fills lacunae in the Law of the Sea Convention by specifying standards and measures for the conservation and management of "straddling stocks" and "highly migratory species" by regional and subregional fisheries management organizations. "Straddling stocks" are those fish stocks, such as cod, that "straddle" the line dividing EEZs from high seas. Highly migratory species are those fish stocks, most prominently tuna and swordfish, which respect no jurisdictional boundaries delimiting the high seas and zones of national jurisdiction and may travel over great expanses of ocean and through numerous zones of national jurisdiction during their lives. Concluded in 1995, the U.N. Fish Stocks Agreement delineates general conservation principles applicable to high seas areas.[88] Signatory parties undertake the obligation to adopt measures to ensure long-term sustainability of stocks, to employ the best scientific evidence in management, to protect biodiversity, and to recognize the special needs of developing and small island states. The Agreement also mandates that the precautionary approach be applied to stocks both on the high seas and within EEZs.[89] Moreover, it requires cooperation between coastal and fishing states to ensure that conservation and management measures for stocks in the high seas and EEZs are compatible.

In addition to strengthening the conservation standards applied by regional organizations, the Agreement breaks sharply from the traditional regimes of high seas freedom of fishing and exclusive flag state jurisdiction in its specification of mechanisms to ensure compliance with and enforcement of such standards. The Agreement departs from the traditional regimes of high seas freedom of fishing and exclusive flag state jurisdiction in numerous ways. First, it provides that only states that belong to a regional fisheries organization or comply with its conservation and management measures can fish for the resources to which those measures apply. This provision is buttressed by the requirement that a state that is not a member of the regional organization shall not authorize vessels flying its flag to fish for stocks subject to conservation and management measures established by the organization.[90]

The "authorization to fish" concept reflected in this second requirement had earlier been codified in the FAO Agreement to Promote Compliance with International Conservation and Management Measures by Fishing Vessels on the High Seas ("Compliance Agreement"), which aimed to bring high seas fishing under more meaningful control.[91]   1993, the Compliance Agreement imposes on all states whose vessels fish on the high seas the obligation to ensure that their vessels do not fish in a manner that undermines a regional organization's conservation and management efforts. States party to the Compliance Agreement must implement a licensing program, or require some other form of authorization, for their vessels to fish on the high seas. In short, the Compliance Agreement tries to create some correlate duties to exclusive flag state jurisdiction and the "right" of freedom of fishing on the high seas.

The U.N. Fish Stocks Agreement does not rely upon flag state enforcement alone. It also authorizes non-flag state enforcement on the high seas, in further derogation of the high seas freedom of fishing and exclusive flag state jurisdiction regimes. Specifically, the Agreement authorizes any party that is a member of a subregional or regional fisheries management organization to board and inspect any other fishing vessel flying the flag of a party to the Agreement in the high seas area covered by that organization, regardless of whether the flag state is a party to the particular fishery organization. In other words, by being a party to the Fish Stocks Agreement, a state consents to enforcement action against its vessels on the high seas.[92]

The U.S. government is now leading the efforts in international diplomacy to implement the principles of the U.N. Fish Stocks Agreement in existing regional and subregional fishery conservation and management organizations. For example, in meetings at both the International Commission for the Conservation of Atlantic Tunas (ICCAT) and the Northwest Atlantic Fisheries Organization (NAFO) the United States is encouraging the adoption of a strong precautionary approach to fisheries conservation and management and enhanced compliance and enforcement mechanisms of the sorts specified in the Fish Stocks Agreement.[93]

As well as delineating principles to be followed by existing fishery conservation and management organizations, the Fish Stocks Agreement called upon states to create regional organizations for conservation and management of straddling fish stocks and highly migratory species where such organizations did not already exist. Based on this mandate, the South Pacific island countries and nations whose vessels fish for tuna in their EEZs and adjacent high seas areas reached agreement on such a regime for tuna in September 2000.[94] In addition, formal international efforts to specify and elaborate guidelines for sustainable development in marine capture fisheries are ongoing. The guidelines build on previous work by the FAO and on the scientific management concepts respecting "reference points" articulated in the Fish Stocks Agreement.[95]

In addition to attempting to reform high seas fisheries management through the Fish Stocks Agreement, the international community has also attempted to reform general fisheries management policy for national EEZ regimes through the U.N. Code of Conduct for Responsible Fisheries ("the Code"), and, thereby, specify fishery conservation and management standards and measures that the Law of the Sea Convention had only adumbrated. In other words, the Code, like the Fish Stocks Agreement, is an elaboration of the Law of the Sea Convention. Adopted by consensus of the FAO Conference in 1995, the Code contains a set of principles and standards covering global fisheries conservation, management, and development.[96] The Code's principles and standards aspire to universality: they are to be used for national programs, international agreements, and by all involved in fisheries. While the Code is universal and transjurisdictional, it is also voluntary. However, the non-binding nature of this agreement allowed for articulation of more demanding and detailed conservation principles than would have been attainable in negotiations over a binding instrument.

Article 6 of the Code enumerates general principles, including sustainable use, excess fishing capacity reduction, management based on best scientific evidence, the precautionary approach, by-catch reduction, and others. The Code is more specific with respect to standards for fisheries management and fishing operations.[97] The Code also provides, in Article 6, that state policies relating to trade in fish and fishery products be consistent with the WTO Agreement. However, the political economy of fisheries make adoption, implementation, and enforcement of effective conservation standards very difficult, and thus the relationship between WTO requirements and trade measures promoting conservation standards will be extremely controversial in the future.

Given the generality of its key provisions and voluntary adoption process, many question how the Code will actually be implemented. Individual countries, and industries within countries, have begun to draw on the Code to develop appropriate codes of conduct for their domestic fisheries. For example, the Canadian fishing industry and Canada's Department of Fisheries and Oceans are developing a Canadian Code of Conduct ("the Canadian Code") for responsible fishing operations. Once finalized, the Canadian Code will be made binding by federal or provincial officials on all participants in a fishery where it has been voluntarily ratified by representative fishing organizations. The Canadian Code will then become a part of the relevant Conservation Harvesting Plan for that fishery, and thereby adherence to the Code will be an explicit requirement for fishing vessels.[98] In the United States, the NMFS has developed an "Implementation Plan for the Code of Conduct for Responsible Fisheries" that commits NMFS to implement Code principles in U.S. domestic fisheries where they have not already been applied.[99] Within some countries, fishing industries have developed their own codes of conduct. The Australian Seafood Industry Council, for example, has developed a "Code of Conduct for a Responsible Seafood Industry," and in the United States, the National Fisheries Institute has developed its own set of "Principles for Responsible Fisheries."[100]

There is reason for cautious optimism that the Fish Stocks Agreement and the Code will succeed in achieving a globalization of conservation standards both on the high seas and within EEZs. Both serve as touchstones for current discussions in international organizations and domestic fishing management agencies. At the same time, it must be acknowledged that the requirement of the Fish Stocks Agreement that measures within EEZs and adjacent high seas areas pertaining to the same stocks be compatible will necessarily exercise more of a normalizing force with respect to straddling stocks and highly migratory species than species that always remain within the same EEZ.

C. Other Mechanisms for Implementation

While not specified in the U.N. Fish Stocks Agreement, the use of multilateral trade sanctions as a compliance and enforcement mechanism is gaining currency in regional and subregional fishery organizations.[101] The United States has strongly supported these efforts in an attempt to refrain from using unilateral trade sanctions and, instead, to "multilateralize" the use of trade sanctions for enforcement of conservation standards. In 1994, ICCAT became the first international fisheries organization to authorize the use of such measures against non-members whose vessels compromise its conservation and management objectives.[102] A year later, ICCAT agreed on a mechanism to impose trade measures on member countries whose vessels fish in contravention of ICCAT conservation and management requirements.[103] NAFO has also discussed the use of multilateral trade measures.[104] The recently agreed upon South Pacific Tuna Convention authorizes the parties to develop procedures for the organization to impose trade sanctions against parties and non-parties that undermine the effectiveness of the organization's conservation measures.[105] The development of multilateral trade sanction mechanisms by regional organization holds great promise for increasing the efficacy of those organizations' conservation and management efforts. However, one commentator has rightly cautioned that "[t]he degree to which such trade measures, as a legal matter, can be reconciled with international trade obligations has not yet been tested."[106]

"Eco-labeling" is a different variant of enforcement strategy and has generated increasing interest in recent years. Given the structural and political impediments to effective implementation and enforcement of conservation standards, environmental organizations seem rightly concerned that state or international action alone may not ensure sustainable fisheries. As a supplement to government action, eco-labeling of fisheries products is emerging prominently in nations engaged in international fish products trade. The most extensive effort underway to date is that of the Marine Stewardship Council (MSC). The MSC was formed in 1996 by the World Wildlife Fund, an environmental organization, and Unilever, an Anglo-Dutch consumer goods company that is one of the world's largest buyers of ground fish which it sells through Birdseye, Gordons, and other frozen fish companies that it owns. Rather than certify products, MSC will certify specific fisheries for their conformance to standards set out in MSC's "Principles and Criteria for Sustainable Fishing." These standards are: (1) the fishery does not lead to overfishing or depletion and recovers those stocks that are overfished or depleted; (2) the fishery is conducted with attention to ecosystem imperatives; and (3) the fishery is subject to a management system that incorporates and enforces governing international, national, and local standards.[107] Certification is not conducted by MSC itself, but rather by MSC-approved independent certification companies who are paid a fee by participants in the fishery. Products from certified fisheries may then carry the MSC label. As of late Fall 2001, MSC-approved certifiers had certified six fisheries and several more were in the process of certification.[108]

MSC seeks to tap into the purchasing power of "green" consumers in Northern Europe and North America. It notes "[m]arket research tells us that there will be greatest consumer and industry demand for certified products in Northern Europe and North America."[109] In the preamble to its Principles and Criteria for Sustainable Fishing, MSC describes "the overarching philosophical basis for this initiative in stewardship of marine resources" as "the use of market forces to promote behaviour which helps achieve the goal of sustainable fisheries."[110] Fisheries producers involved with MSC appear to appreciate the MSC's market-based approach to achieving conservation. An Australian prawn exporter explained that he supported MSC because it would afford his products a "reduction in tariffs for Australian product[s] entering the EU [and] potential to increase market share."[111]

The MSC's efforts have not gone unchallenged. The National Fisheries Institute (NFI), the U.S. commercial fishing industry's primary trade association, recently developed its own organization, named the Responsible Fisheries Society (RFS). The RFS is charged with developing and implementing an alternative eco-labeling program. The RFS provides a set of "Principles for Responsible Fisheries" based on the Code of Conduct, and participating companies can subscribe to and implement these principles.[112] Ocean Trust, a conservation foundation that environmental groups charge is supported by the commercial fishing industry provides certification of company implementation.[113] Critics claim that RFS certification is really self-certification by industry or trade groups, and is therefore not credible.[114] In response to such allegations, the NFI asserts that the RFS certification scheme is a legitimate alternative to what it views as an unduly costly certification program that will direct money from the industry to certifiers. In addition, NFI touts the funding of environmentally beneficial projects by the RFS, in contrast to the leaner operation by MSC. Finally, NFI claims that an impending "market war" over competing eco-labels might lead to more governmental regulation (which NFI opposes). NFI cites as precedent Congress' intervention to define "dolphin-safe" for tuna eco-labels.[115]

How effective eco-labeling will be in promoting globalization of conservation standards and their more effective implementation is difficult to evaluate. Most obviously, this market mechanism is limited in scope due to its reliance on the purchasing power of consumers in the Northern hemisphere; less affluent consumers are unlikely to be willing to pay the premiums charged for "eco-labeled" fish, to say nothing of those who depend on fisheries for their subsistence. At the same time, if eco-labeling becomes the norm for even some of the major fisheries—such as groundfisheries in the North Atlantic—then it can be expected to make a significant contribution to more effective fisheries conservation.

D. Biodiversity Convention Concerns and Prospective Impact on Fisheries

The Convention on Biological Diversity (CBD) reinforces the impact of international agreements on fisheries management, both global and regional, whether through direct enforcement methods or through the specification of general norms and procedural standards. Along with Agenda 21, the CBD is a result of the Earth Summit meetings in Rio, conducted by the U.N. Commission on Sustainable Development.[116] Like the two new U.N. fisheries instruments, the CBD is a globally applicable framework convention providing for the universal application of norms and scientific procedures for the preservation of genetic materials, species, habitats, and ecosystems. The CBD also provides that industrial countries and multinational firms must transfer technology to less developed countries (LDCs) when they exploit the resources in those LDCs. The Convention reaffirms both national ownership and control of genetic resources. It also underscores the concept of the property rights defined in contractual agreements as the final controlling mechanism in the implementation of requirements as to technology transfer and sharing of profits when LDC resources are used. In that sense, it is a conservative instrument.

In another respect, however, the CBD is a bold affirmation of communal, or altruistic, norms as they apply to the common world heritage in natural resources. The U.N. Fish Stocks Agreement and other international instruments—as well as the programs for protection of biodiversity being formulated in individual countries—are addressing the obligation of signatory parties to the CBD to incorporate its norms and principles into their conservation and management regimes. Similarly, the general objectives stated in Agenda 21 are being adopted systematically, albeit in differing ways, in national regulatory programs for natural resources generally and for coastal and marine ecosystems in particular.[117] Just as the Endangered Species Act in the United States is now impinging, and in the Northwest region actually trumping, the established mechanisms and agencies for fisheries management, so too does the a   21 principles have the potential for, at a minimum, forcing the reconsideration of basic regulatory programs in their premises and applications and, perhaps, fortifying conservation standards and buttressing their implementation by regional and subregional organizations.[118]

V. CONCLUSION

The globalization of norms and standards for fishery management in response to a crisis of international fisheries resources has inspired a wide range of responses. The efforts to address these issues since the 1970s have strengthened and reinforced the authority of the individual nation states, most notably in extending jurisdiction offshore to 200 miles in the EEZs. Despite the high hopes that this form of access limitation would lead to more effective conservation regimes, the trend toward overcapitalization, overfishing, and threatened depletion was nearly universal in the EEZs of both individual countries and the European Union; and only in recent years has there been a perceptible slowing of the trend, although the crisis has gone so far in many fisheries that the suspension or radical curtailment of harvesting effort has been the only possible effective response. Where depleted stocks can be restored, this restoration will likely take decades.[119]

The underlying development in the effort to achieve a global and universal response to the fisheries crisis is an effort to define and establish conservation norms: the precautionary principle, biodiversity protection, and other features of reconceptualization that reflect substantive norms. Pursuing the objective of conservationist management that those norms address has also involved considerable reconsideration of basic premises in resource-management science itself—as embodied, for example, in the specification of "reference points" as an improvement on older maximum sustained yield and optimal yield concepts in determining the capacity of stocks to absorb harvesting exploitation.[120] Institutional aspects of the new innovative structures are reflected in the international agreements that seek to apply the new standards.

These agreements also seek to overcome traditional impediments to effective management by specifying new compliance and enforcement mechanisms. How individual nations will translate the obligations of states, including the now common "duty to cooperate," which are embodied in the new international agreements on fisheries, into actual policy is still a matter of speculation.[121] We have noted some mechanisms outside of these framework agreements—including the use of multilateral trade sanctions by parties to regional organizations (actively promoted by the United States as an alternative to the unilateral use of trade sanctions) and the market tool of eco-labeling—that may play a role in ensuring conservation standards are observed. In addition, the imperatives of instruments concerned with preservation of biodiversity may influence, if not control or dictate, implementation of conservation measures by regional organizations. Compulsory dispute settlement in bodies such as the International Tribunal for the Law of the Sea remains less important than the World Trade Organization judicial mechanism, and also less important than the threat or reality of multilateral trade sanctions. [122] It seems likely, however, that one can anticipate a heightened interest in—and perhaps actual accomplishment of—a strengthened role for dispute settlement in bodies that are principally concerned with enforcing the conservationist norms of ocean resource management. If such a strengthened role for conservation-oriented agencies is realized, it will mark an important shift from the present situation, in which ocean-resource disputes are being referred mainly to bodies such as the WTO, which are institutionally designed to give priority to free-trade norms.

Christopher J. Carr is a Partner in the law firm of Stoel Rives LLP, San Francisco; and is a Ph.D. Candidate, Jurisprudence and Social Policy Program, University of California, Berkeley. Harry N. Scheiber is the Stefan Riesenfeld Professor of Law and History, Boalt Hall School of Law, University of California, Berkeley.

Notes
This article is a revision of an article previously published in the Stanford
Environmental Law Journal, 21 *Stanford Envtl. L.J.* 41 (2002) under the title
"Dealing with a Resource Crisis: Regulatory Regimes for Managing the World's
Marine Fisheries." The Stanford E   Law Journal possesses
copyright information. The authors wish to thank Professor Robert A. Kagan,
Professor David Caron, and Dean John Dwyer of the Boalt Hall School of Law,
and Professor David Vogel, of the Haas School of Business, University of
California, Berkeley, for their insightful comments on earlier drafts.

   1. RTE Interactive News, *EU Fisheries Ministers Discuss Fish Quota Cuts,*
Dec. 14, 2000, *at* http://www.rte.ie/news/2000/1214/fish.html (last visited
Nov. 18, 2001).

   2. *See, e.g.,* World Wildlife Fund, *Sulu Sulawesi Seas: Crown Jewel of the
Western   Pacific, at* http://www.wwfmalaysia.org/features/special/Sulu
Seas.htm (last visited Nov. 18, 2001).

   3. Richard Grainger & S.M. Garcia, Chronicles of Marine Fisheries
Landings, 1950–1994: Trend Analysis and Fisheries Potential, U.N. Food &
Agric. Org. Fisheries Technical Paper 359 (1996).

   4. *See* Richard Grainger, *Global Trends in Fisheries and Aquaculture, in
Trends and Future Challenges for U.S. National Ocean and Coastal Policy* 23
(Biliana Cicin-Sain et al. eds., 1999).

   5. *See id.*

   6. U.N. Food & Agric. Org., *The State of the World Fisheries and Aquaculture*
8-11 (1995). The 1998 FAO report, *The State of the World Fisheries, available at*
http://www.fao.org/docrep/w9900e/w9900e02.htm (Dec. 20, 2000), uses
slightly different terms for these categories; but the data and percentages are
essentially the same as in 1995. The forty-four percent category is referred to as
"fully to heavily exploited" in 1995 and as "fully exploited" in 1998;
"overexploited" in the 1995 report is "overfished" in the 1998 report; and an
additional six percent in the 1998 report is cited as "[appearing] to be
depleted".

   7. See Arthur McEvoy and Harry N. Scheiber, "Scientists, Entrepreneurs,
and the Policy Process: A Study of the Post-1945 California Sardine Depletion,"
44 *J. Econ. Hist.* 393 (1984).

   8. *See generally* James R. McGoodwin, *Crisis in the World's Fisheries:
People, Problems, and Policies* (1990); Christopher D. Stone, *Too Many Fishing
Boats, Too Few Fish,* 24 *Ecology L.Q.* 504, 506–44 (1997); Symposium,
"Overfishing: Its Causes and Consequences," 25 *The Ecologist 80 (1995). See
also Marine Fisheries Management and the Law of the Sea: Summary of
Discussion* (Harry N. Scheiber & M. Casey Jarman rapporteurs), *in Ocean
Governance Study Group, Implications of Entry Into Force of the Law of the Sea 92*
(Biliana Cicin-Sain & K. Leccesse eds., 1995) (on interrelationship of national
regimes in the EEZs and regulation under international agreements).

9. Some of these aspects are treated *infra* Part III.

10. William W. Warner, *Distant Water: The Fate of the North Atlantic Fisherman* (1983) provides a vivid historical picture of the depredations. Scientific research indicating extensive trawler damage to habitat and fisheries is summarized in *Will the Fish Return? How Gear and Greed Emptied Georges Bank, Amer. Mus. of Natural Hist. Bio-Bulletin (1999),* at http://sciencebulletins.amnh.org/biobulletin/biobulletin/story1249.html   (last visited Nov. 5, 2001). For essays that contest the argument that trawling has devastated fish stocks and sea floor habitat, see Conservation Law Foundation, *Effects of Fishing Gear on the Sea Floor of New England* (E. Dorsey & J. Pederson eds., 1998), at http://www.clf.org/pubs/effects_of_fishing _gear.htm (last visited Nov. 5, 2001).

11. Committee to Review Individual Fishing Quotas, Nat'l Research Council, Sharing the Fish: Toward a National Policy on Individual Fishing Quotas (1999) and essays in U.N. Food & Agric. Org., Use of Property Rights in Fisheries, U.N. Food & Agric. Org. Fisheries Technical Paper 404/1 (R. Shotton ed., 2000) treat the policy issues and evaluate existing programs' performance records. For an influential private (NGO) study, see Natural Res. Def. Council, Hook, Line, and Sinking: The Crisis in Marine Fisheries (1997). The history of the ITQ and other limited access approaches, in both national and international management, is treated in Harry N. Scheiber & Christopher J. Carr, *From Extended Jurisdiction to Privatization: International Law, Biology, and Economics in the Marine Fisheries Debates, 1937–76,* 16 Berkeley J. Int. L. 10 (1998).

12. The most dramatic recent instances have been the tuna-dolphin issue in the diplomacy of bilateral fishery relations (and U.S. unilateral sanctions) and the subsequent decision of those issues by the WTO judicial body. *See infra* Part IV(A). On GATT decisions on tuna/dolphin as well as other marine resources, *see generally* Richard McLaughlin, *UNCLOS and the Demise of the United States' Use of Trade Sanctions to Protect Dolphins, Sea Turtles, Whales, and Other International Marine Living Resources,* 21 Ecology L.Q. 1 (1994).

13. Some of these interrelations are treated *infra* Part IV. For one example, see Harry N. Scheiber, *Historical Memory, Cultural Claims, and Environmental Ethics in the Jurisprudence of Whaling Regulation,* 38 Ocean & Coastal Mgmt. 5 (1998).

14. The sustainability principle has been challenged recently, especially by competing professional management standards based on notions of economic efficiency. These efficiency-based standards are advanced principally by professional resource economists who have won a sympathetic hearing in an intellectual and political environment heavily influenced by deregulatory and free market ideas. To a significant degree, the movement for efficiency standards, as a challenge to older sustainability norms, has been conflated with the movement for privatization of fishery rights. *See supra* text and citations accompanying note 11.

15. Our subject is the evolution of global *production* (i.e., harvesting) standards for marine capture fisheries. It does not consider *product* standards, but rather is concerned with how the resource itself is harvested. All such production standards for marine capture fisheries are centered around the

principle of "sustainability."

16. "Sustainable development" is a concept that includes resource conservation as well as the maintenance of the fishing industry and its production.

17. Under "freedom of the seas," all vessels could fish beyond territorial limits without any restrictions on the types of gear or techniques they used, or on the species they caught.

18. Marine capture fisheries are distinguished from aquacultural fisheries, which today constitute the source of a significant (and rising) proportion of commercial fish products.

19. Law of the Sea: Convention on Fishing and Conservation of the Living Resources of the High Seas, Apr. 29 1958, 17 U.S.T. 138, 559 U.N.T.S. 285.

20. *See id.* art. 2.

21. United Nations Convention on t   Sea, Dec. 10, 1982, arts. 61, 119, 21 I.L.M.1261 [hereinafter UNCLOS].

22. Agreement of the Implementation of the Provisions of the United Nations Convention on the Law of the Sea of 10 December 1982 Relating to the Conservation and Management of Straddling Fish Stocks and Highly Migratory Fish Stocks, S   1995, 34 I.L.M. 1542. [hereinafter U.N. Fish Stocks Agreement] *See, e.g.,* Moritaka Hayashi, *The 1995 UN Fish Stocks Agreement and the Law of the Sea, in Order for the Oceans at the Turn of the Century 37* (Davor Vidas & Willy Østreng eds., 1999) [hereinafter *Order for the Oceans*].

23. Convention on Biological Diversity, *opened for signature* June 5, 1992, *entered into force* Dec. 29, 1993 (UNEP/Bio.Div/N7-INC.5/4), text reprinted in 31 I.L.M. 818. *See, e.g.,* Harry N. Scheiber, *The Biodiversity Convention and Access to Marine Genetic Materials in Ocean Law, in Order for the Oceans, supra* note 22, at *187.*

24. *See* Ben Boer, Ross Ramsay, and Donald R. Rothwell, *International Environmental Law in the Asia Pacific* 108–112 (1998); Scheiber, *supra* note 23. *See also* sources cited *infra* note 116.

25. Ann L. Hollick, U.S. Foreign Policy and the Law of the Sea 67–95 (1981).

26. Harry N. Scheiber, *Pacific Ocean Resources, Science, and Law of the Sea: Wilbert M. Chapman and the Pacific Fisheries, 1945–70,* 13 *Ecology L. Q.* 510–11 (1986); *Robert L. Friedheim, Negotiating the New Ocean Regime passim* (1993); *Hollick, supra* note 25, *at 62–96.*

27. UNCLOS, *supra* note 21, art. 297(3).

28. UNCLOS, *supra* note 21, art. 286. *See* Bernard Oxman, *The Rule of Law and the United Nations Conventon on the Law of the Sea,* 7 EUR. J. INT'L L. 353, 367 (1996) (explaining the central importance of Article 286).

29. *See* UNCLOS, *supra* note 21, arts. 119, 192.

30. *See, e.g.,* Mark Kurlansky, *Cod: A Biography of the Fish That Changed the World* 177–233 (1997); Suzanne Ludicello et al., *Fish, Markets, and Fishermen: The Economics of Overfishing* 11–26 (1999); *Will the Fish Return? supra* note 10. *See generally* Terry Glavin, *Dead Reckoning: Confronting the Crisis in Pacific Fisheries* (1996).

31. *See supra* note 6.

32. By contrast, an international management agreement protecting fur seals had a successful conservationist record in part because the seals hauled out on rocks and could be counted with a high degree of accuracy, permitting the scientists to assess the condition of the stocks and trends in their population. *See* Convention for the Preservation and Protection of Fur Seals, July 7, 1911, *discussed in Larry Leonard, International Regulation of Fisheries 90–3 (1944).*

33. *See David Cushing, Fisheries Resources of the Sea and their Management* (1975); Harry N. Scheiber, *From Science to Law to Politics: An Historical View of the Ecosystem Idea and Its Effect on Resource Management,* 24 *Ecology L.Q.* 631 (1997). Fisheries management specialists and marine biologists have long been cognizant of basic problems in definition of priorities as well as in achieving objective assessment of the stocks. *See, e.g.,* the classic article by D. L. Alverson and G. J. Paulik, *Objectives and Problems of Managing Aquatic Living Resources,* 30 *J. Fisheries Res. Board Can. 1936–47 (1973).* Theoretical approaches based on ecosystem analysis are surveyed in *Committee on Ecosystem Management for Sustainable Marine Fisheries, Ocean Studies Board, Commission on Geosciences, Environment, and Resources, National Research Council, Sustaining Marine Fisheries 103–121* (pre-publication edition, 1998). Recent scientific and social science writings on "chaos theory" in relation to fisheries exemplify the extent to which uncertainty is a paramount issue in scientific assessments of fish stocks and calculations of optimal harvesting levels. *See* J. M. Acheson, *Environmental Protection, Fisheries Management, and the Theory of Chaos,* Nat'l Res. Council, *Improving Interactions Between Coastal Scien. and Pol'y: Proc. Gulf M p. 155–60 (1995);* J. A. Wilson et al., *Chaos, Complexity, and Community Management of Fisheries,* 18 *Marine Pol'y* 291 (1994). *Contra* Michael J. Fogarty, *Rejoinder: Chaos, Complexity and Community Management of Fisheries: An Appraisal,* 19 *Marine Pol'y* 437 (1995). *See also Global Trends in Fisheries Management* (E. Pikitch et al., eds.) *Am. Fisheries Soc'y Symp.,* No. 20.

34. For the complexity of decision-making in the contentious milieu of the bluefin tuna fishery, see Patrick A. Nickler, *A Tragedy of the Commons in Coastal Fisheries: Contending Prescriptions for Conservation, and the Case of the Atlantic Bluefin Tuna,* 26 B.C. *Envtl. Aff. L. Rev.* 549 (1999).

35. Thus a distinguished fisheries scientist has observed, with reference both to the International Whaling Commission (on which he served) and to fisheries management agencies more generally, that "[s]ince advice comes as a result of evaluation and consensus, it is . . . possible to cause delays by injecting and sustaining controversy in the evaluation stage. How often have we heard 'the scientists cannot agree . . . so we will consider the question again next year, and meanwhile continue behaving as before.' That way, the blue whale and the herring were brought towards extinction." Sidney Holt, "Scientific Advice to International Organizations" (unpublished paper, 1972), *quoted in* Charles B. Heck, *Collective Arrangements for Managing Ocean Fisheries,* 29 *Int'l Org.* 712, 737 (1975).

36. *A.H. Hodel et al., User-Group Participation in Norwegian Fisheries Management* (1994), *quoted in* Geir Hønneland, *Compliance in the Barents Sea Fisheries,* 24 *Marine Pol'y* 11, 12 (2000).

37. Addressing the subsidy issue thus has been one of the keystone policies

on fisheries in the EC. *See* Aaron Hatcher, *Subsidies for European Fishing Fleets: The European Community's Structural Policy for Fisheries, 1971–99*, 24 *Marine Pol'y* 129–40 (2000).

38. This aspect of fishing labor has been explored in the writings of the economist James Wilen. James E. Wilen and Keith Casey, *Impacts of ITQs on Labor: Employment and Remuneration Effects*, in *Social Implications of Quota Systems in Fisheries* 315–34 (Gisli Palsson and Gudrun Petursdottir eds., 1997).

39. *See, e.g.*, Scheiber, *supra* note 26, *passim* (on the focused pressures on the U.S. Congress and the State Department from salmon interests in the Pacific Northwest and from the tuna sector in Southern California).

40. This power is exemplified by the way in which Senator Stevens was successful in protecting Alaskan fishing interests and holding off administrative action under the Endangered Species Act for a full year, despite heavy pressure from the White House and many in Congress to support action that would have placed an immediate moratorium on fishing that was affecting the sea lion population. Senator Stevens accomplished this feat by threatening to delay congressional action on the final Clinton Administration budget and on the entire Congress' adjournment. Robert Pear, *Congress Adopts Spending Measure, Ending Its Work, N. Y. Times*, Dec. 16, 2000, at A1.

Throughout the 1960s and 1970s, Senator Warren Magnuson of Washington, the powerful chairman of the Senate Commerce Committee, advocated extension of U.S. fisheries jurisdiction and exclusion of foreign fishing vessels. Magnuson was the principal author and sponsor of the Fishery Conservation and Management Act of 1976, which extended U.S. fisheries jurisdiction to 200 miles. *See* Shelby Scates. *Warren G. Magnuson and the Shaping of Twentieth-Century America* (1997) 262–63.

The highly focused demands of special interests in fisheries have had great influence, historically and today, in both impelling and constraining U.S. diplomatic objectives in pursuing policies in the international arena as well. For example, the San Diego-based U.S. tuna interests, a distant-water fishing sector, long had an extraordinarily controlling influence on U.S. policy with regard to regulation of highly migratory species, (mainly tuna) in national Exclusive Economic Zones. Similarly, the Pacific Northwest salmon interests had significant influence on negotiations with Canada and Japan as early as the 1953 International North Pacific Fisheries Convention. *See* Harry N. Scheiber, *Origins of the Abstention Doctrine in Ocean Law: Japanese-U.S. Relations and the Pacific Fisheries, 1937–1958*, 16 *Ecology L.Q.* 23 (1989); Scheiber, *supra* note 26, *passim*.

41. *See* M.J. Peterson, *International Fisheries Management*, in *Institutions for the Earth* 249, 259–61 (Peter Haas et al. eds., 1993) (explaining how the fact that each management agency is focused on only one species or fishery makes it difficult to effect compromises by which the agencies and fisheries interests they each manage can make deals that can lead to simultaneous addressing of two or more issues).

42. David A. Dana, *Overcoming the Political Tragedy of the Commons: Lessons Learned from the Reauthorization of the Magnuson Act*, 24 *Ecology L.Q.*

833, 835–37 (1997). We do not mean to imply that fishermen are "anti-conservation," but only that some of them may have different assessments of the status of stocks and measures required for conservation than some others with interests in fisheries, such as regulators and environmental organizations.

43. See Arne Kalland, Management by Totemization: Whale Symbolism and Anti-Whaling Campaign, 46 *Arctic 124 (1993)*.

44. John Gulland, *Managing Fisheries in an Imperfect World, in Global Fisheries: Perspectives for the 1980's, 189* (Brian J. Rothschild ed., 1980). This is likely to be all the more true if the fishing regulations were not developed in a way that achieves the "buy-in" of the regulated, as so many of the "stake holder" processes pervasive in fishery management decision-making hope to do.

45. *See, e.g.,* Garrett Hardin, *Tragedy of the Commons,* 162 *Science 1243 (1968);* Bonnie McCay et al., *From the Bottom Up: Participatory Issues in Fisheries Management,* 9 Soc'y & Resources 237–50 (1996).

46. These monitoring innovations are discussed in Christopher J. Carr, *Vessel Monitoring Systems: A New Technology for the Transition to Sustainable Fisheries, in Ocean Governance Study Group, Emerging Issues in Nat'l Ocean and Coastal Policy 31–34* (H. Scheiber ed., 1999) [hereinafter *Emerging Issues]*.

47. *See generally* David A. Balton, *The Compliance Agreement, in Developments in International Fisheries Law 31–53* (Ellen Hey ed., 1999); Carr, *supra* note 46.

48. For a vivid example of the manner in which an international fishing agreement for sustainable management can be undermined by non-member states that either permit a re-flagging of vessels or simply permit their own citizens to operate in vessels under their flag in a manner evasive of the agreement, see Jean-Pierre Plé, *Responding to Non-Member Fishing in the Atlantic: The ICCAT and NAFO Experiences, in Law of the Sea: The Common Heritage and Emerging Challenges 197* (Harry N. Scheiber, ed., 2000) [hereinafter *Law of the Sea]*.

49. David A. Colson, *Welcoming Remarks, in Report of the Global Fisheries Enforcement Workshop 3* (1994).

50. On the manifold structural changes in, and dynamics of, the tuna industry, see generally *Alessandro Bonanno & Douglas Constance, Caught in the Net: The Global Tuna Industry, Environmentalism, and the State passim* (1996).

51. Similarly, fifty years ago several large Japanese whaling factory ships that had earlier operated in the Antarctic were re-fitted for factory-style tuna fishing operations in the U.S. Trust Territories; and Japanese trawlers were shifted from the China Sea to carry other types of gear in the West Pacific. *See* Harry N. Scheiber, *Inter-Allied Conflicts and Ocean Law, 1945–53: The Occupation Command's Revival of Japanese Whaling and Marine Fisheries 66, 168–69* (Academia Sinica Press, Taiwan, 2000). *See also* F. David Froman, *Note: The 200-Mile Exclusive Economic Zone: Death Knell for the American Tuna Industry,* 13 *San Diego L. Rev.* 707 (1976) (discussing the dilemma of the tuna fleet in light of changing international law (in addition to MMFPA) in the mid-1970s); *Michael Orbach, Hunters, Seamen, and Entrepreneurs: The Tuna Seinermen of San Diego passim* (1977).

52. Powerpoint presentation of Lt. Cdr. Jack Rutz on "Vessel Monitoring System: Leveraging Technology" to the Meeting of the Western Pacific Regional

Fishery Management Council (Aug. 1996) (copy on file with authors).

53. *See generally* M. Harte, *Fisher Participation in Rights-Based Fisheries Management: The New Zealand Experience,* in *U.N. Food & Agric. Org., Use of Property Rights in Fisheries, supra* note 11, at 95, 99–100; J. R. McGoodwin, *Crisis in the World's Fisheries: People, Problems and Policies* (1990).

54. *See, e.g.,* Astrid Berg, Implementing and Enforcing European Fisheries Law (1999).

55. The accuracy of catch data varies from country to country, and even where data may be fairly accurate the flag state government may choose to report them inaccurately to the international management organizations, as has happened most notoriously in whaling regulation. *See* Carr, *supra* note 46, at 32–33 for fuller discussion of the topics in this paragraph. *See supra* textual quotation accompanying note 44; Scheiber, *supra* note 13 at 28 (describing intentional mis-reporting of whale catch data by the Soviet Union).

56. David D. Caron, International Sanctions, Ocean Management, and the Law of the Sea: A Study of Denial of Access to Fisheries, *166 Ecology L.Q. 311* (1989); Steinar Andresen, Effectiveness of the International Whaling Commission, 46 *Arctic* 108 at 113 (1993) (arguing that the deployment of U.S. power, especially in the imposition of sanctions, was the most important factor in the anti-whaling movement's effectiveness).

57. *See infra* Part IV(C).

58. Marine Mammal Protection Act, 16 U.S.C. §§ 1371–1407 (2001). *See generally* Michael J. Bean and Melanie J. Rowland, *The Evolution of National Wildlife Law* (3d ed. 1997) at 116–36, whose text we have followed closely in discussing the tuna/dolphin conflict.

59. On this history, see Laura Lones, The Marine Mammal Protection Act and International Protection of Cetaceans: A Unilateral Attempt to Effectuate Transnational Conservation, 22 *Vand. J. of Transnat'l L. 997, 1006ff.* (1989).

60. The regulatory regime in the Eastern Tropical Pacific was elaborated by the Inter-American Tropical Tuna Commission. The Commission was first established in 1949 to conduct scientific assessments with a view toward imposing regulation when the condition of the stocks warranted it, as happened beginning in 1966 for yellowfin tuna. A full survey and analysis of the first 30 years of East Pacific tuna research and regulation is in *James Joseph & J.W. Greenough, International Management of Tuna, Porpoise, and Billfish: Biological, Legal, and Political Aspects* (1979).

61. MMPA Amendment of 1984, Pub. L. No. 98–364, 98 Stat. 440 (1984) (codified at 16 U.S.C.A. § 1371(a)(2) (2001)).

62. Fisheries Conservation Amendments of 1990, Pub. L. No. 101–627, § 901, 104 Stat. 4465 (1990) (codified at 16 U.S.C.A. § 1385 (2001)).

63. GATT Dispute Settlement Panel Report on United States Restrictions on Imports of Tuna, Aug. 16, 1991, 30 I.L.M. 1594 (1991).

64. *See id.* On historical developments and national rivalries on the tuna grounds before the 1990s, *see The Development of the Tuna Industry in the Pacific Islands Region: An Analysis of Options* (David J. Doulman ed., 1987). Full legal analysis and the economic and regulatory history of the tuna/dolphin issue as of the mid-1990s is in McLaughlin, *supra* note 10.

65. *See* William T. Burke, *The New International Law of Fisheries: UNCLOS*

1982 and Beyond (1994) at 232.

66. GATT Dispute Settlement Panel Report on United States Restrictions on Imports of Tuna, June 16, 1994, 33 I.L.M. 839 (1994).

67. Declaration of Panama, signed Oct. 4, 1995, *available at* http://www.greenpeace.de/GP_DOK_HINTERGR/C10HI19C.HTM.

68. International Dolphin Conservation Program Act, Pub. L. No. 105–42, § 5, 111 Stat. 1125 (1997) (codified at 16 U.S.C.A. § 1385 (2001)).

69. Agreement on the International Dolphin Conservation Program, May 15, 1998, 37 I.L.M. 1246 (1998) (entered into force Feb. 15, 1999). *See Hearing on H.R. 408 to Amend the Marine Mammal Protection Act of 1972 to Support the International Dolphin Conservation Program in the Eastern Tropical Pacific Ocean Before the Subcomm. On Fisheries, Wildlife and Oceans of the House Comm. on Resources,* 105th Cong. (1997) (statement of Mary Beth West, Deputy Assistant Secretary for Oceans) [hereinafter Statement of Mary Beth West].

70. Statement of Mary Beth West, *supra* note 69.

71. *See* Taking of Marine Mammals Incidental to Commercial Fishing Operations; Tuna Purse Seine Vessels in the Eastern Tropical Pacific Ocean, 65 Fed. Reg. 30 (Jan. 3, 2000).

72. *See* Mark J. Palmer, *Dolphin-Safe Label Gutted, Earth Island J.,* Fall 1999, at 11.

73. Brower v. Daley, 93 F. Supp. 2d 1071 (N.D. Cal. 2001), *aff'd* 257 F.3d 1058 (9th Cir. 2001). Other aspects of unilateral sanctions by the United States before 1990 are discussed fully in Caron, *supra* note 56.

74. High Seas Driftnet Fisheries Enforcement Act, Pub. L. 102–582, §§ 101, 102, 104 (1992), 106 Stat. 4901 (codified at 16 U.S.C.A. §§ 1826a-c (2001)).

75. *See* Press Release, U.S. Department of State, Office of the Spokesman, U.S. Satisfied with Italy's Commitment to Stop Illegal Driftnet Fishing (July 15, 1999) (*available at* http://secretary.state.gov/www/briefings/statements/ 1999). Such sanctions are also provided for in multilateral fishery agreements. For example, parties to the Wellington Driftnet Convention of 1990 agreed that they might embargo imports of any fish or fish product caught with a driftnet within the ocean area covered by the Convention's management regime. *See* Ted L. McDorman, *Fisheries Conservation and Management and International Trade Law, in Developments in International Fisheries Law, supra* note 47, at 501.

76. For documentation of this aspect of sanctions and fishery relations, see Tim Eichenberg, *Sea Turtles and Trade, in Emerging Issues, supra* note 46, at 19–24, and Richard J. McLaughlin, *The Recent W.T.O. Decision on Sea Turtles and Its Impact on International Environmental Law, in Emerging Issues, supra* note 46, at 25–30.

77. Earth Island Inst. v. Christopher, 20 Ct. Int'l Trade 1389, 948 F. Supp. 1062 (1996).

78. Inter-American Convention for the Protection and Conservation of Sea Turtles, *opened for signature* Dec. 1, 1996, 37 I.L.M. 1246.

79. WTO Appellate Body, United States—Import Prohibition of Certain Shrimp and Shrimp Products, Oct. 12, 1998 (WT/DS58/AB/R) 38 I.L.M. 118 (1999).

80. *McLaughlin, supra* note 76, at 28.

81. Packwood Amendment to the Magnuson Act, Pub. L. No. 96–61, 93 Stat. 407 (1979) (codified at 16 U.S.C.A. § 1821(e)(2) (2001)).

82. The Pelly Amendment, also known as section 8 of the Fisherman's Protective Act, 22 U.S 1978, authorizes the President to prohibit the importation of products from countries that allow fishing operations or engage in trade that diminish the effectiveness of an international fishery conservation program for endangered or threatened species. Under the Pelly Amendment, the Secretary of Commerce or the Secretary of the Interior are required to determine and certify to the President when nationals of foreign countries are conducting fishing operations that minimize the effectiveness of an international fishery conservation program.

83. See Caron, *supra* note 56, *passim*.

84. See Alf Hakon Hoel, *Regionalization of International Whale Management: The Case of the North Atlantic Marine Mammals Commission,* 46 *Arctic* 116 (1993) (stating an argument that reflects Norway's official position that NAMMCO itself is not a threat to the IWC—a position strongly disputed by the pro-moratorium nations).

85. See David D. Caron, The International Whaling Commission and the North Atlantic Marine Mammal Commission: The Institutional Risks of Coercion in Consensual Structures, 89 *Am. J. Int'l* L. 154, 163–68 (1995). For analyses contending that even in the present day "the legal, political, and economic pressures applied by the U.S." are the key reason for cessation of whaling by other nations, see Steinar Andresen, The International Whaling Regime: Order at the Turn of the Century, in *Order for the Oceans,* supra note 22, at 215, 224. See generally M. J. Peterson, Whalers, Cetologists, Environmentalists, and the International Management of Whaling, 46 *Int'l Org.* 147, 172–74 (1992).

86. U.N. Fish Stocks Agreement, *supra* note 22.

87. For a discussion of the Code, see Gerald Moore, *The Code of Conduct for Responsible Fisheries, in Developments in International Fisheries Law, supra* note 47, at 85–105.

88. This discussion of the U.N. Fish Stocks Agreement draws on two full interpretive studies: Moritaka Hayashi, *The 1995 UN Fish Stocks Agreement and the Law of the Sea, in Order for the Oceans, supra* note 22, at 55, and William T. Burke, *Compatibility and Precaution in the 1995 Straddling Stock Agreement, in Law of the Sea, supra* note 48, at 105.

89. Application of the "precautionary principle" in fisheries management involves shifting the burden of proof to the enterprise that seeks to exploit the resource when definitive scientific prediction of impact is not agreed upon. The greater the uncertainty as to impact, the greater the burden on the exploiting enterprise. *See* Jon Van Dyke, *Sharing Ocean Resources—In a Time of Scarcity and Selfishness, in Law of the Sea supra* note 48 at 3, 29–31. The 1992 Rio Declaration on the Environment and Development expresses what it terms the "precautionary approach" in the following terms: "Where there are threats of serious or irreversible damage, lack of full scientific certainty shall not be used as a reason for postponing cost-effective measures to prevent environmental degradation." Rio Declaration on Environment and Development, *adopted* June 14, 1992, *reprinted in* 31 I.L.M. 874 (1992). On how the Fish Stocks Agreement

addresses the application of the precautionary principle, see Van Dyke, *supra* at 12–13; and, for a very full discussion of the various definitions and emphases in expressions of the principle in international agreements on ocean resources, *see* Stuart M. Kaye, *International Fisheries Management* 163–265 (2001).

90. U.N. Fish Stocks Agreement, *supra* note 22, at arts. 8, 17.

91. Agreement to Promote Compliance with International Conservation and Management Measures by Fishing Vessels on the High Seas, Nov. 24, 1993, 33 I.L.M. 968 (1994) [hereinafter Compliance Agreement]. *See, inter alia,* Balton, *supra* note 47.

92. For a different view, asserting that these provisions actually do not authorize such unilateral enforcement, however, *see* Burke, *supra* note 88, at 110.

93. See "Implementation of the Key Provisions of the United Nations Agreement on the Conservation and Management of Straddling Fish Stocks and Highly Migratory Fish Stocks By Regional Fisheries Management Organizations and Arrangements," prepared by the Government of the United States of America (Sept. 1996) (copy on file with authors).

94. Convention on the Conservation and Management of Highly Migratory Fish Stocks in the Western and Central Pacific Ocean, opened for signature Sep. 4, 2000 (visited Feb. 9, 2002) http://www.spc.org.nc/coastfish/Asides/Conventions [hereinafter "Western Pacific Tuna Convention"]. For an account of the background and the major issues addressed in the Western Pacific Tuna Convention *see* Violanda Botet, *"Filling in One of the Last Pieces of the Ocean: Regulating Tuna in the Western and Central Pacific Ocean,"* 41 VA.J.INT'L.L. 787 (2001).

The negotiations leading to conclusion of the Western Pacific Tuna Convention can also be viewed as part of a larger movement involving bilateral and multilateral agreements, all of which will in future years be impacted by the Biodiversity Convention and other instruments in this region. *See generally,* Ben Boer et al., *International Environmental Law in the Asia Pacific* (1998).

95. For discussion of the most important of such recent efforts, an expert consultation involving Australian and FAO scientists, see S. M. Garcia et al., *The FAO Guidelines for the Development and Use of Indicators for Sustainable Development of Marine Capture Fisheries and an Australian Example of their Application,* 43 *Ocean & Coastal Mgm't* 537 (2000).

96. Moore, *supra* note 87, at 85–106.

97. See Article 7 of the Code of Conduct, *available at* http://www.fao.org/fi/agreem/codecond/ficonde.asp.

98. Canada Dep't of Fisheries and Oceans, Summary Report: Canadian Code of Conduct for Responsible Fishing Operations (1997).

99. U.S. Nat'l Marine Fisheries Serv., Implementation Plan for the Code of Conduct for Responsible Fisheries (1997).

100. Australian Seafood Indus. Council, A Code of Conduct for a Responsible Seafood Industry, *available at* http://www.seafoodsite.com.au/stats/code.htm (last visited Nov. 5, 2001); Responsible Fisheries Soc'y, Principles for Responsible Fisheries, *available at* http://www.nfi.org/organizations/rfs-prf.htm (last visited Nov. 5, 2001).

101. *See* reference to the Wellington Driftnet Convention's terms *supra* note 63. For analysis of the Convention, see Earthtrust, *International Law Concerning Driftnet Fishing on the High Seas,* at http://www.earthtrust.org/dnpaper/intllaw.html (last visited Nov. 18, 2001).

102. *See* Plé, *supra* note 48, at 197, 199–201.

103. *See id.*

104. *See id.* at 197–207.

105. Western Pacific Tuna Convention at Art. 25(12); *see* discussion in Botet, *supra* note 94, at 810 n. 116.

106. Botet, *supra* note 94, at 810 n. 116.

107. Marine Stewardship Council, MSC Principles and Criteria for Sustainable Fishing, *available at* http://www.msc.org.

108. *Id.*

109. Marine Stewardship Council Advisory Board Newsletter 2 (1999).

110. Marine Stewardship Council, Statement of Principles and Criteria for Sustainable Fishing, Arlie House Draft 6 (1998).

111. *Id.*

112. *See* Moore, *supra* note 87.

113. The Earth Island organization, for example, terms Ocean Trust "a faux green group ... run by a former NFI lobbyist." Earth Island, "Shrimp Industry Greenwashing," available at http://www.earthisland.org/eijournal/winter99/ wn_winter99shrimp.html

114. Jane Earley, Chief Executive, Marine Stewardship Council, Remarks at San Francisco Seafood Show Panel on Sustainable Fishing (Nov. 3, 1999).

115. Richard Gutting, President, National Fisheries Institute, Remarks at San Francisco Seafood Show Panel on Sustainable Fishing (Nov. 3, 1999). For discussion of the "dolphin-safe" issues and their relation to U.S. law *see* Bonanno & Constance, *supra* note 50, at 182–95.

116. See generally Symposium, Earth Summit Implementation: Progress Achieved on Oceans and Coasts, 29 *Ocean & Coastal Mgmt.* (1995).

117. *See, e.g.,* M. Haward & D. VanderZwaag, *Implementation of UNCED Agenda 21 Chapter 17 in Australia and Canada: A Comparative Analysis,* 29 *Ocean & Coastal Mgmt. 279 (1995)* (commenting on the national program progress); Harry N. Scheiber, *The Biodiversity Conventon and Access to Marine Genetic Resources in Ocean Law, in Order for the Oceans, supra* note 22, at 187–202. The broad legal and institutional structures that bear on "inter-operability" of the above instruments and also agreements on pollution, coastal protection, etc., is the subject of an insightful study by Rosemary Rayfuse, *The Interrelationship Between the Global Instruments of International Fisheries Law, in Developments in International Fisheries Law, supra* note 47, at 107. *See also* Olav Schramk Stokke, *Governance of High Seas Fisheries: The Role of Regime Linkages, in Order for the Oceans, supra* note 22, at 157–172; and Hans Corell, *Future Role of the United Nations in Oceans and Law of the Sea, in Ocean Policy: New Institutions, Challenges and Opportunities* (Myron Norquist & John Norton Moore eds., 1999).

118. The Convention on International Trade in Endangered Species of Wild Fauna and Flora ("CITES"), 27 U.S.T. 1087, T.I.A.S. No. 8249 [1975], may also

increasingly come to play a role in the implementation of conservation measures by regional and subregional organizations.

119. There is exceptional consensus on the existence of the problem and the attribution of fisheries decline in substantial part to overcapitalization and its effects (interacting, to be sure, with natural disasters, marine pollution, and other factors). There is, however, disagreement on the magnitude of the overcapitalization in terms of excess tonnage over what current fishing harvests would require. For a discussion of the debate, *see U.N. Food & Agric. Org., The State of World Fisheries and Aquaculture* (1998), *supra* note 6 (asserting a probable minimum figure of 30-percent overcapacity). For a summary overview and analysis, *see Year of the Ocean, Discussion Paper: Ensuring the Sustainability of Ocean Living Resources C-2 to C-34 (1998)* (prepared by the U.S. Federal Agencies with Ocean-related Programs), *available at* http://www.yoto98.noaa.gov/.

120. Among especially useful recent scholarly efforts at overviews and analysis of the global situation are Jon M. Van Dyke, *Sharing Ocean Resources—In a Time of Scarcity and Selfishness, in Law of the Sea, supra* note 48, at 3–36 (commenting on the "common heritage" ideal and recent international initiatives); and Ellen Hey, *Reconceptualization of the Issues Involved in International Fisheries Conservation and Management, in Developments in International Fisheries Law, supra* note 47, at 577–88.

121. Assessment of the actual efficacy of the various efforts to establish and implement global conservation standards canvassed here is an undertaking beyond this article's scope. Furthermore, because a number of the international instruments under consideration here were concluded quite recently, data as to their efficacy may not yet be available; the U.N. Fish Stocks Agreement, for example, has not yet come into force.

122. See Thomas A. Mensah, The Role of Peaceful Dispute Settlement in Contemporary Ocean Policy and Law, in *Order for the Oceans,* supra note 22, at 81–94. See generally Tullio Treves, New Trends in the Settlement of Disputes and the Law of the Sea Convention, in *Law of the Sea,* supra note 48, at 61–86; *Developments in International Fisheries Law,* supra note 47, at 159–420 (chapters on implementation issues).

Chapter 4

The Changing Nature of Global Hazardous Waste Management
From Brown to Green?

Kate O'Neill

INTRODUCTION

Safe management of hazardous wastes poses difficult regulatory problems at multiple levels of governance. The major steps—developing more reliable and storage, transportation, and disposal practices and encouraging waste minimization—are costly for industry and difficult and costly for governments to enforce. Changes in recent decades in the problem area, the actors involved and regulatory politics have led to a complex situation, making an overall characterization of whether hazardous waste management is getting better or worse worldwide hard to reach. This chapter, in outlining some of these complex sets of changes, seeks to demonstrate how a more nuanced approach can improve our understanding of this important global environmental issue area.

At least two theses have emerged in the trade and environment literature that aim to shed light on global pollution issues, the examination of which is the subject of this volume. The first of these argues that all else being equal, wastes are likely to be exported to countries with weaker environmental policies than in the home country, and that rich and poor countries alike are less likely to improve regulations as powerful constituencies oppose such moves. In other words, waste makes its way to "pollution havens", and there is a regulatory "race to the bottom" effect as a result—the classic Delaware Effect.[1] Applied to the issue of hazardous waste, as it became more difficult and expensive to site disposal facilities in richer democracies,

156

firms started illegally exporting wastes to poorer countries, rather than minimizing waste generation. For rich countries, exporting wastes to poorer countries solves their problem rather than exacerbating it in the absence of international rules.

A second thesis posits that increased awareness of these risks has created pressures on all governments to control wastes, especially as hazardous wastes are considered among the worst of environmental problems. This in turn leads to the creation of an international regime governing the trade in hazardous wastes, as well as an upward trend in the stringency of national regulations on waste disposal. Competition and tougher regulations advantage larger, multinational corporations who specialize in compliance and may even ally with environmental groups to push governments to adopt stricter rules that they have a comparative advantage in complying with. Unlike the first thesis, this view holds that there is in effect a "race to the top" and a lack of pollution havens.[2]

In this chapter I argue that neither of these theses holds firmly in the case of global hazardous waste management. On the one hand, there is empirical support for upward trends in hazardous waste management regulations across many countries, especially in the rich countries, but also to an extent in poorer countries. Multinational waste management firms have made considerable effort to be seen as a "green" industry, part of the environmental technology solution, not part of the problem, and have taken advantage of their expanded global reach to push for stronger regulations in many cases. More importantly, international governmental organizations—the UNEP and the EU—have been able to develop strong institutional responses to these problems, notably towards restricting the waste trade and modernizing national regulatory systems. At the same time, while stronger regulations are being formulated at national and international levels, serious issues remain about implementation and enforcement, especially but far from exclusively in less developed countries. These include long delays in implementation, weak enforcement capacities of governments and of international agencies and the possibility of regulatory capture in international negotiations over the waste trade. These problems are by no means confined to hazardous waste trading as a global issue—they also afflict many other international environmental regimes. The increased possibility, too, that global waste trading rules could be struck down by the World Trade Organization has helped highlight some of the possible conflicts between the economic and environmental global governance orders.[3]

The reason for the lack of clarity on this debate is linked to changes in global hazardous waste management that make the issue more complex than ever before. In this chapter I outline these changes.

They are first, a shift in the basic "regulatory problem"—from one of a more local nature to the internationalization of waste management issues. Second, there has been a change in the structure of the waste disposal industry worldwide. Third are changes in policies in EU member states. Finally, I outline changes in policies in less developed (emerging) economies. I analyze these changes in the light of the growing involvement of the private sector—namely firms—in international environmental regulation, and of the complex and sometimes contradictory impacts of international regulations on domestic politics. These changing public-private and domestic-international balances in environmental regulation can be seen across many international environmental issue areas—the incorporation of market-based policy mechanisms into the climate change regime is but one example. In the arena of hazardous waste management, I argue in the final sections of this chapter that these changes are a mixed blessing, neither all good nor all bad. In this, I seek to step back from the heated debates, in particular over the role of the private sector in international environmental regulation, and demonstrate the real complexities of these trends and their effects when applied to different policy areas. At the same time, this chapter raises questions about the possible vulnerability of the global system of multilateral environmental agreements to regulatory capture by private interests.

A. REGULATING HAZARDOUS WASTES: FROM LOCAL TO GLOBAL

The first of the changes in international waste management is the shift of the problem and its regulation from one of a local nature to one of a more global nature. The OECD reported in 1994 that its member states collectively generated around 258,266 thousand tonnes of hazardous wastes, a figure that reached 323,411 thousand tonnes in 1997.[4] Incorrectly managed wastes can lead to long term and irreversible damage to human health and local environments. Hazardous wastes disposed in landfill or incinerated can, for instance, lead to harmful releases into groundwater, rivers, oceans, the soil and the atmosphere; and they can remain toxic for hundreds of years. Of particular concern is that many of the wastes categorized as hazardous contain persistent organic pollutants, which remain in the ecosystem for a long period of time and can accumulate in human tissue. Several crisis events, notably Love Canal, in Northern New York State in the 1970s and 1980s and Minamata Syndrome in Japan in the 1950s and 1960s have heightened public perceptions of the dangers posed by hazardous wastes and worsened the siting problem.

Early efforts to regulate waste disposal, both industrial and municipal, were justified on grounds of public goods provision, externality minimization and anti-corruption measures. In many developed countries national framework legislation was passed in the early 1970s, and reflected the view that waste disposal was highly localized in terms of its effects and therefore best dealt with on that level. It was clear in these early years that waste disposal generated significant negative externalities, not only through the effects imposed on communities and ecosystems, but also in terms of the incentive structures facing the key private actors. Waste disposal is unlike many services in that generators, once they have paid to have the waste removed from their hands, and in the absence of liability laws, have no incentive to see that it is disposed of safely as long as they never see it again.[5] Also, many national hazardous waste regulatory programs are considered expensive and unwieldy.[6] In most countries, the regulatory systems that emerged in the 1970s are seen by practically all concerned as complex, arcane, costly and controversial; and many important waste management decisions such as siting new facilities deadlock because communities distrust both industry and government.[7]

Rising costs of waste disposal in most developed countries along with growing social resistance to waste facilities led to the emergence of the international trade in hazardous wastes in the 1970s and 1980s. While caused most directly by domestic economic pressures, the trade was most definitely enabled by the growth of world trade and the opening of domestic markets not only to goods, but also to "environmental bads" from other countries, and an associated fall in global transportation costs.[8] According to one analysis, "the UNEP estimates that the Western European countries annually trade 700,000 tons of hazardous wastes among themselves, and that the USA and Canada each export 200,000 tons, primarily to each other. Moreover, until the new ban's implementation, European countries legally exported about 120,000 tons of hazardous waste to developing countries every year."[9] These are legal transfers; the illegal trade has never been properly quantified, although Greenpeace and the Basel

Action Network have documented cases of illegal dumping extensively.[10] It seems likely now that given the blaze of publicity these cases have aroused and the action taken unilaterally or in groups by less developed countries to ban such imports that the illegal dumping is in fact declining, although this is hard to know for certain.

The international institutional response to the waste trade has been led by the UNEP, the OECD and the EU and facilitated by the work of NGOs, such as Greenpeace International, and the global media. Three main problems triggered this response. First, in the 1980s growing and publicized evidence emerged of "midnight dumping" from wealthy to vulnerable, poorer countries in the global south or Eastern Europe, and dumping of wastes at sea. Second, as the EU expanded its authority, concern grew over the movement of wastes across EU boundaries. It was feared that the creation of the Single Market would create a single market in wastes, and that the weaker southern EU states, such as Spain and Portugal, as well as poorer areas within the richer states would be vulnerable to dumping. Some were also concerned about Germany's continued role as waste exporter, and Britain and France's as importers. Third, but less important on the international agenda, there is an evident lack of capacity in emerging and transitional economies to adequately manage industrial, including hazardous, wastes generated domestically.

The main plank of the international response to the waste trade is the 1989 Basel Convention on the Transboundary Movement of Hazardous Wastes and Their Disposal, one of several UNEP-sponsored multilateral environmental conventions that seek to govern transboundary pollution and pollution of the global commons. These agreements mark a new phase in international cooperation, one that signifies much deeper interaction among states than in earlier eras, and where they have ceded more of their national sovereignty than previously they were willing to do. At the same time, there are strong concerns about the ultimate effectiveness of these agreements: will states comply by changing their national policies, will treaty measures be effectively implemented and monitored, and are they even the right measures to solve the problems?[11] The best progress the Convention has made to date is to help reinforce an international norm against waste dumping on poor countries.[12] How entrenched that norm will become is an issue for future research.

The Basel Convention came into effect in May 1992. Under the original terms of the convention, exportation of wastes should only occur if the exporting country does not have the facilities to dispose of the wastes properly or if the wastes are to be used as raw materials by the importing nation AND if exporters have written consent from government officials in the importing nation under the principle of Prior Notification and Consent. There are several other treaties also seeking to restrict the waste trade. The 1991 Bamako Convention bans waste importation into most of Africa from outside; similar agreements exist in the Caribbean and Pacific.

In 1994, parties agreed voluntarily to ban all exports of wastes from OECD members to non-members, for both disposal and recycling purposes. However, controversies remained. At the 4th Meeting of the Parties, in Malaysia in February 1998, delegates made some progress on drawing up comprehensive lists of hazardous wastes for the purposes of the Convention. They disagreed over which countries should be allowed to belong to continue importing wastes (the Annex VII countries, primarily OECD members), and the availability of bilateral agreements between Annex VII and non-Annex VII countries to continue trading in hazardous wastes. At the 10th Anniversary Meeting of the original convention, held in Basel in December 1999, delegates adopted a draft protocol on liability and compensation for illegal waste dumping. Progress remains slow and disagreements have yet to be resolved. In fact they could lead to the Basel Convention being challenged under World Trade Organization rules as a trade restriction.[13] The ban amendment had by early 1999 been ratified by less than a quarter of parties required for it to come into force; it is likely to be a long time before this happens. As later sections show, the ban is even less likely to be adopted in the near future because it is effectively opposed by a powerful coalition of industry and state actors.

B. CHANGES IN THE WASTE DISPOSAL INDUSTRY

The second important set of changes in international waste management revolves around the structure of the waste disposal industry. Like the problem and its regulation, the waste disposal industry has become more global in its scope. In addition it has become more privatized and concentrated. As these changes have occurred, the industry has also become a political actor in the domestic and international arenas in an attempt to influence the direction of regulations on their operations. Each of these is discussed more fully below.

1. Changes in Industry Structure

Despite conventional definitions, hazardous wastes are hardly "superfluous, refuse, no longer serving a purpose, left over after use".[14] Often they can be reprocessed to obtain valuable "raw" materials or can be highly profitable for firms able to dispose of highly toxic elements.[15] The waste disposal industry has a colorful history.[16] In the USA, it was historically the province of rival ethnic groups, as well as certain organized crime elements; in the UK it began with the rag and bone men, and the first companies were the result of the entrepreneurial skills of lone operators. By the 1970s in most developed countries waste collection and disposal became the responsibility of municipal authorities and a multitude of small local operators either owned by local authorities or contracted to them.[17]

Within the same time frame over which the waste trade emerged, the structure of the waste disposal industry changed in fundamental ways. Three industry-wide trends can be identified most obviously in the US, UK and France: privatization, globalization and concentration. They have followed on more or less chronologically from each other, and were very much facilitated by broader political changes in the 1980s. Globalization of the waste disposal industry began around 1990, and since then, most if not all of the large private firms have established multinational connections. For example, some firms import wastes, while operating within their country of origin, and some (these are not exclusive categories) are horizontally integrated, owning and operating waste disposal plants and collection services in several different countries. Most recently, concentration in global industry structure has been noted since about 1992. Several high-profile mergers in recent years of the bigger firms attest to this fact.[18] This move has been triggered in part by the economies of scale associated with high-end disposal techniques. Many of the main firms are highly diversified, too: concurrent involvement in the construction, energy and water industries is common. This process has left a world market dominated by only a few major players, as Table 1 shows.[9]

Of the group, WMI is the most global. Its parent company, WMX Technologies Inc. is one of the largest North American waste disposal firms. In 1998 WMX was taken over by USA Waste—becoming Waste Management Inc., controlling 22% of the US market.[20] The firm has a 49% interest in Wessex Water Plc. and Waste Management International Plc.[21] In 1996, Waste Management International derived 79% of its revenue from operations in European countries (24% from

Italy alone), 14.3% from the Asia-Pacific region, and 6% from Latin America. Recently it has extended its activities to Hong Kong and Australia, with some success. Many of its UK operations have been carried out by UK Waste, a 1991 joint venture between WMI and Wessex Water, one of the new companies, which emerged from the privatization of the water industry in Britain. Suez-Lyonnaise (SITA), following its purchase of all assets held by the US firm, Browning Ferris Industries Inc. in 1997 became Europe's largest waste service provider.[22] Finally, the big waste multinationals have taken a lead role in less developed countries, siting and building facilities and working with government actors to establish regulatory infrastructures.[23]

Table 1. Waste Companies, World Ranking 1997

Company		Sales ($m)
Waste Management, Inc	USA	9200
BFI	USA	5400
Suez-Lyonnaise	France	2600
USA Waste	USA	2300
Vivendi	France	2450
RWE	Germany	1900
Rethmann	Germany	1700
Republic Waste	USA	900
Allied Waste	USA	900
FCC	Spain	700

Source: "Waste Management Inc: Update on Company Structure, Finances and News", Report for PSI/EPSU (Public Services International/European Federation of Public Service Unions) Meeting, January 29 1999, at www.psiru.org/ipspr/forums/wmiewc/restrict/wmijan99.htm

2. The Waste Industry as Political Actor

Firms in the waste industry, as well as expanding economically, have organized as political actors, with the aim of affecting national and international policies regarding waste management and disposal. As shall be discussed below, various sectors of the industry have played an active role around the negotiation of the Basel Convention and subsequent protocols, and in the evolution of EU waste management policy. They are represented by a number of trade associations at the national and transnational levels, including the European federation of waste management trade associations (FEAD), and the Brussels-based Bureau International de la Recuperation (BIR), the largest international recycling peak association, representing 600 members in over 50 countries.[24]

These activities are in addition to continued lobbying at the national level. They have met with some, though not complete, success in achieving their goals. Their main concerns are to maintain the trade in wastes for recycling purposes, and to advocate the building of new integrated facilities utilizing the advanced technologies for energy and materials recovery. In doing this, they are starting to realize the need to involve public actors.[25] Further, in response to public pressure, a "critical mass" of firms in the industry, at least in the UK, is now seeking certification under recognized environmental management systems, such as ISO14001 or The EU's Environmental Management and Auditing Scheme (EMAS).[26] In the EU the influence of the high-end of the waste disposal industry has been key: some have argued that the EU might have tightened regulations because some firms can meet them, and they are lobbying for tighter restrictions.[27] These firms provide specific sorts of hazardous waste disposal services, including recycling, incineration, and waste collection over a wide area. This strategy also suits the EU's environmental policy mandate, which is as much as possible to harmonize and improve its members' practices.

C. NATIONAL POLICY CHANGES: THE EU AS CASE STUDY
A third set of changes in global waste management has been the shift in national and regional policies in industrialized countries regarding hazardous waste. These have included changes in both policy goals and policy instruments. The goal of waste regulation has evolved from one focused mainly on treatment and disposal to one, which encompasses definitions of hazardous waste and waste minimization. The policy measures used have branched out from reliance on command and control regulations to include market measures, a focus on waste minimization and administrative reorganization. The discussion below outlines these shifts in national policy in industrialized countries with a focus on the European Union, as a diverse and innovative set of national and transnational political and state actors that demonstrates a high degree of divergence from traditional norms of environmental regulation.

1. Regulating Hazardous Wastes: Main Policy Goals
Modern hazardous waste regulation policy has evolved into a highly complex set of rules, norms and practices, affecting large numbers of actors and increasingly crossing many jurisdictional borders. Waste-related policy has a number of goals:[28]

1. Defining, listing or otherwise identifying hazardous wastes.
2. Ensuring safe on-site storage, treatment and disposal (T&D) of

wastes, following the waste management hierarchy: waste prevention, reduction, recycling, treatment, incineration and lastly landfill and ocean dumping.

3. Ensuring environmentally safe transportation, storage and T&D by the waste disposal industry. Rules for licensing or permitting of sites are important, as are liability laws and processes.

4. Moving industry (i.e. waste generators) towards waste minimization, for example through the adoption of new, cleaner technology or other production process change and reuse and recycling initiatives. These can be both within the actual production process and through the wider product cycle, for example, through packaging material recycling. Usually waste minimization policies do not involve actually reducing industrial production.

5. Setting up appropriate national, local and, increasingly, transnational regulatory infrastructures agencies to monitor waste management and mitigate harmful externalities, including clean up of contaminated sites.

The first three are the central planks of the traditional approach to waste management, based on the twin philosophies of dealing with wastes after generation (treating their generation as outside the scope of regulatory authority) and as a local problem.[29] The fourth goal, waste minimization, is much more recent and a more fundamental change. Another defining shift in waste regulation in recent years has been a move to more centralized regulation, and regulation covering larger geographic areas, often transnational. Finally, regulations covering controls on disposal technology have benefited from recent technological advances.

International organizations now provide a main impetus for national change across many aspects of waste management policies and have thus become a regulatory target for actors wishing to influence policy. The pressures vary according to regime: the Basel Convention and associated agreements explicitly governing the illegal waste trade from North to South were initially quite shallow in their impacts on national policies. Ostensibly they deal only with the trade in, not generation of, hazardous wastes. However, as explained below, the regime now has profound implications for the global recycling industry. EU regulations penetrate much more deeply into the policies of members and would-be members, affecting most aspects of waste management, from cradle to grave, including transfrontier movement of wastes. This fits with the EU's desire to expand its role into environmental policies of the member states as part of the overall integration project. The following sections outline these institutional developments, focusing on their desired impacts on the extent and direction of national policy changes, and their likely effectiveness. While the Basel Convention and related agreements remain weak, the EU is proving to be a potent force in modernizing the waste politics of its member states.

Current EU waste policy is based on the 1975 Waste Framework Directive (75/442/EEC) and the 1991 Hazardous Waste Directive (91/689/EEC).[30] These directives have established the framework for waste management structures, along with two types of daughter directives, those dealing with requirements for the permitting and operations of waste disposal facilities, and those dealing with specific types of wastes, such as oils, persistent organic pollutants such as PCBs and titanium dioxide, packaging and batteries. Directives concerning facilities include Municipal Waste Incineration (89/429/EEC), Hazardous Waste Incineration (94/67/EEC) and the Proposal on Landfill (COM(97)105). Finally, the 1993 Directive on the Shipment of Waste (EEC/259/93) deals with transport, import and export of wastes.

Debates over EU waste management policy are occurring within this framework, and affect member state rules and practices much more fundamentally than UNEP regulations. Overall, the EU is concerned with encouraging prevention or reduction of wastes and associated harmful effects through the adoption of clean technology and the recovery of waste and its use as a source of energy. Member states must establish an integrated and adequate network of disposal facilities, and must draw up waste management plans designating the national legislative framework, competent authorities, legal checkpoints, permit procedures, stakeholder involvement and financial considerations.

Regarding hazardous waste specifically, the EU aims to formulate a common definition of hazardous waste across the member states, based on OECD classifications, and to introduce greater harmonization of the management of such wastes.[31] Permitting, packaging and labeling must meet international standards, and inspection is very important. The Shipment of Waste Directive implements the Basel Convention, the OECD Council Decisions on transfrontier movements of waste and the Lomé IV Convention. Therefore export of hazardous waste out of the EU to less developed countries is very difficult. Despite long struggles, there seems to be no final position on the self-sufficiency principle versus the proximity principle in internal (intra-EU) waste trading. This debate is key in understanding EU waste trade politics: if national self-sufficiency were mandated, then the trade would in effect be banned among the member states. Under the proximity principle, supported by Germany, the main exporting state, trade could continue. At the moment, it seems that the EU leadership prefers the latter.[32]

The incineration directive and the proposed landfill directive lay down strict technological standards for new and existing facilities. In particular, all hazardous wastes must be treated prior to landfill, co-disposal—the disposal of hazardous along with non-hazardous wastes in the same site—must be phased out (despite opposition from the UK) and disposal prices must reflect costs of closing the landfill site and at least 50 years of after-closure care.

2. Policy Trajectories in Member States: Market Measures, Minimization and Reorganization

After years of heavy criticism, national regulations within the member states are finally becoming stronger over time as governments and firms adopt more advanced regulatory mechanisms and views of waste disposal problems. While waste management regulations are unlikely to converge towards identity, or in identical ways across countries any time soon, there is convergence along different national paths, responding to particular national needs, prerogatives and demands towards a common set of goals which have been framed by the EU. For example, while Britain is centralizing waste management, Germany is not.[33] Conversely, Germany has made much more progress in reducing the amount of waste generated by its firms. Nonetheless, both the UK and Germany are following the goals set by the waste management hierarchy, and both are responding to EU policy demands.

Trends towards superior disposal technology are also evident across most industrialized countries. These have taken on a number of forms: introducing technology into production processes to minimize waste generation or to recycle materials back through the process; improving existing treatment and disposal technology, often towards integrated treatment processes in large-scale facilities, and the

development of new disposal technologies (often more environmentally sound and/or portable).[34] These technological changes have
in turn been enabled large multinational companies and European
regulators to push for further, and more stringent regulatory change.

The next sections examine more closely three main changes in
regulatory practice as they are playing out across select EU member
states, illustrating the argument that states are moving upwards,
towards stricter regulation, but along different paths.[35] The three on
which the chapter focuses—the use of market measures such as taxes,
the implementation of waste minimization measures and
administrative changes—are indicative of the sorts of regulations often
directly affected by transnational influences. They also illustrate well
the main differences in national approaches to policy reform.

a. Market Measures

One area of variance among EU states is the extent to which they
employ market measures—here, taxes—to move firms up the waste
management hierarchy, most especially to re-route wastes away from
landfill and instead towards incineration or other techniques. Britain
and France have employed landfill taxes—Britain at a much higher
level than France—while Germany, for instance, has not. [36]

In March 1995 the British Chancellor announced a new tax to be
imposed on landfill sites—Britain's first Green Tax—expected to raise
disposal costs by 50%.[37] In its final form, the tax, implemented in
October 1996, was levied at £7 per tonne for special wastes and £2 per
tonne for inactive wastes.[38] In April 1999 it was raised to £10 per tonne
for active wastes, to be raised to £15 by 2004. It is unclear, however,
what the final effect will be on the relative use of landfill compared
with incineration. Early reports on the effects of the tax suggested that
evidence that hazardous wastes have been diverted to illegal disposal
routes (or reclassified as "inactive") and gave few signs that the tax has
boosted practices of waste minimization or recycling. For instance,
reports in *The Guardian* newspaper in early 2000 talk of scandal and
regulatory capture by waste operators.[39] Demands have been made
that it be raised to £30 per tonne and that more of its revenues be
diverted directly to waste minimization or alternative management
measures.[40] In Germany, conversely (and perhaps unexpectedly, as
Germany has traditionally advocated green taxes), a tax not on specific
disposal routes but on hazardous waste disposal in general applied by
two German states, or Länder, Hessen and Baden-Württemburg was

struck down by the Supreme Court in 1998 on the grounds that it runs counter to the federal government waste management concept, which puts more emphasis on cooperation with producers. This decision has far-reaching consequences for the states, who now need to pay the revenues back.[41]

b. Waste Minimization Policies

Waste minimization policies are an article of faith of the new pollution prevention and control policy frameworks.[42] Most often they are designed as part of the set of voluntary approaches to pollution control, where solutions are arrived at through close cooperation with waste generating firms. On the whole, they are not popular, hardly surprisingly, with the waste disposal firms, who feel threatened by potential reduction of their main input. The OECD, which has taken a leading role in coordinating such measures, defines waste minimization as including waste prevention, reduction at source, reuse of products, quality improvements (e.g. reduction of hazard), and recycling.[43] The concept, as a policy measure, does not include energy recovery or pre-treatment of wastes.[44] Policy discussions of waste minimization cross the entire range of waste types, from municipal through industrial to hazardous.

Such measures have been embraced most heartily in Germany, through its *Kreislaufwirtschaft,* or closed-circle economy, ordinance and its emphasis on producer responsibility for waste generation and disposal.[45] However, waste minimization measures are now in place across OECD countries. The majority is voluntary or displays a mix of voluntary and mandatory characteristics. A recent report shows strong similarities in policy priorities across countries, for example for onsite recycling, and for material recycling over energy recovery—energy generation energy from waste incineration.[46] Overall, however, and despite evidence of extensive legislative change, few definitive results are yet out as to the extent to which these measures have been effectively implemented and the impact they are having on waste generation in practice. A study by the German-based Institute for Applied Ecology of EU waste minimization initiatives reported encouraging results in hazardous and industrial waste minimization initiatives by industry and horizontal measures by government. As its results outline "success stories" rather than quantitative data across industrial sectors, there remains room for more extensive analysis.[47]

c. Administrative Reorganization

Many countries—Britain the exemplar—have long recognized that the administrative structures set up in the 1970s for managing hazardous waste regulation were both inefficient and unwieldy. Therefore, administrative reorganization has been evident in Britain, and France, but less so elsewhere. In Britain, overall responsibility for hazardous waste disposal has been removed from the hands of roughly 200 local authorities to the center, with the removal of Waste Regulation Authorities to the supervision of the Environmental Protection Agency, the establishment of stricter inspection policies, and the much-anticipated publication of an overall waste management strategy.[48] Plans have also been laid for a National Transfrontier Shipment Service, to be based in Manchester and run by the Environment Agency.[49] This is a particularly significant development as heretofore the local authorities have been the ones issuing the waste importation permits. These changes have been welcomed by the British waste disposal industry, whose primary concern in the past had been the government's refusal to centralize waste regulation, which would create a "one-stop shop" for industry. France, too, further centralized its regulatory structure beginning in 1982 with the creation of a new tier of government, the Regions. The regions have been slowly, and under conditions of high uncertainty, taking over functions of environmental regulation, but further research is needed to ascertain how this new approach has worked in France.[50]

D. THE "TEMPLATE MODEL" OF POLICY DEVELOPMENT IN LESS DEVELOPED COUNTRIES

The fourth set of changes to global waste management has been the tightening of hazardous waste regulations in the emerging economies of the developing world. It appears as though a model for hazardous waste regulation is being applied, in particular in Southeast Asia. But it is still unclear as to the impact it will have in practice.

A recent study from Resources for the Future examined waste management policies across eight developed and developing countries, yielding results that are generally consistent with the notion that a waste management "template" is being adopted across emerging economies (in this case, Malaysia, Thailand, Indonesia and Hong Kong).[51] This template is characterized by roughly concurrent legislation, national regulatory agencies, public-private partnerships (often with foreign firms) and the construction of modern, integrated disposal facilities, which offer a range of disposal techniques. For example, the Kualiti Alam plant in Malaysia opened in November 1998, with an annual capacity across the different disposal methods of around 50,000 tonnes.[52]

Activity by the big Western firms has been long apparent, and in apparently constructive ways, helping countries with expertise, funding and facility construction. The differences between the programs lie in the extent of foreign involvement and the basic institutional or political structure of the country. For example, Danish firms and environmental consultants have been involved in Malaysia, while Waste Management International has been active in Indonesia.

In addition to these common practices, these countries share a long time frame for policy development, around 10–15 years, and some common problems with waste policy implementation and illegal export. For example, in summer 1998 a Taiwanese firm illegally shipped hazardous wastes to Cambodia, where the drums were dumped in a populated area. This debacle, and the resultant impasse in repatriating and dealing with the wastes sparked a waste management overhaul by Taiwan's EPA and the eventual shipment of the wastes to the Netherlands after several countries, including France and the US refused to take them in.[53]

These practices are comparable to policy adjustments being made in the East and Central European countries that seek to join the EU and are implementing the acquis communautaire, and the more peripheral EU member countries such as Ireland, Spain, and Portugal.[54] However, the question now becomes, how effective is this template model at actually achieving goals of safe waste management in these countries? Preliminary answers to these questions are not encouraging: new facilities rarely operate at full capacity, it is often the case that wastes never reach their destination, and, as Probst and Beierle point out, many less developed countries have yet to develop the "culture of compliance" necessary to effectively manage such schemes. This in turn is not terribly encouraging the argument that less developed countries should try to adopt even minimal standards as a way of escaping being "stuck at the bottom"—as these new plans are above and beyond the sorts of minimum one should expect, and still are not effective.[55] On the other hand, these are long-term projects still at early stages of development. Finally, work remains to be done in this context on two expanding hazardous waste markets: China and India. For example, India's recent policy shifts were cataloged above, in the discussion of the Basel Convention. Also, Tredi, a French-based hazardous waste transport company, which ships around 3,000 tonnes of non-European hazardous waste to France each year is showing interest in China, providing technical advice to the Basel Convention representatives there.[56]

E. ANALYSIS: DOES HAZARDOUS WASTE MANAGEMENT FIT THE THEORETICAL DEBATE?

Three factors define the context facing today's global waste disposal industry and its regulators. First, the hazardous waste management problem and its regulation have become truly global. The international regulatory regime—primarily managed by the UNEP, the EU and the OECD—is quite weak and still in its developmental stage, though, as is the case in the EU, international authorities are now setting regulatory agendas in many places. Second, the industry itself has evolved from a highly competitive, localized industry dominated by small firms with a high level of government involvement to a more concentrated, privatized and indeed global industry which considers itself on the cutting edge of environmental service provision. Third, national regulation specifically of hazardous waste generation and disposal is in transition in most countries, either reforming older practices or developing waste regulations for the first time. This is particularly evident in the EU and in emerging economies.

Under these circumstances, one would expect the "race to the bottom", or pollution haven hypothesis (PHH) to be borne out. In general terms, this would mean firms take advantage of these national and international vulnerabilities to locate their waste disposal activities in poorer, or more venal countries and communities, and to be lobbying relevant authorities to weaken, rather than strengthen national and international regulatory regimes.[57] The PHH is one aspect of the environment and trade literature, and studies examine the extent to which "dirty" industries locate factories or export wastes or environmentally damaging technologies to poorer countries on the basis of their lower levels of environmental regulation. The extent to which this happens is hotly contested in the field, although empirical studies mostly show that the strong version of the PHH—deliberate factory relocation in response to regulatory differences—does not occur.[58]

In much of the activist and scholarly literature on the waste trade, however, the trade is seen as a poster child for a weaker version of the hypothesis: that though firms in developed countries might not want to actually relocate to LDCs, they are willing to illegally export wastes—a cheaper and less labor intensive way of skirting domestic regulations.[59] Data that this is a serious, pervasive and frequent pattern remains inconclusive. Further, such accounts tend to downplay the extent to which poorer countries have organized to resist waste dumping, under the Bamako and Waigani Conventions, for instance.[60]

Many emerging economies are developing models of waste management and regulation, where previously none existed. There are strong similarities across these schemes, leading to the second claim made in this paper, that a "template" of waste management is being applied across many countries, with varied results. However, while waste disposal firms rarely deliberately relocate to take advantage of weak environmental laws, given the level of regulatory capacity and infrastructure in many countries, we could see *unintentional* PHH results, as technologies and practices are put into place without much thought as to how well they will travel.[61] This is a vitally important question that needs further empirical study as these systems evolve.

In the EU cases discussed above, there are many reasons to be optimistic that governments are getting the message about needed reforms. However, again, there is some cause for concern. There are at least three barriers to effective policy implementation across nearly all cases. First, waste disposal costs have increased across EU member states as a result of greater technical stringency. On the one hand, this has advantaged the lead firms in the waste industry. On the other, it can lead to diversion of wastes to illegal disposal routes, including waste dumping within countries (along British motorways for instance) or across borders (to Eastern or Southern Europe). A 1998 report in *The Independent* listed wastes dumped by truck drivers from Germany and Holland along the M-25 motorway in England, including industrial and chemical solvents, low-level radioactive wastes, and human body parts from hospital operations.[62]

Second, policy transformation has also been hampered by slow implementation. Control and monitoring mechanisms are not yet firmly in place in many countries, and the demands of the new policies have diverted regulatory attention from other problems.[63] As one analyst put it, "British players have suffered, not from legislative overkill, but by the void between legislation and its timely, orderly and effective enforcement".[64] A more recent report notes that this is changing: as the EU takes over the reins of waste policy, efforts to fulfill directives are forcing the UK government, for instance, to start setting goals and working out how to meet them, efforts the waste industry appears to be meeting halfway.[65] However, across Europe, slow implementation of EU Directives remains a serious problem. Monitoring too in many countries is weak and often comes under fire, as over-stretched and under-staffed agencies cut back on important regulatory functions, such as on-site inspections.[66]

Further, one of the biggest problems facing waste regulators remains unresolved: communities in most industrialized countries remain unwilling to host new and existing hazardous waste disposal facilities, especially if wastes are to be transported from outside the immediate region.[67] Most countries have internalized at least a minimal consultative approach in siting new facilities. However, and despite some innovative work on voluntary approaches, progress in building new community-based approaches is slow, although in this case it is possible to find the waste industry taking some action.[68]

It is still too early to tell most of the effects of the Basel Convention and associated agreements on national regulatory practices. Some positive trends are discernable. First, public opinion opposes the illegal waste trade. Governments realize they are less likely to get away without bearing some liability, and therefore have in recent years disassociated themselves from these practices. Halting legal waste imports and exports remains, however, far from simple, even for strong governments, as the British failure to implement a ban on legal waste imports shows.[69] Second, the Basel Convention and the work of the OECD Waste Management Group have made many countries take a more technocratic and systematic approach to listing, classifying and publishing data on hazardous waste generation and disposal.

However there is also cause for concern about the extent to which the Basel Convention can change national policies.[70] There are few effective monitoring devices or rules in place to prevent illegal trade. While many actors are concerned with the move towards prohibition among convention supporters, others are concerned with various limits on its scope. For instance, it only tackles the trade, not waste reduction, and it does not cover trading practices among less developed nations. Perhaps most serious is the opposition posed in the on-going negotiation process by the international scrap metal industry and its national/governmental allies to the ban on waste trading for recycling. This cuts at the heart of the issue as to whether recyclable metals are goods or "bads", and represents a different sort of power of globalization in the international sphere: the power of firms and industries to unite across borders and influence inter-state negotiations.

Many industry representatives have lobbied hard against the imposition of the recycling ban.[71] The strategy of directly lobbying the main negotiations, failed at first primarily because the tide of public opinion flowed against it. In recent years, this situation and the political opportunity structure facing these firms has changed. According to Jennifer Clapp, the recycling industry has been able to take advantage of two features of the negotiating structure of the Basel Convention: the technical working group (TWG), which focuses on debates over the definitions and listing of wastes, and the process of ratification of the ban by individual states (the US, for example).[72] The waste and scrap metal industries have been heavily involved at all stages of the negotiations of the Basel Convention, represented by trade associations and the International Chamber of Commerce.

Getting involved in particular in the relatively isolated and specialized TWG marks a significant departure from firms' usual tactics of lobbying their governments to take particular positions, and has proved an effective tool for firms' representatives, who typically have the expertise and the resources to make their voices heard at this level, more so than NGOs. Industry interests have also been able to ally with countries threatening to break ranks—India, for instance, which ended a five year ban on zinc ash imports in August, and is currently considering allowing lead scrap imports—by units with proper recycling and disposal facilities.[73] At stake are large revenue flows: the worth of net exports of scrap metals from the US, excluding iron, is estimated at $2.5bn annually. The TWG meets about twice a year and industry presence is high. In September 1996, of the total 159 representatives there, including government representatives, 49 were from industrial organizations.[74] Their main task has been to lobby to include materials they trade in on List B of the Basel Convention—those wastes that can be freely traded—and redefining their product as "recycled raw materials". They also lobby the waste management policy group of the OECD to change its rules—an important tactic, as the OECD has directed the whole list-building process, affecting both UNEP and EU waste definitions. According to Clapp and to the main NGO following this process, the Basel Action Network, the industry has achieved a good deal of success in this.[75] Indeed, it is looking increasingly unlikely that the waste trade ban will be implemented in its proposed form any time soon.

CONCLUSIONS

The above analysis ends on a negative note, about the vulnerability of the international environmental governance system to regulatory capture by private interests. However, the overall picture it paints of hazardous waste management in this global era is considerably more nuanced. First, hazardous waste regulation needs to be understood at several levels of governance—here, we considered national, regional and global, and how directives from higher levels of government filter down to lower, and are interpreted in different ways. Second, it is evident that the private sector—waste disposal and recycling firms—have become increasingly powerful economic and political actors, both in international negotiations, in working with governments and the EU, and in creating market opportunities in emerging economies. Their activities have on the one hand helped strengthen and modernize national regulatory practices. On the other, they are acting to weaken international regulations governing the international waste trade, especially in recyclable wastes.

The regulatory playing field in hazardous waste management has been irrevocably altered by changes in domestic/international and private/public balances in this arena. Various forces of globalization have evidently had important impacts on this sector, though these are complex and multidirectional. Our theoretical understanding of these processes has yet to catch up with empirical observations, but remains crucial for future analyses of global environmental politics and the effectiveness of global regulation. This piece mostly omitted one particular group of actors from the analysis, namely NGOs and environmental groups. A study of how they ally with or resist private economic actors in this field would be well worth undertaking. The issue of adequate hazardous waste management has by no means been resolved cross-nationally. Further, some of the insights of this chapter could well be applied or compared with other international environmental issue areas, to enhance our understanding of the interaction of multiple levels of governance with newly emerging and strengthened private economic actors.

Kate O'Neill is an Assistant Professor in Environmental Science, Policy, and Management at the University of California, Berkeley.

Notes

A similar version of this article was published as "The Changing Nature of Global Waste Management for the 21st Century: A Mixed Blessing?" *Global Environmental Politics* 1(1): 77–98 (2001). The author would like to thank Jennifer Clapp, Bob Kagan, David Sonnenfeld and David Vogel, other participants in the Globalization workshop, and various reviewers for their invaluable comments on this chapter.

1. Vogel, 1995.

2. Vogel 1995.

3. See Wirth 1998, O'Neill and Burns, 2001.

4. See OECD 1997, Table 2. Countries reported wastes defined as hazardous under national regulations, based on generation figures reported to the OECD for different years. Hazardous wastes are here defined as waste products, often but not exclusively the result of industrial and agricultural activities—which pose particular risks to human health and environments through being reactive, toxic, corrosive or flammable. Nuclear and municipal wastes are mostly excluded from this discussion.

5. Wynne 1987.

6. Wynne 1987, Piasecki and Davis 1987, O'Neill 1998.

7. Munton 1996.

8. Strohm 1993.

9. Montgomery 1995, 4. On the emergence and extent of the waste trade, see also O'Neill 2000.

10. See Vallette and Spalding 1990, and the website of the Basel Action Network at www.ban.org.

11. On compliance and implementation issues see Weiss and Jacobson 1998 and Victor, Raustiala and Skolnikoff 1998.

12. Krueger 2000.

13. Krueger 1999.

14. Oxford English Dictionary, Concise Edition.

15. See Gourlay 1992 and Wynne 1987 for relevant discussions.

16. On the history of the industry, see Crooks 1993, B. Clapp 1994.

17. Brusco et al 1996.

18. Cooke and Chapple 1996, 13.

19. These firms deal with both hazardous and non-hazardous wastes; the sales figures reflect overall sales for these firms, including hazardous waste management.

20. "Waste Management and USA Waste To Merge", *Haznews* 121, April 1998, 1.

21. *Financial Times* Company Brief, Waste Management Inc., October 2 1999.

22. "SITA to be global no. 3 on $1,450m BFI assets purchase", *Haznews* 117, December 1997, 1.

23. See discussion below, and Probst and Beierle 1999.

24. See BIR's website, www.bir.org, for information on their stance regarding the Basel Convention.

25. "Finding an ally in public opinion: A strategy for the waste sector", *Environmental Data Service (ENDS) Report* 296 (September 1999), 24–28.

26. "Facing up to continuous improvement in the waste sector", *ENDS Report* 299 (December 1999), 21–24.

27. Brusco et al 1996.

28. See also Probst and Beierle 1999.

29. On traditional waste regulation policies and structures, see Wynne 1987, Forester and Skinner 1987 and Piasecki and Davis 1987.

30. "The DG XI Guide to the Approximation of EU Environmental Legislation Part 2C: Waste Management", at http://europa.eu.int/comm/dg11/part2c.htm.

31. The OECD classifies wastes into red, green and amber lists. Green-listed wastes are non-hazardous recyclable wastes that can be traded among states most easily; amber and red listed wastes come under much more stringent c   disposal requirements: red-listed wastes, including many persistent organic pollutants are considered "intrinsically hazardous" (Kummer 1995, 162–3).

32. For a history of this debate, see Jupille 1996.

33. O'Neill 2000, Probst and Beierle 1999.

34. See O'Neill 1998 for a brief discussion, extended to the case of Australia.

35. Following Coleman and Grant 1998.

36. Litvan 1995.

37. Reported in *The Daily Telegraph,* March 22 1995.

38. *ENDS Report* 258, July 1996.

39. "£1bn waste scandal as green tax flops", *The Guardian,* April 5 2000.

40. "MPs press for landfill tax increases and reform of tax credits scheme", *ENDS Report* 294, July 1999, and "Less waste than expected leaves £80m hole in landfill tax revenue", *ENDS Report* 274, November 1997.

41. See Stefan Speck, "A Database of Environmental Taxes and Charges: Germany, 1998", from The Eco-Tax Database of Forum for the Future at Keele University, UK.

42. Munton 1996, 4.

43. On OECD approaches to waste minimization see, for instance, "Waste Minimization in OECD Member Countries", Group on Pollution Prevention and Control, Environment Directorate, OECD (ENV/EPOC/PPC(97)15/REV2), released May 1998 and "Waste Minimization Profiles of OECD Member Countries", Group on Pollution Prevention and Control, Environment Directorate, OECD (ENV/EPOC/PPC(97)16/REV2), released May 1998. These documents are available on-line through www.oecd.org.

44. This definition came out of the OECD Workshop on "Building the Basis for a Common Understanding of Waste Minimization" held in Berlin in October 1996.

45. For a full discussion of the measures contained within the Kreislaufwirtschaft in its final version, see Stede 1996, and "New German waste law in force", *Haznews* 104, November, 1996, p. 12. The passage of this legislation was by no means smooth. However, the law was in full force by January 1, 1999.

46. See "Considerations for Evaluating waste Minimization in OECD Member Countries", Group on Pollution Prevention and Control, Environment Directorate, OECD (ENV/EPOC/PPC(97)17/REV2), released May 1998.

47. "EU Waste Minimization Initiatives Surveyed", *ENDS Environment Daily*, October 20 1999. Full report available from http://www.oeko.de/english/depart.htm.

48. Department of the Environment, *Waste Management Planning: Principles and Practice*, London: HMSO 1995. See also *ENDS Report* 234, July 1994, and *Haznews* Number 104 (November 1996).

49. *ENDS Report* 271, August 1997, 11.

50. Bodiguel and Buller 1994.

51. Probst and Beierle 1999.

52. "Malaysia's hazwaste facility official launch" *Haznews* 129, December 1998.

53. "Taiwan proposes waste management overhaul", *Haznews* 134, May 1999, 1.

54. Lynch 2000.

55. See Porter 1999 for the "stuck at the bottom" argument.

56. "Tredi International expanding business?", *Haznews* 130, January 1999, 15.

57. See Copeland 1991.

58. Thompson and Strohm 1996, Clapp 1998 and Porter 1999.

59. See Adeola 2000.

60. The 1995 Waigani Convention bans waste imports into the Pacific Island region.

61. There are arguments that we are seeing other, weaker versions of the PHH playing out in North-south transfers, including continued export of wastes and of risky technologies. See Clapp 1998.

62. "Waste dumped secretly on motorways turns Britain into dustbin of Europe", *The Independent*, August 6, 1998. The M25 is the motorway that rings London.

63. "Agency still not transparent on regulatory performance", *ENDS Report* 295, August 1999, 6.

64. Dr. David Owen, leading waste industry analyst, quoted in *ENDS Report* 248, September 1995, 14.

65. "Signs of Life in the slow-moving world of waste policy", *ENDS Report* 294 (July 1999), "Waste classification scheme takes shape with industry cooperation", *ENDS Report* 295, August 1999.

66. On the UK Environment Agency, see "Agency makes a mess of waste", *ENDS Report* 280, May 1998; on the EU, see Jordan 1998.

67. Munton 1996.

68. "Finding an Ally in Public Opinion: A Strategy for the Waste Sector", *ENDS Report* 296, September 1999.

69. O'Neill 2000.

70. See also Kellow 1999.

71. For the views of industry opponents of the ban, see John C. Bullock, "Hurting Development and Business" *International Herald Tribune*, October 4, 1995 and Alter 1997.

72. Clapp 1999.

73. "India government reviews lead scrap proposal", EnviroLink News Service, October 27, 1999.

74. Clapp 1999, 14.

75. See www.ban.org.

References

Adeola, Francis, 2000. "Cross-national environmental injustice and human rights issues: a review of evidence in the developing world." *American Behavioral Scientist* 43.4: 686–307.

Alter, Harvey, 1997. "Industrial recycling and the Basel Convention." *Resources, Conservation and Recycling* 19.1: 29–53.

Bodiguel, Maryvonne, and Henry Buller, 1994. "Environmental policy and the regions in France." *Regional Politics and Policy* 4.3: 92–109.

Brusco, Sebastiano, Paolo Bertossi, and Alberto Cottica, 1996. "Playing on two chessboards—the European waste management industry: strategic behavior in the market and the policy debate." *Environmental policy in Europe*, edited by Francois Léveque. Cheltenham: Edward Elgar, 1996.

Clapp, B.W., 1994. *An environmental history of Britain since the industrial revolution*. London: Longman.

Clapp, Jennifer, 1998. "Foreign direct investment in hazardous industries in developing countries." *Environmental Politics* 7.4: 92–113.

Clapp, Jennifer, 1999. *The global recycling industry and hazardous waste trade politics.*, unpublished paper presented at the Annual Meeting of the International Studies Association, Washington DC.

Coleman, W. D., and W. P. Grant, 1998. "Policy convergence and policy feedback: agricultural finance policies in a globalizing era." *European Journal of Political Research* 34.2: 225–247.

Cooke, Andrew, and Wendy Chapple, 1996. "EU regulation and the UK waste disposal industry." *Environmental Policy and Practice* 6.1: 11–16.

Copeland, Brian, 1991. "International trade in waste products in the presence of illegal disposal." *Journal of Environmental Economics and Management* 20: 143–162.

Crooks, Harold, 1993. *Giants of garbage: the rise of the global waste industry and the politics of pollution control*. Toronto: James Lorimer and Company.

Forester, William S., and John H. Skinner, eds., 1987. *International perspectives on hazardous waste management*. London: Academic Press Inc.

Gourlay, K.A., 1992. *World of waste: dilemmas of industrial development.*

London: Zed Books.

Jordan, Andrew, 1998. "EU environmental policy at 25: the politics of multinational governance." *Environment* 40.1: 14–20, 39–45.

Jupille, Joseph Henri, 1996. *Free movement of goods and hazardous waste: reconciling the single market with environmental imperatives.*, presented at the Annual Meeting of the International Studies Association, San Diego CA.

Kellow, Aynsley, 1999. *International toxic risk management: ideals, interests and implementation.* Cambridge: Cambridge University Press.

Krueger, Jonathan, 1999. *International trade and the Basel Convention.* London: Royal Institute of International Affairs/ Earthscan Press.

Krueger, Jonathan, 2000. "The Basel Convention and the international trade in hazardous wastes." In *Yearbook of international cooperation on environment and development., 2001,* edited by H. O. Bergeson, G. Parman and O. B. Thommessen (London: Earthscan).

Kummer, Katharina, 1995. *International management of hazardous wastes: the Basel Convention and related legal rules.* London: Oxford University Press.

Litvan, David, 1995. "Politique des déchets: l'approche du Royaume-Uni." *Économie et Statistique* 290.10: 81–90.

Lynch, Diahanna, 2000. *Closing the deception gap: accession to the European Union and environmental standards in East Central Europe,* Working Paper 2.71, Center for German and European Studies, UC Berkeley.

Montgomery, Mark A., 1995. "Reassessing the waste trade crisis: what do we really know?" *Journal of Environment and Development* 4.1: 1–28.

Munton, Don, ed., 1996. *Hazardous waste siting and democratic choice.* Washington: Georgetown University Press.

O'Neill, Kate, 1998. "Out of the backyard: the problems of hazardous waste management at a global level." *Journal of Environment and Development* 7.2: 138–163.

O'Neill, Kate, 2000. *Waste trading among rich nations: building a new theory of environmental regulation.* Cambridge: MIT Press.

O'Neill, Kate and William C.G. Burns, 2001, "Free Trade and Global Environmental Governance: Rules, Actors and Conflicts", presented at Mini Conference on Globalization and the Environment, Annual

Meeting of the American Sociology Association, Anaheim CA, August 17 2001

Organization for Economic Cooperation and Development, 1997. *Transfrontier movements of hazardous wastes: 1992–93 statistics.* Paris: OECD.

Piasecki, Bruce, and Gary Davis, eds., 1987. *America's future in toxic waste management: lessons from Europe.* New York: Quorum Books.

Porter, Gareth, 1999. "Trade competition and pollution standards: 'race to the bottom' or 'stuck at the bottom'?" *Journal of Environment and Development* 8.2: 133–151.

Probst, Kathleen N., and Thomas C. Beierle, 1999. *The evolution of hazardous waste programs: lessons from eight countries.* Washington DC: Resources for the Future.

Stede, Birgit, 1996. "Abfall in der Kreislaufwirtschaft." *Müll und Abfall* .3: 141–152.

Strohm, Laura, 1993. "The environmental politics of the international waste trade." *Journal of Environment and Development* 2.2: 129–53.

Thompson, Peter, and Laura A. Strohm, 1996. "Trade and environmental quality: a review of the evidence." *Journal of Environment and Development* 5.4: 363–388.

Vallette, Jim, and Heather Spalding, 1990. *The international trade in hazardous wastes: a Greenpeace inventory.* 5 ed. Washington: Greenpeace International Waste Trade Project.

Victor, David G., Kal Raustiala, and Eugene B. Skolnikoff, eds., 1998. *The implementation and effectiveness of international environmental commitments: theory and practice.* Cambridge, MA: MIT Press.

Vogel, David, 1995 *Trading up: consumer and environmental regulation in a global economy.* Cambridge: Harvard University Press.

Weiss, Edith Brown, and Harold K. Jacobson, eds., 1998. *Engaging countries: strengthening compliance with international environmental accords.* Cambridge: MIT Press.

Wirth, David A. (1998). "Trade Implications of the Basel Convention Amendment Banning North-South Trade in Hazardous Wastes." *RECIEL* 7(3): 237–248.

Wynne, Brian, ed., 1987 *Risk management and hazardous waste: implementation and the dialectics of credibility.* Berlin: Springer-Verlag.

Chapter 5

Closing the Deception Gap
Accession to the European Union and Environmental Standards in East Central Europe

Diahanna Post

INTRODUCTION

This paper explores the mechanism of convergence via legal institutions in the policy area of environmental standards. The context is the impact of accession to the European Union on environmental standards in three candidate countries—Poland, Hungary, and the Czech Republic.

Since 1989, European Union (EU) member states have struggled over whether, and how fast, to admit the countries of East Central Europe (ECE). EU membership is highly sought after by ECE countries for reasons both symbolic (representing a chance to join the West) and practical (the potential for trade and economic growth).[1] For the EU, the incorporation of ECE countries is an opportunity, but also a tremendous challenge. One of the major stumbling blocks to enlargement has been environmental protection. The EU views its relationship with ECE as a commitment not just to the internal market, but rather a path to a broader set of objectives, including "balanced and sustainable growth respecting the environment."[2] Part of this process is for countries in East Central Europe to adopt the entire body of EU environmental legislation, along with other EU legislation, as a condition of becoming a member.

The environmental dynamics of enlargement encompass different arenas and varying levels of analysis. Some of these have generated significant attention in academic analyses, especially the international agreements and institutions that are the backbone of the enlargement process, and the role of domestic interests—both for and against enlargement—within the member states of the European Union.[3] But other aspects of enlargement have been overlooked. In particular, an understanding of government capacity and of sub-national pressures—domestic interests—in these countries is critical to understanding how enlargement will work.

The focus on capacity and sub-national pressures in these countries leads to a concern with implementation. The recent closure of the environmental chapter in the accession negotiations for Poland, Hungary, and the Czech Republic does not also close the question of implementation. This is because adopting EU environmental legislation is not the same as implementing it. One observer has even referred to the enlargement process as "Potemkin harmonization."[4] A very basic question to ask is, who wins and who loses from enlargement? Who brings pressures to close the gap between adoption and implementation, and who pressures to maintain the gap? I argue that domestic producers and environmental non-governmental organizations are both critical to answering this question. In particular, I suggest that environmental groups may lose the power to set the agenda in their own countries by acceding to the demands of their more powerful European Union counterparts, who are driving the agenda in terms of enlargement concerns. Second, I argue that ECE domestic producers may in fact constitute a force for closing the gap.

My analysis commences with a section on the theoretical framework of the article that considers pressures for "race to the bottom" and "race to the top" in environmental standards and international trade, and suggests a way of conceptualizing the gap between adoption and implementation of legislation. The next section briefly reviews the history of enlargement with a particular focus on aspects of environmental protection. Then, I examine enlargement from the perspective of Poland, Hungary, and the Czech Republic. First, I argue that there is an historical legacy of environmental protection in the post-World War II era in these countries that affects government capacity today. Second, I focus on domestic interests internal to the countries under study, recognizing that an understanding of implementation cannot be complete without a picture of pressures outside the government for and against implementation. Finally, I conclude with some policy implications and questions for further research.

FRAMEWORK FOR ANALYSIS

Much of the research on the relationship between trade and the environment focuses on the impact on environmental standards in wealthy nations, most often the US and northern European states, from free trade with countries which have comparatively lower environmental standards.[5] This literature argues that trade pressures lead to a convergence toward either higher standards (a "race to the top") or lower standards (a "race to the bottom").[6] Within relationships among wealthy nations and between wealthy and non-wealthy nations, however, many analysts agree that the "race to the bottom" argument has become irrelevant due to the increasing pressure "green" states place on their less "green" counterparts through international institutions and agreements, and because the conditions rarely exist under which the "race to the bottom" is supposed to occur.[7]

Convergence toward more stringent standards, on the other hand, can occur when "green" states impose their environmental standards on others as a condition of market access.[8] International institutions and agreements promoting stronger environmental standards are important in this regard, as is the support of domestic public interest groups, sometimes in conjunction with domestic producers for whom stricter regulations are a source of competitive advantage.[9] These conditions exist in the case examined here: the EU is a strong international institution, and both environmental groups and domestic producers within the EU favor strong environmental standards for the applicant countries. According to this viewpoint, then, accession to the EU should lead to higher environmental standards in East Central Europe.

The problem with the viewpoint outlined above is that it does not take into account sub-national pressures in the countries applying for admission to the EU. The EU requires that ECE countries adopt EU environmental law, but what forces in ECE countries will pressure their governments to implement the law, and what forces may be opposed to implementing the law? Simmons' analysis of the internationalization of global capital markets provides a model for this EU-ECE dynamic.[10] Her work begins by assuming that the regulators in the dominant financial market will move first by adopting a new regulation. The dominant market will then decide whether to impose the regulation on other countries; if it does, then the follower countries must decide how to respond. Followers' response is determined by their temptation to defect from the regulation; in return the negative

externalities experienced by the dominant financial center if the
follower countries do not comply drive its determination to impose the
regulation on those countries. That is, if the temptation to defect is
high, and if the dominant market suffers if follower countries do not
adopt the regulation, then the dominant market must exert centralized
pressure on the follower countries.

In the case here, defection—that is, not going through with the
process of acceding to the EU—appears extremely unlikely to be
initiated from the side of the applicant countries, because of the
tremendous benefits, symbolic and material, that come with EU
membership. I argue that rather than asking what might lead the
"follower" countries (that is, the countries applying for admission to
the EU) to defect, a more useful question is asking what might lead
them to deceive, that is adopt but not implement the law? Before
continuing, I should point out that deception is not intended to be a
malicious or pejorative description of the behavior of governments
from ECE. In many cases, they may not have the capacity to implement
the laws that are enacted.[11] Rather, this is a question of who benefits.
Others have maintained that deception is at the heart of the EU-ECE
legal approximation process. Jacoby, for instance, describes the process
as encouraging the East Europeans to build "Janus-faced organizations
in which one element works for an organization's domestic clients
while the other is maintained for the purpose of pacifying its EU
patrons."[12] Public opinion polls indicate that, especially in the Czech
Republic and Poland, the question of whether the EU or the candidate
countries will benefit more from accession is still open.[13]

Here, I will examine pressures to maintain this "deception
gap"—the gap between what is said on paper and what is actually
done in practice—and pressures to close that gap, that is, to foster
compliance with environmental laws and regulations. There are two
linked sets of explanations. The first is prior institutional legacies. EU
environmental laws for the most part do not appear on a "clean slate":
countries' histories with enacting and enforcing environmental
legislation will shape their current efforts.[14] Moreover, lack of capacity
affects government in all of the countries in this study. The second
explanation looks to actors, in particular to domestic producers and
non-governmental organizations. In environmental policy in particular,
observers see external pressure—particularly from the EU, but also
from other international aid agencies—as the main source of
preferences in ECE countries for increased stringency of environmental

standards.[15] This is coupled with a decline in internal pressure for changes as non-governmental organizations (NGOs) in the region become less radical, more professionalized, and more dependent on external funding.[16] What are the implications for policies that are passed because of external pressures, but have no internal constituency to support them?

EUROPEAN UNION ENLARGEMENT AND EAST CENTRAL EUROPE—THE PROCESS

EU relations with East Central Europe over the last decade have been marked by uncertainty and debate internal to the EU over the merits of expanding EU membership ("widening") versus an emphasis on "deepening" relations among existing members. The EU has been reticent to lay out exactly under what conditions it will accept ECE candidates for membership, and the debate continues. The environment has been a main sticking point in negotiations. The official Accession Process was launched only in 1998, nine years after the election of democratic governments throughout the region. Analysts of ECE have termed the EU-ECE relationship an "asymmetric dependency" where "the terms of the policy dialogue are. . .skewed heavily in favor of the EU, leaving little room for consideration of the policy experience of ECE countries."[17] The road has been rocky.

In 1993, the European Council in Copenhagen announced that accession should be the long-term goal for the EU in its relationship with East Central Europe. Among the general criteria for accession, candidate countries are expected to possess the capacity to adopt the *acquis communautaire,* or legal acts of the European Union. The adoption of the *acquis* is the most important part of integration with respect to environmental issues. The EU derives its formal authority to pass regulations on environmental issues from the Single European Act (SEA), adopted by EU member states in 1987. In order to create a single European market, the SEA facilitated the harmonization of national environmental regulations to avoid charges of protectionism or undercutting environmental laws. By the early 1990s, the EU had harmonized standards for a wide range of environmental regulations, including air and water pollution, noise pollution, and conservation. The Maastricht Treaty, ratified in 1993, further aids the harmonization of environmental policy among EU members by strengthening the EU's authority over environmental issues.

In assessing progress toward the goal of accession, the EU has stressed the importance of not engaging in "merely formal transposition of legislation," but rather "establishment of adequate structures for implementation and enforcement."[18] In July 1997, the Commission presented Agenda 2000, the first comprehensive assessment of countries applying for membership in the EU.[19] Agenda 2000 devotes a significant portion of its discussion to progress in non-economic policy areas, including environment. Generally, it notes that ECE countries focus more on "end-of-the-pipe" solutions whereas the EU promotes a preventive strategy that also focuses on non-industrial, non-point sources of pollution. It points out the need for "considerable EU technical and financial assistance" to bring the countries closer to the EU level, particularly in the areas of water and energy-related issues, as well as health-related environmental issues. The gap between the ECE countries and the present member states in terms of environmental standards draws particular comment in Agenda 2000, which points out that "national long term development strategies based on the competitive advantages of low environmental standards would be unacceptable within the Union." Agenda 2000 also requires the Commission to report annually to the European Council on the progress made by candidate countries in preparing themselves for membership.

In its assessment of individual countries' progress thus far, Agenda 2000 noted that Poland was the first country in the region to develop a comprehensive environmental policy in the immediate aftermath of the downfall of the Communist government. The policy was reviewed and assessed in 1995, and a new environmental protection law was passed in 1996. It pointed out that Poland's air pollution standards are higher than those of the EU—"unrealistically high," in the EU's opinion. Secondly, it pointed out that Polish authorities have reviewed legislation for its compatibility with EU legislation since 1991, thus attempting to fulfill their responsibility of ensuring approximation of legislation. It cautioned that the Polish approach to air pollution of regulation primarily through economic instruments needed to be backed up by legislation. Some issues—particularly urban wastewater treatment, drinking water, and some subsets of waste management and air pollution—were highlighted as unlikely to be in compliance until the long term.

With respect to Hungary, Agenda 2000 pointed out that a new environmental policy act was adopted in 1995, which aimed primarily to approximate Hungarian legislation to that of the EU. Water pollution, waste management, and air quality were the three major areas where Agenda 2000 saw deficiencies. While Agenda 2000 praised the extent of the approximation process of environmental legislation in Hungary, it noted that compliance was still a substantial problem. Inadequate supervision and enforcement were cited as the main issues in compliance with legislation. Agenda 2000 also criticized the lack of implementation timetables in the Hungarian environmental accession strategy. As with Poland, urban wastewater treatment, drinking water, waste management and air pollution were deemed to need enough attention that they would only come into compliance in "the long to very long term."

Finally, Agenda 2000's assessment of the Czech Republic noted that air pollution and hazardous and solid waste management posed particular problems. The Czech Republic adopted a framework environmental policy act in 1992 and its level of environmental expenditure in percentage of GDP (gross domestic product) exceeds most of the EU member states. The same problems were mentioned (urban wastewater treatment, etc.) as being achievable only in the long term.

The problems highlighted by Agenda 2000 with respect to the environmental portions of the *acquis* initiated a series of efforts at the EU level. Shortly after putting together Agenda 2000, the European Commission issued a Communication on Accession Strategies for Environment.[20] This Communication was designed to help all ten East Central European candidate countries develop a special strategy for environmental approximation, and also determine what the EU's assistance would be to those countries. It estimated total costs for all ten countries of meeting the environmental *acquis* at 100–120 billion ECU, and promised a number of funding mechanisms from the EU, which will assist countries in approximating their environmental legislation. There were also programs for technical advice and assistance.

The Communication also listed a series of steps to be followed in developing and implementing a national pre-accession strategy for the environment. First, states are to determine the requirements of the environmental portions of the *acquis*, based on an EU-published *Guide to the Approximation of European Union Environmental Legislation*. States are next to analyze their own legislation and determine where it does not meet the *acquis*. This step is called a "legal gap analysis" and uses "tables of concordance" to determine where domestic and EU legislation diverge. Additional steps require analyzing institutional and administrative needs, as well as developing a long-term national strategy to adopt the entire environmental *acquis*. Lastly, states are to set up an implementation timetable and establish formal and structured systems for monitoring, communication and reporting.

A year after *Agenda 2000* was issued, in March 1998, the EU launched the official Accession Process at a meeting in Brussels. As part of that process, the European Commission issued draft Accession Partnerships for Poland, Hungary, and the Czech Republic in 1998 and 1999, and also stipulated that each of the applicant countries must provide a plan indicating how they will go about aligning their legislation with that of the EU. Progress reports on accession issued by the EU in both 1999 and 2000 indicated a number of areas for improvement in terms of environmental protection, and in some cases noted that "little legislative progress" had been made on accession in terms of the environment.[21] But the 2001 reports for the three countries discussed here indicated significant progress in the environmental area of accession.

In 2001, the environmental chapter of the accession negotiations was provisionally closed for all three countries. Each country has transitional periods for several measures, such as urban wastewater and packaging waste. Poland has the largest number of transitional periods, at nine. But just because the environmental chapters have been closed does not mean that questions of implementation have been resolved. It is this gap between adoption and implementation that the remainder of this paper examines.

EAST CENTRAL EUROPE—THREATS TO DECEIVE

Environmental pollution has been and continues to be a problem for the Central and East European region. Rapid industrialization coupled with tremendously inefficient energy use in the post-World War II era led to significant environmental degradation. In the 1980s, levels of sulfur dioxide and nitrogen oxides in Poland and Czechoslovakia ranged far above levels in countries of the Organization for Economic Cooperation and Development (OECD).[22] Emissions of sulfur dioxide per unit of GDP are still the highest in the OECD for all three countries (now OECD members). As recently as 1998, the Czech Republic and Poland were the highest emitters of carbon dioxide per unit of gross domestic product (GDP) among OECD states; however, all three countries also showed among the steepest declines from 1980–1998 in carbon dioxide emissions per capita.[23] In the early 1990s, heavy metal contamination in some parts of Poland was two to five times higher than World Health Organization guidelines.[24] Waste disposal and freshwater and groundwater contamination are also significant problems.

While pollution levels—particularly air pollution—have fallen in recent years, this is usually attributed to a reduction in industrial output. As output climbs again, emissions could re-emerge as a significant problem.[25] Also, increasing use of private automobiles presents different kinds of air pollution abatement challenges than point-source factory emissions. The number of cars per capita from 1994 to 1998 rose by 25% in the Czech Republic and 24% in Hungary; the amount of roadways grew in the same period by 27% in the Czech Republic and a whopping 53% in Poland.[26] Prague now has more cars per capita than Vienna.[27] Also in the Czech Republic, the share of public transportation declined in the period 1990–96 from 65% to 45%.[28] Although Hungary is among the most energy efficient of ECE countries, it still uses energy at approximately twice the rate of Western European countries.[29]

The environmental picture in these countries, however, is not uniformly negative. A long-standing tradition of environmental conservation exists in East Central Europe, and much environmental activism in the 1980s centered on conservation issues. Poland in 1989 had 17 national parks totaling 415,000 acres, and one of the last primeval forests in Europe outside of Scandinavia.[30] The total area of national parks in Poland almost doubled from 1989 to 1994.[31] These protected areas are now under threat both from air pollution and economic pressures, which may encourage them to develop the areas or open them up to poaching. In the accession process, the value of these protected areas is noted by some Western NGOs, who have called on the EU to make biodiversity protection part of EU enlargement.[32]

The point of painting this environmental portrait of the region is neither to suggest a lack of effort at improvement, nor to aver that it has deteriorated significantly since 1990. Many efforts have been made—nationally and internationally, and by government, environmental groups, and industry—to abate pollution and reap the "win-win" benefits of improving the economy and the environment simultaneously. What these indicators are intended to point out is that the state of the environment in these countries is still quite far behind the bulk of EU member states, and that there is reason for concern about how their entry might affect environmental standards in the EU. For these reasons, it is important to the EU that the environmental portion of the *acquis* be adopted.

Two broad factors shape the response of East Central European governments to the environmental aspects of the EU accession process. The first is the historical legacy of environmental law in these countries, and the second is the role of domestic interest groups. EU legislation is not being transposed onto a blank slate. Poland, Hungary, and the Czech Republic, along with most of the other countries in East Central Europe, have developed their own environmental legislation over the past half-century to varying degrees of comprehensiveness. The division of authority and enforcement mechanisms in the law continues to affect the transposition and harmonization process of the *acquis* today.

Environmental legislation passed in the 1970s and 80s in Poland, Hungary and the Czech Republic primarily focused on end-of-the-pipe measures designed to capture and mitigate pollution after its creation, rather than focusing on pollution prevention. These policies generally emphasized fines as an enforcement mechanism, but the fines were often set so low that they did not function as incentives to reduce pollution. In addition, standards were sometimes set so high[33] as to be technically unachievable.[34] This only reinforced the tendency for industries to budget for the fines imposed for non-attainment of standards, rather than attempt to reduce pollution. The problem of ineffective fines persists today, coupled with a lack of experience in administering pollution prevention programs. A related problem is that authors of legislation are unused to including a compliance strategy or timetable, and thus while good principles may exist on paper, there are no concrete plans to implement them.[35]

The conflict of interests at the state level is another legacy of environmental law. Under the Communist regimes, the state was both the source of pollution, through economic activity, and responsible for its prevention, through environmental regulation. In Poland, for example, environmental measures could be suspended for reasons deemed "important," such as achieving a five-year plan goal. Moreover, environmental administrators did not participate in the decision-making of important economic sectors, such as mining and construction. This conflicting set of goals is still salient for government officials today, who may see environmental protection as a subsidiary goal to that of economic recovery and growth. In addition, fragmented authority for environmental protection—both in the administration and in legislation—meant unclear jurisdiction and patchwork responses to environmental problems.[36]

Hungary provides examples of such conflicts of interest and fragmentation today. For instance, environmental inspectors often supplement small salaries by working as private contractors. Yet this can create problems when, say, the Environmental Inspectorate reviews an environmental impact assessment which one of the inspectors was privately hired to prepare in the first place. National authority for environmental issues in Hungary is divided into several functional authorities, leading to fragmentation in policymaking. For example, standards for indoor air pollution and outdoor air pollution are set by different agencies.[37]

These implementation problems can be conceptualized as a "vertical disintegration of policy"[38]: governments in the region are woefully inexperienced at translating general commitments into specific tasks, and particularly at distinguishing costs and benefits of environmental vis-à-vis, for example, economic-oriented legislation. Moreover, whatever capacity for implementation has been developed over the past decade is threatened to be overwhelmed by the tremendous volume of laws these countries are required to adopt to prepare for accession to the EU: roughly 10,000 laws across all sectors. Finally, the past centralization of environmental decision-making has left today's local governments unprepared for adopting the responsibility of environmental enforcement, and left them understaffed as well. The EU has applied pressure to increase capacity, but compliance problems will continue to arise as a result of these already-routinized procedures.

It is not only the historical legacy of poor environmental enforcement that affects the countries of East Central Europe today. Public support for the environment has tapered off as the hardships of post-Communist life have set in, and EU pressure now is the primary driving force behind government prioritization of environmental policy. "Environmental problems are nowhere seen as a high priority and only remain on national policy agendas because of external pressure."[39] Here the "horizontal disintegration of policy" is of concern: "the ability of central government to involve important sectors of the public in policy discussions and, potentially, in mobilizing support for new initiatives."[40]

One important sector of the public is non-governmental environmental groups. Environmental groups are often credited with being visible and influential proponents of democracy in the late 1980s and the immediate period following 1989; they enjoyed broad support from the general public. Numerous analyses give environmental groups partial credit for bringing about the changes that brought down the Communist regimes.[41] By the early 1990s, though, the environmental movement splintered. Today, small, pragmatic, and professional organizations are much more the norm than large grassroots-supported campaigns. A major factor behind this change is increased funding from the EU, the United States, and Western foundations. These new organizations, which receive much of their funding from Western governments and non-governmental organizations, generally adopt a less confrontational attitude in their dealings with government officials than their predecessors.[42]

This shift may have serious implications for the ability of environmental groups to pressure the government to implement EU environmental legislation. In particular, Barbara Jancar-Webster, longtime analyst of environmental issues in Eastern Europe, sees an impoverishment of the political discourse, maintaining that "[t]he great weakness of the development of NGOs today is that they are organized, nurtured and sustained by the West in the name of democracy building. . ..Professionals who head the more successful NGOs risk alienating themselves from a public that no longer sees them as representatives of its interests, but rather as hierarchy and part of the power structure."[43] Moreover, the increased professionalism and pragmatism has not paid off in increased government influence. Whereas in the late 1980s, NGO influence derived largely from the ability to marshal crowds onto the streets, now NGOs neither command that ability nor are they permitted to play a role in setting the government's environmental agenda.[44]

Environmental groups may also resent the EU-driven agenda. In the past few years, the language of EU environmental assistance programs has shifted from "demand-driven" aid to "accession-driven." When Austria recently held the presidency of the EU, the Austrian Environment Minister stated that the countries of East Central Europe should give priority to environmental projects that are needed to fulfill *E U* legislative requirements, particularly environmental infrastructure, investments in drinking water and waste water installations, air pollution abatement and solid and hazardous waste management.[45] He notably did not refer to the specific needs or priorities of the countries themselves. At a meeting of environmental groups from both EU and potential member countries, the ECE environmentalists expressed concern that the EU was pushing the environmental approximation process too fast.[46]

Another important sector of the public is domestic producers. Domestic producers can play an important role in stimulating more stringent government regulation if it is to their competitive advantage. In Hungary at least, there is hope that industry will step in to fill this role. Environmental views among business executives and managers in Hungary to be "comparable" to views of business managers elsewhere—the implication is that Hungarian business executives are more advanced and progressive compared to businesspeople in other countries of East Central Europe. The Hungarian Chamber of Commerce, for instance, has created an environmental position to address environmental issues.[47]

In another study, industrial managers interviewed in the Czech Republic and Poland accepted the objective of overall harmonization with EU environmental policy as part of the process of integration with Europe.[48] At the very least these managers indicated that they do not become involved in systematic lobbying either for or against environmental issues, leading the study's author to conclude that policy making takes place "in a virtual political vacuum."[49] Another study conducted by the Regional Environment Center put hope in the role of industry: "Representatives of various businesses are among those who exert the most aggressive pressure to accelerate the approximation process in the environmental field,"[50] precisely because of competitiveness issues.

Yet the support among domestic producers for coming into compliance with EU law may in fact be threatened by actions on the part of the EU. Since the beginning of the ECE enlargement process, there has been a deep ambivalence within the EU over incorporating East Central European countries. The original mandate given by the European Council to the Commission excluded any reference to potential membership of ECE countries. While the East Europeans always viewed the Europe Agreements as a transitional instrument on the way to full membership, within the European Union there was disagreement over whether they were a long-term agreement in and of themselves. There are two major sets of concerns on the part of the EU: the first is about competitiveness of European industry in the face of cheaper labor; the second is about less stringent environmental standards. The Danish Environmental Protection Agency has warned of economic competitiveness costs to the EU if ECE countries are not required to come into full compliance by the time they accede.[51] This ambivalence could threaten the support among industrial producers in ECE countries for integration with the Union.

Industrial producers in ECE have some cause to be wary of EU trade concession promises. The original Association Agreements excluded agriculture, steel, and textiles—the areas where ECE countries have a comparative advantage—from trade concessions. They also included opt-out clauses for Western European countries.[52] In 1997, Polish environmentalists saw trade barriers behind an EU refusal to import fruit juice on the basis of impure standards.[53] Trade barriers and concerns about dumping continue to be part of the EU-ECE relationship.

Concerns within the EU about enlargement are not restricted to competitiveness, however. The Commission has openly acknowledged that the applicant countries will not be in full compliance with the environmental components of the *acquis* by the time they are admitted to the Union,[54] and the transition periods granted to the countries recognize this fact. Government and non-governmental actors are uneasy about the implications for the high level of environmental protection within the EU. A member of European Parliament worried that, while the political costs of leaving the ECE countries out are too high, there is a slippery slope in letting them in if they have not fully adopted the *acquis*.[55] Environmental groups have also joined in the chorus of caution: the European Environmental Bureau, an umbrella group, expressed concern that admitting the states without full compliance could slow down environmental progress in the EU.[56] EU environment ministers concurred, saying that no special exceptions should be allowed for clean up in the region.[57]

IMPLICATIONS

In order to consider the effect of legal integration on environmental policies, it is important to look beyond the words of an agreement and examine the forces for and against implementation. This is particularly true for countries with a poor record of implementation. Most countries have learned to adopt the language of aid agencies and international donors to obtain the funding they desire, but discerning whether actual commitments to programs are being made is considerably more difficult.

From the EU perspective, a gap between adoption and implementation of environmental laws in ECE may pose a challenge, both in terms of sabotaging current efforts to make the EU even "greener," and also in terms of EU producers who may face stricter compliance efforts, and thus higher compliance costs, than their ECE counterparts. The EU has paid particular attention to implementation problems in the accession process, but its focus appears to be primarily on government capacity. One way the EU has tried to monitor the deception gap is its twinning program, begun a few years ago. This sends member state civil servants to work with their bureaucratic equivalents in ECE. But it is unclear whether EU member states have made efforts to address other parts of the implementation equation, in particular the win-lose coalitions among domestic interest groups. How much does the deception gap matter to the EU? What, if any, are the EU's other options to close the deception gap, if it cannot team up with a domestic ally? Further research that might shed light on these questions involves the success of the less wealthy countries that are already members of the EU in implementing EU environmental law.

CONCLUSION

Convergence of standards is certainly happening in the case examined here; moreover, the convergence is towards the top. Poland, Hungary and the Czech Republic are eager to gain admission to the European Union and they will comply, at least on the face of it, with EU requirements. The deception gap poses a different question, though: will the convergence of standards be followed by implementation of those standards? Previous studies have found that coalitions of domestic producers and environmental groups, so-called "baptist-bootlegger" coalitions, are responsible for promoting higher standards, and elsewhere in this volume the "baptists alone" hypothesis is shown to result in higher standards. But the "baptists" of this case, the environmental groups, are lukewarm about the harmonization process; instead it is domestic producers who, in trying to orient themselves to the EU market, could be a force for closing the deception gap.[58] Thus the mechanism by which the deception gap might be closed is yet to be determined.

Diahanna Post is a Research Fellow at the Brookings Institution and a Ph.D. Candidate in Political Science at the University of California, Berkeley.

Notes
A previous version of this paper has been published in the *Journal of Environment and Development* 9:4 (December 2000). The author thanks David Vogel, Robert Kagan, Beth Simmons, Conor O'Dwyer, and two anonymous reviewers for helpful comments on the paper.

1. Susan Baker and Petr Jehlicka, "Dilemmas of Transition: The Environment, Democracy and Economic Reform in East Central Europe—an Introduction," *Environmental Politics* 7, no. Spring (1998).

2. European Commission, White Paper: Preparation of the Associated Countries of Central and Eastern Europe for Integration into the Internal Market of the Union (EU DG1A, December 1994 [cited 17 August 1999]); available from http://europa.eu.int/comm/enlargement/index.htm.

3. See, for example, Michael J. Baun, *A Wider Europe: The Process and Politics of European Union Enlargement* (Lanham, MD: Rowman & Littlefield Publishers, 2000).

4. Wade Jacoby, "Priest and Penitent: The European Union as a Force in the Domestic Politics of Eastern Europe," *East European Constitutional Review* 8, no. 1–2 (1999). The reference is to Grigori Potemkin's construction of fake villages to assure Russian Tsarina Catherine of her country's prosperity on a visit to the hinterlands.

5. See, for example, Miles Kahler, "Modeling Races to the Bottom" (paper presented at the American Political Science Association, Boston, September 3–6 1998); H. Jeffrey Leonard, *Pollution and the Struggle for the World Product* (Cambridge: Cambridge University Press, 1988); Debora Spar and David B. Yoffie, "A Race to the Bottom or Governance from the Top?," in *Coping with Globalization*, ed. Aseem Prakash and Jeffrey A. Hart (London: Routledge, 2000); and David Vogel, *Trading Up: Consumer and Environmental Regulation in a Global Economy* (Cambridge, MA: Harvard University Press, 1995).

6. The race to the bottom question has been recategorized by some, particularly within the debate on federal vs. state regulation of environment within the United States, as two questions: a question of laxity and a question of desirability. Revesz contends that a race towards laxity is desirable, and that environmental regulation is best left to states, which can set their own levels of protection according to their own preferences. See Richard L. Revesz, "Rehabilitating Interstate Competition: Rethinking the "Race-to-the-Bottom" Rationale for Federal Environmental Regulation," *New York University Law Review* 67 (1992). Swire and Esty, conversely, have argued that the race toward laxity is undesirable because of public choice and measurement problems. See Daniel C. Esty, "Revitalizing Environmental Federalism," *Michigan Law Review* 95, no. 3 (1996); and Peter P. Swire, "The Race to Laxity and the Race to Undesirability: Explaining Failures in Competition among Jurisdictions in Environmental Law," *Yale Law and Policy Review* 14, no. 2 (1996).

7. In particular, the costs of environmental regulations do not appear to be a major factor in firms' siting decisions Kahler, "Modeling Races to the Bottom"; and Leonard, *Pollution and the Struggle for the World Product.*.

8. These conditions assume a large domestic consumer market, which may not hold true for some ECE countries where large segments of the population

do not share in the economic recovery. See Swire, "The Race to Laxity and the Race to Undesirability: Explaining Failures in Competition among Jurisdictions in Environmental Law."

9. See, for example, Spar and Yoffie, "A Race to the Bottom or Governance from the Top?"; and Vogel, *Trading Up: Consumer and Environmental Regulation in a Global Economy*.. Vogel terms the environmental group-domestic producer alliance a "baptist-bootlegger" coalition, referring to the Prohibition era when zealous religious groups promoted prohibition for moral reasons, while bootleggers favored the same goal out of purely economic self-interest. In the environmental case, some producers may prefer similar standards across countries where they do business to low standards in some countries and high in others.

10. See Beth Simmons, "The International Politics of Harmonization: The Case of Capital Market Regulation," *International Organization* 55, no. 3 (2001).

11. I am grateful to an anonymous reviewer for pointing out that the EU also has reasons to be duplicitous and drag out the accession process as long as possible.

12. Jacoby, "Priest and Penitent: The European Union as a Force in the Domestic Politics of Eastern Europe."

13. Questions about who benefits more from relations with the EU—EU member states or the candidate countries—were either split between the two or drew a majority to answer that the EU benefitted more Central European Opinion Research Group Foundation, *Trends in EU, Czech, Hungarian, and Polish Public Opinion on Enlargement: Implications for EU Institutions and Industry. A Report to the European Parliament.* (17 October 2000 [cited November 13 2001]); available from http://www.ceorg-europe.org/brussel2k.html.

14. See, for instance, Paul Pierson, "The Path to European Integration: A Historical Institutionalist Analysis," *Comparative Political Studies* 29, no. 2 (1996).

15. Brian Slocock, "The Paradoxes of Environmental Policy in Eastern Europe: The Dynamics of Policy-Making in the Czech Republic," *Environmental Politics* 5, no. 3 (1996).

16. Michael Waller, "Geopolitics and the Environment in Eastern Europe," *Environmental Politics* 7, no. Spring (1998): 29–52; and Barbara Jancar-Webster, "Environmental Movement and Social Change in the Transition Countries," *Environmental Politics* 7, no. Spring (1998): 69–90.

17. Baker and Jehlicka, "Dilemmas of Transition", 19.

18. European Commission, *White Paper.*

19. European Commission, *Agenda 2000* (EU DG1A, 1997 [cited 16 July 1999]); available from http://europa.eu.int/comm/dg1a/enlarge/agenda2000_en.

20. European Commission, Accession Strategies for Environment: Meeting the Challenge of Enlargement with the Candidate Countries in Central and Eastern Europe Com (98)294 (1998 [cited 17 July 1999]); available from http://europa.eu.int/comm/dg11/docum/98294sm.htm.

21. See, for example, European Commission, *2000 Regular Report from the Commission on Poland's Progress Toward's Accession* (8 November 2000 [cited 8

November 2001]); available from http://europa.eu.int/comm/enlargement/ report_11_00/index.htm., p. 68.

22. Hertzman, *Environment and Health in Central and Eastern Europe*, Tables 3.10 and 3.11.

23. See OECD Environment Directorate, *Key Environmental Indicators* (2001 2001 [cited November 8 2001]); available from http://www.oecd.org.

24. Clyde Hertzman, Environment and Health in Central and Eastern Europe: A Report for the Environmental Action Programme for Central and Eastern Europe (Washington, DC: The World Bank, 1995), Table A5.1.

25. Cole disputes this, citing statistics which show that as Polish industrial production began to increase again in 1992, air pollutant emissions continued to decline. Daniel H. Cole, "Poland's Progress: Environmental Protection in a Period of Transition," 2 *Parker School Journal of East European Law 279* (1995).

26. European Commission, 1999 Regular Report from the Commission on Poland's Progress Toward's Accession; European Commission, 1999 Regular Report from the Commission on Hungary's Progress Toward's Accession; and European Commission, 1999 Regular Report from the Commission on Czech Republic's Progress Toward's Accession.

27. "Clean up or Clear out," *The Economist*, 11 December 1999: 47.

28. "Eastern European Transport 'Unsustainable'," *ENDS Environment Daily*, 14 November 1997.

29. O'Toole and Hanf, "Hungary: Political Transformation."

30. Jeffrey P. Cohn, "Central and Eastern Europe Aim to Protect Their Ecological Backbone: Western Conservationists Send Technical Aid," *BioScience* 42, no. 11 (1992).

31. Barbara Hicks, *Environmental Politics in Poland: A Social Movement between Regime and Opposition* (New York: Columbia University Press, 1996).

32. "NGOs Attack EU Biodiversity Failures," *ENDS Environment Daily*, 7 May 1998.

33. One reason for this was probably ideological, to show that Communist states had stronger environmental protection measures than capitalist ones.

34. See, e.g. O'Toole and Hanf, "Hungary: Political Transformation," 108.

35. Gyula Bandi, "Competence and Harmonization Problems in Hungary," 9 *Connecticut Journal of International Law 607* (1994).

36. Hicks, *Environmental Politics in Poland*.

37. O'Toole and Hanf, "Hungary: Political Transformation."

38. Ibid.

39. Barbara Jancar-Webster, "Environmental Movement and Social Change in the Transition Countries," *Environmental Politics* 7, no. Spring (1998): 76. In Poland, even optimistic observers note that the government has been much less interested in environmental protection since 1992, and that the desire to join the EU is now one of the main motivating forces behind governmental efforts at environmental protection. See, e.g., Cole, "Poland's Progress."

40. O'Toole and Hanf, "Hungary: Political Transformation," 108–9.

41. See, for example, Adam Fagin and Petr Jehlicka, "The Impact of EU Assistance on Czech Environmental Capacity since 1990" (paper presented at the Environmental Challenges of EU Eastern Enlargement, Florence, Italy, May

25–26 2001); and Andrew Tickle and Ian Welsh, eds., *Environment and Society in Eastern Europe* (Essex: Longman, 1998).

42. Waller, "Geopolitics."

43. Jancar-Webster, "Environmental Movement and Social Change," 88.

44. Fagin and Jehlicka, "Sustainable Development in the Czech Republic."

45. Interview with Martin Bartenstein, in European Commission, "Enlarging the Environment: Newsletter from the European Commission on Environmental Approximation," (DG XI, 1998).

46. "NGOs Debate EU Enlargement's Green Challenge," *ENDS Environment Daily*, 28 September 1999.

47. O'Toole and Hanf, "Hungary: Political Transformation."

48. Slocock, "The Paradoxes of Environmental Policy."

49. Ibid, 504.

50. Gyula Bandi and Stanislaw Wajda, "Approximation of European Union Environmental Legislation: Regional Overview," (Budapest: Regional Environmental Center, 1996).

51. "Denmark Warns on EU Enlargement," *ENDS Environment Daily*, 26 August 1997.

52. Janos Martonyi, "The Role and the Impact of the Association," in *Hungary: From Europe Agreement to a Member Status in the European Union*, ed. Ferenc Madl and Peter-Christian Mueller-Graff, European Community Studies Association—Europe (Baden-Baden, Germany: Nomos Verlagsgesellschaft, 1996); and David E. Madeo, "Environmental Contamination and World Trade Integration: The Case of the Czech Republic," *Law and Policy in International Business* 26, no. 3 (1995): 945–977.

53. "Woda zdrowa i bezpieczna?" *Biuletyn Polskiego Klubu Ekologicznego*, April 1997, 16.

54. "Environmental Impasse Feared on EU Enlargement," *ENDS Environment Daily*, 16 July 1997.

55. "EU Enlargement Plan 'Contradictory,' Says MEP," *ENDS Environment Daily*, 6 October 1997.

56. "Green Groups Warn of Risks of EU Enlargement," *ENDS Environment Daily*, 14 August 1997; also "NGOs Issue Austrian EU Presidency Demands," *ENDS Environment Daily*, 10 July 1998.

57. "'No Exceptions' for CEE Country Cleanup," *ENDS Environment Daily*, 20 July 1998; and "Accession Countries Warned on Environmental Rules," *ENDS Environment Daily*, 10 May 1999.

58. Beukel's work suggests that the interests of export-oriented and domestic market-oriented producers may differ on their support of enlargement. See Erik Beukel, "Trade Liberalization and Environmental Regulation: Regional Interests and Ideas in Europe and North America," in *Racing to Regionalize: Democracy, Capitalism, and Regional Political Economy*, ed. Kenneth P. Thomas and Mary Ann Tetreault, International Political Economy Yearbook (Boulder, CO: Lynne Rienner Publishers, 1999), 113–139.

Chapter 6

Environmental Management Standards and Globalization

Magali A. Delmas

I. INTRODUCTION

ISO 14001, released in 1996, is an Environmental Management System (EMS) that can be audited and certified. The development of ISO 14001 as an international standard for EMS is a clear consequence of globalization. The main rationale for the creation of ISO 14001 was that its worldwide acceptance should expedite international trade by harmonizing otherwise diffuse environmental management standards and by providing an internationally accepted blueprint for sustainable development, pollution prevention, and compliance assurance. ISO 14001 is therefore an example of the trading-up hypothesis where market forces are the drivers of increased environmental standards. This chapter analyzes the mechanisms of diffusion of ISO 14001 in Europe and in the United States.

ISO 14001 is an example of procedural harmonized standards where all nations should adopt similar environmental management systems and procedures. However the level of implementation of ISO 14001 differs across countries. In 1998, 52.4% of the 7,887 ISO 14001 certified facilities located in Western Europe and 37% in Asia. On the contrary, American companies, although ahead in many areas of environmental management, seem reluctant to adopt this voluntary standard. U.S. certified facilities accounted for only 3.7% of the total of ISO 14001 certified facilities in the world in 1998 (see Table 1).

ISO 14001 represents a case of a strict standard harmonization with continued divergence in the effectiveness of its implementation. I argue that the main factor that hampers the global diffusion of ISO 14001 is the persistence of national policy divergence in an increasingly globalized economy. This paper analyzes the economic, institutional and normative mechanisms that facilitate or hamper the global diffusion of ISO 14001. It describes in details the role that such factors play in the specific U.S. and European context.

Table 1. ISO 14001 certified facilities worldwide

Region	Country	Certified Facilities	% total
Western Europe		4136	52.4
	UK	921	11.7
	Austria	132	45.4
	Denmark	314	218.1
	Finland	206	70.8
	France	295	204.9
	Germany	651	8.3
	Ireland	96	33.0
	Italy	123	85.4
	Netherlands	341	4.3
	Spain	164	2.1
	Sweden	304	3.9
	Switzerland	360	4.6
	Other	229	2.9
Asia-Pacific		2917	37.0
	Japan	1542	19.6
	Korea	263	3.3
	Taiwan	203	2.6
	Australia	352	4.5
	Other	557	7.1
North America		434	5.5
	Canada	104	1.3
	USA	291	3.7
	Mexico	39	.05
Latin America		144	1.8
Africa/West Africa		138	1.7
Central And Eastern Europe		118	1.5
Total		7887	100.0

Source: International Standard Organization

An environmental management system (EMS) is one of the tools, which organizations can use to voluntary implement environmental policy. It consists of "a number of interrelated elements that function together to help a company manage, measure, and improve the environmental aspects of its operations."[1] However if each company designs its own system to meet its own particular needs, one can see that the resulting systems might differ widely among firms making it difficult to compare their results. To cope with this problem, industry associations have developed codes of practices and some countries have adopted national EMSs.[2] However, without a common international standard, companies would be forced to deal with dozens of separate and potentially incompatible EMSs for every country where they conduct business. This could potentially increase their cost and impose trade barriers.

The ISO 14001 series environmental management systems standards was introduced on the coattails of the success of ISO 9000, which is the series of quality management system standards. ISO 9000 has become a de facto requirement for doing business in many industries.[3] The total number of certifications worldwide has passed 250,000 in 1999. ISO 14001 was created with the idea that it would also become a prerequisite for firms to conduct their business globally.

However, it is not clear how far the internationalization of standardized environmental management systems can go as specific cultural, institutional and organizational issues might hamper the global diffusion of such a standard. These concerns might be more acute for environmental standards as firms might identify regulatory violations during the implementation of the environmental certification. The adoption of the standard might thus be associated with high transaction costs if regulatory agencies were to use such information against firms.

ISO 14001 is voluntary but not free and firms will invest in ISO 14001 if they perceive that it enhances their environmental performance as well as facilitate their business in specific markets. In this chapter, I analyze the characteristics of the institutional environment that favor or discourage the adoption of ISO 14001. I argue that the standard will be adopted in context where regulatory agencies along with stakeholders push for its development. When regulatory agencies provide some guidance for its adoption as well as show some regulatory flexibility to adopting firms, there are more incentives to adoption than in context where regulatory agencies pay little attention to the standard or when there are potential liabilities issues linked to the adoption of ISO 14001. Furthermore, firms will have higher incentives to adopt in context where stakeholders such as distributors, customers, and insurance companies recognize the value of the standard.

European companies benefited from a strong regulatory commitment through the Environmental and Management Eco-Audit Scheme (EMAS) which was a regulation issued by the European Commission to favor the development of a European Environmental Management Standard. This regulatory push favored the development of competencies and environmental resources that privileged the development of environmental management practices among European companies. The analysis is based on a telephone survey of European firms that was conducted for the EMAS assessment by the European Commission.

In contrast American companies, although ahead in many areas of environmental management, seem reluctant to adopt this voluntary standard. This could be linked to American Institutional factors that might impede the diffusion of ISO 14001 in the United States. The analysis is supported by primary data collected from a questionnaire mailed to a representative sample of ISO 14001 certified facilities in the United States.

II. ISO TO REDUCE NON-TARIFF TRADE BARRIERS?

Since 1990 there have been efforts at the national level, within the European Union and at the international level to standardize EMSs by defining the essential elements which such a system should contain. EMS standards such as the British Standard BS 7750 [4], the European Union (EU) Eco-Management and Audit Scheme (EMAS)[5] have been developed to provide organizations with a standardized framework that would allow them to implement an EMS. The international standard ISO 14001 issued in 1996 is more ambitious as it is intended to remove non-tariff barriers to trade linked to environmental practices and to level the international playing field in terms of EMS standard. The development of the ISO 14000 Series was stimulated by two important agreements: the Rio Agreement (1992) and the GATT Uruguay Round Ministerial Decision on Trade and the Environment (1994).

The Global Environmental Initiative in Rio de Janeiro in 1992 was an essential step in the formation of ISO 14000.[6] Over one hundred of the countries attending the United Nations Conference on Environment and Development (UNCED) committed to improving international environmental management programs and petitioned the International Standardization Organization to adopt this cause.

The Uruguay Round Ministerial Decision on Trade and the Environment established a committee in 1994 under the World Trade Organization (WTO) to harmonize environmental and trade policy based on two key factors: (i)"identifying trade and environmental policy linkages to promote sustainable development" and (ii)"avoiding protectionist measures while promoting [the] environmental objective agreed to at the [UNCED]".[7]

On the heels of ISO 9000's success,[8] the International Standard Organization (ISO)[9] responded to the demands to address the field of environmental law and pollution. ISO responded by establishing the Strategic Advisory Group on the Environment (SAGE) to determine whether an international environmental management standard could "promote a common approach to environmental management, enhance an organization's ability to attain and measure improvements in environmental performance, and facilitate trade and remove trade barriers."[10] SAGE assessed the need for an international EMS standard that would encourage responsible environmental management without violating GATT. As a result, Technical Committee 207 (TC 207) was formed in 1993 to develop the ISO 14000 Series.

In September 1996, ISO issued the first edition of the ISO 14000 Series, a set of guidelines for developing systems and practices in six environmental sectors. The Series was divided into six sections, each containing one or more standards:

- ISO standards 14001 and 14004—Environmental Management Systems
- ISO standards 14010 to 14012—Environmental Auditing
- ISO standards 14020 to 14025—Environmental Labeling
- ISO standard 14031—Environmental Performance Evaluation
- ISO standards 14040 to 14043—Life Cycle Assessment
- ISO standard 14060—Environmental Aspects in Product Standards

The first and only edition that was published in 1996 focused on the EMS standard ISO 14001 and the Environmental Auditing standards (ISO 14010—14012)[11].

ISO 14001 is the only certifiable standard in the ISO 14000 Series. All other standards in the Series describe supporting functions, which serve to maximize the effectiveness of the ISO 14001 EMS. However, the implementation of these supporting standards is not required for ISO 14001 certification.

There are five requirements of ISO 14001: formation of a corporate environmental policy and commitment to an EMS, development of a plan for implementation, implementation and operation of the EMS, monitoring and possible corrective action, and top management review and continual improvement.

Worldwide acceptance and incorporation of ISO 14001 should expedite international trade by harmonizing otherwise diffuse environmental management standards and by providing an internationally accepted blueprint for sustainable development, pollution prevention, and compliance assurance. However, if ISO 14001 is implemented unevenly across countries, there is a danger that ISO 14001 may itself serve as a barrier to trade, especially if it promotes preferential selection of certified companies over non-certified ones.

III. WHICH INSTITUTIONAL ENVIRONMENT IS APPROPRIATE FOR ISO 14001?

The institutional environment is an essential influencing factor for firms, as it creates not only the rules of the game but also the market for environmental products and services. [12]

ISO 14001 requires firms to provide information to the certification body that they may consider as 'sensitive'. Once the firm has disclosed this information to the certification body, it cannot take it back. Furthermore, ISO 14001 certification can have potential legal consequences in terms of confidentiality and discoverability. Indeed, the development of the written EMS documentation, identification of regulatory compliance requirements and third party access to sensitive materials, might have legal impacts.

The legal issue that many companies struggle with, and that in some cases could discourage them from implementing ISO 14001, is the potential discovery of regulatory violations that firms had not yet identified or resolved. ISO 14001 inadvertently leads to the discovery of non-compliance with applicable environmental regulations. While compliance with environmental laws and regulations should theoretically be considered a benefit of implementing ISO 14001, the identification of violations during the implementation phase or self- or third party audits can lead to potential liabilities. The violated regulations may involve strict liability (intent or negligence need not be shown) and/or the duty to disclose violations. [13]

Another potential risk of legal liability is that ISO 14001 requires companies to document the details of environmental aspects of their operations that are not related to regulatory compliance in order to track the effectiveness of the system. Audits conducted under ISO 14001 check these documents and may point out weaknesses in the company's handling of environmental matters such as records of system failures and minor spills. These findings, while they may not be governed by any regulations might still be used in legal proceedings as incriminating evidence. Thus, if a company adopts an EMS with a written policy statement on environmental matters which specified targets and objectives, it may also be defining a standard under which it may be held accountable.[14]

IV. ISO 14001 AND THE SEARCH FOR A COMPETITIVE ADVANTAGE

An EMS standard like ISO 14001 can be identified as an intangible resource or a capability since it refers to the organization's set of skills linked to environmental management.[15] The ability to integrate the natural environment into the strategic planning process could potentially offers a firm the opportunity to develop a valuable capability that could be transformed into a competitive advantage. [16]

At present if is not clear how firms can create value by adopting ISO 14001. The standard itself is an intangible resource or capability and can be regarded as more a process standard than a product standard. ISO 14001 certification is therefore not a label that would signal to the market how a product has been produced with environmental sensitivity.[17] This discussion is complicated by the fact that consumers might not identify or understand the advantages of ISO 14001, as the standard does not provide any real measure of environmental performance. Although ISO 14001 requires an organization to measure and track its environmental performance, there are no adopted or commonly accepted Environmental Performance Indicators. Section 4.5.1 of ISO 14001 requires an organization to have procedures to "monitor and measure, on a regular basis, the key characteristics of its operations and activities that can have a significant impact on the environment" as part of the checking and corrective action portion of its EMS. [18] Furthermore, the standard does not establish absolute requirements for environmental performance other than a commitment to compliance with applicable regulations, and it does not identify environmental performance as a factor in the actual certification process.

Due to this lack of definition of precise environmental variables for monitoring purposes, the resulting data may not provide companies, policy-makers, and the public with accurate information they can use to make comparative judgements about organizational environmental performance issues. It is therefore very difficult for consumers to put a value on this resource.

If not a direct signal to customers, ISO 14001 could also signal to other stakeholders such as investors that the management of a certified firm is environmentally sound. The expanding nature of environmental risks and liabilities has led investment and insurance groups to require more thoughtful environmental analysis in the preparatory stages of a transaction. Companies with pollution prevention programs and EMSs like ISO 14001 should be far more attractive risks to insurance underwriters and could gain better rates. However, the difficulty in assessing environmental performance might also be a problem for these stakeholders since they lack tangible elements on which to base their analysis of a firm's environmental performance.

If ISO 14001 is adopted by many firms in one market, and if firms require their suppliers to be ISO 14001 certified, it is clear that the standard will become a requirement for any and all firms wishing to access this market. Certification will function as a barrier hampering a non-certified firm's entry into the market. For example, the large diffusion of environmental management standards such as BS 5570 or EMAS in some sectors of European countries might be a real obstacle to the entry of foreign firms into the European market. Since ISO 14001 is supposed to be applicable on a global scale, it seems obvious that firms wishing to enter such a market would have incentives to obtain ISO 14001 certification.

Although ISO 14001 is open to any company that wishes to invest in obtaining the certification, there is a learning experience curve at the sector or even institutional level that might facilitate the adoption of the certification. It is thus easier for a firm in a particular industry to obtain certification in an environment where other firms in that same industry have already been certified. Since the standard does not offer much guidance, it is important that firms be able to benefit from the experience of other firms in the same sector or from consulting companies which have a proven experience of certification in that sector. In an environment where many firms within the same industry have been certified, the development of knowledgeable consulting companies will be useful for firms in search of certification. In such a context, a certification organization might also be available. ISO 14001 might therefore be a resource difficult to acquire for those firms, which do not benefit from an environment where other similar firms have already had experience with the certification procedure. ISO 14001 is clearly derived from ISO 9000, which is the standard for total quality management. Firms that know how to deal with ISO 9000 should be more inclined to obtain ISO 14001 certification.

In particular, since the standard does not present "tangible" results regarding improvement of a firm's environmental performance, it is necessary that all stakeholders believe in the benefits of ISO 14001 standardization and make a commitment to promote it.[19] Only in this way can firms transform certification into a competitive advantage. Furthermore firms would be more likely to pursue certification if they belong to a sector where process manufacturing as well as pollution prevention are core components of business advantage.

It seems likely that firms would also pursue ISO 14001 certification if they were willing to enter countries where certification was a requirement. Certification would then be similar to, and would function as, a barrier to trade. ISO 14001 could provide a competitive advantage to firms within a given country since it is a resource that is difficult for firms located outside of the country to imitate.

V. THE DEVELOPMENT OF ISO 14001 IN EUROPE

The situation of Europe differs from the one in Asia and in the United States as ISO 14001 could grow on the ground of existing Environmental Management Standards (EMSs). The British BS 7750 and the European EMAS were the first EMSs implemented in the world. This provided Europe with a lead advantage and some experience to build on when ISO 14001 was put into place. Furthermore, EMAS, the European standard developed by the European Commission benefited from a strong support by European authorities that promoted his diffusion into European firms. These two elements, experience and regulatory promotion of the standard would provide a favorable ground to the development of ISO 14001 in Europe by limiting transaction costs associated with the adoption of the standard and favoring the development of potential firm level competitive advantage.

In the course of the assessment of the implementation of EMAS in 1997, a survey was conducted with competent bodies, accreditation bodies, accreditation environmental verifiers (AEV) and EMAS registered sites in the 15 Member States.[20] This part builds on the results of the survey. I first explain how the institutional environment

showed credible commitment to the promotion of the standard there-
fore reducing the costs of acquiring the standard. Second, I show how
EMAS and BS 7750 provided the enough past experience on which
European firms could build to facilitate their certification process.

The threat of a mandatory EMS

It is in the UK, in 1992, that the world's first environmental standard -
BS 7750- was published in March 1992. The standard was subjected to a
2-year pilot implementation program involving almost 500 participants, and was modified on the basis of the feedback obtained from
the program. The modified standard was published in January 1994.

At the same time that the British Standard Institute (BSI) began
work on BS 7750, the European Commission was setting out its
proposal for an eco-audit scheme: the Environmental Management and
Audit Scheme (EMAS). EMAS was adopted by the Council of
Ministers on June 29, 1993. [21] Because EMAS is a regulation, rather than
a directive, it immediately binds all EU Member States. [22]

The European Commission originally intended to pursue
mandatory participation but business lobbying successfully prevented
this. The European Commission did, however, retain the right to adopt
compulsory registration in future, adding power to the legislative
impetus towards environmental audit.[23] The European Commission
also at first required an annual auditing which was changed to a
requirement that the audit will be executed at intervals no longer than
three years.

The EMAS regulation requires the European Commission to review
the progress of the EMAS no more than five years after adoption. Because the original EMAS proposal contemplated a mandatory scheme,
the scheduled renewal in 1999 could result in a mandatory scheme.

The perceived threat of EMAS becoming a mandatory scheme was
also intensified by the choice of "competent certification bodies" that
could be linked to Member States environmental ministries. For
example, in France the choice of competent body has been the cause of
much anxiety in industry with the close link between the inspection
authority (regulator) and competent body leading to concern over
possible increased control of industrial sites, which in turn has raised
the issue of the voluntary nature of EMAS. Therefore in France EMAS
was perceived as a first step to a mandatory standard.

The important difference between EMAS and BS 7750 is that the
later does not have the former's commitment to the publication of

audit findings regarding environmental performance, a disclosure with which companies are often uncomfortable. It has been suggested that BS 7750 would serve to introduce companies to the techniques, allowing them to cut their teeth on the less publicly scrutinized standards of BS 7750 before moving on to EMAS. The similarity between the two schemes should therefore encourage companies to set up an environmental management system and assess their progress before taking the key step to publication of performance.[24]

The early availability of competing national environmental management standards such as BS7750 (which were withdrawn and replaced by ISO 14001 in countries such as the UK) when the EMAS scheme was launched April 1995 is one factor contributing to the current success of ISO 14001.

In brief, in Europe, firms could have been adopting ISO 14001 under the pressure that the European Commission would issue a mandatory environmental management scheme with environmental performance measures. In addition, EMSs in Europe benefited from a strong promotion by competent bodies, which were also granted some regulatory flexibility to EMSs' certified companies.

Promotion of EMAS and regulatory flexibility

According to interviews of EMAS competent bodies conducted in 1997, there have been several measures to inform companies of the requirements of EMAS. Conferences, seminar, brochures, and guidelines were the methods most frequently used by Member States to inform companies of the requirements of EMAS.[25] Six Member States could quantify the financial budget allocated to promote the participation of small and medium companies. The amount was of ECU 35.1 million since 1995 (approximately $34 millions).[26]

Furthermore, in some Member States regulatory flexibility was granted to EMAS certified firms. For example, German authorities have begun to ease administrative enforcement requirements on EMAS certified sites. In the heavily regulated German Länd of Bavaria many industrial sites sought EMAS registration after it was indicated that the environmental regulatory regime would be reduced for EMAS registered sites, this in fact has yet to happen. Within Germany, a political decision was also made to try and keep the competent body for the scheme as close as possible to business. The result was that rather than having one centralized competent body, 44 Chambers of Industry and Commerce and 21 Chambers of Skilled Craftsman were designated as EMAS competent bodies.

In conclusion, in Europe, EMAS was granted a high regulatory credibility and flexibility. Under the threat of a potential mandatory EMAS, firms could use ISO 14001 as a way to learn how to become EMAS certified. This was further facilitated by the increasing compatibility between EMAS and ISO 14001 that was implemented in the revision of EMAS in 1997.

Compatibility of EMAS and ISO 14001

As a result of the European Commission "Decisions on the recognition of ISO14001 and certification procedures for use with the EMAS Regulation", it is now possible for verifiers to avoid duplication of effort when firms seek both EMAS and ISO 14001 certifications. [27]

Although EMAS continues to differ from ISO 14001 in its depth and demand with regard to commitment, transparency and environmental performance, the structure of the environmental management system is to be analogous to the structure detailed in the ISO 14001 standard.

Already in 1997, of the 140 EMAS certified sites that were part of the above-mentioned survey, 47% were also ISO 14001 certified.[28] Only 15% of registered sites of small sized enterprises were not certified ISO 14001. Of the 66 registered sites certified ISO 14001, over a third (38%) had achieved ISO 14001 after EMAS verification and 36% at the same time as EMAS verification.[29] The majority (92%) of the 66 registered sites certified ISO 14001 had their ISO 14001 certification undertaken by the same organization that undertook their EMAS site's verification.[30]

Since there is a high correlation between EMAS and ISO 14001 certification it is valuable to use the results of the survey of EMAS certified facilities to understand the behavior of ISO 14001 certified facilities in Europe. We will look at several aspects of EMS certification. The first one refers to the time to get certification; the second one refers to stakeholder involvement and the third one to the competitive advantage gained through EMS certification.

Time to get EMS certification

EU regulatory credibility also favored the development of certification bodies or "verifiers" and also of the initiation of a market for consulting companies. These elements facilitated the ease of the adoption of EMAS and subsequently ISO 14001 for European firms. Indeed consulting firms knowing the commitment of the European

Commission to promote the standard could invest in consulting services to help firms adopt the standard. This would then reduce firms' costs to get certification as they could rely on a market of consulting firms. In 1997, 254 verifiers have been accredited in 10 Members States, of which 72 (28%) are organizations (as opposed to individuals). Out of the 72 organizations verifiers, 57 (79%) are also certifiers to ISO 14001.[31]

It is however difficult to assess the real cost for EMAS facilities to get certification. The only measures we could gather concern the time firms take to get EMAS certification. 64% of registered sites with EMAS take more than 10 months to implement EMAS.[32] The elements of the certification process that took the most time were the "environmental management system" (39%) and the "environmental review" (29%).[33] Firms that were seeking EMAS and ISO 14001 certification conjointly would take more time to get EMAS certification than firms that were seeking EMAS certification only. However this decreased for the year 1997 with the implementation of the recognition of ISO 14001 in EMAS certification procedures.

Stakeholder involvement

EMAS has more obligations than ISO 14001. It requires firms to provide an "Environmental Statement" that can be disclosed to the public. The Environmental statement is widely distributed. The majority of all registered sites (88%) distribute over 100 and 499 copies of their environmental statement.[34] This figure increases to 94% for large sized enterprises. 45% of all registered sites have had more than 100 of their environmental statement specifically requested. Therefore unlike ISO 14001, EMAS encompasses a public document on the environmental performance of the firm. Firms can use this as a tool to promote their environmental management to stakeholder.

Indeed, all registered sites viewed customers (60%) and the local community to the site (44%) as the main audiences for their sites environmental statement.[35] 60% of all registered sites viewed the environmental statement as a useful communication tool with their stakeholders.[36]

There is therefore a difference between ISO 14001 and EMAS in terms of measurement and diffusion of environmental performance. Firms can use the Environmental Statement to communicate with stakeholders on their environmental policy.

Competitive advantage

In Europe, the European Commission and Member States Ministries promoted EMSs. It is therefore interesting to see how the "market" for environmental standard developed. The survey of EMAS certified facilities provides some responses on how firms perceive the advantages of EMAS. The top three benefits cited by all registered sites were "cost savings" (31%), "better image" (29%) and "improved employee moral" (26%).[37] "Competitive advantage" would be important for only 11% of certified facilities at the same level of "assured regulatory compliance" (11%). In addition to an efficiency rationale, EU firms are seeking to establish good relationships with their stakeholders rather than just seeking a competitive advantage.

In conclusion, European firms responded to a regulatory pressure that favored the development of an Environmental Management Standard. The European institutional environment reduced the potential search and information costs linked to EMAS certification. Furthermore, it facilitated the development of a certification system with "verifiers" and consulting companies. This eased the certification process. Furthermore EMAS with its required "environmental statement" provided a clear and positive signal to stakeholders concerning firms' commitment to improvements in environmental performance. Firms could then use EMAS as a communication tool to improve their relations with stakeholders.

Since ISO 14001 is easier to implement than EMAS, it might be perceived as a good way to get prepared to a potential "mandatory" environmental management standard that could be installed by the European Commission. Furthermore, ISO 14001 with its international dimension provides also economies of scale and may facilitate market entry for multinational companies. Therefore, in Europe, firms could perceive that the benefits of getting ISO 14001 would outweigh its transaction costs.

VI. FIRMS' INCENTIVES TO OBTAIN CERTIFICATION IN THE U.S.

The case of the United States differs strongly from the European one, as there was no previous environmental management standard in place previous to ISO 14001. The U.S. is marked by a very sophisticated command and control system of regulations in which ISO 14001 has difficulty to find a place. Furthermore the adversarial culture between the industry and the regulatory agency does not favor the development of collaborative regulatory schemes.

The number of U.S. certified facilities is low compared to European countries. With 291 certified facilities representing 90 firms in 1998, the United States lagged behind 9 other countries (United Kingdom, Germany, Sweden, Netherlands, Switzerland, Denmark, Japan, France, Australia) (See Table 1.). Within the U.S., many ISO 14001 certification decisions were made by non-U.S. firms. 30.8% of certified firms had their headquarters outside the United States. Of the foreign multinationals that had certified their facilities, the largest percentages were from Japan (19.2%) and the European Union (9.6%).[38] This raises the question of whether there are specific characteristics of the U.S. environment that deter U.S. firms from seeking certification.

To evaluate the drivers and barriers to the implementation of ISO 14001 in the United States, a questionnaire was mailed to 152 U.S. certified companies. Of the 152 questionnaires mailed, a total of 55 responses were received by February 15th, 1999. The responses represent 36% of those surveyed, as well as over 30% of the 200 U.S. ISO 14001 certified firms identified in the Globus International Database as of November 1998. [39] The questionnaire asked managers to state the importance of several factors that led to their decision to become ISO 14001 certified. Two of the questions from the survey were selected for analysis in this chapter. The first question concerns the incentives for a firm to adopt ISO 14001. The second question pertains to the constraints associated with the implementation of ISO 14001 certification.

ISO 14001 and the U.S. institutional environment

Concerning the regulatory framework either favoring or discouraging the adoption of ISO 14001, the variables considered in the survey were: "greater permit flexibility," "revised approach to regulatory inspections," "fewer regulatory fines," and "decreased permit costs." These variables were rated from not important (1) to very important (5). A high majority of firms did not consider these factors to be important incentives to their decision to become ISO 14001 certified. More than seventy-six percent (76%) of the firms in our sample considered "greater permit flexibility" not to be a very important factor in their decision to apply for ISO 14001 certification. Likewise, seventy seven percent (77%) of the firms said that "revised approach to regulation inspections" was not very important; seventy six percent (76%) said the same for "greater permit flexibility"; seventy three percent (73%) for "fewer regulatory fines"; and eighty five percent (85%) for "decreased permit costs" (see Table 2.). According to this survey, it seems clear that the institutional set-up does not provide any incentive for U.S. firms to adopt the standard. In fact, the institutional set-up seems a constraint that hampers firms from adopting the standard.

Table 2. Incentives to ISO certification

	Not important to important (1-3)	Quite important to very important (4-5)
	%	%
Improved management of environmental impacts	28	72
Public demonstration of environmental stewardship	34	66
Reduced pollution	38	62
Reduced environmental risk	38	62
Increased competitive advantage	38	62
Improved compliance with government regulations	45	55
Greater market share	46	54
Improved regulatory compliance	49	51
Increased international trade opportunities	49	51
Improved internal communication among managers	53	47
Access to new markets	57	43
Marketing/Advertising opportunity	57	43
Communication with the community	60	40
Increased shareholder value	64	36
Customer requirement	68	32
Fewer regulatory fines	73	27
Greater permit flexibility	76	24
Revised approach to regulatory inspections	77	23
Decreased insurance costs	85	15
Decreased permit costs	85	15
Greater access to capital	87	13
Buyer requirement	90	10
Lender requirement	94	6
Valid N (list) 53 observations		

In contrast, the variables which represent regulatory constraints, "uncertainty with regulatory agencies' utilization of EMS audit information", and "potential legal penalties from voluntary disclosure", are considered to be important by firms. The five-point scale ranged from "not a constraint" (1) to "a very serious constraint" (5). Sixty two percent (62%) of surveyed firms considered "uncertainty with regulatory agencies' utilization of EMS audit information" to be a constraint. Likewise, sixty percent (60%) indicated that the "potential legal penalties from voluntary disclosure" and sixty nine percent (69%) that the "lack of regulatory flexibility" were also a constraint (see Table 3.).

Table 3. Constraints to the adoption of ISO 14001

	Mild to serious constraint (1-4)	Not a constraint (5)
	%	%
Lack of top management support	77	23
Design costs of ISO 14001 EMS	75	25
Lack of regulatory flexibility	69	31
Registration costs	67	33
Lack of understanding of ISO requirements	67	33
Annual costs of maintaining an ISO 14001 EMS	67	33
Lack of time to implement a quality EMS	65	35
Uncertainty with regulatory agencies' utilization of EMS audit information	62	38
Potential legal penalties from voluntary disclosure	60	40
Lack of personnel to implement/manage EMS	58	42
Valid N (list) 52 observations		

ISO 14001 and the search for a competitive Advantage

It is clear from the survey that, in the U.S. at least, whether or not ISO 14001 is adopted, is not related to stakeholders' requirements. A vast majority of firms considered various stakeholders as non-important incentives in seeking certification: "increased shareholder value" accounting for sixty four percent (64%); "customer requirement" accounting for sixty-eight percent (68%); "buyer requirement" accounting for ninety-percent (90%); and "lender requirement" accounting for ninety-four percent (94%) (See Table 2.). Very few U.S. companies at present require that their suppliers be ISO 14001 certified. IBM is one of the few in this case which might explain the high rate of certification in the electronics industry.[40]

According to the survey results, ISO 14001 certification is better used as a public demonstration of environmental stewardship. Sixty six percent (66%) of the firms in our sample consider "public demonstration of environmental stewardship" as an important reason to get ISO 14001 certification. However, "communication with community" and "marketing/advertising opportunity" are less important for firms as incentives in seeking certification accounting for only forty percent (46%) and forty three percent (43%), respectively (See Table 2.)

One of the main incentives to get ISO 14001 originates from the need to access markets where ISO 14001 is a requirement. The variables representing the potential to gain a competitive advantage from the adoption of ISO 14001 are all considered by the majority of managers as important reasons to seek certification: "increased international trade opportunities" accounting for fifty one percent (51%), "increased competitive advantage" accounting for sixty two percent (62%), and "greater market share" accounting for fifty four percent (54%) (See Table 2.). These results indicate that firms believe that there is a positive link between the adoption of ISO 14000 and the gaining of business advantages.

In conclusion, our results show that:

- Firms that get certified are mostly multinationals with experience in dealing with management standards.
- Firms believe that the U.S. institutional set-up does not facilitate the adoption of ISO 14001 and might even be a constraint to its implementation.
- There is neither demand, nor involvement from U.S. stakeholders to push firms to adopt the standard. U.S.
- Managers do believe that the adoption of the ISO 14001 standard will improve their environmental performance. However, since U.S. stakeholders do not value the standard, it is mainly used to demonstrate environmental stewardship to the public and to increase trade opportunities.

VII. DISCUSSION

In a competitive market in which a contract loss due to non-compliance could irreparably damage the prestige and finances of a company, ISO 14001 offers an organized approach to managing environmental issues. Using this approach, a company can potentially cut environment-related costs and increase profits in a variety of ways.

However, the process of acquiring ISO 14001 certification might be costly if there is uncertainty about regulatory agency commitment to the standard. An EMS audit under ISO 14001 may reveal not only procedural defects, but also environmental performance problems including noncompliance with existing command and control regulations. If companies are required to disclose this information to appropriate enforcement authorities as part of the certification process, and if these authorities do not commit to interpreting these audits in a positive way, then there will be resulting transaction costs for certified companies. These additional costs are potentially a major obstacle to the initiation of ISO 14001 certification.

The European context seems to provide an appropriate ground for the development of EMS standards. The Institutional environment, the European Commission, has been at the origin of the development of EMAS in conjunction with industry. Cultural elements in Europe such as good quality relationship between regulatory agencies and industry have mitigated firms' fears of transaction costs linked to the adoption of the EMS certification.

The lack of cooperation between industry and regulatory agencies in the U.S. most likely accounts for the slow pace of adoption of ISO 14001. The standard stipulates that audit findings from internal or external audits be documented in a detailed written audit report. In the U.S. context, firms might fear that these audit reports would become the new "smoking gun" of environmental litigation. Indeed, it is not clear how corporations would be able to protect the confidentiality of audit reports and other documents solely through the attorney-client privilege and the attorney work product doctrine, which are the two traditional legal privileges that grant confidentiality.[41]

Furthermore the cost of designing and implementing an EMS might be high in an environment where there is little experience to build on within the industry as well as few consulting companies. We have described how the development of the certification scheme for EMAS in Europe favored such experience and facilitated the certification process for firms.

The experience of the firm in dealing with management standards is also important. The time and cost for implementing ISO 14001 depends on whether a site has a functioning ISO 9000 Quality Management System to build on, whether it has implemented Responsible Care (Pollution Prevention, Community Awareness and Emergency Response and Process Safety programs) and if it has systems in place to maintain compliance with state and federal regulations. European firms are well ahead their American counterparts in terms of the adoption of ISO 9000 standard. [42] This might also be one of the element explaining the difference between the two continents in the difficulty of the implementation of ISO 14001 in the U.S.

Although commitment to improved environmental performance and compliance with existing command and control regulations are prerequisites to ISO 14001 certification, the ISO 14001 standard does not provide any real measure of environmental performance. It is therefore difficult for stakeholders to assess the value of such a standard. Furthermore, since ISO 14001 is a process standard and is not linked to any eco-labeling standard, it does not send a clear signal to customers regarding a firm's environmental improvements. In addition, as the standard is not linked to any life cycle analysis it might not encourage a firm to actively research innovative and lucrative solutions to environmentally sensitive components of the production process. However, ISO 14001 is a resource that might allow a firm to penetrate foreign markets where EMS standards are already requirements.

The survey of U.S. certified firms supported these propositions. Firms seem to perceive that American regulatory institutions do not provide enough regulatory flexibility to allow the smooth development of ISO 14001. Stakeholder pressures to push the adoption of the standard are still weak. The data indicate that firms are using the certification more to increase trade opportunities than to obtain a competitive advantage within their own market. In conclusion, it is not clear in the United States whether the competitive advantage gained from the adoption of the ISO 14001 standard offsets its potential associated transaction costs.

This paper has compared the diffusion of ISO 14001 in Europe and in the United States. It would be very interesting to compare these cases to the Asian context in which the diffusion of ISO 14001 seems quite rapid. Like in Europe, Asian regulatory agencies have actively pushed the development of ISO 14001. Many Asian countries have government funded ISO 14001 support programs already in place and some of them are hoping that in the long run, an ISO 14000 system will assist them in monitoring industry. [43]

VIII. CONCLUSION
Spearheaded by the International Organization for Standardization,

with the participation of 50 of its 111 member nations, ISO 14001 is a voluntary environmental management and procedural standard. However the implementation of ISO 14001 is not even between countries as there is continual divergence in the effectiveness of its implementation. This paper has described the economic, institutional and normative mechanisms that are favoring or discouraging the diffusion of ISO 14001 in specific national contexts.

Since ISO 14001 is voluntary, firms will seek certification if the potential transaction costs of acquiring the certification are offset by the advantages the certification will ultimately provide to the firm. This chapter has analyzed how a specific institutional context can impact firm's incentives to adopt an EMS standard. The role of regulatory agencies is key to reduce the costs that are linked to firms seeking certification. I have shown how European governments have been providing assistance to firms seeking certification. Furthermore, since the standard does not present tangible results of actual improvement of environmental performance to a firm's stakeholders, it is therefore necessary that all stakeholders believe in the benefits of the ISO 14001 standardization and promote it. With such a demand from stakeholders firms are more likely to transform certification into a potential competitive advantage. In conclusion, without the support of regulatory agencies, the dynamics of market or competitive forces alone may not be sufficient drivers to promote the diffusion of ISO 14001 and guaranty the convergence of voluntary environmental standards.

It seems that ISO 14001 are more likely to be adopted when government believe in the competitive advantage that their firms will gain out of ISO 14001 certification. Regulatory agencies by setting up a system that facilitates the adoption of ISO 14001, provide the ground for their firm to be ahead of competition in "lagger" countries. This is the case of some Asian and European countries where regulatory agencies compete for the adoption of a standard that might create barriers to trade for their industry.[44] This is consistent with the trading-up hypothesis developed by Vogel.[45] Such competitiveness rationale can promote a race to the top concerning voluntary environmental standard.

Apparently this incentive was not present in the US. U.S. firms seem quite hesitant to enter this race, as the EPA does not facilitate the development of the standard. Firms are therefore reluctant to adopt a standard, which does not provide much benefits on their national market. U.S. ISO 14001 certified companies are mostly multinational companies operating on European and Asian markets. There is still some skepticism in the U.S. with regards to self-regulation which might be seen as a legitimate instrument. As ISO 14001 is diffusing rapidly in other countries it is not clear how long U.S. regulatory agencies will be able to resist the trend.

Magali A. Delmas is an Assistant Professor at the Donald Bren School of Environmental Science and Management, University of California, Santa Barbara.

Notes

1. Welford, R., ed. 1996. Corporate Environmental Management, Systems and Strategies. London: Earthscan. P. 61

2. Examples of Industry codes of practice are the US Chemical Management Association's Responsible Care program; the Global Environmental Management Initiative (GEMI), the Environmental Self Assessment Program, and many others. Great Britain is the first country which developed a national EMS' standard: British Standard 7750 in 1992.

3. Struebing, L. (1996). '9000 standards.' Quality Progress 29(1): 23–28.

4. In 1990, the British Standard Institute (BSI) started to consider the question of third party assessment of environmental performance. BSI had tackled the issue of quality management using a system approach producing the quality system standard BS 5750 (subsequently replaced by the ISO 9000 series of standards) and was of the opinion that environmental performance within organizations could be tackled using a similar approach, i.e. by the introduction of an environmental management system standard. The draft version of British Standard 7750 was published in March 1992. See Welford, R., ed. 1996. Corporate Environmental Management, Systems and Strategies. London: Earthscan.

5. Europe's Eco-Management and Audit Scheme (EMAS) followed the development of BS 7750. EMAS was adopted by the European Union (EU) on June 29, 1993, and became effective April 10, 1995. The Commission originally intended to pursue mandatory participation but business lobbying successfully prevented this. Eden, Sally. 1996. Environmental issues and business: implications of a changing agenda. Chichester ; New York: John Wiley.

EMAS is a site-based registration system (i.e. the certification is granted for individual industrial sites) but considers off-site activities that may have a bearing upon environmental management at the registered site. EMAS is primarily aimed at the industrial sector.

6. Von-Zharen, -. W.-M. 1996. ISO 14000 : understanding the environmental standards.: Government-Insts.

7. Hall, R. M. J., and K. A. Tockman. 1995. International corporate environmental compliance and auditing programs. Environmental Law Reporter

25:10395–10407.

8. The ISO originally focused on product technical standards. Then in 1979, the ISO decided to address quality management and assurance standards. As a result, ISO 9000 was published as a final standard in 1987. This system establishes standards for quality management in all areas of business and a process for registration or verification of compliance. ISO 9000 is voluntary, yet market forces have mandated ISO 9000 compliance as a virtual passport to international business. Up to the end of December 1997, at least 226,349 ISO 9000 certificates have been awarded in 129 countries worldwide.

9. The International Organization for Standardization (ISO) was founded in 1946 to "promot[e] standardization and related activities in order to facilitate international exchange of goods and services." There are 111 member countries within the ISO and each country has 1 official representative. The United States' representative is the American National Standards Institute ANSI.

10. Tibor, T. 1996. ISO 14000: a guide to the new environmental management standards: Irwin.

11. The other sections were published in draft and are still being revised by TC 207.

12. Reinhardt, F. L., and R. Vietor, H. K. 1996. *Business Management and the Natural Environment.* Cincinnati, Ohio: South-Western College Publishing.

13. Wilson, R. C. 1998. What you don't know can definitely hurt you. *Pollution Engineering,* 30 (12):33–34.

14. Mostek, M. 1998. Limited privilege and immunity for self-evaluative environmental audits. *Creighton Law Review:* 545.

15. Hart, S. L. 1997. Beyond greening: Strategies for a sustainable world. *Harvard Business Review* 75 (1):66–76.

16. Hoffman, A. J. 1997. *From heresy to dogma : an institutional history of corporate environmentalism.* New Lexington Press ed. San Francisco, California: The New Lexington Press management. Esty, Daniel. C., and Michael. E. Porter. 1998. Industrial Ecology and Competitiveness. *Journal of Industrial Ecology* 2 (1):35–43.

17. ISO 14001 is not linked to ISO 14020 to ISO 14025 which are the environmental labeling standards under discussion under the supervision of Technical Committee 207.

18. ISO 14031 (*Guidelines on Environmental Performance Evaluation*) contains over 100 examples of measures and indicators, but it does not propose a core set of metrics for comparison and benchmarking of performance, nor does it establish performance levels.

19. Delmas, M. 2001 "Stakeholders and Competitive Advantage: the Case of ISO 14001," *Production and Operations Management.* 10(3): 343–358

20. 14 representatives of Member State Competent bodies or Ministries were interviewed. Competent Bodies in DK, FR, IR, LUX, NL, SW, the UK , Belgium, Spain. Ministries for the Environment in AU, FIN, GR, P were interviewed. Germany did not provide answers to these questions. The interviews were conducted during the time period 23/10/1997 to 5/11/1997.

140 registered EMAS sites in 12 Member States (11.6%) were interviewed by phone. Population data from EMAS Help Desk (31/12/97): 1211 EMAS sites

in 12 Member States. GR, LUX and P had no registered sites. Population size in AU, DK, FR, FI, DE, NK, SE and UK meant EMAS sites were randomly selected for a minimum representative sample of 10%. The interview time period was 2/2/1998 to 23/2/1998.

The registered sites interviewed were distributed across three years: 9% for 1995, 44% for 1996, 47% for 1997.

21. Council Regulation 1836/93, art. 1(1), 1993 O.J. (L 168) 1, 2.

22. Directives and regulations are two methods of legislation in the European Union. Directives are most common in the Environmental area. By 1992, there were almost 200 environmental directives but only forty regulations. Once passed, a directive requires " harmonization" of the various Member States through national legislation passed in accordance with the directive. Various levels of harmonization are possible, sine Directives are binding, but only as to the result to be achieved. They leave to the national authorities the choice of form and methods.

23. Ashford, N.A. 1994. An Innovation-Based Strategy for the Environment. *The Industrial Transformation Paradigm*:275–314.

24. Gilbert, M. 1994. BS 7750 and the eco-management and audit regulation." *Eco-Management and Auditing* 1(2): 6–10.

25. Question G.4.a: "What measures have been taken to inform companies of the requirements of EMAS?" Respondents 14 representatives of Member State Competent Bodies or Ministries.

26. Question G.6.: " What financial budget (and over what time period) has been allocated to informing companies and the public?". Respondents 14 representatives of Member State Competent Bodies or Ministries.

27. As published in the Official Journal OJ L104 22 April 1997.

28. Question S.2a: "Is your site certified to ISO 14001?"

29. Question S3: " Was the certification to ISO 14001 undertaken before, at the same time, or after EMAS validation?". Responses 26% before EMAS verification, 38% after EMAS verification and 36% at the same time as EMAS verification.

30. S4:" Was the certification undertaken by the same organization that undertook your site's verification?" The 8% of sites which used different organizations for their site verification and their ISO 14001 certification were all of large sized enterprises.

31. Question A.2.a " To date, approximately how many verifiers has your organization accredited?" Question A.2.b.: How many of these verifiers are organizations?". A.2.c. " How many of these accredited verifier organizations are also verifiers for ISO 14001?"

32. Question S5ab:" Could you estimate how long achievement of EMAS took from the start of EMAS implementation to the verification of the site?"

33. Question S.6.b "What element of EMAS took the most time to implement?"

34. Question S.13a. " How many of your site's environmental statements have you distributed in total so far?"

35. Question S.14a. "What in your opinion, are the 3 main audiences (or stakeholders) for your site's environmental statement?" Question s.14.b. " Which are the 3 main groups that have actually requested copies of your site's

environmental statements?" The overwhelming majority (79%) of requests for environmental statements came from researchers and people in education/schools. Consultants (34%) are the second highest group requesting site environmental statements.

36. Question s.15. " In your opinion, has the site's environmental statement been a useful communication tool with the site/company stakeholders that you have mentioned?"

37. Question S.16a. " What are the 3 main benefits of EMAS implementation?"

38. Bansal, P. 1999. Taking Stock of ISO 14001 certifications. Final Report. Washington D.C.: Environmental Protection Agency.

39. The population of certified firms was so small (180) that it was almost impossible to compare it to a representative sample of non-certified companies since they were so numerous (billions of firms).

40. Zuckerman, A. 1999. Using ISO 1400 as a trade barrier. *Iron Age New Steel* 15 (3):77.

41. Delmas, M. 2000 "Barriers and Incentives to the Adoption of ISO 14001 in the United States." *Duke Environmental Law and Policy Forum.* Fall: 1–38.

42. In December 1998, Western Europe accounts for 157,016 ISO 9000 certified facilities, 56% of the 279,583 worldwide certified facilities. The United States with 24,987 certified facilities account for 10% of the total.

43. These countries include: Japan, China, South Korea, Taiwan, Hong Kong, Thailand, Malaysia, Singapore, Indonesia, Vietnam, and Sri Lanka . Among these countries, Singapore, Thailand, South Korea, Japan and China also offer technical or financial assistance to companies taking up ISO 14000. Some pro-active countries even had their pilot project put in place prior to the official publication of ISO 14001, to prepare their national certification bodies and industry for a quick implementation of the standard. OECD. 1998. What do Standards for Environmental Management Systems Offer? Background paper: Review of the Development of International Environmental Management Systems -ISO 14000 Standard Series-. Paris: Organisation for Economic Co-operation and Development.

44. Esty, D.C., and D. Geradin (1998). 'Environmental Protection and International Competitiveness: A conceptual framework', *Journal of World Trade,* 32(3), pp. 5–46.

45. Vogel, D. 1995. *Trading up: consumer and environmental regulation in a global economy.* Cambridge, Mass: Harvard University Press.

Chapter 7

WTO Efforts to Manage Differences in National Sanitary and Phytosanitary Policies

David G. Victor

INTRODUCTION

One measure of the success of the postwar trading system is that tariff trade barriers have declined sharply. But the reduction in tariffs has exposed the many non-tariff barriers that remain, and in many cases governments have kept protectionism in place by simply shifting from tariff to non-tariff measures. Included in the broad category of non-tariff barriers are differences in technical standards such as labeling requirements and environmental regulations. The focus in this paper is on one subset of these technical barriers: measures for sanitary (animal, including human) and phytosanitary (plant) protection. Such rules include import bans that are intended to prevent pests from moving across borders along with trade goods, fumigation regimes that are intended to kill harmful pathogens, and sundry other systems.

Sanitary and Phytosanitary (SPS) measures often have huge effects on trade; yet managing them is not easy. SPS measures vary across and within nations because preferences and circumstances vary. Simply requiring nations to harmonize the SPS measures to a single standard is neither technically nor politically feasible in the global context. Some nations seek tight protection while others readily consume riskier foods; some pristine environments are vulnerable to pest infestations and require elaborate quarantines for imported products, but other countries are already overrun with pests. It would be difficult to design a single set of international standards that could accommodate such varied preferences and circumstances. Even if that were technically possible it would be politically impossible in the global context because harmonization of standards would transfer political power to international institutions.

The 1994 World Trade Organization (WTO) *Agreement on the Application of Sanitary and Phytosanitary Measures* ("SPS Agreement") is the most significant global effort to reduce trade distortions caused by differences in national SPS protection policies. The negotiations leading to that agreement rejected harmonization as technically and politically infeasible; instead, the architects of the SPS Agreement sought to strike a balance between the need to accommodate differences in local preferences and circumstances while also barring SPS measures that are merely impediments to trade. The Agreement urges the use of international standards as benchmarks but allows countries to deviate from international standards provided that national SPS policies are based on risk assessment and meet other criteria.

This paper examines the first five years' operation of the SPS Agreement and explores the three questions raised in the introduction to this book:

1. Are the rules of the SPS Agreement having an effect on national standards?
2. Is the Agreement leading to harmonization of national SPS policies or diversity?
3. Is the Agreement leading to national SPS policies that are stricter ("trading up") or weaker ("trading down")?

The answers will help improve the debate about globalization. International free trade agreements, such as those in the WTO, are designed to promote globalization. International agreements are also often cited as the best remedy for the ills of globalization, such as the fear that fully free trade will lead to a "race to the bottom." The SPS Agreement is one of the few in the are of "trade and the environment" where there is some track record that makes it possible to determine whether agreements are fostering or hindering trade, and whether they are also harmonizing or changing the stringency of national SPS protections.

In brief, I argue that the effect of the SPS Agreement on national regulatory standards has been remarkably small. Benchmarking appears to be having little effect because the SPS Agreement allows countries to deviate from international benchmarks provided that the *process* by which countries set their SPS measures meets certain minimum standards. In particular, the SPS Agreement is requiring that countries establish a "rational relationship" between assessments of SPS risks and the measures that they impose. Moreover, it has required that they impose comparable levels of SPS protection in comparable situations. In practice, these process requirements have been vague and elastic. They have probably led to the use of SPS measures that are less restrictive of trade, but they have had no significant effect on the *level* of SPS protection. Indeed, the SPS Agreement was designed so that it would not require countries to reduce (or increase) their level of SPS protection. In a few cases countries are removing highly restrictive SPS measures, but doing so has had no appreciable effect on SPS protection. The "rational relationship" test is probably leading to more use of risk assessment and greater attention to risk management, which may lead to more diversity in SPS measures and levels but no systematic trend toward tighter or looser SPS measures. Neither "trading up" nor "trading down" is observed.

The SPS Agreement is still young and there are no other global examples of this strategy with which to make useful comparisons. The approach taken here is to examine the major elements of the SPS Agreement and the three international SPS standard-setting processes that are explicitly mentioned in the SPS Agreement (section I). Then I review the major elements and decisions of the three WTO disputes that have concerned SPS measures, which help reveal how the WTO system is interpreting the SPS Agreement (section II). Finally, I explore a few conclusions that emerge (section III).

I. THE SPS AGREEMENT: MAJOR ELEMENTS

The basic obligations for members of the world trading regime have not changed since the first GATT agreement in 1947: members must give equal treatment to exports from all members, and members are barred from discriminating between locally produced and imported products. Exceptions were allowed for tariffs on specific products, which were "bound" at specific levels. Numerous other "general exceptions" were also allowed for many national policy purposes, such as protection of human, animal or plant life or the conservation of exhaustible natural resources. But those general exceptions—listed in the famous Article XX—were described only briefly. A system of "dispute panels" emerged to handle conflicts. In principle, the dispute panel system could have clarified the scope of Article XX; but in practice any GATT member could block adoption of a GATT panel report and the panel system was often inactive, erratic in operation, and ineffective in major cases.[1] Enforcement that did exist was mainly through reciprocity imposed by GATT members themselves. But the blunt instrument of unilateral reciprocity was poorly suited for working out and applying the complex legal interpretations that would be needed to make Article XX workable. In the early decades of the GATT, tariffs were the largest barriers to trade. The main result from each of the first 6 rounds of negotiations to strengthen the GATT was to revise the list of tariff bindings and reduce the tariff impact on trade. Non-tariff measures remained in shadow.

For the last thirty years, attention to non-tariff measures has grown. The 1979 "Tokyo Round" agreements, which resulted from the 7th round of negotiations, included a separate "standards code" that imposed discipline on technical barriers to trade. But the code, like the GATT agreement, was backed by little enforcement; although all GATT members were bound by the GATT's core rules, they were largely free to pick and choose among "code" rules. The result of the Tokyo Round's "GATT a la Carte," most experts agree, was little effect on lowering technical barriers to trade.

The failures of earlier efforts were addressed head-on in the most recent (8th) Uruguay round of negotiations. By 1986, the year that the Uruguay round began, nearly 90% of US food imports were affected by nontariff barriers to trade, up from only half in 1966.[2] Exporters had a growing interest in taming these barriers. The main legal products of the Uruguay round were adopted in 1994: an updated version of the GATT ("GATT 1994") along with 14 other agreements on textiles, subsidies, technical barriers to trade, SPS measures and other topics. The Uruguay round also produced a stronger dispute resolution procedure and a mechanism that reviews trade policy in all member countries on a regular basis. Together, these agreements form a single, integrated package of obligations that constitutes the core obligations of a new international organization: The World Trade Organization (WTO).[3] Countries were no longer free to pick and choose their free trade commitments.

The most important element of the WTO concerning SPS protection is the *Agreement on the Application of Sanitary and Phytosanitary Measures* ("SPS Agreement"). The Agreement's central purpose is to promote international trade by limiting the use of SPS measures as disguised barriers to trade. The Agreement's basic rights and obligations (Article 2) underscore that WTO Members have the right to impose SPS measures as necessary "for the protection of human, animal or plant life or health (Articles 2.1 and 2.2)." But the agreement bars countries from using SPS measures as disguised barriers to trade (Article 2.3). These basic rights and obligations are quite general and thus efforts to interpret them have focused on the more detailed provisions of the SPS Agreement (in particular Article 5, which is detailed below). In addition to restraining the SPS policies that countries may develop on their own, the SPS Agreement urges members to implement international standards. Countries that apply international standards are automatically deemed in compliance with the SPS Agreement. Countries may deviate from international standards if there is scientific justification for doing so.[4]

Thus WTO members face a choice. The Member may simply implement international standards,[5] where they exist. Or, it may deviate from those standards. In order to examine how the Agreement affects the SPS measures that countries implement it is thus necessary to examine both outcomes: (1) how international standards are established, and (2) the exceptions that permit a country[6] to deviate from those international standards. I will address these in reverse order because the exceptions are the most elaborate portion of the SPS Agreement, and all of the disputes involving the SPS Agreement, have focused on how to interpret the exceptions.

Before turning to international standards and exceptions, it is important note that the SPS Agreement includes several important obligations that extend the Agreement's influence beyond simply the setting of SPS levels and measures. In particular, Article 4 of the SPS Agreement requires importers accept the SPS measures of exporters:

> . . .as equivalent, even if these measures differ from their own or from those used by other Members trading in the same product, if the exporting Member objectively demonstrates to the importing Member that its measures achieve the importing Member's appropriate level of [SPS] protection. (Article 4.1)[7]

Assuming that exporters have an interest in identifying the least trade restrictive measure, this "equivalence" requirement could automatically ensure that SPS rules are not more discriminatory than necessary. In essence, equivalence could ensure that trade liberalization (which is the central goal of the WTO) is achieved without reducing (or raising) SPS protection.

The Agreement also requires that countries make their SPS policies transparent both through publication and creation of national "enquiry points" that can answer any reasonable question about that country's SPS rules (Articles 5.8 and 7, and Annex B). In addition, the Agreement creates an international "SPS Committee" that meets on a regular basis to consider relevant topics and periodically review the performance of the SPS Agreement (Article 12).

The Exceptions

One of the most controversial aspects of the debate over opening trade has been the fear that free trade will force all countries to harmonize their national standards into a straitjacket of international standards. Especially vocal in the development of the WTO rules on SPS protection were governments and interest groups who feared that international standards would be weaker than national SPS policies; the straightjacket, they feared, would require "downward harmonization." In the name of freeing trade, the WTO would require compromising hard won rules that protect consumers and the environment.[8]

Because of this heated debate, fully under way when the WTO agreements were negotiated, the SPS Agreement permits countries to adopt SPS protection policies that deviate from international standards, provided that the Member bases its SPS measures on "scientific principles" (Article 2.2) and can provide "scientific justification" for choosing a higher level of SPS protection (Article 3.3). These general requirements are quite broad and thus, in practice, the Panels and Appellate Body decisions in the three WTO disputes related to the SPS Agreement have turned to Article 5 for a more detailed description of what qualifies as "scientific" determination of SPS levels and measures.[9]

Article 5 essentially creates five rules that countries must follow when they impose SPS measures that deviate from international standards (or when no international standards exist):

- The country must obtain a risk assessment (Articles 5.1, 5.2, 5.3, and 5.7);[10]
- The SPS measures imposed must be "based on" that risk assessment (Articles 5.1 and 5.7);
- The country must not discriminate or create disguised trade barriers by requiring different *levels* of SPS protection in comparable situations (Article 5.5);
- A country may adopt more stringent measures if scientific

information is incomplete, provided that the measures are temporary and a process is established to provide the missing information (Article 5.7). This is one of the few specific applications in international law of what is often termed the "precautionary principle."

- The measures must not be more restrictive of trade than necessary to reach the level of SPS protection that the country desires (Articles 5.4 and 5.6).

As we will see below, the exact meaning of these five requirements is not obvious. However, Article 5 is the linchpin of the SPS Agreement—it puts discipline on SPS protection policies that countries adopt without requiring the politically impossible task of harmonization.

There is a curious tension in Article 5 and other related provisions of the SPS Agreement.[11] Article 5 is mainly concerned with ensuring that countries base their SPS *measures* on risk assessment and that they not adopt measures that are more restrictive of trade than necessary. It is largely silent on the *level* of SPS protection that a country seeks. Indeed, as already mentioned, several provisions of the SPS Agreement underscore that countries are free to set their own level of SPS protection, even if that level of protection is different from the level that would be afforded by international standards (e.g., Articles 2.1 and 3.3). The only provision in the SPS Agreement that specifically constrains the *level* of SPS protection that a country may set is Article 5.5, which requires that countries seek comparable levels of SPS protection in comparable situations.[12] Thus to determine whether a country's level of SPS protection is legitimate one must *look inside the country itself*—at whether the country consistently seeks a particular level of SPS protection. It is possible to interpret the requirements that SPS *measures* be based on a risk assessment (Articles 5.1, 5.2, 5.3 and 5.7) as also a requirement that a country's SPS *levels* also be based on risk assessment. Indeed, how can one assess the risks of SPS measures without assessing the risks associated with the level of protection as well? Levels and measures are two sides of the same coin.[13] This remains a hotly contested issue because it concerns perhaps the most politically sensitive aspect of the SPS Agreement—whether it will encroach on a nation's sovereign right to determine its own SPS protection level.

International Standards

While most of the SPS Agreement is focused on exceptions, its principal objective—stated in the preamble—is to promote harmonization of national standards.[14] The SPS Agreement explicitly urges countries to adopt the standards set in three international processes: the *Codex Alimentarius* Commission (food safety), the Office International des Épizooties (animal safety, also known as the World Organization for Animal Health) and the various organizations and processes that operate under the International Plant Protection Convention (plant safety). It also empowers the SPS Committee to identify other appropriate standards, guidelines and recommendations; so far the Committee has been silent on that matter.

The Codex Alimentarius *Commission*[15]

In the aftermath of the Second World War the European nations created several institutions that were designed to promote trade and cooperation. Their architects hoped that the resulting economic integration would widen and deepen—by focusing on making money, European nations would form a binding political union that would avert future war. The institutions included the European Coal and Steel Community (a predecessor of today's European Union) and the *Codex Alimentarius Europaeus,* established in 1958 to help harmonize methods for testing food safety in Europe. At the same time the World Health Organization (WHO) and Food and Agriculture Organization (FAO), spurred by the European dairy industry, created a committee to harmonize milk standards and thus open trade in milk and milk products. In 1962 WHO and FAO loosely merged these activities into the *Codex Alimentarius* Commission.

The Commission's mandate was to develop and adopt food standards that would allow firms and countries to realize their self-interest: world trade in safe food products. From the outset the emphasis was on participation and consultation, especially with industry; engagement, the *Codex* architects hoped, would lead these stakeholders to harmonize their activities without the need for international enforcement. Thus *Codex* standards are developed by committees of government representatives and stakeholders through an 8-step cycle. Technical committees evaluate evidence and elaborate standards, which are then subjected to the approval of the full *Codex Alimentarius* Commission, which meets every two years. The process is designed to obtain wide input and yield consensus. Participation in the committee and Commission meetings has been open to any stakeholder; yet only rarely have consumer and other public interest groups attended the committee meetings where standards are elaborated. The process is driven by industry, and the vast majority of *Codex* standards attract essentially no attention from other interest groups.

The Commission adopts three types of standards: (1) residue standards, which define acceptable levels of pesticides and food additives, (2) commodity standards, which define what qualifies as a particular commodity (e.g., what is a "canned peach" or "bottled water"), and (3) codes of conduct and other guidelines that recommend, for example, good practices in the use of veterinary drugs or methods for risk assessment. To date the Commission has adopted about 3000 standards; I describe the standard-setting process in more detail elsewhere.[16]

So far, only *Codex* standards for residues have been directly involved in WTO disputes over the application of the SPS Agreement. These standards codify a value for an acceptable residue (the "maximum residue level (MRL)") of a food additive or contaminant for a particular food. The standards are set by identifying an acceptable daily intake (ADI) of the residue or food additive in question. Typically ADIs are established by identifying an animal that best mimics the most dangerous possible human response to the residue or food additive and determining the "no effect" level in that animal. What is meant by "no effect" and how it translates to human effects has not been rigorously defined or quantified. The ADI for humans is set by adjusting for the mass, diet and lifetime of a typical human being compared with the test animal. (In the case of the bovine growth hormones, which will be used as examples here because that WTO case involved a *Codex* residue standard, the typical human is 60 to 70 kg and the diet is generously assumed to be 500 grams of bovine meat per day over an entire lifetime.) The ADI also includes a large safety factor. (In the bovine growth hormone case, the ADIs are 100 times lower than they would be without the safety factor.) A maximum residue level (MRL) is then calculated that would ensure that the ADI is not exceeded. If guidelines for "good practice" in food production would yield residues that exceed the MRL then those guidelines are brought into line.[17] In the case of bovine growth hormones, one expert testified that the MRLs adopted by the *Codex Alimentarius* Commission would result in a cancer risk of between 0 and about one-in-a-million;[18] but that was a guess because the *Codex* system does not have a standard level of risk that guides its standard-setting activities.

Determining ADIs and MRLs is a highly technical process. Experts are needed to review the raw data from scientific studies and to calculate ADIs and MRLs. The *Codex* system has drawn on the recommendations of two joint WHO/FAO committees that are independent of and external to the *Codex* system: the Joint Meeting on Pesticide Residues (JMPR) and the Joint Expert Committee on Food Additives (JECFA). Both provide advice not only to *Codex* but also to many other activities of WHO, FAO and the UN system. In the *Codex*, JMPR and JECFA recommendations are used mainly by the three committees that set residue standards (i.e., MRLs): The Committee on Pesticide Residues, Committee on Food Additives and Contaminants, and Committee on Residues of Veterinary Drugs in Foods.

Commodity standards are more complex and make less extensive use of independent expert information. Instead, they are set mainly through a "bottom up" industry-driven process that codifies what is considered to be good practice for supplying safe food. In the past, commodity standards have been inconsistent—some simple while others define a wide array of food characteristics (size, shape, color). Since 1991 the Codex system has been simplifying and harmonizing commodity standards so that they are less complex and focus on elements that are critical for food safety; in part, this revamping of commodity standards is an effort to make the standards more useful for promoting trade and more relevant to application under the SPS Agreement (which Codex members knew would be a likely outcome of the WTO Uruguay Round by the late 1980s).

Finally, codes of conduct and guidelines are looser and are intended to augment application of the core standards rather than as principal standards themselves; in some cases, such standards have been adopted when agreement was not possible on a commodity or residue standard. If the SPS Agreement is interpreted broadly then these looser norms will have potentially binding application. However, that matter of legal interpretation has not been resolved nor tested in any WTO disputes.[19]

For all three types of *Codex* standards the working committees make recommendations, which they forward to the full *Codex Alimentarius* Commission for decision. To speed its work, the Commission allows for simple majority voting when adopting a standard. Prior to 1994—when the SPS Agreement came into force—the mere adoption of a Codex standard had no international legal consequences for Codex members. Thus it was rare for *Codex* standards to require a vote because a country could simply ignore an unfavorable standard. Indeed, standards were not binding unless the *Codex* member gave its formal "acceptance." The acceptance process allowed countries to pick and choose which standards they wanted to apply rigorously within their nations. For pesticide residue or food additive MRL standards, a country faced a simple binary choice: accept or not. For more complicated commodity standards, countries could accept the standard "with specific deviations," which gave them the opportunity to unilaterally tune the commodity standard to their own local conditions and preferences.

The combination of extensive consultation in standard-setting, simple majority decision-making, and the acceptance process make it difficult to assess what impact Codex standards have actually had on national food safety standards and trade. The only hard data come from acceptances, which are not impressive. Table 1 shows that by 1993—on the eve of incorporation into the WTO—only 12% of the *Codex* standards had been accepted. Moreover, the pattern of commodity standard acceptances suggests that international standards followed rather than shaped national standards: in industrialized countries, which typically already had elaborate commodity standards in place when *Codex* norms were developed, nearly all acceptances were "with specific deviations."[20] Deviations allowed them to tune international standards to meet existing local standards; when the needed deviation was large the country could choose simply not to accept the international standard.

Voluntary standards and the acceptance procedure were designed to give states and stakeholders maximum control over which standards they adopted which, in turn, dampened potential conflicts. Today, after the incorporation of *Codex* into the WTO, standards are no longer viewed as completely voluntary. For purposes of the SPS Agreement, a standard is now considered "adopted" when it has been approved by the *Codex Alimentarius* Commission. The requirement of acceptance, which previously was the way that countries ensured that no *Codex* standard would be imposed against its wishes, no longer plays a role. Because of majority voting rules, in principle the result may be a large number of standards adopted against a country's wishes. Industrialized countries have been especially worried about that outcome because those countries governments are under strong

Table 1. Acceptances of the *Codex Alimentarius* Standards
(163 standards × 138 countries = 22494 possible acceptances)

	Developing countries (114 in '93)	OECD countries (24 in '93)	Total
Actual acceptances	2,175	559	2,734
Possible acceptances	18,582	3,912	22,494
Acceptance rate:	12%	14%	12%
Type of Acceptance			
Full Acceptance	1,215 (56%)	100 (17%)	1,225
Acceptance with specific deviations	228 (10%)	252 (45%)	480
Free distribution	732 (34%)	207 (37%)	939
TOTAL	2,175 (100%)	559 (100%)	2,734

Source: Compiled by author from 1989 Acceptances, vol 14 of *Codex Alimentarius* Commission; updated 1991 & 1993.

pressure from public interest groups who are worried that *Codex* standards will force the lowering of national food safety rules. In practice, however, *Codex* standards have largely reflected risk management procedures in the advanced industrial countries. They are developed with extensive input from industry, mainly (but not exclusively) in the advanced industrialized countries. The industry's interest has been to ensure that international standards are consistent with national practices—they seek international standards that mirror those already in place in major markets or in "good practice" standards developed by industry associations.[21] Similarly, the large safety margins and the desire to set MRL standards at the "no effect" level reflect the goal of the advanced industrialized countries, which is to set food safety risks as close to zero as is practical. Thus the greater worry, perhaps, should be by developing countries that, if forced to apply *Codex* standards, would be implementing food safety approaches that reflect the preferences of industrialized nations. In practice, however, we will see that the real story is that *Codex* standards are not mandatory and there is no strong pressure for harmonization.

Nonetheless, participants in the *Codex* process think that the standards are more relevant now than they were in the past, and that has increased the level of controversy in the standard-setting process. Floor debates at the *Codex Alimentarius* Commission are common, and a greater fraction of draft standards are now put to a vote at Commission meetings than in earlier years when the *Codex* system was viewed as entirely voluntary. Rising conflict in standard-setting bodies should not necessarily be lamented. It is the byproduct of a shift from a voluntary (often ineffective) system of standards to a scheme that may have more binding impact. Until the application of *Codex* standards through the SPS Agreement touched off the systematic effort to streamline and harmonize the *Codex* system, nobody knew exactly what safety levels *Codex* assured and nobody had tried to assure that *Codex* standards attained a specific level of protection. Probably it is a good sign that countries are paying closer attention to the implications of the standards they are adopting.

One negative aspect of the new controversy in *Codex*, however, is that it greatly slows the process of standard-setting; in some politically charged cases, it has caused gridlock. The result is an absence of timely standards, or broad and meaningless guidelines that are equally useless, in areas where *Codex* otherwise would have been able to adopt standards. That could lead to less trade and to less effective SPS protection, especially in developing countries. Historically, the one situation in which *Codex* standards have been consistently influential has been when they fill gaps in areas of food law where nations did not already have standards in place. As shown in table 1, developing countries lodged more "full acceptances" of *Codex* commodity standards, but industrialized countries—especially those with the most advanced SPS protection systems—employed principally "acceptances with specific deviations." The explanation for this difference is that developing countries had few SPS measures already in place; when they wanted to raise food safety levels they simply adopted *Codex* standards—the standards were a fluid that filled gaps (when countries let the fluid flow). In the industrialized countries, however, the "acceptances with specific deviations" reflected efforts to adjust international standards to the already existing local ones.

The worry is that as markets open the number of gaps—especially in countries where administrative capacity is low—will grow, at least in the short term until countries catch up with the process of national risk assessment and management. International standards could thus play an especially important role in opening trade to new markets, new products and new methods of SPS protection. Examples currently on the agenda of the World Trade Organization include genetically modified organisms (GMOs), labeling, and a scheme for more consistent implementation of SPS measures known as hazard analysis and critical control point (HACCP). However, if nations are gridlocked in *Codex* because they fear binding application in the WTO they won't have adequate international standards to guide their efforts to address new SPS threats and new opportunities for improved SPS protection.

In sum, what began as a voluntary body has been transformed into a very different purpose. Conflicts that should have affected the standard-setting process—such as different views on the acceptable level of risk for products, food additives and residues of veterinary drugs and pesticides—were latent in the *Codex* system but have now developed fully. In the three Commission sessions that have been held since the SPS Agreement was concluded (1995, 1997 and 1999)—the Commission's work is increasingly mired in controversy because it is now viewed as more relevant to trade.

The Office International Des Épizooties (OIE)

The Office International Des Épizooties (OIE) is an intergovernmental body established in 1924 with the purpose of protecting animal health. It serves as the umbrella for numerous commissions that prepare codes, protection strategies, and manuals. Some commissions work on specific diseases (e.g., fish diseases or foot and mouth disease); others work on problems of specific geographical regions. The OIE periodically revises the *International Animal Health Code*,[22] which applies to mammals, birds and bees; it is also the model for a separate *International Aquatic Animal Health Code*.[23] Both codes include the requirement that countries analyze and manage risks of diseases that are transmitted across borders via international trade and give special attention to adopting measures for controlling diseases that have minimum adverse effects on trade. As with the SPS Agreement itself, the codes also require that countries make their risk analysis transparent and be able to justify their import decisions. In short, the codes thus provide a basis for establishing quarantines and other sanitary measures and for adjusting the severity of the measures according to the economic risks. However, the requirements only strictly apply to diseases listed in each code; the lists are incomplete and thus offer only a starting point—countries are free to identify other diseases and regulate risks associated with them as well.

In addition to the codes, the OIE also produces guidelines for disease testing and surveillance programs and serves as a clearinghouse for current information on particular diseases (e.g., outbreaks). The work of these commissions is approved by the International Committee, the OIE's main decision-making body. The OIE is also the umbrella for numerous other collaborations help develop reference standards; various working groups promote debate that could lead to standards in areas such as biotechnology and wildlife. As of December 1999, 155 countries were members of the OIE.

International Plant Protection Convention

The International Plant Protection Convention (IPPC) entered into force in 1952 and was amended in 1979. It is intended to promote international coordination of measures necessary to limit the spread of plant diseases. The IPPC obliges countries to identify, assess and manage risks to plants, including risks from plant pests that are carried through international trade. "Guidelines for Pest Risk Analysis," developed within the framework of the IPPC, provide detailed information on how to assess and manage pest risks and require that countries develop import restrictions for protecting plant safety in conjunction with a broader plan for risk management.

The Convention requires nations to create official plant protection organizations that perform inspections, conduct research and disseminate information. (Most countries would have such organizations in place even without the Convention.) As with the SPS Agreement, it requires that countries adopt phytosanitary measures only to the extent necessary for phytosanitary protection. Countries must use the least restrictive trade measures, avoid unnecessary delays during inspection and quarantine, and ensure that phytosanitary measures are transparent.[24] The IPPC probably aids coordination of national plant protection policies—although some of that would occur anyway among those countries that want to coordinate—but it has not engaged in detailed standard-setting to the degree of the *Codex Alimentarius* Commission or the OIE.

II. THE SYSTEM AT WORK: THREE CASES

A full-blown assessment of how the SPS Agreement has affected the use of SPS measures should focus country-by-country, measure-by-measure. That is impractical. The number of trade measures that could be affected by SPS disciplines is potentially huge. So far, only a small fraction has been subjected to international scrutiny. Many changes to national SPS policies will be time consuming to implement; yet only four years have passed since the WTO agreements went into effect on 1 January 1995.

Thus the approach here is to examine the three WTO dispute settlement cases that have concerned SPS measures: the European Community's ban on imports of bovine meat produced with growth hormones ("EC meat hormones"),[25] Australia's ban on imports of fresh and frozen salmon ("Australian salmon")[26] and Japan's ban on imports of numerous varieties of fruits and nuts ("Japanese fruits and nuts").[27] These cases reveal how the SPS Agreement has been interpreted to date and thus are the most instructive means available for beginning to assess the impact of the SPS Agreement.

Prior to the WTO the dispute settlement procedure had few teeth and was, in essence, voluntary. Any GATT member could block adoption of a dispute panel report and thus block the formal remedies that might help to achieve compliance with trade rules and resolve the dispute. In practice the system was not completely anarchic, but nonetheless it was severely hobbled. The WTO system is more elaborate, has stronger tools at its disposal, is governed by strict timetables that help keep disputes from dragging out over years, and is less vulnerable to dissent. The WTO's Dispute Settlement Body (DSB) manages the process that begins with consultations and other efforts to resolve the dispute. If they fail then the DSB convenes a panel of three experts (the "Dispute Panel") to hear the arguments of the parties and third-parties, consult experts, interpret the relevant WTO obligations, and issue a report with rulings. Either party may appeal the rulings; three members of the standing seven-person Appellate Body reviews such appeals and issues a report with final rulings. The DSB must decide whether to adopt Panel and Appellate Body reports; only a consensus of WTO members may block adoption. (To date, no Panel or AB report has ever failed adoption.) Once the final report is adopted the offending country must comply within a "reasonable period of time."[28]

Formal disputes are important not only because they often address important trade barriers themselves but also because they create interpretations of the law, focus expectations on how the WTO system will handle possible future disputes, and deter other violations. If disputes demonstrate clear discipline and a credible threat to dismantle trade barriers then countries will be more likely to remove illegitimate SPS measures on their own. There is significant evidence that the extended effect may be significant—beyond the three measures that have been the subject of formal disputes, the SPS Agreement has been a "broader catalyst" that has induced some nations to remove illegitimate SPS measures.[29] Moreover, as with any properly functioning enforcement system, well-handled disputes can deter countries from imposing illegitimate SPS measures in the future. These extended and deterrent effects can be extremely important multipliers of the effect of individual disputes, but they are also difficult to assess. More work is needed to extend the results of this study—which focuses on three cases—to the systematic effect of the SPS Agreement.

The discussion here will present the basic facts and arguments in the cases.[30] In the next section I will suggest the major issues and conclusions that should be drawn when examining the whole system: The SPS Agreement, the international standard-setting bodies, and these three cases.

EC meat hormones[31]

The first case concerns an EC Directive, imposed in 1981 and strengthened in 1988 and 1996, to ban imports of meat from farm animals that had been administered natural or synthetic hormones. Exceptions were allowed for hormones that are used for therapeutic purposes but not for hormones used to promote growth in cows. American, Canadian and other beef producers used hormones to accelerate growth that reduced costs and yielded higher quality (leaner) meat. The United States had challenged the EC ban under the Tokyo Round "code" on technical barriers to trade, but the EC had blocked formation of an expert panel to examine the dispute. The conflict festered and became symbolic of why the voluntary Tokyo round codes and non-mandatory dispute settlement were incapable of imposing discipline on non-tariff barriers to trade.

At issue was whether the EC ban, which concerned 6 hormones, was compatible with the SPS Agreement. In 1995 the *Codex Alimentarius* Commission adopted standards (by narrow majority vote) for 5 of the 6 hormones in the dispute. The standards were based on the work of the Codex Committee on Veterinary Drugs in Foods and the recommendation of JECFA, which had reviewed the scientific evidence related to hormones twice. The *Codex* standards did not impose MRLs for the three natural hormones in question (oestradiol-17ß, progesterone and testosterone) because naturally-produced residues would far exceed the additional residue caused by "good practice" use of these hormones for promoting growth in cows. For the other two synthetic hormones (trenbolone and zeranol, which mimic the biological activity of natural hormones) the MRLs adopted were far below the residue that would be expected if good veterinary practices were followed. There were no *Codex* standards for melengestrol acetate (MGA), a synthetic hormone administered as a feed additive that was included in the EC ban.

The EC argued that the SPS Agreement explicitly allows WTO Members to adopt standards that are stricter than international norms if those standards are based on an assessment of risks. Every risk assessment of these hormones had shown that growth hormones applied according to good veterinary practices would result in no significant harm to humans—those assessments included two major reviews by JECFA (1988 and 1989) and at least two reviews commissioned by the EC itself.[32] The EC argued that although those studies suggested that there was no objective risk, numerous highly publicized incidents since the early 1980s during which hormones entered European food markets had made European consumers wary of beef.[33] A ban, the EC argued, was necessary to restore confidence in the market.[34]

The WTO Dispute Panel ruled against the EC on three grounds. First, it argued that the EC's measure was illegal because more permissive international standards existed for five of the hormones. The Panel interpreted Article 3.1 of the SPS Agreement, which declares that ". . .Members shall base their sanitary or phytosanitary measures on international standards" as a requirement that SPS measures *conform* with international standards.[35] In perhaps its single most important ruling on SPS-related issues the WTO Appellate Body explicitly overturned this interpretation, preferring instead the more common-sense definition of "based on:" a measure can be based on international standards without conforming with those standards. Instead of conformity, the Appellate Body pointed to Article 3's fundamental purpose: to promote the use of international standards while allowing countries to deviate from those standards if those deviations conform with Article 5 which pertains to the use of risk assessment.[36] This approach of the Appellate Body, although obviously more consistent with the purpose of the SPS Agreement than the narrow interpretation imposed by Dispute Panel, was nonetheless a watershed—it removed a legal interpretation that could have resulted in international standards becoming the feared straitjacket.

Second, the Dispute Panel and Appellate Body also ruled that the

EC measure was not based on a risk assessment as required in Article 5 of the SPS Agreement. The Panel and Appellate Body found that for five of the hormones that the EC had obtained assessments of some risks—in particular, a 1982 Report of the EC Scientific Veterinary Committee (the "Lamming Report") and two reports (in 1988 and 1989) by JECFA.[37] The Appellate Body underscored that risk assessments need not be based entirely on research in the physical sciences; nor must risk assessments examine only quantitative risks. However, the EC measure failed because the EC had not applied risk assessment techniques to the particular risks that the EC claimed were the basis of its SPS measures (an import ban). All of the valid risk assessments showed that "good practice" application of growth hormones was safe. The EC had argued, however, that a ban was necessary because misuse of hormones could cause excessive risks; the Appellate Body concluded that the EC had not actually presented an assessment of such risks.[38] Not only is there a procedural requirement to *obtain* a risk assessment; also, the Appellate Body declared: "The requirement that an SPS measure be 'based on' a risk assessment is a substantive requirement that there be a *rational relationship* between the measure and the risk assessment."[39] Because the EC failed to examine the risks its measure failed the "rational relationship" test, but the AB never explained the exact contours of would pass or fail.

For the sixth hormone (MGA) no valid risk assessment existed and thus, by definition, the EC measure was not "based on" a risk assessment.[40]

Third, the Panel found that the EC had violated Article 5.5 of the SPS Agreement by demanding different levels of SPS protection in comparable situations. Notably, the EC allowed carbadox and olaquindox to be used as antimicrobial feed additives that promoted the growth of pigs; yet the EC banned the use of hormones as growth promoters in cows although the hormones resulted in similar (or lower) risks to humans. The Appellate Body overturned that decision by declaring that the SPS level required by a country would be incompatible with Article 5.5 if it failed *each* of the following three tests: (1) the country did not require comparable levels of protection in comparable situations, (2) the failure to apply comparable measures in comparable situations is arbitrary and unjustifiable, and (3) the such measures result in discrimination or a disguised restriction on international trade.[41] The Appellate Body found that the EC had, indeed, applied different SPS levels in comparable situations and thus failed the first test.[42] The EC ban also failed the second test because the EC could not justify this difference in treatment. But the Appellate Body argued that the third test—whether "arbitrary or unjustifiable" differences in SPS levels harmed trade—was most important, and the complainants provided insufficient evidence that the EC measure failed that test. Allowing carbadox and olaquindox as feed additives on the one hand while barring hormones for promoting growth in cows on the other was not by itself evidence of a disguised barrier to trade. The Appellate Body concluded that the "architecture and structure" of the EC Directives was not the purpose of the EC rules that created this incongruous situation. The EC applied the same level of SPS protection (with a ban on hormones as growth promoters) equally to imports and domestic production. Nor had the United States or Canada submitted adequate evidence that the different treatment had resulted in "discrimination or a disguised restriction on international trade."[43]

In sum, the Panel viewed the SPS Agreement as requiring strict adherence to international standards and sharply limiting a nation's right to determine its SPS levels and measures. The Appellate Body, which is more attuned to the political and social context in which the SPS Agreement and the WTO operate, gave importers much greater autonomy in setting SPS policy. Whereas the Panel found three main reasons to rule against the EC, the Appellate Body endorsed only one—the EC's failure to base its SPS measures on a risk assessment.[44]

Having lost the case the European Union has not complied. Politically, it would be extremely difficult for some democratically elected governments in Europe to reverse course and let hormone-treated beef on the market. If some countries are strongly opposed then it will be difficult for any European country to open its borders to these products as borderless trading within the EU would expose all to hormones. So, rather than comply the EU has been subjected to retaliatory tariffs by Canada and the U.S. In an effort to compensate for lost exports, the EU is negotiating preferential access for hormone-free beef from North America to the European market. However, it has taken a long time to certify the mechanisms that will be used to guarantee that exports are truly hormone-free; moreover, disputes have erupted over the level of concession that will be needed to offset the loss of the hormone-treated market.

Australian salmon

This dispute, the second involving SPS measures to result in a Panel decision, concerned an Australian regulation dating from 1975 that bans imports of fresh or frozen salmon in order to prevent 24 fish-borne diseases from spreading into Australia's pristine environment. Many of the diseases could adversely affect trout, which are vital to Australian sport fishing and tourism as well as Australia's small trout aquaculture industry. And the diseases could also harm the Atlantic salmon aquaculture farms, first established in 1986 in Tasmania, that export high value salmon to world markets and also sell their product on the local Australian market. To combat the threat, Australia required heat treatment for all imports from regions where fish might become infected with the diseases.

The Office International des Épizooties (OIE) listed two of these 24 diseases in the *International Aquatic Animal Health Code* category of fish diseases that are particularly dangerous threats for spreading. Such transmissible diseases "are considered to be of socio-economic and/or public health importance within countries and that are significant in the international trade of aquatic animals and aquatic animal products."[45] The OIE also listed four of the diseases in a category of fish diseases that are less well understood but potentially dangerous. For diseases on either list, OIE "Guidelines for Risk Assessment" require countries to undertake analysis to examine the "disease risks associated with the importation" and to tailor particular import controls to the real world situations in the country.[46] The remaining diseases were not listed by OIE and thus no special OIE guidelines were applicable.[47]

Canada, a major exporter of fresh and frozen salmon, challenged Australia's regulation. Canada did not dispute that Australia had the right to preserve a pristine environment—that is, in the jargon of the SPS Agreement, Australia had the right to determine its own "appropriate level of SPS protection." Canada argued that the quarantine was arbitrary because Australia did not apply similarly strict quarantine measures against other practices that could also spread disease in Australia. Australia had allowed imports of frozen herring bait fish and live ornamental fish that could much more easily transmit many of the 24 diseases into Australian waters, but it barred Canadian salmon. Bait fish are, by design, disposed directly into Australian waters where disease could easily pass to other fish. Ornamental fish often escape their ponds and aquaria; when they die they may be disposed without care for the risk of transmitting diseases to other fish in Australian waters. In contrast, headless and eviscerated fresh or frozen salmon from Canada had low incidence of the diseases and could transmit the disease into the Australian fish population only through a long and implausible chain of events.[48] None of the several existing risk assessments supported the Australian argument. As the EC argued in the Meat Hormones case, Australia maintained that although the risks were low, it could not be certain that headless eviscerated fish would not spread disease.

The Panel and Appellate Body ruled against the Australian measure largely on three grounds. First, the Appellate Body determined that Australia's ban on imports of fresh and frozen Canadian salmon was not based on an assessment of risks. In doing so, the Appellate body established a three-pronged test for what would qualify as a risk assessment: (1) identification of the diseases and possible biological and economic consequences of their entry or spreading; (2) evaluation the likelihood of entry, establishment or spreading; and (3) evaluation of the impact of SPS measures on the likelihood of entry, establishment or spreading of the diseases.[49] Australia's "1996 Final Report," which established the ban on imports of fresh and frozen salmon, met the first requirement. But the Appellate Body said that Australia had failed the other two. This finding overturned the Panel, which had ruled that the 1996 Final Report did constitute a "risk assessment." The Panel had followed the cue of the earlier Appellate Body report on EC meat hormones, which had suggested that the requirement of the SPS Agreement be "based on an assessment" allowed WTO members to include many diverse factors. But the Panel had wrongly assumed that that permissive standard also meant a low threshold for what qualified as a "risk assessment." The Panel concluded that the 1996 Final Report "to some extent evaluates" the risks and risk reduction factors and thus qualifies as a risk assessment, but the Appellate Body established a stronger test for compliance.

Second, the Panel and Appellate Body found that the salmon import ban was a disguised restriction on trade. Both the Panel and the Appellate Body stressed that Australia was free to determine its own level of SPS protection; however, they found that Australia did not apply that high level of protection in other comparable situations. By allowing imports of bait and ornamental fish, Australia exposed itself to greater risk than if it had permitted salmon imports; not treating these comparable risks in comparable ways revealed that the salmon import ban was a disguised restriction on trade. To reach this decision the Panel applied the three-step test that the Appellate Body had developed in the EC meat hormones case: (1) it decided that the situation of disease risks from salmon imports was comparable with the disease risks from ornamental and bait fish because they involved similar diseases, media and modes propagation; (2) such different treatment for salmon and other disease risks was "arbitrary or unjustifiable;" and (3) the different treatment for salmon resulted in a disguised restriction on international trade. Whereas the third element of the test failed in the EC meat hormones cases, the evidence was much stronger in the salmon case. The evidence included the fact that the draft of Australia's salmon rules would have permitted the importation of ocean-caught Pacific salmon under certain conditions; but the final rule—based on substantially the same risk assessment, but issued *after* stakeholders such as the Australian salmon industry had commented—barred imports. That factor, compounded by many other "warning signals," led the Panel and Appellate Body to decide that the import ban was, indeed, a disguised restriction on trade.[50]

Third, the Panel decided that the particular SPS measure required by Australia—heat treatment of salmon prior to export to Australia—was more trade-restrictive than necessary to achieve Australia's level of SPS protection. Heat treatment, in effect, barred Canadian salmon from a lucrative segment of the market because heat treatment, by definition, converted fresh or fresh-frozen fish into less valuable heat-treated fish. (Moreover, some experts consulted by the Panel suggested that heat treatment might actually raise the disease risks because elevated temperatures were not high enough to kill all pathogens and could cause some to grow more rapidly.) An alternative sanitary measure—requiring the beheading and evisceration of fish—would yield a similar level of SPS protection for Australia with a much less deleterious impact on Canada's exports. The Appellate Body appeared to be inclined to agree with the Panel, but it overturned this aspect of the ruling. The AB argued that SPS measure at issue was not heat treatment but rather the import ban on fresh and frozen salmon from Canada. (Because of that ban, the only means available to Canada to supply salmon to the Australian market was heat treatment.) The Appellate Body overturned the Panel because it could not be determine Australia's "appropriate level of protection." The Appellate Body underscored that "determination of the appropriate level of protection. . .was a prerogative of the Member concerned [Australia]. . .."[51]

Having lost on the central aspects of the case, the Australian government changed it rules. In 1999 it allowed limited access to the Australian market for fresh, chilled and frozen salmon from Canada. Early in 2000 a WTO Panel ruled that this limited access still violated WTO rules; in May 2000, the Australian and Canadian governments reached a settlement that allowed much wider access to the Australian market, including for "consumer ready" fillets and steaks from fresh wild caught and farmed fish.[52] That final agreement resolved the case.

Japanese fruits and nuts

The final case concerns a Japanese regulation that had the effect of requiring exporters of various fruits and nuts to submit each new variety they intended to export to Japan to an extensive regime to verify that fumigation with methyl bromide would effectively kill the eggs and larvae of coddling moths.[53] The case focused on four species (apples, cherries, nectarines and walnuts) although potentially had application to others.[54] The United States challenged the requirement as not based on an assessment of risks; it also argued that the varietal testing requirement imposed excessive costs and delays and thus was more trade-restrictive than required. The US contested only the measures that Japan had applied; it explicitly did not question Japan's right to determine its "appropriate level of SPS protection"—that is, for Japan to ensure that its pristine islands remain free of coddling moth.[55]

The Panel found that the Japan's testing requirements were inconsistent with the SPS Agreement for three reasons. First, the varietal testing requirement was not based on a risk assessment. (The failure to employ risk assessment also violated the IPPC's requirement to base plant protection measures on risk assessments. However, in practice, the IPPC's requirements were redundant of the SPS Agreement's obligation to base measures on risk assessment; thus the IPPC played no significant role in this dispute.) In particular, the Panel concluded that "it has not been sufficiently demonstrated that there is a rational or objective relationship between the varietal testing requirement and the scientific evidence submitted to the Panel."[56] Japan claimed that its goal was to ensure that new varieties would impose no danger of coddling moth infestation that was greater than the infinitesimal risk of infestation from varieties that had already undergone extensive testing. Each variety must be tested individually, Japan argued, because there may be a chance (although extremely small) that differences between varieties of fruits and nuts could lead to ineffective treatments that would let a coddling moth slip through. However, the Panel found that ". . .so far not a single instance has occurred in Japan or any other country, where the treatment approved for one variety of a product has had to be modified to ensure an effective treatment for another variety of the same product."[57] Moreover, the United States as well as experts advising the Panel had shown that varietal differences did not influence the efficacy of quarantine methods, and Japan had not presented adequate evidence to the contrary.[58]

Japan argued that Article 5.7 allowed countries to adopt stringent measures when "relevant scientific evidence is insufficient." The Panel underscored that Article 5.7 is an exception to the general risk assessment obligations of the SPS Agreement (i.e., Articles 2.2 and 5.1) that applies only to *provisional* measures. The language of Article 5.7 itself suggests that such provisional measures must meet four cumulative requirements:

- the measure is imposed where "relevant scientific information is insufficient;"
- the measure is adopted "on the basis of available pertinent information;"
- the Member must "seek to obtain the additional information necessary for a more objective assessment of risk;" and
- the Member must "review the . . . phytosanitary measure accordingly within a reasonable period of time."[59]

The Panel concluded that Japan had failed on at least both the third and fourth requirements.[60]

Second, the Panel also found that the varietal testing requirement was more trade restrictive than necessary and thus violated Article 5.6 of the SPS Agreement. Because there is no significant difference in the efficacy of fumigation techniques across different varieties of the same product, alternative measures—such as setting fumigation requirements on the basis of the easily measured "sorption level" of new varieties, rather than a full re-testing of each variety—would be less restrictive of trade yet still achieve the level of SPS protection that Japan requires.[61] The Appellate Body overturned this ruling because it was based on evidence marshaled by the Panel itself and thus the Panel had over-stepped its authority;[62] the United States had not, first, presented a *prima facie* case that a measure based on determination of sorption levels would have achieved the same level of protection that Japan demanded.[63] Since the U.S. had not made *prima facie* case, Japan could not be obliged to rebut it.

Finally, the Panel and Appellate Body found that Japan had violated the requirement to make its SPS measures transparent, especially the requirement in Article 7 that measures publish their SPS measures. The Japanese varietal testing requirement was based on numerous de facto rules that were not easily understood by outsiders, which made it difficult for exporters to understand and comply with the requirements of the Japanese market.

Having lost this case, the Japanese government changed its fumigation rules and notified the WTO in January 2000 that it was in formal compliance with the SPS agreement.

III. WHAT CAN WE LEARN?

It is difficult to draw strong conclusions about the effect of the WTO's SPS Agreement on the stringency and harmonization of national SPS protection policies. The Agreement has been in operation for only 5 years; many developing countries were not required to implement the agreement fully during that period; and only a handful of disputes have allowed some interpretation of the Agreement's critical provisions. Thus here I speculate on the lessons learned and focus on the same closely interlocking questions that I posed at the outset:

- What is the impact on national standards?
- Is the agreement leading to harmonization or diversity?
- Is there any trend toward tighter or looser standards ("trading up" or "trading down")?

It is clear that the Agreement is not leading to strict harmonization of SPS measures and levels. The Dispute Panel in the hormones case attempted to interpret the Agreement as requiring such strict harmonization, but the Appellate Body decisively rejected that interpretation. Indeed, the Appellate Body has interpreted the original Agreement as allowing even greater flexibility for nations to set their own SPS measures than a strict reading of the SPS Agreement would imply. For example, the Appellate Body has made an expansive interpretation of the term "risk assessment" and has created an elastic "rational relationship" test for assessing whether a nation's SPS measures are based on risk assessment.

Nor has the SPS Agreement resulted in much impact on national standards by transferring decision-making authority away from national governments and toward international standard-setting bodies such as the *Codex Alimentarius* Commission. Many critics had feared this outcome because these international bodies, they charged, were undemocratic and captured by industrial interests.[64] Understandably, public interest groups have been worried that their voices won't be heard when the *Codex* determines standards—with few exceptions, they have been poorly represented at *Codex* meetings.[65]

In each of the three WTO panel cases, international standards were referenced in the resolution of the disputes. But *none* of the outcomes from the disputes was affected by the existence of an international standard. The EC hormones case made most extensive use of international standards, but that was because the *Codex* system—in particular JECFA (which is formally external to *Codex*)—had extensively reviewed the science related to hormones. Even so, the dispute panels did not rely exclusively on the JECFA reviews. Rather, the Panel (advised by experts it had retained) looked at the entire scientific literature, which included several non-JECFA reviews of hormone risks. The JECFA reviews were helpful and set a clear benchmark for quality scientific assessment, but the other scientific reviews came to the same conclusions. Moreover, by overturning the narrow interpretation of the SPS Agreement as requiring *conformity* with international standards, the Appellate Body underscored that international standards were at best a starting point for countries that wanted to deviate from them. Indeed, the existence of international standards was irrelevant for the main line of legal reasoning that decided the EC meat hormones case—the failure for the EC to have some "rational relationship" between risk assessment and the measures it imposed. The lack of any international standard for one of the six hormones (MGA) did not excuse the EC from the obligation to base even its ban of that hormone on a risk assessment. The AB's decision on MGA was the same as for the 5 hormones for which *Codex* standards existed.

The minimal influence of international standards is even more evident in the Australian salmon and the Japanese fruits and nuts cases. In those cases the OIE and IPPC, respectively, had few, if any, standards that were directly applicable to the issues in the disputes. Only a few of the fish diseases on the lists of diseases are in the OIE's *International Aquatic Animal Health Code,* and thus only for those did

OIE specifically enable trade restrictions. For the other diseases, OIE was largely silent. Both OIE and the IPPC promulgated general standards for risk assessment that could be applicable in those cases where more specific international methods and standards did not exist, but those guidelines were so broad as to be essentially irrelevant to the resolution of these two cases. Since there is little evidence that international standards have had much impact on behavior—at least in these three disputes—it may also be true that these standards are not a conduit for a harmonization of SPS protection rules. In these three cases there is no evidence of harmonization "up" or "down." It is possible, as I suggested earlier, that the controversy over standard-setting has led to less useful standards and, in turn, to lower levels of SPS protection on emerging issues, especially in developing countries—but that remains a quite hypothetical argument (and deserves closer attention).

Perhaps the fact that SPS measures were struck down in all three cases is evidence that the WTO system is prone to find violations and is thus causing downward pressure on standards. However, the outcome—three cases and three defeats—is easy to explain: launching WTO disputes is extremely costly, and governments are unlikely to bring them unless they are confident of winning. Offending governments don't abandon the cases because SPS policies are politically extremely sensitive. And thus the WTO system is prone to yield winner cases that are shrouded in rhetoric claiming that the WTO system is leading to a decline in SPS protection. If the science is believable, however, in all three of these cases alternative SPS measures were available that would lead to the same *level* of SPS protection with less distortion of trade.

Are these cases are creating a dark precedent—a deterrent effect that is leading countries to adopt less stringent SPS measures in a host of other cases? This question is harder to answer because deterrence is hard to measure. One answer is found by observing the brewing trade dispute over genetically modified (GM) foods. The case appears to parallel closely the basic facts of the hormones dispute. The science about safety of GM foods is incomplete but, so far, remarkably consistent in upholding the safety of those products that are on markets already. Consumers are increasingly concerned about the safety of GM foods; their rising concern reflects the contagion of public concern more than the appearance of new scientific evidence. In addition, European farmers could lose if they are forced to compete with more efficient overseas producers. Some countries (e.g., Austria) have vehemently opposed allowing imports of GM foods while others are more tolerant, but the single European market requires a single European regulatory approach. Mired in controversy, the European Commission has adopted a *de facto* moratorium on approval of new genetically modified foods—which hurts exports from firms in the U.S. and elsewhere that produce and grow GM crops—and is under pressure to ban all imports of GM products. Does the hormone case demonstrate that Europe will be forced to open its doors more widely to GM foods? Mindful that it lost the hormones case, is Europe's reluctance to impose an outright ban on these foods—which most consumer groups in Europe are demanding—evidence of the chilly deterrent that is exposing European consumers to risks that they don't want?

Indeed, the GM case shows that the SPS Agreement is having an effect—on *procedures* for setting trade-related SPS measures, but not on the *level* of food safety. Mindful of the SPS Agreement, governments are "playing the SPS game" differently. For new uncertain risks, such as GM foods, the game is to adopt provisional measures and then to establish a (never-ending?) process to complete the scientific assessment of risks. That approach, within some (still unclear) limits, is permissible under Article 5.7 of the SPS Agreement. This is the first serious application of the "precautionary principle" in a trade agreement, and it is mirrored in the Biosafety Protocol adopted in early 2000. Furthermore, to the extent that European regulators are worried about the risks to consumers from GM foods they will likely require labeling of GM products. The validity of such labels is an issue for the Technical Barriers to Trade (TBT) Agreement of the WTO and is outside the scope of this paper, but as a matter of food safety they allow individuals to make their own choices. If some choose to consume these products then trade will increase; food safety for those that avoid products is not harmed.

Thus the SPS Agreement has not required weakening of SPS measures that countries apply to protect humans, animals and plants. But it may have a different, much larger effect on how countries manage risks. In all three of the disputes one of the critical complaints has been that import bans were arbitrary—challengers argued that the importers had used less restrictive measures in other comparable situations. Although not all of those complaints were successful, the intense focus on ensuring comparable treatment has put all members of the world trading system on notice that they must be able to justify SPS regulations that were previously regarded as purely internal policy matters.

If countries are under constant pressure to justify that they adopt comparable SPS measures in comparable situations then they are likely to give much greater attention to internal alignment of risk assessment and management policies—in other words, they are more likely to ensure that comparable levels required in comparable situations. They are also more likely to ensure that the particular measures they impose are based on risk assessment. The consequences of these external pressures will include much greater application of risk assessment and more transparent national SPS rules. That could be a boon for those who advocate the making of public policy according to sober assessment of risks. It will be difficult to discern how much of this shift towards risk management is the consequence of the SPS Agreement rather than simply the consequence of the spreading norm that favors rational risk management as one pillar of good government. The recent decision by the European Commission to create an independent group of expert advisors on food safety matters illustrates the problem in assessing cause and effect. That expert group should allow more rational management of risks, which should reduce the tendency for EC rules to run afoul of the SPS Agreement. However, the decision to create that group was mainly the consequence of declining public confidence in food safety regulation after the poor handling of the BSE ("mad cow disease") crisis, rather than the result of international pressure related to the SPS Agreement.

The net effect of much greater transparency and internal alignment of risk management should result in more *trade*, but the effect could be very small. Greater transparency should facilitate trade by making it easier for importers to identify and comply with applicable rules; the Japanese fruits and nuts case makes is clear that transparency requirements in the SPS Agreement will be enforced strictly. Greater transparency may also make it easier for exporters to declare that they have imposed SPS measures that are "equivalent" to the SPS protection required by importing countries. In democratic societies, more transparency may also make governments less likely to adopt rules that would be embarrassing and vulnerable to attack. The requirement that SPS measures not be more trade restrictive than necessary should also facilitate trade. The requirement that governments align risks at "comparable levels" will eliminate grossly protective SPS measures—as in the three cases reviewed here—which should open trade.[66]

However, greater use of risk management and the requirement to align risks at "comparable levels" may have little net effect on SPS protection levels. Some measures may not be adopted because of fears that they will violate the SPS Agreement, but we have already seen that countries enjoy extensive freedom to devise ways to avoid conflicts with the Agreement. In some cases, more attention to risk alignment may lead to tighter SPS protection. One of Australia's main responses to the argument that allowing imports of potentially disease-carrying live ornamental fish was incompatible with their ban on imports of fresh and frozen salmon was to point out that it was reviewing the rules that govern imports of ornamental fish (and other potential disease carriers).[67] Similarly, the European Community's response to the inconsistency between allowing the use of known carcinogens (carbadox and olaquindox) while prohibiting hormones used for growth promotion was to underscore that the carcinogens were under review and might be regulated more tightly.[68]

More generally, increased attention to evaluating risks is likely to result in a greater number and diversity of SPS measures. As societies have become more aware of risks and better able to afford risk management they have demanded more stringent social regulation. Within this context, international rules that force countries to look more closely at their SPS policies are likely to yield more SPS measures by accelerating the tendency for countries to impose SPS measures. And, the SPS measures that countries do adopt are more likely to be tuned to local conditions and interests if they are explicitly based on risk assessment. It is thus plausible—perhaps even likely—that the result of greater attention to SPS measures will be *greater diversity* in SPS levels and measures, not harmonization.

IV. CONCLUDING THOUGHTS

This paper has reviewed the provisions of the 1994 SPS Agreement and all three WTO Disputes that have related to the application of the SPS Agreement. It has argued that large areas of interpretation remain open. However, the cases to date have underscored that nations have wide latitude in setting their SPS protection levels and measures. Thus far from imposing a strict harmonization between national and international standards—which was the main fear of the Agreement's detractors—the Agreement actually allows diversity to flourish. Harmonization of SPS *levels* and *measures* is not under way. Nor is there evidence of any significant change—towards stringency or laxity—in

SPS protection levels.

However, the agreement is having two procedural effects. One is harmonization of national SPS *procedures,* such as the requirement for risk assessment. The other, not evident from these three cases but likely as governments ponder the lessons from these cases, is to favor increased use of the "precautionary principle" (Article 5.7) when governments try to defend SPS policies that are based on dubious or incomplete risk assessments.

To close, I note that procedural harmonization without the strict requirement for harmonization of levels and measures may help to mute the backlash against globalization that, in part, is animated by the fear that national sovereignty is being lost to undemocratic international standard-setting bodies. Such harmonization could be an attractive model for other areas of national policy—such as environmental regulations—that both serve legitimate purposes as well as pose potential trade barriers. The SPS Agreement shows how such a system could be designed, but it also underscores that there are no easy remedies for the backlash against globalization. In the hormones case, even the wide latitude afforded to European regulators did not avert the backlash caused by strong consumer support for the hormone ban. Nor is there an easy way to promote free trade by taming nontariff trade barriers. The clearest conclusion from this study is not that the SPS Agreement is trampling national freedom of action but, rather, how little influence it has exerted.

David G. Victor is Director, Program on Energy and Sustainable Development at Stanford University.

Notes

1. For a comprehensive treatment of the cases that were handled, see: Hudec, R.E. 1993, *Enforcing International Trade Law: The Evolution of the Modern GATT Legal System* (Salem: Butterworth Legal Publishers).

2. A. Tutwiler, 1991, "Food Safety, the Environment and Agriculture Trade: The Links," International Policy Council on Agricultural Trade, Discussion Papers, series no. 7, June, p.2, cited in: David Vogel, 1995, *Trading Up: Consumer and Environmental Regulation in a Global Economy* (Cambridge: Harvard University Press). For a current overview of all technical barriers to trade in U.S. agriculture exports see: Donna Roberts and Kate DeRemer, 1997, "Overview of Foreign Technical Barriers to U.S. Agricultural Exports," *ERS Staff Paper,* No. 8705, Economic Research Service, Commercial Agriculture Division, U.S. Department of Agriculture.

3. In addition, the WTO agreement included four "plurilateral" agreements (on aircraft, government procurement, dairy products, and bovine meat) that were adopted in 1994 along with the Core WTO agreements. Unlike the "multilateral" obligations that all WTO members must implement, plurilateral agreements are optional. They are not necessarily useless because an agreement—even if voluntary—helps to signal proper conduct and facilitate cooperation. Moreover, often voluntary agreements lay the groundwork for later agreements that are binding and backed by an enforcement mechanism. For example, the conclusion of the 7th round in 1979 included a plurilateral code on technical barriers to trade; the failure of that code to have much effect led to the creation of similar, but binding, multilateral TBT and SPS agreements that were adopted in 1994 along with the other WTO agreements.

4. The Agreement's preamble underscores the goal: "*Desiring* to further the use of harmonized sanitary and phytosanitary measures between Members, on the basis of international standards, guidelines and recommendations developed by the relevant international organizations. . .." The Agreement declares that "Members shall base their sanitary and phytosanitary measures on international standards, guidelines or recommendations. . .. (Article 3.1)." When a member imposes SPS measures that conform with international standards, guidelines or recommendations, those measures will automatically be "presumed to be consistent with the relevant provisions of this Agreement. . . (Article 3.2)." However, countries may introduce measures that are stricter than international standards "if there is a scientific justification, or as a consequence of the level of [SPS] protection a Member determines to be appropriate in accordance with the relevant provisions. . .of Article 5 (Article 3.3, emphasis added)." The SPS agreement also includes a footnote at this point: "For the purposes of paragraph 3 of Article 3, there is a scientific justification if, on the basis of an examination and evaluation of available scientific information in conformity with the relevant provisions of this Agreement, a Member determines that the relevant international standards, guidelines or recommendations are not sufficient to achieve its appropriate level of sanitary or phytosanitary protection." Although the obligations and reasoning are a bit convoluted, this footnote has been interpreted as meaning that measures that deviate from international standards are acceptable if based on a risk assessment—that is, if they meet the requirements of Article 5, which includes the requirement of a risk assessment (Article 5.1). In plain language: Article 3 promotes harmonization with international standards. And Article 5 allows countries to escape the straitjacket of international standards, provided that an assessment of risks is the first step in setting such stricter SPS measures.

5. For simplicity, hereafter I use the term "international standards" to denote "international standards, guidelines, or recommendations." While the full term is important for legal purposes because it is broader, the simpler plain English term is most appropriate for this paper. One of the remaining gray zones in applying the Agreement concerns just how broadly to apply this definition. For example, as I review below, the *Codex Alimentarius* Commission adopts not only specific standards (e.g., on food additives) but also more general standards for commodities and advisory guidelines. Does the WTO

Agreement apply to all three, even though *Codex* guidelines were never designed nor intended to have binding application?

6. For simplicity I will use the terms "country" and "WTO Member" interchangeably. For purposes of discussing legal obligations I will also treat countries as single units. However, some SPS measures (e.g., quarantines) apply only to certain parts of countries and thus have trade effects only for imports (from outside as well as inside the country) into that part of the country. Examples include quarantines for many exports to Hawaii, which are stricter than exports to the rest of the United States. Moreover, although the obligations of the WTO agreements are imposed on "Members," it is not necessary that *governments* perform all of the required tasks. Often risk assessments and trade controls are implemented by NGOs (especially private firms, industrial associations and scientific laboratories), with government acting only a supervisor. (See SPS Agreement, Article 13.)

7. The SPS Agreement also includes a specific application of the "equivalent" requirement, which is especially important for SPS measures: pest- and disease-free areas. Countries that can demonstrate that all or some of their country is free from a hazard are allowed to circumvent SPS measures that are intended to block diseases on products from that country. (See Article 6.)

8. For example, see Silverglade, Bruce A., 1998, "The Impact of International Trade Agreements on U.S. Food Safety and Labeling Standards," *Food and Drug Law Journal*, vol. 53, pp. 537–541; "Consumer Groups, Officials Demand Strong U.S. Action at Codex Commission Session," *World Food Chemical News*, vol. 4, No. 5, p.3; Jacobson, Michael F., 1997, "Comments of the Center for Science in the Public Interest," Consideration of Codex Alimentarius Standards, Advance Notice of Proposed Rulemaking, U.S. Department of Health and Human Services, Food and Drug Administration, Docket 97N-0218. There have been numerous letters to the President of the United States, responses to proposed rulemaking, and other political actions based on similar arguments.

9. The legal reasoning is a bit convoluted because the SPS Agreement is also convoluted and layered on this point. For the link between Article 3.3 and Article 5 see Article 3.3 itself, which specifically cites Article 5 as a justification for deviation from international standards. (However, the citation is odd because it suggests that a Member may employ a "scientific justification" *or* Article 5 when, in fact, they have been interpreted as the same.) Moreover, see the footnote to Article 3.3 cited above (ref. 4). For a statement on the need to examine Article 5 in order to interpret the basic rights and obligations enumerated in Article 2 see: Appellate Body, "EC Measures Concerning Meat and Meat Products (Hormones)," WT/DS26/AB/R & WT/DS48/AB/R (16 January 1998), AB-1997–4, which argues that: "Articles 2.2 and 5.1 should constantly be read together. Article 2.2 informs Article 5.1: the elements that define the basic obligation set out in Article 2.2 impart meaning to Article 5.1. (para 180)." In addition, the same report (para. 212) notes that Article 2.3 must be read together with Article 5.5—the former declares a general obligation, and the latter elaborates "a particular route" for determining whether the general

obligation has been met.

10. The WTO disputes related to risk assessment have focused on Articles 5.1 and 5.2; Article 5.3 is also relevant because it outlines the type of information that should be included in a risk assessment. Article 5.7 concerns provisional measures taken when information is insufficient and is an extension of the basic risk assessment requirements in Articles 5.1, 5.2 and 5.3. In the EC Meat Hormones case the WTO's Appellate Body noted that Article 5.7 is a reflection of the precautionary principle—in particular, strict measures may be put into place on a temporary basis if information is insufficient (similar statements are found in the sixth paragraph of the preamble and in Article 3.3). However, the precautionary principle and Article 5.7 do not override the requirement to base measures on a risk assessment as denoted in Articles 5.1 and 5.2. See WT/DS26/AB/R & WT/DS48/AB/R, paras 120–125. For more on the tests that must be met to qualify under Article 5.7 see the discussion of the Japanese fruits and nuts case, below.

11. The other related provisions are, in particular, Articles 2 and 3 and the definitions in Annex A.

12. There is a small qualifier to this statement. Article 3.3 also says that Members may impose SPS measures ". . .which result in a higher level of [SPS] protection. . ." *if* one of two conditions is met: the measures are based on a "scientific justification" or the measures are in conformity with Article 5. The concept of "scientific justification" is defined in a footnote (see ref. 4) such that, in practice, "scientific justification" means based on a risk assessment. The provisions for risk assessment are outlined in Article 5 and in Annex A ("definitions") of the SPS Agreement. Thus the discipline on the *level* of SPS protection that a country may establish funnels through Article 5, and the only part of Article 5 that explicitly addresses the *level* of SPS protection is Article 5.5.

13. This is especially evident in the EC's meat hormones ban and Australia's ban on imports of fresh and frozen salmon, which are the only two cases where a country's *level* of SPS protection has been challenged directly. In both cases, the level of protection that the importing country sought was zero risk because the country had imposed a ban on imports. Thus testing whether the bans were consistent with the requirement to base SPS measures on risk assessment was, de facto, a test of whether the goal of zero risk was based on risk assessment.

14. Two statements in the preamble make this point: "*Recognizing* the important contribution that international standards, guidelines and recommendations can make in this regard. . ." and "*Desiring* to further the use of harmonized sanitary and phytosanitary measures between Members, on the basis of international standards. . .." In contrast, the preamble does not mention risk assessment or rules to govern deviations from international standards as principal objectives.

15. This section is based mainly on Victor, David G., 1998, "The Operation and Effectiveness of the Codex Alimentarius Commission," in: *Effective Multilateral Regulation of Industrial Activity: Institutions for Policing and Adjusting Binding and Nonbinding Legal Commitments*, Ph.D. Thesis, Department of

Political Science, Massachusetts Institute of Technology. For the early history of Codex see: Leive, D.M., 1976, *International Regulatory Regimes: Case Studies in Health, Meteorology and Food*, 2 volumes, (Lexington: Lexington Books for the American Society of International Law); Kay, D.A., 1976, *The International Regulation of Pesticide Residues in Food* (Washington: American Society of International Law). And for a study with particular attention on pesticide (residue) standards see: Boardman, R., 1986, *Pesticides in World Agriculture: The Politics of International Regulation* (New York: St. Martin's Press), chapter 4.

16. See Victor (1998), *op cit.* ref. 15 and also Victor, David G., 2000, "Risk Management and the World Trading System: Regulating International Trade Distortions Caused by National Sanitary and Phytosanitary Policies," in: *Incorporating Science, Economics and Sociology in Developing Sanitary and Phytosanitary Standards in International Trade: Proceedings of a Conference* (Washington: National Academy Press), ch. 6, online at: http://www.nap.edu/catalog/9868.html; and see Victor, David G., 2000, "The Sanitary and Phytosanitary Agreement of the World Trade Organization: An assessment after five years," *New York University Journal of International Law and Politics*, vol. 32, No. 4 (summer), pp. 865–937.

17. The process also ensures that the MRLs adopted are consistent with testing equipment and practices for food safety inspection so that the standards are relatively easy to implement.

18. See statements by the experts in "Annex: Transcript of the Joint Meeting with Experts, held on 17–18 February 1997," WT/DS26/R/USA, for example paras, 743, 819, 824, and 826.

19. See ref. 5.

20. Most of the full acceptances by advanced industrial (OECD) nations were notified by the least developed of the OECD members, such as Portugal.

21. Office International Des Epizooties, *International Animal Health Code* (Seventh Edition, 1998).

22. Office International Des Epizooties, *International Aquatic Animal Health Code* (Second Edition, 1997).

23. The statements here apply strictly to the 1952 IPPC (with revisions that came into force in 1991). A New Revised IPPC was adopted by the FAO Conference in 1997, but it has not entered into legal force. The new treaty explicitly aligns the requirements of the IPPC with the SPS Agreement, but in practice that has required few significant deviations from the 1952/1991 IPPC Agreement. One significant revision is that the new treaty will create a Commission on Phytosanitary Measures that can provide a standing body to address issues that arise; that body could be important for fine-tuning plant-related SPS issues since such matters will probably be more technical than would be appropriate for handling within the SPS Committee (created by the SPS Agreement). Although the new IPPC is not in effect, guidelines for Pest Risk Analysis—adopted in 1995 in parallel with development of the new treaty—probably do apply, regardless of their legal status, because the SPS Agreement has an expansive requirement to base SPS measures on "international standards, guidelines, and recommendations developed by the relevant international organizations.. . ."

24. ˙ This is actually two cases—one originating from a US complaint and one from a Canadian complaint. But both were heard by the same panel, employed the same experts, were conducted on parallel decisionmaking tracks, and had the same outcome. See World Trade Organization, "EC Measures Concerning Meat and Meat Products (Hormones), Complaint by the United States," Report of the Panel, WT/DS26/R/USA (18 August 1997); World Trade Organization, "EC Measures Concerning Meat and Meat Products (Hormones), Complaint by Canada," Report of the Panel, WT/DS48/R/CAN (18 August 1997). Both of these cases were appealed, and the WTO Appellate body issued a single report on the two measures: World Trade Organization, "EC Measures Concerning Meat and Meat Products (Hormones)," Report of the Appellate Body (AB-1997-4), WT/DS26/AB/R, WT/DS48/AB/R (16 January 1998). Finally, the question of what constituted a "reasonable period of time" during which the EC must bring its measure into line was submitted to binding arbitration, which determined that the EC must comply no later than 13 May 1999 (15 months after 13 February 1998, the date of the adoption of the Appellate Body and Panel Reports by the WTO's Dispute Settlement Body). For the outcome of the arbitration see: World Trade Organization, "EC Measures Concerning Meat and Meat Products (Hormones)," Arbitration under Article 21.3(c) of the Understanding on Rules and Procedures Governing the Settlement of Disputes, WT/DS26/15, WT/DS48/13 (29 May 1998).

25. World Trade Organization, "Australia—Measures Affecting Importation of Salmon," Report of the Panel, WT/DS18/R (12 June 1998). The case was appealed: World Trade Organization, "Australia—Measures Affecting Importation of Salmon," Report of the Appellate Body (AB-1998-5), WT/DS18/AB/R (20 October 1998). Citations to the Appellate Body Report are in the form of page numbers because paragraph numbering is not accurate in the available (online) version of that Report.

26. World Trade Organization, "Japan—Measures Affecting Agriculture Products," Report of the Panel, WT/DS76/R (27 October 1998); World Trade Organization, "Japan—Measures Affecting Agriculture Products," Report of the Appellate Body WT/DS76/AB/R (22 February 1999).

27. See "Understanding On Rules And Procedures Governing The Settlement Of Disputes," Annex 2 of "Agreement Establishing the World Trade Organization." On the matter of a "reasonable period of time"—which is intended to be typically no longer than 15 months—see the Arbitrator's report in the EC meat hormones case at ref. 24.

28. Roberts, Donna, 1998, "Preliminary Assessment of the Effects of the WTO Agreement on Sanitary and Phytosanitary Trade Regulations," *Journal of International Economic Law,* pp. 377–405, esp. pages 396–398.

29. The discussion of the cases is purposely simplified. The goal here is not to identify the twists and turns in the legal and technical arguments. Rather, it is to identify the main arguments that proved to be most important in resolving the case and thus are likely to have the strongest value as precedents for future cases. The excerpts are based on analysis of the full Panel and Appellate Body reports (cited at refs. 24, 25, and 26).

30. For more on the origins of this dispute see David Vogel, 1995, *op. cit.* ref.

2, chapter 5; for more on the WTO aspects of the dispute see Steve Charnovitz, 1997, "The World Trade Organization, Meat Hormones, and Food Safety," *International Trade Reporter*, vol 14, No. 41 (15 October), pp. 1781–1787; Donna Roberts, 1998, *op. cit.*, ref. 28.

31. *32nd JECFA Report*, published in 1988 ("1988 JECFA Report"); *34th JECFA Report*, published 1989 ("1989 JECFA Report"); Report of the Scientific Group on Anabolic Agents, Interim Report, 22 September 1982 ("Lamming Report"); EC Scientific Conference on Growth Promotion in Meat Production, 29 November to 1 December 1995 ("1995 EC Scientific Conference"). For a conclusion from the 1995 EC Scientific Conference that starkly states that growth hormones are safe see Maddox, J., 1995, "Contention Over Growth Promoters," *Nature*, vol. 378, p. 553.

32. The EC did cite some risk assessments that pointed to a risk of cancer due, broadly, to hormone exposure. However, those assessments did not examine the risks associated with particular hormones and were not treated as relevant evidence by the Panel, especially as numerous other more focused assessments showed no particular risk.

33. For the arguments, including quotes from European Parliament reports favoring a ban, see WT/DS26/R/USA, paras 2.26–2.33.

34. In particular, the Panel decided that "based on" meant that the SPS measure should afford the same level of SPS protection as the international standard. See WT/DS26/R/USA, para 8.72.

35. See WT/DS26/AB/R & WT/DS48/R, paras 160–177.

36. Other reports were also presented by the EC and other members as "risk assessments" but they were discounted. Some were cursory examinations of the issues. In particular, the EC's strongest evidence that hormones caused risks were in reports (the "IARC Monographs") that examined only categories of hormones or the hormones at issue in general. Those studies were discounted as not adequately focused. See WT/DS26/AB/R & WT/DS48/R, paras 195–202.

37. WT/DS26/AB/R & WT/DS48/R, paras 207–208.

38. WT/DS26/AB/R & WT/DS48/R, para 193 (emphasis added).

39. WT/DS26/AB/R & WT/DS48/R, para 201. Due to the lack of evidence, the EC might have maintained the ban on MGA as a "provisional" measure under Article 5.7 of the SPS Agreement. However, the WTO Dispute Panel dismissed that argument because the EC did not claim the measure was "provisional" and concluded that the ban on MGA still would need to comply with the other provisions of the SPS Agreement (e.g., the requirement to conduct a risk assessment). See WT/DS26/R/USA, para 8.248 to 8.249 and paras 8.250 to 8.271. The EC might have overturned at least part of that ruling on appeal which could have, perhaps, allowed the MGA ban to stand under Article 5.7's allowance for strict measures in the face of uncertainty (in essence, the "precautionary principle"). However, this was not a central issue in the appeal and the AB did not rule on that particular argument (i.e., Article 5.7) directly; and generally the AB did not view the "precautionary principle" as giving countries wide latitude (see ref. 10).

40. The Appellate Body derived this three-part test in part from Article 5.5,

which requires that "each Member shall avoid arbitrary or unjustifiable distinctions in the levels [of SPS protection] it considers to be appropriate in different situations." The interpretation of that requirement requires, in part, looking to Article 2.3 of the SPS Agreement which is part of the Agreement's basic rights and obligations: "Members shall ensure that their sanitary and phytosanitary measures do not arbitrarily or unjustifiably discriminate between Members where identical or similar conditions prevail, *including between their own territory. . .* (emphasis added.)" For the three-part test see WT/DS26/AB/R & WT/DS48/AB/R, paras 210–246.

41. In addition to allowing the use of carbadox and olaquindox while banning growth hormones in beef, the WTO Panel had also suggested that there were many other examples where the EC had not applied comparable levels of protection in comparable situations. The Panel drew particular attention to the fact that the natural residues of these hormones were higher in some foods—such as eggs and broccoli—than would occur if applied as growth promoters. The Appellate Body rejected these comparisons because the addition of hormones for growth promotion was different from the natural presence of hormones in food—the former concerns an intervention by humans in the food production process, whereas the latter is a fact of nature that humans can't alter without a "comprehensive and massive governmental intervention in nature." See WT/DS26/AB/R & WT/DS48/AB/R, para 221.

42. For the third part of the test see WT/DS26/AB/R & WT/DS48/AB/R, paras 236–246.

43. Of course the dispute also touched on many other issues—here I have raised only the most important ones that related directly to the interpretation of the SPS Agreement and the effect of the SPS Agreement on nations' SPS policies. Among the other issues is the burden of proof. The Panel argued that the importing (defending) country had the obligation to prove the consistency of its SPS levels. The Appellate Body argued that the complainant must first establish a *prima facie* case that the defending country violated the SPS Agreement; only then must the defender disprove the claim. The Appellate Body also addressed procedural issues related to the handling of matters related to the WTO's dispute settlement procedures and whether a dispute could be prosecuted for measures, including the EC hormone ban, that were imposed before 1 January 1995 (the date when the WTO Agreements came into force).

44. Office International Des Epizooties, *International Aquatic Animal Health Code* (Second Edition, 1997), Section 1.1.

45. The Guidelines are codified in the *International Aquatic Animal Health Code*. See: Office International Des Epizooties, *International Aquatic Animal Health Code* (Second Edition, 1997), Sections 1.4.2.1 through 1.4.2.3.

46. The *International Aquatic Animal Health Code* does include a more general requirement that countries conduct "import risk analysis to provide importing countries with an objective and defensible method of assessing the disease risks associated with the importation of aquatic animals, aquatic animal products, aquatic animal genetic material, feedstuffs, biological products and pathological material." (Section 1.4.1.1). A liberal interpretation of the *Code*

would suggest that that requirement applies generally to imports and not only to listed diseases. However, the *Code* explicitly allows countries to determine their own methodology for conducting such analysis; countries can use procedures outlined in OIE reference documents for conducting such analysis, but they are not required to do so (Section 1.4.1.3). Moreover, the broad requirement to conduct import risk analysis also exists in the SPS Agreement. Finally, the definition of "disease" in the *International Aquatic Animal Health Code* strictly applies only to diseases that are included on one of the *Codes* two lists.

47. An example of the chain of events required: a disease-ridden fish carcass would be disposed in the sewers, sewage would leak into waterways, and waterways would then carry the disease (perhaps via an intermediate host) into the Australian fisheries. Canada argued that the probability of each step was low and, in total, the probability of the full chain of events was extremely low. The case focused on pacific wild salmon, which were the most important potential Canadian export and had been the subject of a special effort by Canada and the United States to perform a risk assessment and obtain export permission from Australia. Later that same risk assessment process would be extended to other species. Such risk assessment must differentiate between populations and species because the incidence of disease and risk of transmission probably vary.

48. The three-pronged test is based on Article 5.1 and Annex A (paragraph 4) of the SPS Agreement. For the test see WT/DS18/AB/R, page 73.

49. The Panel's ruling on all the major issues in this case was developed by focusing on ocean-caught Pacific salmon because those were the first that Canada sought to export. However, similar issues arose for other salmon since the import ban applied to all Canadian fresh and frozen salmon, and where possible the Appellate Body extended its ruling to cover other salmon as well. (Salmon stocks must be considered separately because some of the disease risks vary with the ecosystem in which the salmon are caught.) For the three part test applied to ocean-caught Pacific salmon see WT/DS18/AB/R, pages 80–93. For the test applied to other salmon see WT/DS18/AB/R, pages 108–111.

50. The ambiguity reflects that Australia's measure (the import ban) was not based on a risk assessment—in particular, it failed to assess the risk reduction that might be caused by alternative SPS measures. Australia maintained that its level of protection was "very conservative" (Panel report, para 8.107); but its prohibition on imports suggested that the actual level of SPS protection that Australia sought was zero-risk. On ocean-caught Pacific salmon see WT/DS18/AB/R, pages 93–104; for other salmon see WT/DS18/AB/R, page 112. For the quotation here see page 99.

51. "News Release: Canada and Australia Reach Agreement on Salmon," Office of the Minister for International Trade, Government of Canada, Ottawa (16 May 2000).

52. The case also included attention to non-fumigation techniques (cold treatment). The treatment varies not only with the characteristics of the fruit/nut but also the season of harvest because coddling moths exist in different forms (e.g., eggs, larvae, adults) in different seasons. Different

varieties have different harvest times, and thus Japan argued that test results for one variety were not applicable to another.

53. The United States challenged the Japanese varietal testing requirement for all "US products on which Japan claims that coddling moth may occur," which included apricots, pears, plums and quince. But the US had not provided a *prima facie* case that the Japanese testing requirement was maintained "without sufficient scientific evidence." The US met that standard for apples, cherries, nectarines and walnuts but not for the other four fruits. See WT/DS76/AB/R, paras 132–138.

54. Ensuring that Japan would remain "free" of coddling moth is, of course, impossible to guarantee. Japan's requirement is that all 30,000 insects at the most resistant stage in their development die in large-scale fumigation tests. Japan considers that efficacy as equivalent to at least a 99.9968% ("probit 9") treatment efficacy. See WT/DS76/R, paras 2.15 and 2.23. In addition to this large-scale mortality test there are preliminary ("basic") small-scale tests and on-site confirmatory tests. The Japanese varietal testing requirement obliged exporters to perform the basic test and on-site confirmatory tests for each variety, but the large-scale mortality test need not be repeated for each variety. See WT/DS76/R, paras 2.23 and 2.24.

55. WT/DS76/R, para 8.27.

56. ibid.

57. ibid. Data did exist to show that the measurements which are typically used to determine quarantine efficiency varied across tests on different varieties. However, the United States argued (and experts advising the Panel confirmed) that the differences were easily due to differences in testing conditions and did not indicate substantive differences in the efficacy of the varietal testing requirement. The Appellate Body endorsed the conclusion that the Japanese testing requirement was not based on a risk assessment; echoing Article 2.2. of the SPS Agreement, the Appellate Body found that the testing requirement was maintained "without sufficient scientific evidence." However, as in the hormones and salmon cases, the Appellate Body also avoided creating any standard for "sufficient" or "rational relationship;" instead, they found, "[w]hether there is a rational relationship between an SPS measure and the scientific evidence is to be determined on a case-by-case basis and will depend upon the particular circumstances of the case, including the characteristics of the measure at issue and the quality and quantity of the scientific evidence." WT/DS76/AB/R, paras 76 and 84.

58. SPS Agreement, Article 5.7.

59. WT/DS76/R, paras 8.49–8.60.

60. WT/DS76/R, paras 8.70 to 8.104. The Appellate Body agreed: see WT/DS76/AB/R, paras 86–94.

61. The idea for a "determination of sorption level" approach derived from suggestions from the experts advising the Panel (see Panel report, para 8.74).

62. WT/DS76/AB/R, paras 123–131.

63. See ref. 8.

64. See Victor, 1998, *op. cit.*, ref. 15.

65. Of course a nation could align risks so as to support a grossly protective

measure. But I discount that possibility for two reasons. One is that it would require massive distortion of trade, perhaps across many sectors, which would become apparent and vulnerable to challenge both in internal political processes as well as through the WTO. The other is that even if SPS risks are aligned internally they must be based on a risk assessment (SPS Agreement, Article 5).

66. World Trade Organization, "Australia—Measures Affecting Importation of Salmon, Report of the Panel," WT/DS18/R (12 June 1998), para 4.190.

67. WT/DS26/AB/R & WT/DS48/AB/R, para 234.

Chapter 8

Globalization, Federalism, and Regulation

R. Daniel Kelemen

I. INTRODUCTION

Globalization has given rise to a number of conflicts that are familiar to students of federal systems.[1] It is no coincidence that terms used in the study of globalization, such as "race-to-the-bottom" and "California effect," stem from the study of a federal system. Processes of economic and legal integration within federal systems have generated both general tensions between promoting legal uniformity and protecting state autonomy and specific conflicts between free trade and social regulation. The conflicts between free trade requirements and social regulations that have emerged between states in the international arena have already been played out within the context of federal systems.[2]

Given these similarities, examining the experiences of federal systems may provide important insights into the dynamics of globalization. However, federal polities are not only models for globalization, they are also subject to it. State-level regulatory autonomy has been attacked by international trading partners, who claim that regulatory diversity within federal systems can constitute a non-tariff barrier to trade. For instance, the EU complains that the diversity of regulatory requirements in the U.S.'s 50 states often constitutes an unfair impediment to trade.[3] State-level social regulations have been attacked as trade violations in the context of the WTO, NAFTA and the EU.[4] State officials have begun to fear that globalization could endanger their regulatory autonomy. The North Dakotan Attorney General expressed the fears of many state officials in the US, stating, "NAFTA and other trade agreements present the greatest challenge to state sovereignty that we have."[5] In response to such perceived threats, state governments have fought to defend their interests in the face of globalization. From India, where three state governments sued the federal government for violating state's rights by signing the Uruguay Round Agreement,[6] to the US, where state governments demanded and won special exemptions to protect existing state laws from attack under NAFTA, state governments are pressing their federal governments to protect their regulatory autonomy.

This chapter examines the impact of globalization on social regulation in federal polities. Is globalization likely to lead to a reduction in state regulatory autonomy, as many states rights advocates fear? Or will the regulatory diversity within federal systems persist and dampen the effect of globalization on federal polities? In other words, will globalization undermine federalism, or will federalism undermine globalization? Finally, we must ask what impact globalization has had, and is likely to have, on regulatory standards within federal systems. Many supporters of social regulation in advanced industrialized societies fear that globalization will lead to a diminution of regulatory standards. Some critics contend that we are experiencing a battle of "Globalization vs. Nature" in which, "[the WTO's] victims include dolphins, sea turtles, clean water, clean air, safe food, family farms and democracy itself."[7] Are these fear justified, or do they misjudge the likely impact of globalization? Might globalization actually serve to enhance environmental standards?

For the purposes of this chapter, I view both regional trade blocs, such as NAFTA and the EU, and international trade institutions such as the GATT and WTO as manifestations of globalization. I divide globalization into two components, legal integration and economic integration. Legal integration refers to the establishment of common, international rules and legal institutions to govern trade and regulation. Economic integration refers to the integration of markets. In this chapter I focus primarily on legal integration, examining its impact on domestic social regulations, and on federal polities specifically.

I argue that international legal integration encourages the centralization of regulatory power within federal polities. However, the impact is modest, and may in some cases be overwhelmed by developments rooted the internal dynamics of particular federal systems that work in the opposite direction. The impact of legal integration on regulatory standards has also been mixed. Decisions made by supranational dispute resolution bodies have attacked social regulations set by national and sub-national governments in some cases; however, the impact of these decisions has been limited. Counterbalancing this downward pressure on standards, regulatory commitments made internationally (e.g. through multi-lateral environmental agreements) or regionally (e.g. in the context of the EU) have in many cases led to increases in regulatory standards.

The chapter proceeds as follows. Section II examines the dynamics of legal integration. Section III explores the dynamics of legal integration in the context of the WTO, NAFTA and the EU. Section IV briefly discusses the impact of economic integration. Section V concludes.

II. LEGAL INTEGRATION
Legal integration involves the establishment of common, international rules and legal institutions to govern trade and regulation. Legal integration can affect social regulation through two processes—negative integration and positive integration. Negative integration relies on the selective removal of national (or sub-national) regulations that impede trade in order to secure a "level regulatory playing field". Positive integration involves the harmonization of regulatory requirements through the enactment of common regulatory standards. To assess the net impact of legal integration on social regulation, we must consider the impact of both forms of legal integration and the interaction between the two of them.

Negative integration can occur in the context of international agreements, such as NAFTA, the GATT and the EU Treaties, in which states commit themselves to establishing free trade. Negative integration occurs when dispute resolution bodies attached to the international agreements rule that a particular domestic social regulation constitutes a non-tariff barrier that violates free trade rules and should be removed. Most critics of globalization focus exclusively on this aspect of legal integration, decrying the fact that "faceless bureaucrats" have the power to declare domestic regulations illegal violations of international trade law. Cases in which GATT and WTO panels have made such rulings have attracted intense criticism from consumer and environmental protection advocates, who voice fears that the WTO constitutes a grave threat to national social and environmental regulations. Such criticisms misjudge the likely impact of negative legal integration in two respects.

First, such criticisms ignore the fact that supranational courts and dispute resolution bodies, like all courts, have an interest in maintaining their legitimacy. To do so, they must avoid making decisions that will spark disobedience or political attacks. They understand that many social and environmental regulations are popular with important constituencies in powerful states. Accordingly, they recognize that if they consistently make decisions that antagonize these constituencies, governments may defy their decisions or launch a more aggressive political attack on their jurisdiction or overall legitimacy. The greater the political threat posed by a state's (or a group of states') potential defiance, the more likely the court will adjust its decision to suit the state's (the states') preferred outcome.[8] Certainly, we can expect dispute resolution bodies to continue declaring some domestic regulations invalid, and sub-national governments (i.e. states in federal systems) will generally pose less of a threat of political retaliation than national governments and, therefore, will be more susceptible to having their social regulations overturned.[9] While negative integration will occur, political considerations will prevent dispute resolution bodies and supranational courts from launching a wholesale attack on domestic social regulations.

Second, a narrow focus on negative integration obscures the fact that negative and positive legal integration are often closely linked, and that positive integration may serve to increase regulatory standards. Positive harmonization occurs when states make multi-lateral commitments to adopt social regulations. Negative and positive harmonization are often linked, because pressure for negative harmonization often sparks efforts at positive harmonization. Governments that see their strict regulations attacked as NTBs may respond by promoting international agreements that serve to pressure other states to adopt their standards. International agreements on matters of social regulation and the institutions established to monitor the implementation of such agreements place pressure on governments to raise their regulatory standards. Thus the net effect of legal integration on regulatory standards will depend on the balance of negative and positive integration. In contexts where the effects of negative integration are not counteracted by a process of positive integration, globalization will tend to decrease regulatory standards. However, where the effects of positive integration outweigh those of negative integration, globalization will encourage increases in standards.

Both forms of legal integration encourage the centralization of regulatory authority in federal systems. Because federal governments are held accountable for state-level violations of free trade agreements, they have an incentive to prevent state governments from adopting laws that are prone to be challenged as trade violations. Similarly, in the realm of positive harmonization, only national governments can participate in the negotiation of such agreements, and only they are held responsible to implement regulatory commitments. Therefore, an increase in treaty making activities by federal governments will tend to concentrate regulatory authority in the hands of federal governments at the expense of state governments.

III. LEGAL INTEGRATION IN THE GATT/WTO, NAFTA, AND THE EU

GATT/WTO

Negative Integration
WTO dispute resolution panels and the WTO Appellate Body (and their predecessors, the GATT dispute resolution panels) have the power to declare national or sub-national social regulations illegal under the GATT.[10] While a number of cases have examined conflicts between free trade and national social regulations, to date GATT/WTO decisions have had a minimal impact on sub-national regulations. Only two GATT panels have directly considered sub-national regulations.

The first case, *Beer II*[11], arose in the context of an ongoing Beer War between the US and Canada. In 1991, Canada brought the case before the GATT, arguing that a tax break for micro-breweries that Minnesota had instituted discriminated against Canadian brewers and, therefore, violated the GATT. The law was not facially discriminatory, as both Canadian and Minnesotan microbreweries could benefit from the tax breaks. However, the Canadian government suggested that the law constituted indirect discrimination, in that it put Canada's large breweries at a disadvantage. The GATT panel ruled for Canada, holding that Minnesota should remove the tax credit or extend the same tax rates to all Canadian brewers. The USTR accepted the panel ruling and encouraged Minnesota and other states to comply.

The *Beer II* decision, and the USTR's reaction, increased concern among state government officials in the US regarding the impact that international trade regimes could have on state autonomy. These concerns surfaced in the debates over ratification of NAFTA and the Uruguay Round of the GATT. [12] State officials demanded and won assurances that the federal government would consult with state governments whenever state laws were attacked before the WTO. Legislation implementing the Uruguay Round Agreement in the US establishes detailed procedures to be followed in the event that legal proceedings are brought against a US state law. USTR must notify a state within 7 days after a WTO member requests consultation (or formal adjudication) on a state law alleged to violate the GATT. Moreover, the Uruguay round implementation legislation also requires the USTR to consult with Congress at least 30 days before it attempts to overrule a GATT-inconsistent state law.[13]

In September 1998, the EU and Japan brought a case before the WTO challenging a Massachusetts law that denied state contracts to firms that did business in Burma (Myanmar). The Massachusetts law applied equally to US and foreign firms. However, as more European and Japanese firms do business in Burma than America firms, the EU and Japan argued that the law indirectly discriminated against them and therefore violated a Government Procurement Agreement (GPA) signed as part of the Uruguay Round.[14] The WTO never had to decide this potentially explosive case. Before the WTO panel had ruled on the Massachusetts law, the National Foreign Trade Council brought and won a suit against the Massachusetts law before a federal District Court in Boston. The court declared the law to be an unconstitutional exercise of foreign affairs power by Massachusetts. In the wake of the District Court ruling, the EU and Japan suspended their case before the WTO. In June 1999, the US Court of Appeals—First Circuit, upheld the District Court's judgment on appeal.[15]

More cases against state laws are likely to arise in the future. The US's trading partners have identified numerous state regulations that violate GATT rules. For instance, in its 1994 report on US trade barriers, the EU highlighted many state laws that might violate GATT rules, including California's Proposition 65.[16] Proposition 65, placed on the ballot by an initiative process, established the Safe Drinking Water and Toxics Enforcement Act of 1986 requiring stricter labeling of products containing carcinogenic substances than is required under federal law. The law requires foreign manufacturers to apply special labels to any products sold in California containing substances that the state of California deems hazardous; manufacturers who fail to label products may be sued by private litigants on behalf of the state.[17]

Proposition 65 is likely to be an early target of a WTO case. Recycling requirements are other likely targets. As part of the Beer War between the US and Canada mentioned above, the US objected to an Ontario recycling law that it claimed sought to protect Canadian beer makers from U.S. competitors.[18] Many states, including California, Wisconsin, Oregon and Connecticut have minimum recycled content requirements for glass containers and newsprint. Such requirements can be argued to advantage local suppliers of recycled content and may be challenged before the WTO. Also, state regulations, such as those in Idaho and Oregon, prohibiting the export of raw logs, are easy targets.

While there have been very few cases in which a national or state social regulations have been declared illegal under the GATT/WTO, many critics of the WTO suggest that the very potential for such rulings has a *"chilling effect"* on the enactment of new laws. Examples from the area of animal welfare illustrate this dynamic. A 1991 EU regulation[19] promised to ban the import of certain animal pelts from countries that used leg-hold traps. The ban was due to come into effect at the beginning of 1996. However, the US and Canada threatened to take the EU to the WTO if the ban was enforced.[20] The EU delayed implementing the ban and initiated negotiations with the US, Canada and Russia, in the hopes of convincing them to agree to a gradual phase out of the traps in exchange for the EU's not implementing the ban. In June 1997, the Commission reached an agreement with Canada and Russia, in which they agreed to phase out the use of steel-jawed leg-hold traps.[21] In November 1997, the Commission reached a similar, though non-binding, agreement with the US.[22] Animal rights advocates argued that the agreements reached with Canada, Russia and the US were inadequate and accused the EU of caving into the threat of a WTO suit.[23] However, viewing the leg-hold trap episode simply as an instance of the chilling of EU standards ignores the impact the dispute eventually had on the EU's trading partners.[24] The EU understood that the US and Canada preferred to avoid confrontation over an EU ban, because of the negative publicity a case concerning leg-hold traps could have generated for the WTO. Knowing this, the EU had leverage to pressure Canada and the US (along with Russia) to phase out the use of steel-jaw leg-hold traps in exchange for the EU's not instituting a ban on fur imports. Thus, while the EU was dissuaded from implementing its ban, its trading partners were pressured into raising their regulatory standards.

Subsequent developments concerning animal rights in the EU seem to support the view that the EU feels threatened by the potential for WTO suits. In May 1998, the European Commission issued a proposal for a law requiring labels on egg containers to indicate whether hens were free range or caged. Concern over a potential WTO challenge to the law in the wake of the conflict over leg-hold traps led the Commission to restrict its application to EU eggs. Imported eggs will not be required to use the labels.[25] Similarly, the Commission has resisted calls from animal welfare advocates to ban the use of ingredients tested on animals because of fear that the US could successfully challenge the law as a non-tariff barrier before the WTO.[26]

Finally, in the US, domestic pesticide regulations are beginning to include references to Codex standards, international standards that the GATT and NAFTA are guaranteed to uphold. For instance, amendments to the Federal Insecticide, Fungicide, and Rodenticide Act and the Federal Food Drug and Cosmetic Act passed in the summer of 1996 state require that the relevant administrator use the codex standard for maximum residue level, or, if not, offer a reasoned explanation for divergence from the international norm. Given that Codex standards are generally laxer than US standards, this too can be interpreted as an instance of the chilling effect.[27]

While these examples suggest that some "chilling" of new regulatory initiatives has occurred at the federal or EU level, it is important to note that governments continue to enact far-reaching environmental and social regulations. Thus far legal integration has not led to a roll-back of social regulation, rather, its primary impact has been to discourage the use of import bans as a means of pursuing the objectives of social regulation, as in the cases of free-range chickens and animal testing mentioned above. Moreover, as the ongoing EU ban on hormone treated beef demonstrates, where governments are willing to take a strong stand in defense of their social regulations, they remain in place despite even the greatest legal integration pressures.

Positive Integration

The WTO lacks any legislative body that could produce harmonized regulatory standards at the international level. However, outside the WTO framework, national governments have negotiated numerous multi-lateral agreements concerning issues of social regulation, most prominently environmental protection where approximately 120 international agreements have been signed.[28] While such agreements are not directly connected with the WTO, many are linked to trade disputes. Governments that see their social regulations attacked as non-tariff barriers sometimes respond by promoting multi-lateral agreements, as the US did in the wake of the Tuna-Dolphin dispute with Mexico. Many multi-lateral environmental agreements (MEAs), such as CITES (the Convention on International Trade in Endangered Species) and the Basel Convention on the Control of Transboundary Movements of Hazardous Wastes and their Disposal, establish common environmental standards for traded goods, thus averting trade disputes that might arise from unilateral measures. Finally, many MEAs use the threat of trade restrictions as an enforcement mechanism.

MEAs can have a significant impact on federal-state relations in federal polities. Australia provides the most striking example of how a federal government used commitments made in MEAs to strengthen its own powers vis-à-vis state governments. Section 51(xxix) of the Australian Constitution gives the Commonwealth Parliament the power to make laws with respect to external affairs. The Constitution does not indicate what should be done in cases where this power comes into conflict with policy areas reserved for state governments. The federal government in Australia has used its "external affairs" power as a constitutional justification for expanding into a number of new areas of policy-making, including worker rights, civil rights and environmental protection.[29]

The use of the external affairs power to justify federal policy-making came into the spotlight during the Tasmanian Dam crisis of 1982–83. The government of the state of Tasmania supported the construction of a dam in the Western Tasmanian Wilderness, an area that had been listed as a World Heritage Site under an international agreement (the World Heritage Convention). The Commonwealth government intervened to block the construction of the dam, arguing that it was obliged to do so in order to comply with the World Heritage Convention. The Tasmanian government challenged the Commonwealth's jurisdiction, arguing that the construction was a land use issue subject to state authority. In its *Franklin Dam*[30] decision, the High Court ruled that the Commonwealth was justified in acting to block the dam in order to fulfill Australia's obligations under an international agreement. The Franklin Dam ruling secured the use of the external affairs power as a justification for Commonwealth jurisdiction in environmental policy. This justification was also used as the constitutional basis for many other pieces of Commonwealth legislation, such as the National Parks and Wildlife Conservation Act 1975 (taken pursuant to the Convention on International Trade in Endangered Species), the Ozone Protection Act 1989 (taken pursuant to the Montreal Protocol), and Protection of the Sea (Prevention of Pollution from Ships) Act of 1983.

Federal treaty making power also has the potential to expand federal power vis-à-vis states in the U.S. In a 1920 case, *Missouri v. Holland*,[31] the U.S. Supreme Court established the principle that the 10th Amendment's protections of state powers against federal intrusion could not serve to limit the Federal government's treaty making powers. The case involved a conservation treaty signed between the US and Great Britain to protect birds migrating between the US and Canada.[32] Missouri argued that the Migratory Bird Treaty Act of 1918, which served to implement the treaty, intruded on an area of regulation reserved to the states and therefore violated the 10th Amendment. The Supreme Court held that the 10th Amendment did not protect states' rights in this case, because the federal law in question had been passed pursuant to an international treaty, and therefore fell within the federal government's foreign affairs power. From the mid-1930s until the mid-1990s, while the Supreme Court interpreted the Commerce Clause to give Congress nearly plenary power in all areas of social regulation, the doctrine established in *Missouri v. Holland* did not have an impact on policy. The federal government did not need to rely on its treaty making authority to expand its regulatory powers, because it could simply rely on its power to regulate interstate commerce. However, since the mid-1990s, as the Supreme Court has resurrected the 10th Amendment and placed increasing limits on federal regulatory power, the federal government may need to rely on its treaty making powers to justify some federal legislation. For instance, in light of *Lopez*[33] some portions of the Endangered Species Act may be found to exceed the scope of federal power under the Commerce Clause. If so, the Act's constitutionality may depend on the fact that it serves to implement international treaties on wildlife preservation that the US has signed.[34]

NAFTA

Negative Integration
NAFTA provides greater protection for national and sub-national social regulations in some areas than does the GATT/WTO; however,

because it allows private parties to bring suit against governments NAFTA also poses greater threats to social regulation. While NAFTA does call for the use of international regulatory standards as a guideline when judging trade disputes over national or sub-national standards, NAFTA stipulates that the international standard should only be applied if it would not reduce consumer or environmental protection compared to the disputed domestic standard.[35] NAFTA provides more protection for the standards set by sub-national governments than does the GATT/WTO, in that NAFTA includes a grandfather clause allowing state government regulations in force before NAFTA entered into force to remain in place.[36] Such protections for state government standards notwithstanding, NAFTA provides greater opportunities for negative integration than the WTO. Where the WTO permits only national governments to challenge social regulations as non-tariff barriers, NAFTA empowers both governments and private parties to bring legal challenges before arbitration panels. Under NAFTA's Chapter 11 investor protection provisions, investors may demand compensation from signatory governments for losses they suffer as a result of regulatory policies and actions that have the effect of "expropriating" their investment.

Direct confrontations between national governments before NAFTA panels have been rare. Trucking safety regulation is one area where a national government (Mexico) has directly challenged the national (and state) regulations of another signatory (the U.S.) As part of NAFTA, the U.S. agreed to recognize Mexico's commercial driver's licenses, and to allow Mexican trucks open access to US highways, in border states by December 1995, and nationwide by January 1, 2000. After NAFTA went into effect, California continued to enforce its licensing requirements on Mexican vehicles. Not wanting to be held responsible for California's violation of the agreement, the US federal government initially pressured California to accept the Mexican licenses.[37]

However, the US federal government soon took a different approach to Mexican trucking. As the December 1995 deadline for opening up trucking in border states approached, the US government backed out of its commitment, citing concerns over safety problems documented in the Mexican trucking fleet.[38] Thereafter, US states were able to enforce their trucking regulations on Mexican fleets. In 1998, the Mexican government requested the establishment of an arbitration panel under NAFTA in the hope of pressing the US to open its border to Mexican trucking.[39] As the second NAFTA deadline (January 1,

2000) for opening the US market passed, the US restated its refusal to open the US market to Mexican trucking, again citing continuing concerns over the safety of the Mexican trucking fleet and demanding that Mexico improve its safety record.[40] Finally in December 2001, after an arbitration panel had ruled that the US should open its market to Mexican trucking by January 1st 2001, the U.S. adopted legislation opening the entire U.S. market to Mexican trucking firms and establishing inspection systems and safety standards for Mexican trucks in the U.S.[41]

National governments are likely to limit the number of cases they bring before NAFTA panels challenging social and environmental regulations in neighboring countries. Such cases can easily generate political backlash from consumer and environmental advocates that may undermine free trade and, therefore, government representatives are likely to seek negotiated compromises where possible. However, individual firms are far less likely to consider the potential political repercussions of bringing cases. NAFTA's Chapter 11 enables investors to bring cases against governments to recover losses suffered due to government expropriations of their investments. This provision has provided grounds for lawsuits challenging regulatory acts as illegal "expropriations" and demanding compensation for them. The ability of firms to bring such cases has the potential to generate a host of challenges against national and sub-national regulations.

In the first such case, Ethyl Corporation, a US company with a Canadian subsidiary, has sued the government of Canada for $250 million under NAFTA Article 1110 on expropriation and compensation.[42] Ethyl charged that a Canadian ban on the import and transport of a gasoline additive that it produced, MMT, is not based on scientific evidence that the product is harmful. Ethyl had supplied MMT to the Canadian market until 1997 when Parliament banned its import and inter-provincial transport. Ethyl argued that the ban lacked any scientific basis and therefore constituted an unjustified, "expropriation" of their investment in manufacturing the product for the Canadian market. Rather than risk losing the case, Canada chose to revoke its ban on MMT and settle with Ethyl, paying the company $13 million in compensation.[43]

Canada's reaction to the Ethyl case provides a clear example of the "chilling effect". Subsequently, other firms have followed Ethyl's lead. After U.S. firms threatened to challenge a Canadian ban on the exports of PCB-contaminated waste, Canada ended the ban. S.D. Meyers, a

U.S. PCB treatment company, sued Canada under Chapter 11 for losses it suffered while the PCB export ban was in place.[44]

In a similar case, Metalclad Corporation, a U.S. firm, sued the Mexican government for losses it sustained due to a decision made by a Mexican state government. Metalclad had planned to build a hazardous waste treatment facility on a site approved for that purpose in the Mexican state of San Luis Potosi. Later, just before the site was to open, the state government blocked the project and declared some of the land in the area to be a nature preserve. Under NAFTA, firms can sue only national governments, not state or local governments, and in 1997 Metalclad sued the Mexican federal government, demanding $90 million to compensate it for losses it sustained on the project due to the actions of the state and local governments.[45] In 2000, a NAFTA arbitration panel ruled in favor of Metalclad, awarding the company $16.7 million. Mexico initially appealed the ruling in a Canadian court, but later settled with Metalclad for $16 million.[46]

In a fourth case, Methanex, a Canadian manufacturer of MTBE, has brought a suit for $970 million losses it would suffer as a result of California's announced phase-out of MTBE, which it argues constitutes an expropriation of its investment.[47] However, where Canada backed down in the Ethyl case and repealed its PCB ban when faced with subsequent threats, California is standing firm behind its planned phase out of MTBE.[48]

Canada, the US and Mexico have debated limiting the scope of Chapter 11 since 1999, but no action has been taken.[49] As of 2001, 17 Chapter 11 cases had been filed, ten of which involved attacks on environmental regulations.[50] The federal governments of the U.S., Canada and Mexico recognize that a proliferation of such suits could both severely undermine public support for NAFTA and cost governments billions. As it being invoked by private parties, NAFTA's chapter 11 constitutes a "regulatory takings" compensation measure that goes beyond any provisions the three governments have in place. If left unchecked, Chapter 11 could have a considerable "chilling effect" on new state and federal environmental and social regulations.

Positive Integration

NAFTA's mechanisms for positive legal integration do not match its Chapter 11 mechanisms for negative integration. Unlike the EU, NAFTA does not establish the law-making institutions that would be necessary to craft an extensive body of social regulation to match that produced by the EU. In the NAFTA context, the institutions most likely to encourage positive harmonization were established in the context of the North American Agreement on Environmental Cooperation (NAAEC), more commonly known as the NAFTA environmental side agreement, came into force on January 1, 1994. The side agreement promised to complement NAFTA's free-trade focus by encouraging cooperative environmental protection efforts among the NAFTA signatories and by ensuring that they enforced their existing environmental laws.

The agreement established the North American Commission for Environmental Cooperation (CEC) to oversee implementation. The CEC can hear challenges regarding failures by NAFTA signatories, or their sub-national units, to enforce domestic environmental legislation. In addition, the CEC has the power to impose sanctions against states that systematically fail to enforce their own environmental laws. Thus, while NAFTA cannot create new laws for all of North America, it can pressure governments to apply their existing laws.

However, to date this body has not played a role in pushing for an "upward harmonization" of environmental policy enforcement. Mexican, American and Canadian environmental organizations have brought thirty-two cases before the CEC. [51] The CEC has dismissed most of these cases, while others are still pending. Only two cases have proceeded to the final stage of the CEC process, which involves the preparation of a "factual record" detailing the facts surrounding an alleged enforcement failure. The first was a complaint regarding construction of a pier at Cozumel, Mexico that threatened to destroy a coral reef.[52] Mexican environmental groups argued in their submission to the CEC that the Mexican government had failed to enforce its own environmental laws on environmental impact assessment in connection with the construction of the pier. In October 1997, the CEC issued a "final factual record," in which it agreed with the Mexican environmentalists that the Mexican government had failed to enforce its environmental laws. However, the CEC called for no censure of the Mexican government.[53]

In a second case, which is still pending, the CEC has moved to establish a factual record regarding a complaint brought by a Canadian environmental group, Friends of the Oldman River, that Canada has failed to enforce habitat protection provisions of the Fisheries Act and the Canadian Environmental Impact Assessment Act.[54] Friends of the Oldman River argues that the federal government of Canada has abdicated legal responsibility for enforcing these federal statutes to the provinces, which are not doing an adequate job. When Canada signed the environmental side agreement, it agreed only to be bound for matters that fell within federal jurisdiction. The federal government worried that it might be held responsible for an enforcement failure in one of the provinces.[55] The Friends of the Oldman River submission, may reveal whether these fears were warranted and whether the federal governments effort to shield itself from blame in such cases can be sustained.

While environmental organizations are increasingly making use of the CEC's citizen submission procedure, this procedure has proven far weaker than the Chapter 11 procedure. While other aspects of the economic integration process may encourage higher environmental standards, in terms of legal integration, NAFTA clearly produces more pressure for negative integration than it does for positive integration. Finally, both Chapter 11 and the CEC submission procedure hold federal governments accountable for the actions of their state governments, thus giving the central governments more incentive to centralize control over regulatory policy making.

THE EU

Negative Integration

In contrast to NAFTA, legal integration in the EU has produced very little negative harmonization and a great deal of positive harmonization. In cases that pit free trade requirements against an EU Member State's strict environmental regulations, the ECJ has generally supported environmental concerns. The Danish Bottles[56] case marked the first time that the ECJ had been asked whether a Member State could justify a violation of Article 30 on environmental grounds. The case centered on a Danish law on the recycling and reuse of beer and soft drink containers. The European Commission viewed the Danish law as a violation of the Community's free trade principles. In December 1986, the Commission, with the support of the UK, brought a case against Denmark charging that the recycling law violated Treaty Article 30, in that it discriminated against producers in other Member States by making it more difficult for them to sell their beverages in the Danish market.

The ECJ's ruling upheld most aspects of the Danish recycling law, including the law's mandatory collection requirements. The Court ruled only one element of the law invalid, a quantitative restriction that the law placed on the volume of non-approved containers a manufacturer could sell. In upholding the recycling law, the Court established that environmental protection concerns could justify restrictions on intra-community trade. While restrictions on trade with a more direct bearing on human health had been upheld previously, this decision marked the first time that an environmental provision with less direct relevance to human health was upheld. Along with its decision the ECJ set out a list of conditions which such environmental barriers to trade must meet: they must not serve as disguised protectionism, must not discriminate against foreign goods or producers (nondiscrimination) and may only impede trade as much as is necessary to achieve the environmental objective in question (proportionality).

In 1992 the ECJ ruled on the *Walloon Waste*[57] case concerning a Wallonian decree dating from 1987 that banned the import of waste intended for disposal into the Belgian province of Wallonia. The Commission challenged the law as an unjustifiable violation of Article 30. Given that the law explicitly barred imports, the Commission's case seemed strong. The ECJ upheld the Walloon waste ban as it applied to non-hazardous waste.[58] The Court ruled that because of environmental principles such as the need to rectify environmental damage at its source, local waste had an inherently different character than foreign waste and could be subject to different regulatory requirements.[59] This decision continued the line of pro-environment case law established in Danish Bottles.

A 1994 case tested a state's ability to maintain higher national standards where harmonized Community standards were already in place.[60] The *PCP*[61] case concerned a German ban on the use PCP (pentachlorophenol), a chemical used as a wood, leather and textile preservative, releases cancer causing dioxins. The Community had enacted a regulation (91/173/EEC) limiting the use of PCP in 1991. At the time, German domestic law already provided for stricter limits on PCPs, which amounted practically to an outright ban. Germany and three other states advocated enacting such strict standards at the EU level as well, but were outvoted by states that favored less stringent restrictions. Germany notified the Commission of its intention to keep its existing national ban on PCPs in place and the Commission gave Germany its approval in December 1992.

France, supported by Belgium, Italy and Greece, brought a

complaint before the ECJ against the Commission's decision to approve the German measure. France viewed the regulation as a disguised trade barrier, particularly against leather goods. France argued that the Commission had not provided sufficient scientific justification for the German ban and had not examined alternatives to a ban suggested by France.

In May 1994, the ECJ ruled that the Commission had failed to demand sufficient justification for the German rule and had failed to examine other, less trade-restrictive alternatives.[62] Germany might indeed be justified in maintaining a stricter law, in accord with the Article 100a(4) exemption for stricter national standards, but the Commission had failed to follow the procedures necessary to ensure that the German measure was justified. This decision established the precedent that strict procedural rules had to be followed, while at the same time leaving open the possibility that the German ban might eventually be approved. Subsequently, after conducting an investigation in adherence with the procedural requirements set out by the ECJ, the Commission re-approved the ban. The episode demonstrated that states could gain environmental exemptions under Article 100a(4) where they could provide adequate justification.

In another recent trade-environment decision, the ECJ ruled once again to allow a green Member State to maintain an environmental regulation that impinged on free commerce. The *Danish Bees* case[63] concerned a Danish ban on the importation of yellow honey bees to the Danish Island of Laeso. The government had declared the remote island a protected endangered species habitat, as it was the home to a rare species of brown honey bee, that could disappear through cross breeding with yellow bees. The case arose after an immigrant from the mainland began raising yellow bees on the island, where they could take advantage of the island's abundant heather. The islander's were weary of competition and anxious to protect the brown bees that had made Laeso's honey famous across Denmark.[64] The ECJ upheld the Danish ban, saying that the protection of endangered species, which was the central aim of the measure, took precedence over incidental effects on trade. Again, as in most of the cases it has heard pitting free trade requirements against national environmental regulations, the ECJ has allowed national standards to remain in place.

Positive Integration
In addition to liberalizing trade and striking down Member States'

non-tariff barriers, the EU has also adopted a wide-range of regulatory measures at the supranational level that create harmonized regulatory standards in areas including food and drug safety, workplace safety and environmental protection. EU social regulations have pressured laggard Member States to increase their standards. Moreover, in the case of EU Member States with federal systems, the EU has pressured federal governments to hold their state governments accountable for satisfying EU requirements. These developments are evident in the area of environmental regulation, where the EU has adopted a wide range of directives and regulations addressing all the major areas of environmental policy. EU environmental policy has driven up the regulatory standards of many laggard Member States. In states such as Spain, Portugal and Greece, national environmental policy consists of little more than application of EU directives. Where the EU has harmonized standards at the supranational level, it generally permits Member States to maintain stricter national standards if they chose to do so.

Article 130t of the 1986 Single European Act (SEA) allowed Member States to maintain or introduce more stringent regulations than those adopted at the EU level, as long as they do not constitute a disguised restriction on trade.[65] Similarly, Article 100a(4) allows states to maintain higher national standards when environmental harmonization measures relating to the functioning of the internal market are taken. These provisions were included in the SEA at the insistence of high standard states like Denmark. The safeguards provided by these "upward escape clauses" were important to winning the support of Denmark and other high standard states for the Treaty.

EU environmental policy has also pressured some of the greener Member States to adopt stricter regulations. In the case of federal polities within the EU, this has encouraged federal governments to centralize regulatory authority and has placed pressure on sub-national jurisdictions to increase their regulatory standards. The impact of EU environmental policy on the German federal system illustrates this dynamic.

Pressure from the EU has encouraged the shift of legislative competence to the federal level within Germany. Most EU laws are transposed into German law as federal regulations or guidelines.[66] Some EU directives, particularly those that focus on procedural issues, required the introduction of laws that took an approach far different from the traditional policy style in Germany.[67] The EU directives on environmental impact assessment[68] and freedom of information on the environment[69] are two prominent examples.

To transpose the EU's environmental impact assessment directive into national law, the German federal government enacted the Act on Environmental Impact Assessment (*Gesetz über die Umweltverträglichkeitsprüfung — UVPG*) in 1990. In accord with the requirements of the EU directive, the Act establishes the procedures to be followed by state and local officials in conducting environmental impact assessments and establishes an extensive list of the types of projects for which assessments are required. The German government transposed the EU's directive on freedom of access to information on the environment into national law in 1994 by enacting the Environmental Information Act (*Umweltinformationsgesetz — UIG*). The Environmental Information Act required environmental authorities and regulated entities across Germany to release information that had previously been inaccessible to the public.

The German federal government, and a number of German states, have resisted implementing some of the procedural requirements of these directives, and the Commission has brought a series of legal actions against Germany as a result.[70] Beyond these two directives, the Commission has clashed with Germany regarding the use of non-binding administrative guidelines as a means of implementation. While the use of such guidelines by federal lawmakers to direct the implementation activities of state officials was long standard practice in Germany, the Commission maintains that such guidelines do not provide citizens with sufficient legal certainty. The Commission brought a case before the ECJ challenging the Germany's use of an administrative guideline (*TA Luft*) to implement an EU directive on air quality. The ECJ ruled for the Commission, holding that the administrative guideline did not provide the necessary legal certainty to constitute a sufficient means by which to implement EU law.[71]

EU directives have forced the German federal government to introduce stricter deadlines into its regulations and to introduce more detailed requirements in some areas. Traditionally, German regulations had not contained action-forcing deadlines. The presence of deadlines in EU directives has encouraged the federal government to centralize more authority, since such deadlines must be met nation-wide. Failure of any state to meet an EU directive's deadline could result in an infringement action being brought against the federal government. Some EU directives have introduced detailed requirements into areas of German law that had historically been subject to only loose controls. For instance, water pollution control had been one of the less detailed areas of German environmental law. However, German regulations concerning drinking water, nitrate levels in water and bathing water have all become far more detailed in light of EU requirements. Also the EU waste directive set out detailed requirements regarding the regulation of landfills, where state governments had previously enjoyed great discretion.[72]

EU enforcement actions have brought pressure to bear on German states. The German federal government traditionally relied on informal means to pressure states to implement federal laws effectively. By contrast, the Commission regularly employs a more formal, adversarial procedure, the Article 169 infringement procedure. The Commission can only bring cases against the German federal government. Nonetheless, it is clear to all parties involved when the implementation failure is actually attributable to one or more state governments. If the German federal government comes under pressure from Brussels, then it in turn pressures state government officials to redress the implementation problem. If such an infringement case comes before the ECJ, the German federal government makes it clear to the German public which state is to blame. Like national governments, German state governments prefer to avoid being marked as violators of EU law.[73]

IV. ECONOMIC INTEGRATION

The second set of forces that may influence both regulatory standards and the allocation of regulatory authority in federal systems stem from economic integration. According to common wisdom and some scholarly observers, economic liberalization generates a regulatory race-to-the-bottom, while according to David Vogel and others economic liberalization has just the opposite effect, encouraging a regulatory race-to-the-top.[74] These dynamics are not mutually exclusive when social regulation is taken as a whole; they could be at work simultaneously in different areas of regulation. I do not attempt here to determine which of these dynamics is dominant. Rather, I focus on the ways in which either of these dynamics may have a distinctive impact on federal polities.

Within federal systems, sub-national jurisdictions compete with each other to attract and retain investment. Thus, there may be "race-to-the-bottom" pressures within a federal system, even in the absence of globalization. Nonetheless, sub-national jurisdictions have generally not engaged in "races-to-the-bottom" in social regulation.[75] Historically, there have been instances in which trade liberalization has impeded the establishment of social regulations, most famously in the case of US state child labor laws. In the field of environment, before the introduction of federal laws, US states with powerful coal industries tended to ignore the environmental consequences of coal mining.[76] Despite such examples, there is little empirical evidence in support of the race to-the-bottom hypothesis in the area of environmental or social regulation.[77] The primary reason is that such regulatory standards do not make up significant proportion of total production costs for most industries. For instance, according to a number of studies, environmental compliance costs for most industries are minimal, rising to only approximately 3% for the heaviest polluting, most strictly regulated industries.[78] Both in the US and EU, where minimal standards (floors) that apply across the common market have been enacted, greener states continue to maintain stricter standards.

One would expect economic globalization to contribute to domestic competitive pressures between sub-national jurisdictions within federal systems. Will this lead sub-national units that had not previously engaged in a "race-to-the-bottom" to begin one? This seems highly unlikely. Market integration and inter-jurisdictional competition within federal systems generally far exceeds that at the international level. The competitive pressures added by globalization are minimal compared to those that already exist within the federal system. There is no reason to believe these added pressures will drive states within federal polities into a "race-to-the-bottom" competition with one another.

While there is little evidence to support the race-to-the-bottom hypothesis, there is some evidence that opponents of social regulatory initiatives have used global competitiveness concerns to successfully oppose new regulatory initiatives. Whether or not race-to-the-bottom pressures are an economic reality, they constitute a powerful rhetorical tool. Opponents of regulation can feed on fears of race-to-the-bottom pressures to argue that environmental and social regulations are simply untenable 'in the competitive global economy'.[79] Though it was not a regulatory initiative *per se*, Clinton's Btu tax proposal was a potentially significant environmental initiative that was shot down largely due to competitiveness concerns. Clinton proposed the energy tax in February 1993, promising that it would reduce pollution and increase energy conservation. However, the legislation was defeated in Congress with opponents citing the damage the tax would cause to the competitiveness of US industry.[80] A similar carbon tax proposal in Australia was also abandoned due to competitiveness concerns.[81] EU proposals for a carbon/btu tax have been stalled because of fears of the competitive disadvantages it could create vis-à-vis the US and Japan. Globalization need not generate domestic opposition to new regulatory initiatives. However, where opponents of regulation can successfully invoke the perceived demands of "global competition" to justify their position, this will aid their efforts to reduce regulatory standards.

As its name suggests, the "California" effect holds the promise that economic integration may allow a sub-national government to see its strict standards spread to other jurisdictions. Until recently, the scope for the California effect to occur internationally has been limited primarily to product standards.[82] Initial GATT jurisprudence on trade-environment disputes indicated that states could restrict imports only on the basis of product standards, not on the basis of how a product was produced (production process measures (PPMs).[83] However, more recent WTO case law has overturned this interpretation. In the Shrimp-Turtle case, the WTO ruled that, in principle, a state could restrict imports on the basis of PPMs.[84] To the extent that states can restrict trade on the basis of PPMs, they can create pressure amongst their trading partners to adopt strict process regulations. How far this principle will be stretched remains to be seen. If it is given a wide reading by future dispute panels, it could significantly increase the scope of the California effect.

V. CONCLUSIONS

Globalization will not undermine federalism. The evidence presented above indicates that globalization encourages the centralization of regulatory power in federal polities. As federal governments are accountable for violations of international trade or environmental agreements committed by sub-national jurisdictions, they have an incentive to restrict the autonomy of these jurisdictions. However, while globalization has an impact on the internal dynamics of federal systems, it does not determine their course. The domestic dynamics of federal systems may work in opposite directions. For instance, in the 1990s, while the U.S. has been imbedding itself in regional and global trade agreements that encourage the concentration of power in federal hands, the U.S. Supreme Court has been reinterpreting the

Constitution to hand power back to state governments. Globalization has an impact on federal polities, but it clearly does not have an overwhelming effect.

The impact of globalization on regulatory standards is less clear. Supranational dispute resolution bodies have attacked some social regulations set by national or sub-national jurisdictions. While the immediate impact of these decisions has been limited, there is some evidence that they have inspired a more widespread "chilling effect". The impact of dispute resolution processes that rely on states suing one another (as in the WTO) is limited by the restrictions in the volume of litigation that such processes can handle.[85] A system that empowers private litigants to challenge states' social regulations and to recover damages for "regulatory takings", such as that which exists under NAFTA's Chapter 11, promises to generate far more litigation and a far greater chilling effect.

Positive regulatory commitments made in EU directives and international agreements, such as MEAs, have led to increases in federal and sub-national standards in a number of cases. In the EU, these positive commitments have certainly outweighed any downward pressure on standards that European integration has generated. By contrast, in the context of NAFTA positive integration through the channels established in the Commission for Environmental Cooperation (CEC) has thus far proven very weak.

R. Daniel Kelemen is a University Lecturer in Comparative European Politics and a Tutorial Fellow in Politics at Oxford University.

Notes

1. Farber and Hudec 1994.

2. Stewart 1992.

3. See, for instance, European Commission 1999.

4. See Section II below.

5. Evelyn Iritani, "Trade Pacts accused of subverting U.S. Policies," *Los Angeles Times*, February 28, 1999.

6. "Dilemma-of-Politics", Business India, AP *Worldstream*, April 5, 1998.

7. "Globalization v. Nature," paid advertisement, *New York Times*, November 22, 1999.

8. Kelemen 2001.

9. Harvey Berkman, "As GATT Gains, Will States Wane?" National Law Journal, November 14, 1994.

10. Hoekman and Kostecki 1995.

11. United States—Measures affecting alcoholic and malt beverages, adopted 19 June 1992, DS23/R, BISD 395/206.

12. Sager 1999.

13. Uruguay Round Agreements Act, Pub. L. No. 103–465, 103 (codified at 19 U.S.C. 3512 (1994).

14. Michael Lelyveld, "US may defend, oppose state's sanctions law," *Journal of Commerce*, February 3, 1999.

15. European Commission 1999.

16. European Commission 1994.

17. O'Reilly 1997.

18. Vogel 1995:229–231.

19. Council Regulation No. 1254/91.

20. "EU urged to curb fur imports," *Financial Times*, March 3, 1997.

21. "Brussels reaches pact on leg-hold traps," *Financial Times* May 29, 1997.

22. "New offer by US on leg-hold traps." *Financial Times*, November 30, 1997.

23. "Brussels under US pressure," *Financial Times*, February 16, 1999.

24. Vogel 2001:338.

25. Keith Nuthall, "Trade rules harm animals," *The Independent*, May 24, 1998

26. "Brussels under US pressure," *Financial Times*, February 16, 1999.

27. General Accounting Office, *International Food Safety: Comparison of U.S. Codex Pesticide Standards* (Aug. 1991; "Harmonization Alert: International Harmonization of Social, Economic and Environmental Standards," Public Citizen, http://www.harmonizationalert.org/harmbk.htm#N_46_

28. Vogel 2001:340.

29. Boardman 1990.

30. *Commonwealth v. Tasmania (Franklin Dam Case)* (1983) 158 CLR.

31. 252 U.S. 416 (1920)

32. See Scheiber 1993 for a discussion of the case.

33. *United States v. Lopez* 115 S. Ct. 1624 (1995).

34. Bradley 1998; Villareal, 1998.

35. Orbuch and Singer 1999.

36. NAFTA Sec. 102(b)(1)(B)(i). See Sager 1999:11.

37. Ibid. Also see State Government News, "NAFTA Rewrites Status of States," 10, 13, May 1994.

38. Kevin G. Hall, "Mexico-US Truck Talks to go Another Round," *Journal of Commerce*, Aug. 21, 1998; Mary Sutter, "Mexico Asks Arbitration to Force Open Border," *Journal of Commerce Special*, Sept. 24, 1998.

39. Kevin G. Hall, "Clinton resists easing of rules," *Journal of Commerce*, Oct. 12, 1999.

40. Esther Schrader, "U.S. move to ban Mexican trucks is causing rift," *Los Angeles Times*, October 19, 1999; Scott Bowles, "Loads of worry about open borders," *USA Today*, October 20, 1999; Robert Kuttner, "Globalization and U.S. Highway Safety," *San Diego Union-Tribune*, October 24, 1999

41. "President Bush signs Mexican truck bill," Agence France Press, December 19, 2001.Also see, Lyzette Alvarez, " Senate Votes to Let Mexican Trucks in U.S," *New York Times*, December 4, 2001.

42. Andrew Tellijohn, "Canadians Fear Sovereignty Loss as NAFTA Suit Progresses," Corporate Legal Times, July 1998.

43. Evelyn Iritani, "Trade Pacts accused of subverting U.S. policies," Los Angeles Times, Feb. 28, 1999.

44. Ibid.

45. Joiel Millman, "Metalclad Suit is First Against Mexico Under NAFTA Foreign Investment Rules," Wall Street Journal, October 14, 1997; John O'Dell, "O.C. firm files first Mexico NAFTA claim,"Los Angeles Times, October 15, 1997.

46. Evelyn Iritani, "Ruling in Canada Strikes at Companies' NAFTA Trade Suits". Los Angeles Times, May 5, 2001; Danielle Knight, "Environmentalists urge pesticide fight," Inter Press Service, January 29, 2002.

47. Robert W. Benson, "Constitution? Forget it! Nafta rules," Los Angeles Times, June 24, 1999; Terence Corcoran, "The Push to Gut Nafta," The Ottawa Citizen, June 24, 1999.

48. See supra, note 46.

49. Courtney Tower, "NAFTA considers curb on claim from "green" laws," Journal of Commerce, February 23, 1999; "Americas leaders to discuss free trade pact progress amid protests," Agence France Press, April 17, 2001.

50. See supra, note 46. Also see Mann 2001.

51. NAFTA Commission on Environmental Cooperation, Registry of Submissions on Enforcement Matters, Commission on Environmental Cooperation, site visited on Nov. 1, 1999. http://www.cec.org/templates/RegistryFront.cfm?&format = 2&varlan = English

52. SEM 96–001 Comité para la Protección de los Recursos Naturales, A.C.; Grupo de los Cien Internacional, A.C.; Centro Mexicano de Derecho Ambiental, A.C v. United Mexican States.

53. Construction of the pier was complete by the time the CEC issued its report.

54. SEM 97–006, Friends of the Oldman River v. Canada.

55. Subsequently, the federal government negotiated with the provinces to bring them under the NAAEC framework. The negotiations resulted in the Canadian Intergovernmental Agreement (CIA) on the NAAEC, which would allow signatory provinces to both benefit from and be subject to the NAAEC. By signing provinces could use NAFTA's Commission on Environmental Cooperation to challenge enforcement practices in the US and Mexico. However, provinces would also subject their own enforcement practices to scrutiny by the CEC. Only three provinces, Alberta, Québec and Manitoba, have signed the agreement thus far.

56. C-302/86, Commission v. Denmark, ECR [1988] I-4607.

57. C-2/90, Commission v. Belgium, ECR [1992] I-4431.

58. The Commission had also argued that the Belgian law violated a Community Directive (84/631) on transfrontier shipments of hazardous waste. The Court agreed with the Commission regarding hazardous waste, noting that the directive allowed states to stop hazardous waste shipments only on a case by case basis, rather than with an across the board ban as Wallonia had done.

59. Jupille 1997.

60. This practice was to be permitted under Art. 100a(4).

61. C-41/93, *France v. Commission*, ECR [1994] I-1829.

62. "Commission Wrong to Authorize German ban on PCPs" Reuter European Community Report, May 17, 1994.

63. C-67/97, *Kriminalretten i Frederikshavn v. Denmark*, ECR [1998] I-8033.

64. Patrick Smyth, "Flight of the bumble bees case to create quite a buzz in Luxembourg," Irish Times, October 24, 1997.

65. Interestingly, the original Commission proposal did not contain an "escape clause" equivalent to Article 130t. This is understandable given the Commission's preference for harmonization. Community measures lose significance if strict Member States can ignore them and maintain national standards. (See Krämer 1990:93).

66. In some areas, such as urban wastewater treatment, EU directives are transposed into German law by state level regulations. Interview, European Commission DG XI, March 1998.

67. Héritier et al 1994; Knill 1998; Knill and Lenschow 2000:261.

68. Dir. 85/337 [1985] OJ L175/40.

69. Dir. 90/313 [1990] OJ L 158/56.

70. Knill and Lenschow 2000; Kimber 2000; Wessels and Rometsch 1996.

71. *Commission v. Germany*, C-361/88, [1991] ECR 2567.

72. Interview, German Permanent Representation to the EU April 3, 1998.

73. Ibid.

74. See Vogel 1995; Esty and Geradin 2001; Drezner 2001; Swire 1996; Stewart 1993; Porter 1999 for reviews of the literature on this subject.

75. Revesz 1992.

76. Rodden and Rose-Ackerman 1997. Also see Engel and Rose-Ackerman 2001.

77. Esty 1994; Drezner 2001.

78. Stewart 1993; Esty and Gentry 1997.

79. Esty 1994:162–3.

80. Zarsky 1997.

81. Ibid.

82. Swire 1996.

83. United States—Restrictions on Imports of Tuna, circulated on 3 September 1991, BISD 39S/155.

84. United States—Import Prohibition of Shrimp and Certain Shrimp Products, WT/DS58/AB/R, 12 October 1998

85. "Constitutional Federalism," *State Legislatures*, February 1999, Vol. 25 (2).

References

Bermann, George. 1998. Constitutional Implications of U.S. Participation in Regional Integration. *American Journal of Comparative Law* 46:463.

Boardman, Robert. 1990. *Global Regimes and Nation States: Environmental Issues in Australian Politics.* (Ottawa: Carleton University Press).

———. 1992. *Canadian Environmental Policy: Ecosystems, Politics, and Process.* (New York: Oxford University Press).

Bradley, Curtis A. 1998. The Treaty Power and American Federalism. *Michigan Law Review* 97(2):390.

Drezner, Daniel. 2001. Globalization and Policy Convergence. *International Studies Review* 3(1):53–78.

Esty, Daniel. 1994. *Greening the GATT.* Washington, DC: Institute for International Economics.

Esty, Daniel and Bradford Gentry. 1997. Foreign Investment, Globalization, and Environment. In OECD Proceedings, *Globalisation and Environment: Preliminary Perspectives* (Paris: OECD).

Esty, Daniel C. and Damien Geradin, eds. 2001. *Regulatory Competition and Economic Integration.* Oxford: Oxford University Press.

European Commission. 1999. Report on United States Barriers to Trade and Investment—1999. European Commission: Brussels.

European Commission, Report on United States Barriers to Trade and Investment, Doc I/194/94, Brussels, April 1994. Cited in, Paul M. Orbuch and Thomas O. Singer, "International Trade, the Environment, and the States: An Evolving State-Federal Relationship," Working Paper, Western Governor's Association, http://www.westgov.org/wga/publicat/tradepap.htm

Farber, Daniel A. and Robert E. Hudec. 1994. Free Trade and the Regulatory State: A GATT's-Eye View of the Dormant Commerce Clause. Vanderbildt Law Review 47:1401.

Friedman, Barry. 1994. Federalism's Future in the Global Village. Vanderbildt Law Review 47:1441.

Goldsmith, Jack L. 1997. Federal Courts, Foreign Affairs and Federalism. Virginia Law Review 83: 1617.

Héritier, Adrienne et al. 1994. Die Veränderung von Staatlichkeit in Europa: Ein regulativer Wettbewerb: Deutschland, Grossbritannien und Frankreich in der EU. Opladen: Leske + Budrich.

Hoekman, Bernard M. and Michel M. Kostecki. 1995. The Political Economy of the World Trading System. Oxford: Oxford University Press

Jupille, Joseph. 1997. Contracts, Contingencies and Coordination: The European Court of Justice and the EC's Green Market," Manuscript, University of Washington.

Kelemen, R. Daniel. 2001. The Limits of Judicial Power: Trade-Environment Disputes before the ECJ and WTO. *Comparative Political Studies* 34(6): 622–650.

Kimber, Clíona. 2000. Implementing European environmental policy and the Directive on Access to Environmental Information. In Knill and Lenschow, eds. *Implementing EU Environmental Policy: New Directions and Old Problems.*

Knill, Cristoph. 1998. European Policies: The Impact of National administrative Traditions. *Journal of Public Policy* 18 (1):1–28.

Knill, Cristoph and Andrea Lenschow, eds.. 2000. *Implementing EU Environmental Policy: New Directions and Old Problems.* Manchester: Manchester University Press.

Krämer, Ludwig. 1990. *EEC Treaty and Environmental Protection.* London: Sweet and Maxwell.

Mann, Howard. 2001. *Private Rights, Public Problems: A guide to NAFTA's controversial chapter on investor rights.* Washington, DC: International Institute for Sustainable Development and Worldwide Fund for Nature.

O'Reilly, James T. 1997. Stop the World, we want our own labels: Treaties, state voter initiative laws and federal pre-emption. *Journal of International Economic Law* 18:617.

Orbuch, Paul M. and Thomas O. Singer. 1998. "International Trade, the Environment, and the States: An Evolving State-Federal Relationship," Working Paper, Western Governor's Association. Available at: http://www.westgov.org/wga/publicat/tradepap.htm

Porter, Gareth. 1999. Trade Competition and Pollution Standards: "Race to the Bottom" or "Stuck at the Bottom"? *Journal of Environment and Development,* V. 8(2):133.

Revesz, Richard. 1992. Rehabilitating Interstate Competition; Rethinking the "Race-to-the-Bottom" Rationale for Federal Environmental Regulation, 67 *NYU Law Rev.* 1210.

Rodden, Jonathan and Susan Rose-Ackerman. 1997. Does Federalism Preserve Markets? *Virginia Law Review.* Vol. 83:1534.

Sager, Michelle A. 1999. From Conflict to Cooperation: International Trade Agreements and American Federalism. Paper Prepared for 1999 Annual Meeting of APSA, Atlanta, GA, Sept 2–5, 1999.

Scharpf, Fritz. 1999. *Governing in Europe: Effective and Democratic?* Oxford: Oxford University Press.

Scheiber, Harry N. 1993. International Economic Policies and the State Role in U.S. Federalism: A Process Revolution? In Douglas M. Brown and Earl H. Fry, eds. *States and Provinces in the International Economy.* Berkeley: Institute of Governmental Studies.

Steinberg, Richard H. 1997. Trade-environment negotiations in the EU, NAFTA, and WTO: Regional trajectories of rule development. *American Journal of International Law* 91(2):231.

Stewart, Richard B. 1977. Pyramids of Sacrifice? Problems of Federalism in Mandating State Implementation of National Environmental Policy, 86 *Yale Law Journal* 1196.

————. 1992. International Trade and Environment: Lessons from the Federal Experience, 49 *Wash. & Lee L. Rev.* 1329.

————. 1993. "Environmental Regulation and International Competitiveness," *Yale Law Journal,* Vol. 102:2039.

Straight, Samuel. 1995. Gatt and Nafta: Marrying effective dispute settlement and the sovereignty of the fifty states. *Duke Law Journal* 45:216.

Swire, Peter. 1996. The Race to Laxity and the Race to Undesirability: Explaining Failures in Competition Among Jurisdictions in Environmental Law. *Yale Law Journal and Yale Journal on Regulation* Symposium Issue: 67.

Villareal, Gavin R. 1998. One Leg to Stand On: The Treaty Power and Congressional Authority for the Endangered Species Act After United States v. Lopez. *Texas Law Review* 76:1125.

Vogel, David. 1995. *Trading Up: Consumer and Environmental Regulation in the Global Economy.* Cambridge: Harvard University Press.

————. 2001. Environmental Regulation and Economic Integration. In Daniel C. Esty and Damien Geradin, eds. *Regulatory Competition and Economic Integration.* Oxford: Oxford University Press.

Wessels, Wolfgang and Dietrich Rometsch. 1996. "German administrative interaction and the European Union: the fusion of Public Policies," In Yves Meny et al. *Adjusting to Europe,* New York: Routledge.

Zarsky, Lyuba. 1997. Stuck in the Mud? Nation-States, Globalisation and Environment. OECD Proceedings, *Globalisation and the Environment: Preliminary Perspectives.* Paris: OECD.

Chapter 9

Feminism, NGOs and the Impact of the New Transnationalisms

Joyce Gelb

I. INTRODUCTION

This article suggests that transnational interactions concerning ideals and norms may generate external pressures on nations to conform. Such interactions may also strengthen internal political actors advocating the enactment of national policies that implement those norms. Nations that feel compelled, either through treaties, participation in international conferences or other transnational interactions, to seek acceptance in or to join a larger global community will tend to "race toward the top" in enacting policies that conform to emerging norms of gender equality. Thus transnationalism[1] has had an impact on national policies related to gender equity, although the impact has been far from consistent and uniform. This essay will focus on the impact of globalization on three nations: Japan, Britain and the U.S.

New developments related to government and governance strategies, propelled in part by globalization, are creating a more pro-active policy related to gender equality in some nations. [2] This argument reflects the work of other scholars, including Friedman and Hochstetler, Clark, Risse and others, who argue for increased attention to the role of nongovernmental access to global institutions, emphasizing as well their interaction with other NGO's and national states.[3] Subsidiary effects of internationalism, such as pressure for greater transparency and other forms of democratization, may also impact positively on women's opportunities.

The dual emergence and interrelationship of transnational feminist activism and supranational political systems has been significant for national gender and gender equality policy making especially in nations that have been most eager to join international systems. The development of feminist policy communities and efforts toward achieving international and regional integration and agreements have accelerated this trend. This analysis will explore the emerging impact of informal pressures on national policy through the confluence of non-governmental organizations (NGO's) that advocate gender equality and international organizations and treaties that support such goals.

Feminists have utilized three types of institutions in order to generate international norms for gender equity and to pressure nation states to adopt them. In ascending order of level of significance in terms of direct authority and potential impact, they are:

I.   The creation of new international forms and venues such as world women's conferences. Feminists from countries that have been unresponsive to demands for change have incentives to participate actively in such forums.

II. The "capture" or attempted "capture" of the machinery of the United Nations both to lend its institutional sponsorship to gender equity norms and to the draft and "market" binding treaties.

III. Persuading transnational institutions with more direct legal and political power over nation states, most prominently the European Union (EU) to promulgate gender equity directives, or, (via the European Court of Justice—ECJ) to issue judicial rulings requiring member states to conform to EU gender equity norms.

Because the first two involve the least direct authority, they may have a less potent impact on the gender equity policies of nation states. They may therefore be most likely to be ignored or to produce merely symbolic policy change. Nations that are not subject to international norms at all such as the United States, would be likely to demonstrate the least responsiveness to *international* gender equity norms.

Changes in policy considered in this essay will include increased attention to gender related issues, discursive changes, as well as new policy approaches that are adopted into law. The gender equity policies to be considered relate primarily to equal opportunity in the labor market, although these vary in terms of costs of compliance, which may be used as an indicator of the degree of change they entail. Thus the policies may be grouped, according to specific policy and costs of compliance as follows:[4]

Table 1.

Policy	Cost of Compliance/Enforcement
maternity leave	low (unpaid) to high (paid)
child care	moderate- high
equal pay	moderate
antidiscimination	low -moderate
affirmative action(positive discrimination)	low (depending on job retraining)
sexual harassment	low

Invoking European and international legal standards, gender equity feminists have pressed governments and employers to reform their policies and practices, threatening potentially higher costs and liabilities through expanded litigation, public embarrassment and/or loss of face. With respect to the three case studies in this chapter, the most profound impact of globalization and NGO activism has been felt in Britain, primarily due to its membership in the EU. Some change has occurred in Japan due to compliance with the United Nations (UN) Convention on the Elimination of Discrimination Against Women (CEDAW; Women's Convention) which resulted in the passage of the Equal Opportunity Employment Law (EEOL). The least impact has been felt in the US, which has not been a party to transnational treaties related to gender equality. It should be noted, however, that those nations that have accepted inclusion of women's rights in some form of international agreement have agreed on a minimum standard for goals but not necessarily on specific policies or implementation.

II. INTERNATIONALISM AND FEMINISM: CREATING NEW FORUMS AND VENUES AND THE PROCESS AND OUTCOMES TO DATE

The increased significance of international organizations, combined with the emergence of second wave feminism as a world wide movement, have contributed to a new role for gender equality on the global stage. With the end of World War II, the discourse that shaped women and women's issues changed dramatically as the nature of world politics changed, the state system was expanded, and human rights- with women's rights as a central component—was placed on the international agenda.[5] The world polity created transnational bodies through the UN and associated agencies, and these began to deliver specific instructions to member nations to modify existing laws, create new organizational structures, and undertake new research and development approaches.[6] The Commission on the Status of Women (CSW) was created in 1945. The UN Declaration on Human Rights was adopted in 1948 and called for equal pay for equal work.[7] In dialogue with such bodies as the International Labor Organization (ILO), an interwar creation, the CSW helped develop new international standards for employed women and to expand concepts of economic rights.[8] The idea of using all societal resources equally—a human capital approach—became widely accepted as a basis for encouraging women's full economic, political and social participation in society. "Standard setting" of new norms—through the drafting of international treaties such as 1979 Convention on the Elimination of Discrimination against Women (CEDAW; hereafter referred to as the Women's Convention) which followed a 1967 Declaration, proved to be very significant. Borrowing language from an earlier treaty, the Convention on the Elimination of All Forms of Racial Discrimination, the Women's Convention's purpose is to "ensure" that gender does not impede women's ability to exercise rights basic to international human rights law, rather than guaranteeing identical treatment for women and men.[9]

The Women's Convention deals with civil rights, the legal status of women, and reproductive rights and emphasizes non-discrimination in education, politics, employment, and economic and social life. It asserts norms of gender equality with regard to choice of spouse, parenthood, personal rights, and command over property. It declares that intentional or unintentional rules that treat women differently from men cannot be tolerated. States have the obligation to provide services that facilitate combining family responsibilities with family and public life.[10]

The importance of the enactment of such international conventions, pressure on nation states to ratify them, and the establishment of monitoring systems (e.g. annual meetings held at the United Nations) cannot be overstated. By 1990, the Women's Convention had been ratified by over 100 nations (including Japan to be discussed below): "many countries that have focused little if any attention on women's rights in the past do so today largely because of the treaty." [11] Two "equality in employment" conventions adopted by the ILO in the 1950's were ratified by 112 and 110 countries respectively by 1991 (true of only 8 of 157 prior ILO conventions).[12] Even more impressive is the proliferation of national legislation that incorporates equal pay principles during the period after 1960. By the 1970's these had been adopted by over half the world's nations in contrast to just 10% prior to the convention's codifications.[13] These were followed by equal pay for equal value policies, and then "equality of opportunity" legislation.

For some, the rapid and general acceptance of the Women's Convention implies the recognition of gender equality as an international norm. Its function of monitoring and scrutinizing state policy may result in positive change. For example, Canada strengthened its sexual harassment laws as a result.[14] Anther example of a national policy relying on the Women's Convention is in Tanzania where a court found in favor of women's land ownership based partly on the ratification of CEDAW.[15] The new Columbian constitution, adopted in 1991, incorporates provisions derived from CEDAW as well.[16] Australia has relied upon CEDAW in a court ruling dealing with sexual harassment,[17] while embarrassing testimony pressured both the Australian and Korean governments to commit themselves to legislative change.[18] The impact of CEDAW as a policy making instrument was enhanced by the passage of the "optional protocol" by the 1999 UN General Assembly, which permits individual women to lodge complaints pursuant to the treaty before international bodies.[19]

However, the evidence is far from conclusive, or at best incomplete and ambiguous, with regard to change. Over 40 of the 133 parties to the Convention (as of 1994) have made a total of over 100 reservations to it as the price of ratification, suggesting considerable undermining of its integrity.[20] This convention is one of the most heavily reserved in implementation.[21] Some critics have contended that the Women's Convention has contributed to the marginalization of women's issues in "mainstream" human rights bodies, and that its implementation and obligations are weaker than in other human rights instruments.[22]

"Human rights advocacy relies primarily on publicity and shaming" rather than enforcement.[23] The Convention establishes only one enforcement mechanism, CEDAW. Implementation and enforcement have been impeded by several factors. States do not report progress in a timely fashion, resulting in a backlog of complaints; there is no one standard for evaluation; and the there is no mechanism to enforce individual complaints.[24] Some difficulties are mitigated by the work of the CSW, the Women's Commission—which is more proactive, aggressively investigating violations. However, it also has weak enforcement powers.[25] Even national governments that have not opted out are free to ignore provisions at will. "Ratification in and of itself does little to liberate women"[26] although it may create a lever through which to press for national changes or enforcement of existing laws.

III. INTERNATIONALISM AND NGO'S

A significant and symbiotic relationship has developed between NGOs representing the international women's movement and new transnational structures and institutions, resulting in such events as the International Women's Year (1975) and Decade of Women (1976–85). They are representative of new subjects and actors in international politics and law: individuals and non-state actors make new claims that go beyond national citizenship.[27] NGO's have acted as catalysts for social change, often bringing expertise to bear on specific rights and providing information concerning rights in specific countries. There are now well over 15,000 NGO's that operate in three or more countries and draw their financial support from more than one country.[28] New communications technologies (fax, email, the Web) have helped to further interaction and relationships unthinkable in earlier eras. Electronic space has been seen as the contested province of global capital and multiple new social forces, the latter emphasizing its openness and lack of hierarchy and central control.[29] Conferences and institutional settings such as the UN and EU also provide spaces through which to discover, collectively construct and organize new entities.[30] Jane Connors of the UN Division of the Advancement of Women (DAW) contends that, "Women's human rights groups have seized political space and United Nations and other international conferences in a way that no other group has".[31] Lacking any equivalent to bureaucratic labor and socialist organizations, international women's organizations define themselves in relation to the state, global forces (including those who seek to limit their influence) and each other.[32]

Transnational advocates seek to change the behavior of nation states and international organizations.[33] Through shared values, common discourse, as well as dense exchange of information (and services), they seek to frame new issues, attract attention and insert them into favorable institutional venues.[34] The UN aided the creation of the international women's movement and helped the development of new relationships among women's NGO 's, national states and international networks.[35] Thousands of new non-official participants began to attend international events in advocacy roles. In particular, feminists from countries unresponsive to national women's movements have had particular incentives to throw their energies into such forums, appealing to international organizations and citizens in order to pressure their own governments to take action.[36]

The UN and CSW provided new contexts in which women's movements could meet, lobby and mobilize campaigns. Among their demands was pressure for international conferences on the advancement of women. In 1976, an International Tribunal on Crimes Against Women was one of the initial attempts at an international public hearing by feminists and an early effort to focus on violence against women.[37] The UN Decade for Women was initiated by 1975 as International Women's Year (IWY), and increased attention to issues of women's equality. World conferences devoted to women under UN sponsorship began to convene every five years, beginning in 1975 in Mexico City. By 1980, prior to the Copenhagen meeting attended by 8,000 women, 60 nations signed onto CEDAW. This conference marked the beginning of the international importance of NGO's as well as a new consensus on the importance of changing domestic, national laws through an international feminist movement.[38] In 1985, the Nairobi conference, attended by 15,000 women, the second largest world conference ever, adopted a document entitled "Forward Looking Strategies for the Advancement of Women" toward the year 2000 (FLS) and embraced an explicitly feminist outlook.[39] The 1995 Beijing women 's conference' s NGO Forum was attended by close to 40,000 women.[40] There were 900 NGOs in consultative status before the Beijing meeting—550 more groups had provisional status related to issues of sustainable development. According to one analysis, there were over 300, 000 attendees and 3000 accredited NGO's at the Beijing meeting.[41] Their face-to-face interaction, information sharing and discovery of common concerns led to enhanced international and regional networking, and new impetus for national legislation. They participated in preparatory meetings, formed new caucus structures and negotiated effectively with national delegations.[42] At Beijing, NGO's and network representatives had significant impact by monitoring issues and inserting language into the conference's final document.[43]

Beyond world conferences and events specifically related to gender, feminist advocates have become a presence at conferences on food, population, (Cairo, 1994) human rights (Vienna, 1993), environment, and sustainable development. The 1993 World Conference in Vienna expanded the legitimacy and integration of gender concerns into the entire human rights system through its transnational organization labeled the "most coherent force at the Conference"[44] while the Cairo conference in 1994 saw the formation of an international women's coalition to influence the outcomes.[45] At these and subsequent conferences, an NGO Women's Caucus and other women's caucuses have met daily to assess conference proceedings and to monitor the drafting process.[46]

The impact of world conferences has been to prod nation states to take action, including their ratification of such international treaties as the Women's Convention. The final document issued by the Beijing Fourth World Conference on Women, entitled the Beijing Platform for Action, provided a new international instrument by which to measure the commitment of nation states to women's rights. Ninety percent of UN members have subsequently established some sort of national machinery that, at the very least, has increased access to political and economic resources for women.[47] Women activists have increased their ability to lobby and monitor with impact at the UN and within their national governments. The conjunction of international feminist activism and the internationalization of women's rights issues has also produced many new international women's organizations. A surge in international women's NGO's began during the UN Decade for Women.[48] These include the Women's International Network (WIN), ISIS (International Women's Information and Communications Service, International Women's Rights Action Watch (ISIS), and the International Women's Tribune Center. Numerous regional groups have developed as well while some have gained a foothold at the UN itself. Groups network through fax and now the internet, using new technology to foster a sense of international community. These efforts have contributed to better data collection and measurement related for several aspects of women's participation.[49] "Producing more standardized knowledge in a rationally planned and monitored way has been one of the main contributions of the modern campaign on women's issues ... to the world."[50] Of course, the NGO sector is not monolithic; groups span the political and social spectrum, and vary in access to power and resources. Furthermore, they range from unstructured associations to large professionalized organizational entities.[51] The latter include the Women's Environment and Development Organization (WEDO) which created a network of women's groups after the 1992 Rio UN Conference on Environment and Development (UNCED) and whose voice has been forceful in lobbying for inclusion of women's rights in all major international documents and conferences.[52]

The argument advanced here suggests that feminist NGO's have forcefully pressed the concept of "women's rights as human rights" in international arenas. As Hochstetler, Clark and Friedman suggest: "NGO's challenge to the nation state has garnered some results since the 1995 conference"[53] The remainder of this article will be devoted to three case studies , to analyze the extent of actual implementation at the national level. As mentioned earlier, the three countries were chosen to represent a range of different outcomes. While the case studies do not provide entirely conclusive findings, they point to the significance of transnational as well as national factors in determining outcomes.

IV. GENDER EQUALITY IN JAPAN: THE LIMITS AND POTENTIAL OF CEDAW

Japan's experience with regard to internationalization of gender equality issues demonstrates both the significance of international pressure in creating new approaches and the limits of symbolic response. In Japan, there would have been little change without international pressure. However, the thrust of the changes made is subject to state interpretation and the limitations imposed by national policy making. The Japanese experience tests the potential of gender equality policy emanating from international forums and UN machinery.

The Japanese government ratified the ILO Convention on Equal Remuneration for Men and Women Workers for Equal Value (#100) in 1967 and the CEDAW in 1985.[54] Japan's decision to participate formally in the newly developing international norms related to gender equality may have been at least partially due to a desire to be considered a "modern" nation, worthy of prestige and acceptance.[55]

The activism of Japanese feminist groups also may have "embarrassed" the Japanese government into signing the treaty, as they sought to prod the government into action through expanding norms of gender equity.[56] In a 1980 meeting of the Cabinet, it was decided that Japan would ratify the Women's Convention by July 1985,[57] in the final year of the UN Decade for Women. The Japanese government began to review its statutes in terms of the Convention to reconcile its demands for gender equality, seeking a balance with national customs and law. In addition to the Equal Employment Law reviewed here, the government amended its Nationality Law to permit acquisition of citizenship through a Japanese mother married to a non- Japanese national. It also modified educational curricula that required only women to take compulsory home economics courses.[58] After protracted negotiations in the consultative committee, or *shingikai*, the tripartite group essentially accepted the views of employers, who insisted on a weak law, with provisions merely to "endeavor" to attain gender equality, as the price for acquiescing to any law.[59] The Equal Employment Opportunity Law (EEOL), passed in 1985, became effective the following year, meeting the UN deadline. While the Japanese government acknowledged this as a "historic" opportunity,[60] it concurrently amended the Working Women's Welfare Law of 1972 and Labor Standards Law of 1947, to limit protective legislation for women, a move opposed by many women's groups. Karube views the "international force of social change", as exemplified by the UN Decade for Women and the Women's Convention, as failing to achieve true gender equality in Japan.[61]

Nonetheless, signing on to the treaty and the subsequent passage of the EEOL did produce some changes in Japanese society including some that were unforeseen. Among these was an increase in women attending four-year colleges, and an increase in hiring of female college graduates during the period of the "bubble economy", in the late 1980's. The law has certainly helped to increase the number of qualified women who can fulfill managerial and professional responsibilities.[62] Some women albeit few, were able to gain access to the managerial or career track (*sogo shoku*), which involves transfers and more responsibility as well as higher wages, promotion and benefits. However, many large companies introduced a "two track system" after the law's adoption, to essentially limit women to clerical tasks (*ippan shoku*). The combination of increased education and aspirations that resulted from the law's passage, led to more women applying for full time employment. A combination of the collapse of the bubble economy and continued discrimination by employers led the government to open prefecturally based offices to investigate complaints of discrimination and harassment.[63] They have received 20,000 complaints per year since 1994.[64]

The non-coercive weak law that was adopted essentially left unchallenged the male dominated, seniority-based system, replete with gender distinctions. The EEOL prohibited employers from discriminating against women in education, training and benefits and with regard to mandatory retirement based on marriage, childbirth or age. Weaker provisions seek only good faith efforts for recruitment, hiring, job assignments and promotion. A prefectural mediation process was put in place to resolve complaints but required the approval of both employee and employer. As a result, this process proved difficult to implement. Not surprisingly, only one mediation was accepted at the prefectural level, and its outcome disappointed the women complainants because it lacked concrete remedies that led to more reliance on litigation. As of 1995, women earned only 57.7% of men and women held only 1.5% of managerial positions (many of which may be only token titles), suggesting that the concept of equal pay for work of equal value, although accepted through treaty ratification, is a long way off in reality.[65]

Encouragement of shared family and work responsibilities as mandated by the UN and ILO was not incorporated into the EEOL and did not lead the Japanese government to limit long working hours. In 1995, Japan ratified ILO conventions 195 and 196, which called for equal opportunity and treatment for male and female workers with family responsibilities.[66] Prompted at least as much by the declining birth rate as international strictures, the Child Care Leave Act of 1992 provided unpaid leave or reduction of work hours for either parent. In 1995, a Child Care Benefit system was established which provided for 25% of leave to be paid. A Part Time Work Law, passed in 1994, sought to improve the lot of part time workers, most of whom are women, by providing them access to unemployment insurance and special programs, including skills training.[67]

The impact of international women's activism began in 1975 - International Women's Year—somewhat after the beginnings of a new wave of feminism in Japan.[68] The impact was far greater in Japan than in the US, where "it was hardly noticed by an already active women's movement".[69] By the time of the 1995 Beijing meeting, 6000 Japanese women attended.

Participation in international meetings has increased women's litigation and activism related to the EEOL in Japan as well as other activities.[70] The Japanese based Asian Women's Forum is one example; founded in 1977, its focus is the elimination of sexual exploitation of Asian women and the creation of stronger links between Japanese women and women throughout Asia .[71] The Asia Solidarity Network on Forced Military Comfort Women Problem was created in 1992 and involved groups in Japan, Korea, Indonesia and the Philippines. [72] Further evidence is seen in the activism of such groups as the Working Women's Network based in Osaka, which brought its complaints regarding the ineffectiveness of the EEOL before the ILO and Commission on the Elimination of Discrimination against Women, as well as the UN Human Rights Committee, in an effort to gain media and public attention to embarrass the Japanese government and force greater compliance. [73]

These efforts may have helped pressure the Japanese government into revising the EEOL through amendments, effective April 1999, that now mandate equal opportunity in recruitment, hiring, assignments, training and promotion (excluding on the job training).[74] The amendments also permit mediation to go forward through a request from only one side, and names of recalcitrant employers are to be publicized. All remaining overtime protections of the Labor Standards Act were repealed at the same time. The changes do not create an independent agency, restructure the mediation process or provide more enforcement powers. Furthermore, there is no consideration of indirect discrimination, penalties for infringements of the law, requirements for positive action, consideration of mediation based on positive action or sexual harassment or attack on the "two track system." The amendments do require increased "consultation" regarding positive action and sexual harassment; subsequent Ministry of Labor Guidelines stress prevention of verbal or physical harassment, including a broad definition of "workplace" that encompasses after hours activity. [75]

Much of what is occurring embodies symbolic elements, but there may be elements of real change emerging, filtered through the lens of national policy making and the continued preeminence of business pressure in this policy arena. At the very least, the recourse of Japanese feminists, to pursue international gender equality norms through ratification of CEDAW and the subsequent enactment of legislation, has raised awareness and influenced activism and litigation.[76]

V. REGIONAL SUPRANATIONAL ORGANIZATION AND WOMEN'S RIGHTS

Another significant instance of the impact of transnationalism is to be found in the European Union (EU). Similar to the international community discussed above, the regionally-based EU has also provided a political arena for networking and contacts, research sharing, single issue campaigns and practical actions. [77] Article 119 of the Treaty of Rome that established the European Community (hereafter referred to as the EC, to apply to all European Union references) endorsed the concept of equal pay. This part of the treaty remained a dead letter for many years, as it was not implemented by member states, too weak in wording and context to have resonance immediately for women's equality in Europe.[78] However, in the early 1970's, it was reactivated by three European court cases, which stated for the first time that it was binding on member states. In addition, an Equal Pay directive in 1976 prohibited discrimination in promotion, benefits and training.[79] While initial debates around Article 119 failed to consider the interests of women or social justice—it was activist women who transformed the debate into a demand for equal rights.[80] A further step toward recognition of women's rights came with the announcement of the 1974 EEC Social Action Program, in which three Equality Directives were adopted which explicitly extended the concept of women's rights beyond equal pay to the equal treatment in social security, and statutory and occupational equal treatment in employment. This included access to employment, training, promotion and working conditions and entailed the absence of indirect discrimination and connection with family or marital status.[81](For the first time, a broader ILO formulation of "equal pay for work of equal value" was utilized, which mentioned the relationship between paid labor and family roles.)[82] A subsequent directive dealt with equal treatment for self-employed women and the protection of pregnant women's right to leave from work before and after pregnancy. The European Court of Justice (ECJ) granted private litigants the right to draw on EC laws to challenge both governments and private employers on issues encompassed by Article 119 and the Equal Treatment Directive. Other community policies exhort member nations to promote equality with reference to sexual harassment, child care, positive action and vocational training. [83]

The ECJ has been called second only to the US Supreme Court in its power, as it establishes the primacy of European over national laws. It is one of the most active tribunals in the development of international human rights jurisprudence.[84] The Court has turned the Treaty of Rome into a Constitution that limits European governments just as the US Constitution constrains governmental action. [85] The EC has brought infringement proceedings against Britain for failure to fulfill treaty obligations. The ECJ has interpreted the Directives more broadly than the British legislation they spawned, permitting individual claimants to reverse adverse rulings under British law through appeal. ECJ decisions have forced the British parliament to amend laws in order to bring its practices in harmony with EC law and British courts to harmonize domestic law with European law. [86] In 1976, a decision of the ECJ found that Article 119 was directly binding on all member states, creating a firm legal base for women's rights in years to come. Together, Article 119 and the Directives constitute an "advanced legal framework" with considerable force in European nations. [87] The EC has, however, sought to maintain a balanced position, leaving national courts to develop their own approaches within the larger framework of advancing equality for women in an evolutionary manner.[88] The specific implementation of EC policy with reference to Britain will be discussed below.

An increased European focus on women's employment issues and beyond was enhanced in the 1980's by several factors: the new progressive majority in the European Parliament after 1984, an OECD conference on women in the labor market in 1980 and the activity around the UN Decade for Women discussed above.[89] From 1982–95, three EC action programs, coordinated by the since renamed Women's Bureau, the EC's Equal Opportunities Unit, maintained policy initiatives. The Commission on Women's Rights orchestrated a strong European parliamentary lobby that presented thorough analyses of women's status and pressed for specific demands.[90] A European\Women's Lobby, established in 1990, represents Europe-wide and country-specific women's groups. Women's groups and their allies have focused on the EC as a vehicle for change. And have achieved many positive developments related to gender equity: for example, the EC Third Action Programme on Women emphasis on "mainstreaming" the concept of equal treatment into all appropriate

EC programs and policies. Gender related policy machinery has been put in place: The European parliament has a women's committee and "women's policy" now has a budget and a unit; advisory groups have been established; and research and workshops have been funded. The expanding transnational women's network has helped to prevent erosion of hard fought policy gains, as cost cutting and deregulation have taken hold almost universally. [91]A major impact of the EC's interest in equality has been the establishment of official and nonofficial networks of women who have gained roles in decision-making and have established an extended infrastructure that is difficult to dismantle or eliminate.[92] It is at the regional level that internationalism is likely to be practiced most intensively," according to one observer. [93]

Other analysts take a more critical stance and stress the limitations of women as transnational actors within the EC. [94] They point to the relative remoteness of EC decision-making and its distance from second wave feminists. In addition, women's entry, particularly in the social field, was late and limited, so their foothold is somewhat tenuous. [95]The number of policy initiatives has been relatively small and there has been difficulty getting the EC to focus beyond the framework of paid labor, and equal pay and treatment issues to a "difference" approach that deals with matters of family responsibility and organization.[96] The obdurate British government and the increasingly powerful transnational business community challenged new gender equality efforts, and a weakening labor organization was unable to fight back.[97] The efforts of the former were able to retard action on parental leave and part time work for a number of years.

Nonetheless, the 1989 Social Charter marked a new recognition in Europe of the need for equal treatment for men and women. It extended the notion of "equal opportunities" and developed measures to recognize differences through positive action, and the work/family divide. The ratification of the Maastricht Treaty in 1993, suggested a new approach to integrating issues of social policy with those related to workplace activity.[98] One observer points to a three stage theory involving gradual broadening of EC policy on women: the first stage, (1957- 69) focused on economic equity and equal pay to prevent competitive disadvantage to any one member state; the second (1970–79) prioritized the impact of social policy for women; and the third (1980–86) emphasized newly broadened policy concerns including parental leave, rights for part time workers and positive action.[99] While its restricted scope and partial implementation continue to limit the EC's role as emancipator of women,[100] its potential as a force for equal citizenship should not be dismissed. For many British women, EC membership has meant a significant strengthening of civil and social rights as the next section will suggest.[101]

The European Union's legal system has provided domestic groups with mechanisms that can be used to impose new costs on their government, giving weak interest groups the political leverage to directly influencing national policy.[102] ECJ legal precedents create new material and political costs for government and private actors. [103] A change in EU policy is much harder for national governments to reverse than legal victories based on domestic law, because such reversals would require legislative consensus at the European level.

VI. THE EU AND GENDER EQUITY IN ENGLAND

The English experience with gender equality reflects both the limits of supranational politics on state autonomy and the impact of transnationalism in shaping British policy innovation. This section will illustrate how the gradually adopted gender equity policy to the "standard setting" initiatives developed by the direct authority of EC directives. Ultimately, EC law permitted women's rights advocates to force an unwilling British government to change public policy.

Under Thatcherite Conservative government, England resisted full inclusion in the new united Europe and refused to adhere to the Directive mandating parental leave and leave for family reasons. When proposed by the EC in 1983, it was vetoed by Britain and then adopted despite British opposition in 1993.[104] The Conservative British government also opted out of the Maastricht social policy agreement that provided three month parental leave for child care purposes as well as steps toward positive action for working women.[105] Lacking unanimous support, the Social Protocol was unable to acquire treaty status. The British government also opposed two out of three directives on atypical (non-full time, regular) employment.[106] In addition to refusing to participate in and lobbying against policies it viewed as abhorrent, the British government delayed compliance with and ignored certain EU directives. In the face of repeated demands and treaty obligations, it stalled, leading Lord Lester to observe that the government's delay in implementing an ECJ judgment on equal pay dating from 1982, "amounts to a continuing denial in the United Kingdom of the fundamental human right to sex equality in pay." [107] The Tory British government ignored some rulings until forced to do otherwise, responded slowly, and was outright obdurate, as in its refusal to comply with the directive for pregnant workers and equalization of retirement and pension ages.[108]

From its inception, the EC has been reluctant to interfere in the internal affairs of member states—although it is within the competence of the EU to intervene, the requirement of "subsidiarity" means that such authority should be exercised only if member states cannot achieve collective objectives.[109] Nonetheless, there is a good case to be made for the significance of the EC on numerous aspects of British policy toward gender equality. The EC's supranational safeguards played a major role in preventing backsliding and eroding women's rights during recession.[110]

Gender equity feminists and the Equal Opportunities Commission (EOC) had considerable success in forcing a reluctant Conservative government to accept significant changes in equality policy.[111] Women's interest groups, and later trade unions as well, mobilized around a litigation strategy, national judicial support obtained and follow through maintained to show the costs of not changing national policy.[112] While the passage of the Equal Pay Act (EPA) of 1970 and Sex Discrimination Act (SDA) of 1975 (and amendments to them) had multiple sources and only the latter occurred when Britain was an EC member , the importance of compliance with the Treaty of Rome , the Equal Pay (1975) and Equal Treatment Directives (1976) of the EC and various ILO conventions must be acknowledged.[113] It is possible that it was EC membership that forced the UK into its relatively forward-looking role regarding sex discrimination laws.[114] Similarly, EC pressure led to a strengthening of the equality machinery established by the SDA, the Equal Opportunities Commission (EOC). In order to comply with EU directives, resources (however limited) were made available to the EOC to promote sex equality and to accelerate the implementation of sex equality objectives. While the EU brought judicial proceedings against the UK to correct defects and exclusions in national legislation, the EOC used its legal resources to support a series of cases before the ECJ that clarified the rights conferred by European law.[115] These changes became part of the 1983 Equal Value (Amendment) regulations and the Sex Discrimination Act of 1986, which together removed loopholes from the original legislation and strengthened the principle of equal pay for comparable work.

The EOC has become an effective advocate for British women, successfully sponsoring cases that advance equality rulings and invalidate portions of British law.[116] The UK has one of the highest levels of anti-discrimination litigation in the EC, most of it funded by the EOC or trade unions.[117] The EOC is thus providing a significant resource for legal redress by complainants as well as to appeal for more favorable case court interpretations. The EC is also helping to diffuse the EC's equality principles to national laws through the large number of referrals from British Courts to the ECJ and the widespread reporting of the impact of the referrals. Domestic court rulings have become more willing to find in favor of women as a result.[118] A publication, the Equal Opportunities Review—regularly reports on the significance of national and supranational rulings.[119]

VII. SPECIFIC POLICY IMPACTS [120]

ECJ rulings have narrowed exceptions to the SDA, incorporated "equal value" into the EPA, made retirement subject to discrimination law, and enabled married women to be eligible for the British Invalid Care Allowance.[121] In the *Marshall* case in 1986, the ECJ found that differential retirement ages for men and women was a violation of the Equal Treatment Directive, which led to subsequent amendments to the law, all favoring women. The Court has also ruled that sex discrimination in pensions was contrary to European law in *Barber v. Guardian Royal Exchange Assurance Group*. In *Enderby v. Frenchay Health Authority*, it ruled that a female employee's pay should be equal to males in different job categories and covered by Article 119 on equal pay. British policy makers are currently addressing other policies recommended by the EU, including rights for part time workers and independent taxation of married couples.[122] *Webb v. EMO Air Cargo* ruled that employers could not dismiss pregnant workers. To comply with EC directives, the UK's Sex Discrimination Act of 1986 extended the scope of the law to cover all employers, extending coverage to those with fewer than 5 employees and to prohibit laws that force women to retire from employment at different ages than men. The Employment Act of 1989 reduced exceptions to the prohibition on sex discrimination, and the Pensions Act of 1995 equalized male and female pension provision (but not until the year 2020!).[123] A 1996 amendment to the SDA permitted industrial tribunals (which hear many British sex discrimination complaints) to award compensation for indirect discrimination.

Consideration of sexual harassment led to statements that it is already outlawed by the EU Equal Treatment Directive; national tribunals are relying increasingly on the Commission's Recommendation and Code of Practice. The Equal Treatment Directive obliged member states to review all protective measures and make changes where the "concern for protection that originally inspired them is no longer founded".[124] The British government complied by abolishing the ban on women in mines and on cleaning machinery. Other protective measures have given way to the principle of equal treatment except where pregnancy and maternity create particular risks for women. In the *Johnston* case, the ECJ raised questions regarding the use of protective legislation based on reproductive hazards and other biological and physiological distinctions that may lead to further changes in British practice.[125] The ECJ also abolished an upper limit on back pay in sex discrimination cases in *Marshall v. Southampton*, 1993. This bore concrete application when the British Ministry of Defense was found to have summarily dismissed pregnant personnel and they were able to receive large settlements (in cases supported by the EOC).

EC infringement proceedings against the UK alleging inadequate compliance have resulted in amendments to British laws. The EC has also been empowered to conduct formal investigations and has judicially reviewed national legislation, including the UK's Employment Protection (Consolidation) Act, which had prevented claims for unfair dismissal from those who worked less than 16 hours per week. They found that treating part timers differently amounted to indirect discrimination. Its 1996 ruling altered the structure of statutory maternity pay (SMP), increasing its value to women.[126]

It is difficult to establish a causal relationship between legal changes and material behavior. Female/male pay ratios have remained about the same (about 75%) and occupational segregation has remained at the same levels during the period under review. Nonetheless, the EC gave British feminists virtually their only enforceable mechanism to improve and seek more favorable interpretations of domestic legislation, particularly under neo-liberal domination. It provided a vehicle for intervention and regulation on gender equity issues in a period of deregulation and anti-rights primacy.[127]

VIII. GENDER POLICY IN BRITAIN SINCE BLAIR

The election of Tony Blair and the electoral victory of Labour appeared to have the potential of altering the previous government's obduracy toward gender based issues. Reinforcing the notion that national government still plays a key role in regulating gender-based policy, shortly after the election, Britain did sign on belatedly to the Social Chapter of the EU. This bound it to the parental leave, part time work and protection of pregnant women directives of the EC (the latter's impact preceded the Labour victory in 1996). Three months unpaid parental leave and provision for time off for caring responsibilities have been introduced into the UK. Pregnant women are eligible for forty weeks leave with six weeks paid at 90% of wages; a further twelve weeks may be paid at the same level as sickness benefit. Eligibility is conditional on two years employment with the same employer, of over sixteen hours per week.[128] Maternity leave has been standardized at 18 weeks for all with the right to return to work.[129] The government has adopted the EU Burden of Proof Directive to be implemented within three years, requiring an employer to justify any rules that have a greater adverse impact on one sex.[130] The government has committed itself to implementing "fairness at work" policy in line with the Part Time, Working Time and Young Workers Directives of the EU, which will also protect against unfair dismissal.

IX. THE UNITED STATES—PROGRESS ON GENDER EQUALITY IN A NATIONAL CONTEXT

The argument presented here suggests that United State, initially a world "standard setter" regarding norms of workplace gender based equality, is currently falling behind in comparison to other nations, particularly with respect to acceptance of new norms that provide a more holistic approach to equity for working women. In contrast to Japan and Britain, the US has been slower to adopt emerging international norms of gender equality. The US has resisted ratification of CEDAW and other treaties, regarding the US Constitution as the preeminent safeguard of similar rights and freedoms.[131] It has been alienated from international legal strictures, preferring to operate within its own system.

Even if ratification were to occur, the US would impose significant reservations,[132] such as noting the primacy of the US Constitution and rejecting the principle of women in the military, comparable worth to set remuneration, and maternity leave with pay or comparable social benefits without loss of employment and seniority.[133] Because of its reluctance to submit to supranational rules, US policy on gender equality, unlike Britain and Japan, although impressive in many ways, has not benefited from a dialogue with the dual forces of transnationalism and feminism.

For example, in response to the 1995 Beijing UN Fourth World Women's Conference, the US established an Interagency Council on Women. By and large, its role has been symbolic, leading to little actual policy reevaluation and change.[134] However, subnational governments, including San Francisco and Maine, have passed legislation endorsing CEDAW within their jurisdictions, "standard - setting" efforts that may impact on the national government at a future time.[135]

In the US, despite the defeat of the Equal Rights Amendment to the Constitution in 1982, women's rights were steadily expanded through Title VII of the CRA, which extends the prohibition on employment discrimination to discrimination based on sex. The enforcement body established by the CRA, Equal Employment Opportunities Commission (EEOC) whose brief deals with racial minorities and women, and was initially more active in litigating cases and issuing guidelines than its British counterpart. In recent years, the two agencies have arguably have become more similar, with the UK's EOC taking on a larger role discussed above.[136] Prodded by feminist groups, the EEOC came to see sex discrimination as a priority issue. The EEOC can investigate and conciliate complaints and grant complainants the right to seek remedies in court.[137] It can also bring class action suits and issue *amicus* briefs, strengthening its role in policy. It has issued guidelines and advanced the gender equality agenda on affirmative action, pregnancy, insurance premiums, and sexual harassment. While there has been much disappointment with the agency, relating to the huge case backlog, turnover of personnel and charges of ineffectiveness, it has realized occasional major victories such as the $40 million settlement in the AT&T case in 1973.

The Equal Protection clause of the 14th Amendment has been interpreted to include gender inequity although sex based classifications have been subject only to intermediate scrutiny. Judges in the US have often played an active role in enforcing Title VII and awarded substantial remedies, although the conservative appointees to the judiciary and bureaucracy after 1980 in the US and the liberalizing impact of the EC in Britain narrowed the gaps between the two nations.[138] Feminists and trade unions have sometimes been more effective advocates for change than their counterparts abroad, litigating and lobbying with impact at the state and national levels. Presidential executive orders 11246 and 11375 prohibited federal contractors from engaging in sex based discrimination and established affirmative action in hiring, in efforts to result in greater inclusion of women and minorities. Recalcitrant employees face the threat of funding cut off. Affirmative action and the impact of private class action suits vigorously prosecuted by women, advocacy groups and their activist attorneys through the structure of American law enforcement have produced dramatic gains for American working women.[139]

At present, women comprise just 5% of top managers in the United States, although their numbers as administrators and managers have increased dramatically from 19% in 1970 to over 45% in the late 1990's, male wages in the 1990's, perhaps related in part to the fact that they tend to hold less high paying positions in these fields making American women perhaps the most successful in the world in holding high level positions.[140] Still, their incomes continue to lag behind those of men; they earned 71–75% of male wage in the 1990's, due in part to the fact that they tend to be employed in fields that pay less.

The major difficulty for American working women lies in the absence of other policies that might support them outside the workplace. For example, the US lacks a national comprehensive child care policy or mandatory maternity assistance. Since 1993, the Family and Medical Leave Act has provided for a three-month unpaid parental leave policy in companies with over 50 employees; while Japan has partially paid leave and Britain's emerging paid parental leave policy. Unlike other nations more attuned to emerging gender equity norms, there has been no attention in the US to the plight of part time workers, who are primarily women

Unlike Japan, a non-Western relative newcomer to international norms, the US, a proud, self confident hegemonic state , refuses to be "embarrassed" into signing most international treaties, including those related to emerging norms of gender equity. There may be several explanations: 1) the US may feel it has already leads the world in enacting gender related policy, 2) it is reluctant to relinquish judicial power to international courts; and, 3) American feminist advocates have not aggressively pressed for treaty ratification. In addition, the US has been reluctant to sign on to treaties because legal rules are often enforceable in courts by private parties, courts are unpredictable and independent and judicial remedies are very strong.[141] Because of the reluctance to engage in the new international community effort on gender, some contend that, currently, access to the EC has meant a higher level of continuity for British gender equity policy related to women and work than has been true in the US.[142]

X. CONCLUSION

This analysis has provided evidence for the growing force of international gender equity norms within nation states, citing its concerns over sovereignty. The impact of three factors have been considered: the role of feminist NGO's in negotiating and "capturing" transnational institutions, the development of new international forums and treaties, and the promulgation of gender equity policies which may produce change within nation states (a product of the interaction between the first two). In none of the instances considered here has change occurred as a result of the "negative externalities" experienced by nations thought to be world leaders in gender equity policy e.g. Sweden and the United States. Such nations have no economic incentive to pressure others to move toward gender equality.

This examination of three countries has shown that the United States' failure to participate in the new international system has meant that it is least affected, Japan has been affected to some extent by the weaker and less direct authority of UN based international treaties, while the EC approach, which involves the most intervention in member states, has produced the most change in a member state.

The issue of costs to government and business will affect the rate of acceptance of new policy, as Table One suggested. Governments and private sector organizations will be most likely to accept exhortations with limited costs and maximum symbolic resonance to avoid the costs of compliance with new international standards, particularly those with which it is most expensive to comply. In this regard, they are most likely to agree to minimal, general appeals for anti discrimination policy. The extent of resistance to strict implementation by the Japanese business community of the equal employment law (which still controls much of the political process) and by the British Tory government and business community to compliance with EC directives suggests that these actors view compliance with new international gender equity norms as having considerable costs. They can be expected to oppose efforts to institutionalize paid maternity or child care leave, mandate equal pay and promotion or provide new affirmative action opportunities, unless they can be persuaded that the short term costs will be justified by utilizing a more qualified and enduring labor force. However, they may prefer complying with more stringent equality policies if they know they will lose in the courts. Indeed, the threat of a legal case and potential liability, as well as adverse media coverage, can be a weapon in itself, altering the behavior of government and firms.[143] In the British case, lobbying by women's advocates and their allies created significant political and financial costs, including large settlements to sex discrimination plaintiffs. This process has been slower to develop in Japan, though there have been several recent settlements in cases involving discriminatory salary and promotion as company policies. Further study of the implementation of new gender equity directives within nation states is needed in order to assess the full impact of change.

Britain has been increasingly receptive to European approaches to gender issues, with an interactive process emanating from within government (the EOC), regionally-based transnational activists (feminist NGO's) as well as transnational and national courts and legislative bodies. Women's rights groups have been able to gain greater leverage over domestic policy through appeals to an overriding transnational institution. The EC has clearly acted as a "standard setter" which has changed national norms. This has led one of the most powerful nations in Europe to alter some of its policies and to increase regulation, suggesting a "race to the top" related to gender equity policy. The costs of violating and reversing EC directives have created significant incentives for compliance for government and employers.

In Japan, national and international pressures emanating from the UN, international treaties and women's NGO's have increased the government's attention to gender equality. The Japanese case may provide support for the "Baptists Alone" hypothesis: that laggard nations concerned about their international reputation and "keeping up" with other world democratic powers may adopt new human rights policies as a result. This appears to have resulted despite the absence of negative externalities and pressure from multinational corporations. The Japanese response to the desire for new international stature (as well as domestic pressure from women's rights groups) has been to adopt the trappings, if not reality, of new standards and regulation related to gender issues. National policy making, still reliant on business, the Liberal Democratic Party (LDP) and bureaucrats, has tended to invoke the symbols of gender equality with limited attention to serious implementation of change. Yet, changed expectations among women and the nation's continued, expanded exposure to the international community have created momentum which has resulted in some modifications to existing practice and maintains pressures for more regulation of practices related to gender equity regulations. Continued concern for "losing face" due to adverse publicity generated by women's rights advocates has imposed new, albeit limited, costs on government and employers. One result has been the enactment of Amendments to the Equal Employment Law effective in April 1999 .The Japanese case suggests that the acceptance of even weak international norms may have an impact on gender policy change.

The US, in many ways a "standard setter" in the twentieth century's struggle for gender equity, has remained aloof from the strictures of international treaties, in the interests of national sovereignty. As a result, it has fallen behind in setting new standards for working women as it does not view itself as subject to the demands of global feminism and international rule making.[144] By ignoring important social policies that support working women who must balance home and work responsibilities, US policy making has neglected important aspects of gender equity.

Joyce Gelb is a Professor of Political Science and Director of the Program in Women's Studies and the Center for Research on Women in Society at the Graduate Center, City University of New York.

Notes

1. See Boyle and Preves, forthcoming.

2. Held, 26

3. Friedman, and Hochstetler, 2 ; Clark, Friedman and Hochstetler, 2; Risse, 185–88, 204.

4. The list of costs must remain speculative lacking specific data for each country.

5. Berkovitch, 100
6. Ibid, 101.
7. Ibid, 103, 105, 110.
8. Ibid, 104
9. Wang, 1995, 906.
10. Mahoney, 1996, 799.
11. Jacobson, 1992, 444.
12.
13. Ibid, 117.
14. Wang, 917.
15. Ibid.
16. Plata and Espriella, 1995, 401.
17. Landsberg –Lewis , 1998, 23.
18. Interview, Connors, DAW, 10/6/99.
19. Ibid.
20. Mahoney, 799.
21. Wang, 917.
22. Mahoney, 799.
23. Copelon and Petchesky, 363.
24. Wang, 917.
25. Wang, 920.
26. Staudt,
27. Sassen, 21, 96.
28. Axtmann, 17.
29. Sassen, 177, 194.
30. Waterman, 159.
31. Interview, 10/99.
32. Waterman, 154, 59.
33. Keck and Sikkink, 2; see also Boyle and Preves.
34. Ibid.
35. Sienstra, 110; Keck and Sikkink , 150.
36. Boyle and Preves.
37. Hoskyns, 36.
38. Jaquette, 50.
39. Sienstra, 144.
40. Keck and Sikkink, 169.
41. Clark Freidman and Hochstetler, 9.
42. Clark Friedman and Hochstetler, 16.
43. Ibid. , 188.
44. Dorsey, 344.
45. Copelon and Petchesky , 348; Romany, 543.
46. Chen, 150.
47. Sienstra, 109.
48. Berkovitch, 160.
49. Ibid., 151.
50. Ibid., 152.
51. Silliman, 1999,25.

52. Ibid., 39.
53. Hochstetler, Clark and Friedman.
54. Hayashi, 1990, 19.
55. Gelb, 1998,42; see also Boyle and Preves.
56. Mackie, 271.
57. Kamiya, 1995,40.
58. Ibid; Karube, 12.
59. Ibid. , 18.
60. Ibid. 19
61. Ibid., 20.
62. Molony, 298.
63. Gelb, 1998, 50; Karube, 27.
64. Gelb, ibid.
65. Hayashi, 1995, 40; JWIE, 22.
66. WWN Went to the ILO,1997, 94.
67. Ibid.
68. Molony, 282.
69. Ibid.
70. Gelb, 1998, 52.
71. Buckley, 132.
72. Keck and Sikkink, 180.
73. Buckley, 68.
74. Gelb, 58.
75. Ministry of Labor ann.#20 , 1998, 1–2.
76. Buckley, 72.
77. Hoskyns, 15–16.
78. Ibid., 155; Reinalda, 213.
79. Kenney, 80.
80. Ibid. ,57. See also Reinalda, 213.
81. Hoskyns, 103; Meehan and Collins, 224.
82. Reinalda, 213.
83. Meehan and Collins, 224.
84. Wang, 906; Kenney, 60.
85. Kenney, Ibid.
86. Kenney, 82.
87. Ibid. 92–3; 113.
88. Ibid. , 83.
89. Ibid. 142.
90. Ibid.
91. Colgan and Ledwith, 1996, 297.
92. Hoskyns, 196; O'Donovan and Szyszczak,195.
93. Waterman, 162.
94. Reinalda, 214.
95. Ibid.
96. Ibid. and Hoskyns.
97. Hoskyns, 145.
98. Hanmer, 142.

99. Colgan and Ledwith, 300.

100. Reinalda, 215.

101. Lister, 8/98, 324.

102. Alter and Vargas, forthcoming.

103. Ibid.

104. O'Connor et al. , 1998, 86.

105. Hoskyns, 134

106. Burchell et al , 224.

107. Q. in Forbes , in Norris and Lovenduski, 150.

108. Meehan and Collins, 232.

109. Elman, 9.

110. O'Donovan and Szyszczak, 208.

111. Alter and Vargas.

112. Ibid. .

113. Lovenduski and Stetson and Mazur, 118.

114. Meehan and Collins, 233.

115. Ibid., 124.

116. Kenney, 99.

117. Kilpatrick in Gardiner, 38.

118. Forbes, 150.

119. Forbes, 150.

120. This section relies extensively on Meehan and Collins ,1996, 223–36

121. Meehan and Collins, 234.

122. See Bashevkin, 60, for a discussion of specific cases.

123. Fourth Report to CEDAW , 17, 96. This extensive compilation of data related to women, probably for the first time, demonstrates as well the importance of Britain's ratification of the Women's Convention.

124. Meehan and Collins, 229.

125. O'Donovan and Szyszczak, 198.

126. Fourth Report to CEDAW,1999,92.

127. Bashevkin, 15.

128. O'Connor et a. , 84.

129. Ibid., 85,

130. Ibid., 19.

131. Mayer, 740.

132. Ibid. , 753.

133. Ibid., 802–4

134. *U.S. Follow Up,* May 1996.

135. Landberg –Lewis, 26–8.

136. Kenney, 140.

137. O'Connor at al , 92.

138. Kenney, 140.

139. Gelb, 1989; McCann, and Saguy.

140. O'Connor et al , 98; Spain and Bianchi , 1996.

141. I am indebted to Robert Kagan for this additional insight.

142. Bashevkin, 236.

143. Alter and Vargas, op cit.

144. This view was vigorously articulated by all panelists at the Annual Justice Ruth Bader Ginsburg Distinguished Lecture on Women and the Law , "Panel Discussion on Current Topics in International Human Rights" December 13, 2001, Association of the Bar of the City of NY and NOW Legal Defense and Education Fund.

References

Alter, Karen and Jeanette Vargas "Explaining Variation in the Use of European Litigation Strategies: EC Law and UK Gender Equality Policy" . forthcoming, *Comparative Political Studies*. June 2000.

Axtmann, Roland. "Globalization, Europe and the State: Introductory Reflections" in Axtmann, Roland. *Globalization and Europe*. London: Wellington House, 1998.

Bashevkin, Sylvia. *Women on the Defensive*. University of Chicago Press, 1998.

Berkovitch. Nina. *From Motherhood to Citizenship*. Baltimore : Johns Hopkins University Press, 1999.

Blair, Tony. *The Third Way*. London: Fabian Society, 1998.

Blossfield Hans Peter. "Women's Part Time Employment and the Family Cycle" in Blossfield and Catherine Hakim . *Between Equalization and Marginalization*. Oxford: Oxford University Press. 1997. 315–320.

Boyle, Elizabeth Heger and Sharon Preves. "Sovereign Autonomy V. Human Rights: The Case of Anti-Female Genital Cutting Laws" *Law and Society Review.* 34: 2000. 703.

Burchell, Brendan, Angela Dale and Heather Joshi, "Part Time Work among British Women" in Blossfield, 210–42.

Chen, Martha Alter. "Engendering World Conferences: The International Women's Movement and the UN" in Thomas Weiss and Leon Gordenker *NGO's , the UN and Global Governance*. Boulder: Lynne Rienner 1996. 139–158.

Clark, Ann Marie. Elizabeth J. Friedman and Kathryn Hochstetler, "The Sovereign Limits of Global Civil Society : A Comparison of UN World Conferences on the Environment , Human Rights and Women" *World Politics* 51:1. 1998, 1–35.

Copelon, Rhonda and Rosalind Petchesky. "Toward an Interdependent Approach to Reproductive and Sexual Rights: Reflections on the ICPD and Beyond" in Margaret Schuler ed.

From Basic Needs to Basic Rights. Washington DC: Institute for Women Law and Development. 1995.

Colgan Fiona and Sue Ledwith. "Movers and Shakers- creating organizational change" in Ledwith and Colgan eds. *Women in Organizations: Challenging Gender Politics*. Houndsville: Blackwell, 1998, 278–300.

Delphy Christine " The European Union and the Future of Feminism" in Amy Elman ed. *Sexual Politics and the European Union*. Providence: Berghahn Books , 1996.

Delivering For Women: Progress So Far London: Cabinet Office. Women's Unit. November 1998

Dorsey, Ellen. "The Global Women's Movement: Articulating a New Vision of Global Governance" in Paul Diehl ed. *The Politics of Global Governance*. Boulder: Lynne Rienner, 1997. 335–360.

Forbes, Ian "The Privatization of Equality Policy in the British Employment Market for Women" in Frances Gardiner ed. *Sex Equality Policy In Western Europe* . Routledge 1997. 161–79.

———. "The Privatization of Sex Equality Policy" in Lovenduski and Norris, 145–62.

Fourth Report of the United Kingdom of Britain and Northern Ireland CEDAW, January 1999.

Friedman Elisabeth J.. and Kathryn Hochstetler." Sovereign Limits and Regional Opportunities for Global Civil Society in Latin America" 2001. v.36# 3, pp 7–31.

Gardiner Jean "A New Gender Contract?" *Soundings* Summer 1997, 69–76.

Garrett Geoffrey and Peter Lange , "Internationalization, Institutions and Political Change" in Robert Keohane and Helen Milner eds. *Internationalization and Domestic Politics,* Cambridge: Cambridge University Press ,1996. 48–78.

Gelb Joyce "The Equal Employment Opportunity Law: A Decade of Change for Japanese Women?" *Law and Policy* . October 2000. v. 22#3–4. 385–408.

———. *Feminism and Politics*. Berkeley: University of California Press. 1989.

Hanmer, Julia. "The Common Market of Violence" in Elman ed. 131–47.

Hayashi, Hiroko. "Sexual Harassment In the Workplace and Equal Employment Legislation" *St. Johns Law Review* , 69 Win-Spr. 1995, 27–60.

Held David. "Globalization: The Timid Tendency" *Marxism Today* Nov/Dec 1998, 24–27.

Hoskyns, Catherine. *Integrating Gender : Women Law and Politics in the European Union.* London:Verso , 1996.

———. "The European Union and the Women Within " An Overview of Women's Rights Policy" in Elman ed. , 13–22.

Japan Institute of Workers Evolution *Working Women in Japan* . Tokyo ,1998.

Japan's Working Women Today , Tokyo 1995.

Jaquette Jane "Losing the Battle, Winning the War" in Ann Winslow ed. *Women Politics and the United Nations.* Westport : Greenwood Press. 1995, 45–60.

Kamiya, Masako. "A Decade of the Equal Employment Act in Japan : Has is Changed Society?" *Law in Japan* , 25, 1995 , 40–83.

Karube, Keiko. "The Force of Social Change: :A Case Study of the Equal Employment Law in Japan" unpub. paper delivered Association for Asian Studies meeting , Washington DC , April 8 1995

Keck , Margaret and Katheryn Sikkink. *Activists Without Borders* . Ithaca: Cornell University Press, 1998.

Kenney, Sally. *For Whose Protection? Reproductive Hazards and Exclusionary Policy in the United States and Britain.* Ann Arbor: University of Michigan Press, 1992.

Keohane Robert and Helen Milner "Internationalization and Domestic Politics: An Introduction" in Keohane and Milner, *Internationalization and Domestic Politics.* Cambridge: Cambridge University Press, 1996, 3–24.

Kilpatrick, Claire. "Effective Utilization of Equality Rights: Equal Pay for Work of Equal Value in France and the UK" in Gardiner ed. 1997. 25–25.

Landsberg-Lewis, Illeana. *Bringing Equality Home : Implementing CEDAW* . New York : UN Development Fund for Women. 1998.

Lister, Ruth. "From Equality to Social Inclusion: New Labour and the Welfare State" in *Critical Social Policy* , 18,2 .May 1998. 215–25.

———. "Vocabularies of Citizenship and Gender" *Critical Social*

Policy, 18, 3 .August 1998. 309–31.

Lovenduski, Joni. "Sex ,Gender and British Politics" in Lovenduski and Norris 1996, 3–18.

Mackie, Vera. "Feminist Critiques of Modern Japanese Politics" in Monica Threlfall ed. *Mapping the Women's Movement.* London:Verso. 1996. 260–87.

Mahoney, Kathleen. "Theoretical Perspectives on Women's Human Rights and Strategies for their Implementation" 21 *Brooklyn J. Intl Law,* 1996, 799.

Mayer, Ann Elizabeth. "Reflections on Proposed US Reservations to CEDAW" 23 *Hastings Const. Law Q,* Spring 1996, 727–823.

Mann, Michael "Is there a Society Called Euro?" in Axtmann, 184–207.

McCann, Michael . *Rights at Work: Pay Equity Reform and the Politics of Legal Mobilization.* Chicago: University of Chicago Press, 1994.

Meehan , Elizabeth and Evelyn Collins "Women , the European Union and Britain" in Lovenduski, Joni and Pippa Norris eds. *Women in Politics* . Oxford : Oxford University Press. 1996. 223–37.

Molony, Barbara. "Japan's 1986 Equal Employment Law and the Changing Discourse on Gender" *Signs,*20,21 Winter 1995, *268–301.*

O'Connor, Julia. Ann Shola Orloff and Sheila Shaver. *States Markets Families* . Cambridge: Cambridge University Press, 1999.

O'Donovan Katherine and Erika Szyszczak. *Equality and Sex Discrimination Law* . Oxford: Blackwell, 1988.

Plata Maria Isabel and Adriana de la Espriella. "CEDAW, Colombia and Reproductive Rights" in Schuler ed. , 401–08.

President's Interagency Council on Women. *U.S. Follow -Up to the Fourth World Conference on Women* . May 1996.

Prime Minister's Office. *Japanese Women Today.* Tokyo, 1995.

Reinalda, Bob. "*Dea ex Machina* or the Interplay between national and international policy making: a critical analysis of women in the EU." in Frances Gardiner ed. *Sex Equality Policy in Europe* . London: Routledge 1997. 197–215.

Risse, Thomas. "The Power of Norms versus the Norms of Power : Transnational Civil Society and Human Rights" in Ann M. Fiorini ed. *The Third Force : The Rise of Transnational Civil Society.*

Tokyo: Japan Center for International exchange and Washington DC : Carnegie Endowment for International Peace . 2000. 177–210.

Romany, Celina. "On Surrendering Privilege: Diversity in a Feminist Redefinition of Human Rights Law" in Schuler ed. . 543–54.

Saguy, Abigail. "Employment Discrimination or Sexual Violence: Defining Sexual Harassment in American and French Law." *Law and Society Review* 2000 . 34:1091.

Sassen, Saskia. *Globalization and Its Discontents.* New York: New Press, 1998.

Sienstra, Deborah. "Organizing for Change: International Women's Movements and World Politics" in Francine D'Amico and Peter Beckman eds. *Women in World Politic.* Westport: Bergin and Garvey, 1995. 143–54.

Silliman, Jael. "Expanding Civil Society: Shrinking Political Spaces—the Case of Women's Nongovernmental Organizations" *Social Politics* . 6,1 Spring 1999. 23–53.

Snyder, Margaret. "The Politics of Women and Development" in Anne Winslow ed. *Women Politics and the United Nations* . Westport, Conn.: Greenwood Press , 1995. 95–116.

Staudt Kathleen. *Policy Politics and Gender.* West Hartford, Conn.: Kumarian Press, 1998.

Stetson Dorothy and Amy Mazur. *Comparative State Feminism.* Thousand Oaks, Calif.: Sage, 1995.

Taylor, Judith. "Case X: Irish Reproductive Policy and European Influence" in *Social Politics* 6,2, Summer 1999. 203–229.

Teeple, Gary. *Globalization and the Decline of Reform.* Toronto: Garamond Press, 1995

Wang Shirley. "The Maturation of Gender Equality in to Customary International Law" 27. *New York University Journal of International Law and Politics,* Summer 1995, 899–32.

Waterman Peter. *Globalization, Social Movements and the New Internationalisms.* London: Mansell, 1997.

Working Women's Network, *WWN Went to the ILO* Osaka, 1998.

Chapter 10

A Race to the Bottom, a Race to the Top or the March to a Minimum Floor?
Economic Integration and Labor Standards in Comparative Perspective

Daniel P. Gitterman

INTRODUCTION

Economies around the world are becoming increasingly integrated as globalization promotes trade and mobility of capital and labor. An expanding network of trade and investment is bringing nations and societies with different rules and norms that govern working conditions and industrial relations into closer and more frequent contact with one another. The regulation of labor markets has been traditionally a sovereign national matter, determined by voters, domestic groups, and governments, without regard for its effect on standards in other nations. Now, an emerging "race to the bottom" (RTP) logic predicts that if a nation's labor market protections are high or social protections generous, it will experience an outflow of capital to nations with lower labor costs, depressing compensation and placing downward pressure on domestic standards. With the free movement of factor inputs, goods, and services, analysts predict, noncompetitive cost differentials will be competed away. Much less scholarly attention has been given to the impact of economic openness on labor standards. This essay highlights the political response to race to the bottom claims and examines the impact of one mechanisms of globalization—agreements and institutional pressures—on labor standards.

What is all too often missing from the literature is an explanation that highlights political and institutional factors, and whether international and regional labor agreements have any impact on domestic standards. I conclude that globalization has not been driving regulatory standards in a race to the bottom or a race to the top: rather, national heterogeneity prevails, with some movement toward minimum norms and principles. The essay explains how different groups of nations respond to the real and perceived distributional implications of deeper integration and the impact that these labor agreements have on domestic standards within and across the following cases: European Union (EU), North America (NAFTA), the Common Market of the Southern Cone (MERCOSUR), the Association of Southeast Asian Nations (ASEAN), the World Trade Organization (WTO), and International Labor Organization (ILO).

Labor markets involve much more than the exchange of a worker's labor for payment in the form of a wage. National governments, through either collective bargaining or legislation, establish domestic labor standards (regulations or protections) to assure freedom of association and minimal conditions of employment for workers. For example, in some EU member states, labor market protections are restrictions on the ability of economic agents to enter and exit formal, contractual employment relationships. "Core" standards, within the ILO, are typically rules on freedom of association, collective bargaining, prohibition of forced labor, elimination of child labor, and nondiscrimination. For comparison across these cases and various labor market areas, this paper broadly defines labor standards as the "rules and norms that govern working conditions and industrial relations" (OECD 1996).

The conventional wisdom in the literature suggests that labor agreements are "weak" and have little impact on domestic labor standards. While it is difficult to prove that standards would be lower in the absence of such agreements or that governments and firms would behave dramatically differently, their impact is not neglible. These agreements account for increasing flows of information and sharing of best labor market practices, create a minimum floor of rules and norms (with difference enforcement mechanisms) for competition while allowing nations to adopt higher standards, and encourage nations to improve oversight and enforcement of their domestic standards. While increased trade, capital, and labor flows require new trade-offs, nations maintain their own regulations to govern working conditions and industrial relations. There is limited evidence of convergence: despite integration, governments maintain distinct labor standards if they (and their voting citizens) are willing to bear the costs. Rather than a race to the bottom or the top, the outcome is an incremental march toward minimum regional and international norms and principles.

The first three sections of this essay review existing explanations that account for "race to the bottom," "no race at all," and "race to the top" outcomes, and explain why nations have an incentive to retain their comparative advantage and respond to the real and perceived distributional implications of greater economic openness. The next section highlights variations in institutional mechanisms and the impact of these five labor agreements on domestic standards. The final section concludes that globalization has not produced convergence at the bottom or at the top: national differences remain substantial. While nations have a strong incentive to retain their comparative advantage, this essay explains why there are increasing efforts to develop labor agreements in conjunction with new forms of regional and international economic openness. Rather than a race to the bottom or the top, integration appears to result in an incremental march toward common regional and international minimum rules and norms.

MARKET PRESSURE AND THE "RACE TO THE BOTTOM": A REVIEW OF THE EVIDENCE

Globalization, according to some, is forcing nations into a race to the bottom (RTB), as it increases the costs of domestic labor market institutions and of maintaining higher labor standards in advanced economies. According to the RTB argument, integration fosters dysfunctional competition among national rules and firms, leading to regime shopping, competitive deregulation, and social dumping. Social dumping are outcomes disadvantageous to existing social and labor market protection that could result from the operation of a single market or free trade zone encompassing wide variations in social and labor costs (Erickson and Kuruvilla 1994).[1] Governments will be required to either offer market-pleasing, business-friendly policies or sacrifice growth and employment to nations more responsive to the needs of capital. As competition occurs as goods, services, or factors move easily, if not totally freely, within different geographical areas, the prediction is that standards will be selected according to their relative attractiveness for investors and firms (Gatsios and Holmes 1999).

The race to the bottom prediction is that without harmonized labor standards, "low" labor standards in exporting developing countries will artificially depress labor costs, lead to unfair competitive advantage, and place downward pressure on "high" labor standards in advanced industrialized countries. For example, assume one nation does not regulate a minimum wage but all others do. Firms in the countries with a minimum wage would be at a competitive disadvantage compared with those in the country without a minimum wage. Just as Northern firms feared capital flight to the South in the early twentieth century United States. Governments will be pressured by capital to lower or repeal its existing minimum wage. Alber and Standing (2000) refer to this as "labor cost" dumping, in which legislation that cuts employer obligations or makes it easier to bypass such obligations enables firms to reduce their wage and nonwage labor costs. Thus, standards in any one country end up lower than they would have been in the absence of an external economic pressure (Alber and Standing 2000). Thus, worldwide, workers in the "North" (i.e., United States, Germany) will have to accept standards that are low enough to prevent footloose capital from deserting them for the "South" (i.e., Mexico, Portugal).

A review of empirical evidence suggests that integration has not led to a race to the bottom in standards simply because the "cheapest" labor market regimes appear to offer cost savings. A principal finding of a major 1996 OECD study reports no evidence that countries with low labor standards enjoy better global export performance than high-standard countries (OECD 1996; 2000). On the basis of observed patterns of foreign direct investment, Rodrik (1996) reports that multinational firms invest principally in the largest, richest, and most dynamic labor markets; countries without "core" labor standards receive a very small part of global flows. In sum, there is no robust evidence that low-standard countries provide a haven for foreign firms (OECD 2000). Krueger (2000) concludes that imperfect mobility of capital, labor, goods, and services will further limit the pressure of globalization on labor standards.

Much of the empirical evidence focuses on the EU. Evidence on the labor cost incentive for capital movement in manufacturing within the EU shows that capital flows to the lower labor cost countries are actually not much larger than capital flows to the higher labor cost countries, despite differences in unit labor costs (Erickson and Kuruvilla 1994). Adnett (1995) reports that although there is potential for social dumping in the EU, they are unlikely to be significant in the long run. Overall, there has been little evidence of North-South social dumping, and few signs that Southern member states are eager to exploit their lower standards as a competitive tool (Ross 1995). Southern European producers with low productivity tend to specialize in different products from those in Northern Europe and thus, do not place downward pressure on existing standards (Adnett 1994). In addition, in the low-wage sectors in the EU, it is really only in textiles and clothing that there is much international competition. Even then, the most intense competition comes from developing nations outside the EU, where wage costs are exceptionally low (Bazen and Benhayoun 1995).

A review of the evidence also suggests that compensation costs alone do not determine competitiveness. The competitiveness of similar products made in different nations often varies greatly, because firms establish different mixes among infrastructure, skills, training, and technology (Mosley 1990). As Mosley (1990) has noted, high-wage countries (in the EU) are likely to have compensating advantages over low-wage countries, such as a more skilled workforce, better infrastructure, and perhaps productivity that is high enough to offset the disadvantage of higher labor costs. In several sectors, cross-national differences in labor costs are apparently compensated for by differences in the systems by which these costs are paid and by the productivity arising from different skill levels and the quality of technology; thus, per-unit cost of production does not reflect differences in labor costs (Lange 1992; Adnett 1995). Many EU member states have come to see labor relations as a strategic factor in strengthening national competitiveness and product innovation (Kluth 1998).

In summary, existing evidence suggests that integration will lead to neither a race to the bottom nor a race to the top in labor standards (Adnett 1995; Andersen, Haldrup, and Sorensen 2000; Krueger 2000). A number of recent studies, as reviewed by the OECD, also suggest there are major constraints on a race the bottom outcome (OECD 2000). In fact, Freeman (1994)argues that any nation that prefer higher labor standards can purchase them for itself, regardless of other countries, by either currency devaluation (more difficult in a monetary union), a direct downward adjustment in wages, or an increase in taxes to pay for the cost of higher standards. In addition, redistributive or technical assistance mechanisms from advanced economies can help developing countries increase compliance, as they may not have the resources to meet higher standards. Thus, the race to the bottom need not occur.

COMPARATIVE ADVANTAGE, HETEROGENIETY AND NO RACE AT ALL

Much of the literature on the impact of globalization on labor markets (i.e., of trade on wages) focuses on the employment and wages of less-skilled workers in advanced economies (Freeman 1995; Wood 1995)—whether they have been (or will be) determined by the global supply of less-skilled labor rather than by domestic labor markets (Freeman 1995). As labor costs are one factor in competitiveness, one view among economists is that globalization does indeed put pressure on wages and employment in labor-intensive industries in advanced economies. Another view rejects the notion that trade in one sector can determine labor outcomes in an entire economy and others suggest the deleterious effects of trade on demand for less-skilled workers are modest enough to be offset through redistribution funded by the gains from trade (Freeman 1995).

Less attention focuses on the institution side: does integration mean that all countries must adopt the same institutional structure and labor standards? Rodrik (1996) argues that much of the economics literature has focused on identifying the magnitude of the downward shift of the demand curve for low-skilled labor rather than on the consequences of that demand's greater elasticity. Deeper integration of nations with high and low labor costs can be thought of as an enlargement of the effective labor supply. In an economy that is more open to trade and investment, the demand for labor will be generally more elastic: employers (and consumers) can substitute for foreign workers either by investing abroad or by importing products made abroad (Rodrik 1996). Thus, the greater substitutability of labor can alter the nature of bargaining between workers and their employers. Most importantly, Rodrik suggests that increased trade and foreign investment makes it more difficult for workers to force other groups in society, employers in particular, to share in the costs.

With greater integration, labor markets have a wide variety of characteristics that influence trade flows, and both capital and labor mobility. While there are significant differences in real wages and labor costs between developed and developing countries, it is not conceptually or empirically clear that higher labor standards means higher labor costs (Freeman 1994). In addition, some differences in labor practices have no effect on labor costs. Other costly differences are shifted back to workers. Other costly differences are shifted to entire population through currency devaluation (Freeman 1994).

Rodrik (1999), however, suggests that low-standard countries tend to have low labor costs, controlling for labor productivity, and a strong revealed comparative advantage in labor-intensive manufactures. According to economic theory, the mobility of capital is assumed to allow capital-labor ratios to equalize across nations, and thus to equalize marginal productivities of capital and labor (Ehrenberg 1994).

An analytical focus on the impact of globalization on labor standards is critical because labor costs are a big part of trade and comparative advantage. Economists predict that nations at different levels of income will choose different standards. Standards should thus naturally vary across countries, depending on such factors as endowments, income growth, and culture or values. For example, this logic assumes that trade is driven by differences in factors' endowments, with one country (i.e., Mexico or Portugal) relatively abundant in low-skill labor, and the other country (i.e., U.S. or Germany), in high-skill labor. The more different nations are, the more they stand to gain from trading with one another: thus, they have an incentive to retain their comparative advantage and protect the heterogeneity in their labor standards and costs.

The simple Heckser-Ohlin model predicts that expansion of trade will reflect specialization based on factor endowments.[2] The theory of comparative advantage claims that nations can profit from differences in endowments of technology, capital, skilled labor, unskilled labor, and other inputs. As barriers to trade are removed and competition intensifies, they will seek to improve their competitiveness, which depends upon relative unit labor costs of producing a unit of output compared to those borne by competitors.[3] In terms of efficiency and mutual gain, there is limited incentive for either advanced or developing economies to harmonize standards: this artificially raises labor costs and reduces the comparative advantage of nations with relatively large supplies of unskilled labor, thus reducing the benefits of trade for all (Ehrenberg 1994).

Thus, if we assume that governments respond, at least in part, to efficiency concerns and the aggregate gains, we should observe them protecting their comparative advantage and reacting individually to changes in their respective environments. Globalization should produce neither a race to the bottom nor a race to the top, but strong market pressures for nations to preserve their comparative advantage and labor market diversity. Each country therefore will have a strong incentive to choose the "right" level of labor standards, given its preferences and level of economic development. With greater economic growth and development, labor standards in developing countries will eventually rise in due time.

For the most part, harmonization of labor standards has not been viewed as a necessary condition for integration across these cases, but groups of nations have sought ways to respond to the real and perceived distributional implications of economic openness. Policies and events originating in one nation are increasingly viewed to have distributional effects on the welfare of citizens and level of regulation in other nations; and thus, in response, there are increasing political demands on governments to confront the real or perceived "efficiency" and "equity" trade-off. One mechanism of globalization, regional and international rules or institutions, attempts to foster and recognize norms or principles as a floor under competition within the context of continued national regulatory diversity.

MARKET OR INSTITUTIONAL PRESSURE AND A RACE TO THE TOP

A recent and growing literature on the impact of globalization on national regulatory standards specifies market and institutional conditions in which integration results in convergence toward more stringent standards, or a race to the top, often focusing on the case of environmental regulation. In Vogel's (1995) trading-up analysis, the key market, institutional, and political variables predicting a race to the top are: internationally oriented producers for whom stricter regulations are a source of competitive advantage; international agreements and institutions; and Baptist-bootlegger coalitions of domestic producers and public interest groups. In challenging the claim that liberalization leads to a lowering of standards, Vogel (1995) argues that integration can actually lead to strengthening of consumer and environmental standards, as greener states export their higher standards or harmonize their standards through international or regional agreement. The result is thus more akin to a race to the top than a race to the bottom.

As Vogel and Kagan acknowledge (this volume), the impact of globalization is likely to vary across policy areas. Existing political economy arguments contend that harmonization or convergence of labor standards can be explained, not by the presence of Vogel's internationally oriented producers or Baptist-bootlegger coalitions as is true in environmental standards, but by protectionist demands of labor groups (and import-competing firms) in advanced economies to prevent competition from developing countries based on comparative advantage (Hansson 1983; Bhagwati 1994; Srinivasan 1994).[4] While much of the benefit from integration accrues to society as a whole in the form of lower prices for consumers, the losses fall heavily on particular groups and industries from certain geographic areas. By requiring competitors to improve or harmonize their standards, these pressures groups, according to rent-seeking theories, strategically increase prices of goods produced by labor-intensive technologies by increasing the cost of labor.[5]

This paper argues that domestic group demands do affect the behavior of nations, and such political variables clearly must be central to any analysis of the effects of globalization on standards. Globalization, no matter how much in the national interest, inevitably has different effects on various domestic groups. As Frieden and Rogowski (1996) have noted, aggregate benefits will be distributed across groups within countries in predictable ways, creating relatively clear lines of cleavage.[6] The winners prefer to maintain or accelerate change; the losers aim to impede or reverse change.[7] However, unlike political economy of rent-seeking arguments, not all outcomes can be explained by the wasteful influence or pervasive success of pressure groups or particular coalitions. Governments must be willing to accommodate demands and supply particular outcomes. Rather than regulatory capture of outcomes or cleavages determining outcomes, demand-side influences are filtered through domestic politics and institutions: national preferences are then aggregated within the decision rules of existing agreements.

Simmons (this volume) posits the impossibility of a race to the bottom, as a dominant power or powers has the ability to impose their preferences on other nations if necessary to maintain the "effectiveness" of their own standards. The heterogeneity of regulations generates strong negative externalities for the dominant country, since it is adversely affected if other countries do not adopt equally stringent standards.[8] Simmons suggests this insight can be useful in accounting for other areas in which there is a great imbalance of standards or of economic or political power among countries. Powerful polities that might experience adverse effects from other nations' laxity are likely to pressure those countries to adopt similarly "high" standards.

However, in contrast to Simmon's power asymmetry explanation, nations that seek to harmonize standards must do so within existing decision rules, which often require unanimity or a majority (or qualified majority) voting or allow only for voluntary nonbinding decisions. Thus, this prevents even the most powerful nations from unilaterally imposing their preferences and standards on other nations. Within interstate bargaining, strategic and collective choices about preference aggregation and decision rules, and formal governance and enforcement mechanisms within agreements, are primary factors in explaining why high-standard nations are not able to secure harmonization or upward convergence of standards. Thus, we see no race to the top in standards.

I argue that national governments are faced with conflicting economic and political incentives. While globalization offers obvious opportunities for aggregate and mutual economic gains, it also fosters distributional consequences. This creates electoral and political risks for governments, as domestic groups and the public often fear a race to the bottom outcome. Governments pursue different strategies for coping with risk. The first is protectionism. Assuming the choice is to pursue economic openness, the second strategy is linking deeper integration with provision of domestic compensation or social insurance. Developing countries, however, may remain protectionist because they lack the resources for internal transfer programs to cope with risks. Reliable mechanisms of compensation are strategically important for domestic stability as exposure to international trade expands (Rogowski 1989).

A third strategy, highlighted and explained here, is to respond with formal rules or informal mechanisms to set *minimum* standards or norms that govern working conditions and industrial relations. As Spar and Yoffie (2000) emphasize, races, even after they are launched, can be curtailed by the establishment of common standards. As these cases show, globalization has led to neither a race to the bottom (due to social dumping claiming) nor by any means a race to the top (due to market or institutional pressures)). Instead, globalization has produced political demands and institutional responses aimed at establishing norms or principles as a floor under competition while perpetuating national diversity and protecting comparative advantage.

The nature of the institutional response to distributional concerns and impact of labor agreement on standards varies across the cases, depending on the national *preferences* of the member states or trading partners (and political parties with control); the formal institutional and *decision rules* for aggregating policy preferences; and the *collective action* problem of joint decision making among many governments. National preferences—a balance of electoral self-interest and loyalty to core domestic groups—vary according to the governments (and political parties) that exist at critical points in time. It is important to note that these responses emerge within agreements that vary significantly in terms of level of integration that have (or aim to reach), and in terms of the disparities in real wages and labor costs between them.

THE EUROPEAN UNION

The EU is an important case because its process of integration has proceeded over several decades and has recently been reinforced by the creation of the Single European Market and the European Monetary Union (Andersen, Haldrup, and Sorensen 2001). Labor, capital, goods, and services can now flow freely across borders, and most countries share a common currency. The EU is far more than a free trade zone: it possesses characteristics of a supranational entity, including extensive bureaucratic competence, overriding judicial control, and significant capacity to develop or modify member state rules.[9] If a member state fails to incorporate a EU directive into domestic law, individuals can seek enforcement against the member through the ECJ. The Commission monitors the performance of members and may initiate enforcement proceedings.

Over time, negative integration—policies eliminating restraints on trade and distortions of competition—has not been challenged, as all EU member states signed the treaties, all national parliaments ratified them, and all agreed to create a common market. Positive integration—policies that shape the conditions under which markets operate—has been more difficult, as it depends on member agreement in the Council of Ministers and thus is subject to all the collective action problems of intergovernmental decision making (Scharpf 1997). My focus here is solely on the adoption of legislation aimed at improving labor standards and workers' rights in the European Union and its impact on domestic standards.

Within the EU, even the most powerful regulatory "leaders" cannot just impose their standards on the "laggards": any harmonization or transfer of regulatory authority is the result of a dynamic interaction among domestic groups, EU-wide associations, member states, and Community institutions *within the* parameters of existing decision rules. The preferences of member states in the Council of Ministers and the European Council are influenced by the demands of domestic interests as well as EU associations, the European Trade Union Confederation (ETUC), and the Union of Industrial and Employers' Confederations of Europe (UNICE). Governments have had to balance which groups to accommodate and which to resist over time. Currently, fourteen of the fifteen EU countries have center-left governments.

In the years prior to the treaty, there was concern about the distributive implications of a newly integrated economic area. The six original members (Belgium, France, Germany, Italy, Luxembourg, Netherlands) had achieved similar levels of economic development, and the consensus view among them was that only minimal harmonization was required for a customs union (Teague and Grahl 1990). Under the 1957 Treaty of Rome, members committed themselves to economic and social cohesion: the goals were to raise living standards and improve employment conditions in member states.[10] As part of the Treaty, decision rules required the Council of Ministers to act unanimously before any social or labor protection proposal could be approved.

The EU has promoted free mobility of labor ever since its inception. In the early period, members acted to promote labor mobility by removing non-tariff barriers to the free movement of labor rooted in national labor market regimes, and harmonizing education and training of workers. Over time, members have unanimously agreed to harmonize through a series of EU "market-making" directives and resolutions that allow citizens to move between nations, to maintain residency in other nations after employment, to be eligible for all social insurance programs in other nations on the same terms as citizens of those nations, and to receive recognition of professional qualifications across member states (Ehrenberg 1994).[11] Since July 1986, citizens have been entitled to employment in any other nation on equal terms and conditions with residents.

With Denmark, Ireland, and the UK joining the EC in 1973, and Greece in 1981, and Spain and Portugal in 1986, there was intensified political concern (and demands) within the EU as members with higher labor standards confronted greater heterogeneity in standards and costs between more- and less- advanced economies. Deeper integration thus generated new pressures for the creation of a "social" dimension and the greater harmonization of "market-breaking" policies within the Community. First, at the 1972 Paris Summit, members committed to a social agreement, and the EC launched the 1974 Social Action Program with three *goals:* full and better employment, improved working and living conditions, and greater participation of workers in EC decisions (Teague and Grahl 1989). During the 1970s and early 1980's, members agreed to approximate standards only for equal pay and specific worker protections.[12] In the 1980s, a number of directives proposed by the Commission were not approved by the Council as pro-regulatory members were constrained by the preferences of the least ambitious member in a minimum winning coalition (i.e., Britain), reflecting a lowest-common-denominator outcome.

By the early 1990s, the dominant view of member governments was that the extension of European integration—the goal of economic convergence—required harmonization of labor market and goods market regulation (Adnett 1995). Nations with "higher" standards—Belgium, Denmark, France, and Germany—pushed for harmonization, as the incongruity of rules and the increased wage and non-wage costs of heterogeneity would expose their systems as a competitive cost liability, leading to a "race to the bottom."[13] Nations with "lower" standards—Portugal, Greece, Ireland, and Spain—would be losers, as harmonization would raise their existing labor standards but would not reflect national production cost structures (Lange 1993). Spain's socialist government supported harmonization, though the country was similar to the other "lower" standard nations in socioeconomic terms.

UK and Portugal, supported by UNICE and domestic employer groups, opposed harmonization, as it would prevent or delay the adjustment process necessary for improving national economic performance (Rhodes 1991). The harmonization of labor market protections, and changes in the direct and indirect labor costs to firms and the rules governing relations with workers, would have a direct and negative impact on national competitiveness. The British government, with period support from some of the less economically developed members, pushed for greater labor market flexibility. Britain attributed its success in creating jobs to flexible labor markets (Rhodes 1991). Since its admission, the UK has had an uneasy relationship with other members due to its preferences for deregulation and labor market flexibility (Hargreaves 1997). To preempt action, in conjunction with Italy and Ireland, it launched the Action Program for

Employment Growth, proposing a redirection of policy toward greater labor market flexibility.

Historically, EC decisions have been made on the basis of unanimity voting. Britain strategically manipulated these decision rules, particularly the unanimity rule, to impose its preferences on others and block any efforts toward common regulatory standards. Britain opposed any change in the decision rules, particularly any that might require it to accept a decision from a qualified majority, within the EU. Unanimous decision rules were modified slightly by Article 118A of the 1986 Single European Act (SEA), which allowed for qualified majority voting (QMV) for directives relating to "the working environment as regards the health and safety of workers."[14] In negotiations leading up the SEA, members agreed in Article 100a to extend QMV for measures that have "as their object the establishment and functioning of the internal market." However, this was conditional on Article 100A(2), where the members states required that the rights and interests of employed people still a matter for *unanimous* voting only (Bercusson and Van Dijk 1995).

The regulation of worker health and safety has been the area in which the EU has had the greatest authority to act, and there has been significant agreement among all the member states to harmonize regulatory standards (Ross 1995). Health and safety rules are concerned with "goods" rather than "people": they are product rather than labor market regulations. The UK and employer groups viewed harmonization of health and safety rules as important for securing the single market, and regarded comparable regulatory costs as essential to level the playing field for competition among EU firms. The British originally agreed to QMV, believing their "existing system of worker health and safety standards to be higher than those of other members" (Friedholm 1999). On the other issues, the UK, domestic employers, and EU-level employer groups opposed encroachment on national autonomy and demanded a strict interpretation of treaty law; the Commission, backed by a majority of the member s, and domestic and EU-level labor groups, sought ways to gain a more expansive interpretation of treaty law (Rhodes 1995).[15]

To address the political demands of members with more significant labor market protections, Jacques Delors, originating with the 1987 Belgian presidency, pushed for members to adopt *minimum* norms or conventions. The Community would influence national collective bargaining and labor market protections without Europe-wide harmonization (Teague and Grahl 1989). For high standard nations, the original proposal did not impose new labor market protections but rather established their existing rules at the EU level (Teague 1999). This represented convergence in goals rather than harmonization of rules and norms that govern worker conditions and industrial relations (Teague and Grahl 1989). With the 1989 EC Charter on Fundamental Social Rights (Social Charter),[16] the subsequent Action Program, and their consolidation in the 1991 Social Protocol of the Maastricht Treaty, members agreed to *minimum regulatory standards only in specific labor market areas* (Baldry 1994). While the it guaranteed "rights" to freedom of expression and collective bargaining, the Action Program ruled out any harmonization in this area, as member states believed the responsibility for implementing these provisions rested with the members in accordance with their "national traditions and policies."

Prior to the Protocol, a majority of member states pressed to adopt directives from the Action Program, on labor market issues such as part-time work, organization of working time, contents of employment contracts and proof of their existence, information and consultation with workers with EC-scale companies, and protections for pregnant women and new mothers. Britain refused to relinquish control and opposed any changes in decision rules that would subject such directives to adoption by QMV (Lange 1994). Due to opposition from Ireland and Portugal, the Action Program also failed to establish a minimum pay directive, proposing only an opinion instead. Minimum pay was not mentioned directly, but members were asked to take appropriate measures, through either legislation or collective bargaining, to ensure that the right to an "equitable" wage was respected (Bazen and Benhayoun 1992).

In the end, eleven members signed the Declaration of Principles, which guaranteed twelve fundamental social rights (Britain opted out).[17] They agreed, in accordance with national rules and practices, to guarantee the rights in the Charter and implement the necessary measures to accomplish this (Teague and Grahl 1992). The 1991 Protocol specified issues on which the eleven could avoid British vetoes by allowing QMV in several labor market areas (Van Wenzel Stone 1995). Since Maastricht retained the provisions of the Treaty of Rome and the SEA, all members could still make policy together, but with majority voting limited to only the harmonization of health and safety. Most important, members retained direct control over industrial relations and collective employee rights—the right to pay, the right to association, and the right to strike or impose lockouts.[18]

By joining the Protocol, Portugal, Greece, Ireland, and Spain made themselves potentially vulnerable to standards that could be adverse to their national competitiveness (Lange 1993). Thus, the EU provided compensation to them in the form of structural funds to offset costly new steps toward deeper integration. In other words, side payments were offered to lessen political opposition in "lower" standard nations and allow these members to adjust to the short-term costs of new EU standards. The transfers provided short-term cover to governments who saw integration as important to their long-term economic growth and preferable to EU exclusion (Lange 1993). Delors won over these nations with promises of more structural funding, and in the case of Spain, with direct solidarity appeals to the socialist government (Moravcsik 1998).

After eighteen years of British veto threats, the new Labor Party signaled a preference to join the 1991 Protocol. Before assuming control in 1997, the Blair government led the way in negotiating the 1997 Amsterdam Treaty, but warned that Britain would oppose any harmonization measures that would place excessive burdens on British firms (Rice-Oxley 1997). The Amsterdam Treaty, which was signed in 1997 and entered into force in 1999, was a significant agreement among *all* members states to accept majority voting on issues beyond worker health and safety standards (McGlynn 1998). Following the example of the 1961 European Social Charter and the 1989 Community Charter of the Fundamental Social Rights, the treaty refers to fundamental social rights: promotion of employment, improved living and working conditions, proper social protection, dialogue between management and labor, the development of human resources with a view to lasting high employment and combating exclusion.[19] However, a unanimous vote was still required for many issues, and the rights to association, strike, and lockouts were specifically excluded (EU 1999).[20]

A central feature of the 1991 Social Protocol, which became applicable to all EU countries as a result of the UK signing the Amsterdam Treaty, is that EU trade unions and employer associations can propose directives. Thus, the EU's reforms empowered these social partners, shifting authority and decision rules at the very moment the Council of Ministers was adopting QMV. Bercusson (1994) suggests that the "principle of subsidiarity will be interpreted to imply a greater role for the process of social dialogue and collective bargaining at national and transnational levels, supplementing the Commission's role in the lawmaking process." With the social partners playing a greater role in EU decisions, the new approach involves the introduction of a framework agreement that is intended to advance minimum standards but requires parallel implementation in each of the member states.[21]

With the Treaty of Amsterdam, which consolidated the mechanisms set in place by the Maastricht Treaty, members also agreed to promote a new series of priorities at Community level, especially in the area of employment. These are only guidelines for both the Community and the member states intended to promote employment and improved living and working conditions (EU 1999).[22] Members agreed at the Luxembourg Jobs summit in November 1997 that the objective is to reach a "high level of employment" without undermining competitiveness in the EU. In order to attain it, the Community was charged with developing a "coordinated strategy" for employment. Benchmarking plays a key role, as members highlight best labor market performances and aim to identify, evaluate, and disseminate good practices in the field of employment and labor market policy (Commission of the European Communities 2001).

As the Treaty qualifies fundamental social rights as only "guidelines" for activities, there was increasing pressure for member states to agree to a European Union Charter of Fundamental Rights, which they did at the 2000 Nice European Council meeting.[23] While France pushed for fundamental social and economic rights, Britain viewed the Charter as a "statement of policy," and opposed incorporating the Charter within the Treaty, which would make it binding with stronger legal status. While preferring to endorse rather than veto, Britain successfully negotiated amendments to prevent any new economic or social rights that would undermine British labor laws, impose new costs on firms, or undermine their competitive advantages (Herald Tribune 2000; Financial Times 2000). Britain specifically opposed language on a workers' right to strike and a requirement that employers consult with employees at all levels about matters that concern them. In its final form, the right to strike remains in national law and practices, which was of particular concern to the Confederation of British Industry (Financial Times 2000). Currently, these are principles rather than binding rights, and it will have to be decided whether and how the Charter should be integrated into the Treaties (Commission of the European Communities 2000).

In summary, the EU member states do not harmonize worker

protection and industrial relations, but agreed to minimum harmonization of rules and norms only in specific areas. The EU sets minimum standards and norms from which national departures are acceptable, thereby preserving policy autonomy and diversity. Members retain control over the form and method of implementation, and implement directives through collective bargaining agreements as well as through statutory or administrative regulation, to allow flexibility. Many members have used their control over the legal mechanisms through which directives are incorporated into national law to limit the overall impact on domestic standards. Thus, a significant gap exists between directives and their implementation in national law. In other areas, regulatory diversity prevails.

NAFTA

Unlike the EU, whose member states commit to minimum and enforceable standards under a Treaty, sovereign trading partners in North America agreed only to improve oversight and enforcement of existing labor and employment standards, and to participate in a dispute process as a supplemental part of the agreement. NAFTA, ratified in 1993, implements free trade between two highly developed economies and one developing economy within fifteen years, with no provision for labor mobility.[24] The agreement contains only one formal clause on standards, discouraging trading partners from reducing environmental or health and safety standards to attract investment; however, the North American Agreement on Labor Cooperation (NAALC), ratified in 1993 as part of NAFTA, represents the first labor side-agreement directly linked to a trade treaty. In a final framework, the partners created a Commission for Labor Cooperation (CLC) to promote enforcement of each nation's labor and employment laws (Garvey 1997).

The U.S. preference for a side- agreement arose out of the need to respond to domestic political demands. The centrist Clinton administration, supported free trade and had incentives to capture the aggregate gains, but also had a political incentive to respond to the demands and fears of organized labor (as well as environmental and consumer groups) to harmonize regional standards. Thus, the United States pushed for three supplemental accords to NAFTA on labor, the environment, and import surges. Labor (AFL-CIO, UAW) preferred regional labor rights—collective bargaining (i.e., free association) and health   and   safety,   child   labor,   and   minimum   wage standards—enforceable through domestic courts and if needed, through Commission authority. Business (Business Roundtable, Chamber of Commerce, National Association of Manufacturers, and U.S. Council on International Business) supported the formation of a "consultative" commission, but opposed any delegation of investigative and enforcement authority, particularly the power to issue trade sanctions, to it. The U.S. negotiating position balanced labor and business demands: labor did not capture the outcome, as the rent-seeking theories would predict, and win an agreement that imposes U.S. standards on Mexico.

Mexico refused to renegotiate NAFTA, but fearing NAFTA's defeat in the Congress, did agree to negotiate a labor side-agreement. Mexico's preference was for each nation to maintain control over standards, and for a regional commission to have no authority to issue trade sanctions (Mayer 1998). Mexico had incentives to maintain the corporatist system of labor relations, and labor groups there resisted any change that threatened their monopoly of labor movement representation (Cameron and Tomlin 2000). Mexico pushed for a compensation mechanism to aid with adjustments (a North American Development Fund), but the U.S. refused to support any structural or regional fund (Cameron and Tomlin 2000). Mexico opposed harmonization, particularly any mechanism that would erode the benefits of free trade and undermine their comparative advantage.

During the bargaining, the trading partners diverged: the United States favored a commission with authority to issue sanctions; Mexico preferred no transfer of authority or weak enforcement; and Canada supported a commission for oversight but insisted that it remain firmly under national control. Both Canada and Mexico rejected trade sanctions and supported monetary sanctions only as a final punitive measure. The United States proposed that complaints go to national administrative offices (NAOs) within each nation rather than to a regional commission. Each partner would retain full control over whether complaints had sufficient merit to require trilateral consultation or dispute resolution.

In balancing economic and political demands, the United States proposed that each partner commit only to enforcing its existing labor and employment standards. Mexico held firm on consultation only on health and safety standards, while the United States and Canada preferred consultation on labor relations, a minimum wage, and child labor. In a final negotiation, Mexico accepted the U.S. proposal that fines of up to $20 million could be imposed for failure to enforce domestic labor and employment rules, and trade sanctions could be issued *only* if a trading partner failed to pay the monetary fine. Thus, Mexico could claim that trade sanctions would never be imposed for an enforcement violation while the United States could signal to labor groups that the agreement included trade sanctions for non-enforcement of domestic labor standards. Mexico agreed to fine and sanction authority only for enforcement of health and safety standards; disputes over minimum wage and child labor standards would be referred to an Evaluation Committee of Experts (ECE) for recommendations. Cooperation on labor relations would be limited only to consultation and information sharing. The U.S. preference was that minimum wage, child labor, and labor relations standards be subject to the same enforcement mechanisms as health and safety standards. In a final bargain, Mexico agreed to subject child labor and minimum wage enforcement to the same dispute resolution process as health and safety, and to link its minimum wage to national productivity increases. The United States acceded to Mexico's wish that labor relations be exempt from any dispute resolution process.

In the final agreement, each partner retained full regulatory control to establish or modify its labor and employment standards. Through the NAALC, the partners cooperate on seven objectives, including improving working conditions and living standards and promoting eleven labor principles to protect, enhance, and enforce workers' basic rights. The partners agreed to six obligations that define effective enforcement and hold one another accountable through the mechanisms of consultation, evaluation, and dispute resolution. The obligations are non-voluntary (i.e., the governments cannot choose the areas of law to which they will apply) and enforceable by sanctions in only those three specific labor market areas (child labor, health and safety, and minimum wage).[25] The NAALC contains substantial references to improving the availability of information: "transparency" and "sunshine" are considered important features of the agreement and one's the trading partners claim will lead to real improvements.[26]

In summary, within the NAALC, trading partners are able to lower their standards by statutory change and did not agree to harmonization of their standards even at a minimum level. The process reflects the trading partners' ability to agree to solve labor disputes only through informal coordination and to confront conflicts through dialogue and consultation, initially at the NAO and later at the ministerial level. Due to divergent preferences, the labor market issues that may be raised at subsequent levels of review is limited and was designed to exclude the first three labor principles (freedom of association and protection of the right to organize, the right to bargain collectively, and the right to strike) so as not to interfere with national autonomy and comparative advantage, and more important, to prevent coalitions of free trade opponents from using the process for protectionist purposes.[27]

MERCOSUR AND ASEAN

Similar to NAFTA, MERCOSUR (the Common Market of the Southern Cone) and ASEAN (Association of Southeast Asian Nations) represent new and evolving regional arrangements. The 1991 Treaty of Asuncion launched the process for MERCOSUR, with Brazil, Argentina, Uruguay, and Paraguay as its members, nations (and regions within) at different levels of economic development. MERCOSUR envisioned that a free trade area for labor, services, goods, and capital would be established by 1994, but as of 1995, the region had organized itself as an imperfect customs union in which members have a common external tariff covering imports from third countries, with largely tariff-free trading among themselves. Members agreed to a five-year program to perfect the customs union, standardizing trade-related rules and procedures and moving toward harmonization of economic policies.[28]

Brazil, the most advanced economy, and Uruguay advocated for a Social Charter of Fundamental Rights, and trade unions from the four countries, organized as the Southern Cone Central Labor Coordination, fought to have negotiations opened to worker organizations. Employer groups remained resistant to harmonization of labor standards. In response to political demands from labor groups, members created a tripartite 1992 MERCOSUR Working Group on Labor Relations, Employment and Security. While the 1994 Protocol of Ouro Preto established a permanent institutional structure for MERCOSUR, the governments at first rejected demands for a social charter with enforceable labor rights. Instead, members created an Economic and Social Consultative Forum in which business, labor, and other sectors can make only non-binding recommendations to governments on labor rights and standards.

In December 1998, members adopted a Social and Labor Declaration, responding to pressures that integration could not be restricted to economic and commercial areas. While the declaration does not provide for uniform regional standards, members commit to promoting *principles* through national legislation and practice as well as through collective agreement and conventions. The declaration's twenty-five articles are grouped into three broad categories dealing with individual rights, collective rights of employers and workers (i.e., freedom of association, collective bargaining, strikes), and procedures addressing implementation and follow-up. A tripartite Social and Labor Commission promotes implementation but has no sanction authority (OECD 2000).[29] In summary, the member agreed to respect a minimum level of worker rights, mainly those that emerged from the 1998 ILO Declaration of Fundamental Rights.

Similarly, ASEAN joined the regionalism tends when in 1992 these nations agreed to implement a free trade area (AFTA) by 2007 (Lawrence 1996). The members have been unwilling to transfer any authority to regional institutions: there are no central monitoring or third party enforcement mechanisms (Mattli 1999). East Asian nations originally formed ASEAN as a political association, with relatively few programs designed to promote intra-ASEAN trade. With the exception of Singapore, the economies of the nations are very similar: there is no regional "leader," little scope for mutually beneficial exchange, and only weak demand for deeper integration. By 1999, ASEAN encompassed all ten countries of Southeast Asia by admitting Cambodia (Brunei Darussalam in 1984, Vietnam in 1995, and Laos and Myanmar in 1997). Although all are export oriented, the nations have small shares of their trade with one another.

Despite limited intra-ASEAN trade, members agreed to coordinate on labor affairs with the 1976 Declaration of the ASEAN Concord.[30] The First Meeting of the ASEAN Labor Ministers introduced an Ad-Hoc Committee to examine areas of informal cooperation in labor and manpower policy. The declaration noted that coordination be undertaken "with emphasis on the well being of the low-income group and of the rural population, through the expansion of opportunities for productive employment with fair remuneration." At the sixth summit in December 1998, members responded to domestic pressures and formally recognized that the financial crisis had a social dimension, and at the 1999 Meeting of ASEAN Labor Ministers, they agreed "to share and exchange best practices" in developing social protection and social security systems; promote tripartite cooperation through increased consultation between social partners and strengthen tripartite institutions and mediation/consultation mechanisms; and enhance the capacity to design *active* labor market policies and retraining.[31]

At the ASEAN+3 Summit (Brunei Darussalam, Cambodia, China, Indonesia, Japan, Korea, the Lao People's Democratic Republic, Malaysia, Myanmar, Philippines, Singapore, Thailand, and Vietnam), members acknowledged, with the 1999 Joint Statement on East Asia Cooperation, the importance of "social and human resources development for the sustained growth of East Asia by alleviating economic and social disparities within and between nations."[32] At the May 2001 ASEAN Labor Meetings, the members, fearful that the low labor cost comparative advantage they enjoyed was being eroded by new economies, stressed the need for coordination on human capital issues. For the most part, ASEAN cooperation on labor markets is limited only to sharing information and coordinating "active" labor market policy, such as human capital investment. With the rapid integration of ASEAN in the Free Trade Area (AFTA), the Investment Area (AIA) and the Framework Agreement on Services (AFA), members agreed to develop a technical assistance program for Cambodia, Laos, Myanmar, and Vietnam (CLMV) to help these countries to integrate into ASEAN. Similar to structural funds in the EU, technical assistance could be interpreted as an effort to deal with regional disparities and encourage economic growth as well as social progress without resorting to any form of harmonization.

THE WTO/ILO

From 1947 to 1994, GATT (General Agreement on Trade and Tariffs) was the forum for negotiating lower customs duty rates and other trade barriers; since 1995, the updated GATT has become the WTO's umbrella agreement for trade in goods. Members are required to negotiate the reduction of tariffs, eliminate nontariff barriers, and refrain from discriminatory treatment. The WTO is the primary arena for negotiating and settling disputes. The GATT/WTO system has remained largely free of labor standards; the sole provision is one on prison labor in GATT Article XX(e). The original International Trade Organization (ITO) Charter has an Article (VII) on labor standards, which states, "all countries have a common interest in the achievement and maintenance of fair labor standards related to productivity." That is, rather than through harmonization, national efforts to raise domestic standards will be linked to productivity increases.

In the 1990s, the issue of trade and labor linkage led to intense political conflict among the WTO's 130 member nations. Since the 1994 Uruguay Round, there have been pressures from advanced economies such as the United States, Canada, and the EU member states (and demand from labor groups within them) for "social clauses" in trade agreements. At the signing of the treaty that formed the WTO, the Ministerial Conference of the 1994 Marrakesh GATT, the Conference Chairman reported no unanimity among member nations. The collective action problems of so many member nations with different preferences prevented the WTO from coming to any agreement on a trade and labor linkage.

The EU and U.S. preference was for the WTO to address core labor standards. At the WTO's General Council session, which preceded the Seattle Ministerial Conference, the United States proposed a WTO Working Group on Trade and Labor, and the EU pushed for a joint WTO/ILO Standing Working Forum on trade, globalization, and labor issues. Canada proposed a WTO working group to report on the relationships among appropriate trade, developmental, social, and environmental choices members faced in adjusting to globalization (ILO 2000). Members were able to agree in the 1996 Singapore Declaration only to a set of principles, including: respect core labor standards; support the ILO; affirm that trade helps promote higher standards; oppose the use of standards for protectionist purposes; and acknowledge that the comparative advantage of countries—particularly low-wage developing countries—must in no way be put into question.

The official 1999 WTO Ministerial Conference agenda did not include labor standards, but this became again the main conflict between developed and developing nations, dominating the WTO's agenda. The United States warned "that trade liberalization can occur only with domestic political support; that support will surely erode if we cannot address the concerns of working people and demonstrate that trade is a path to tangible prosperity."[33] In contrast, developing nations, such as Singapore, Pakistan, and Mexico, saw a strategic trade and labor linkage as a disguised instrument of protectionism among advanced nations. Countries such as Hong Kong (China), Morocco, Malaysia, Nigeria, Botswana, Panama, Nicaragua, and Zimbabwe argued that bringing labor standards into the WTO would undermine the comparative advantage of low-wage countries. The WTO members could only agree to issue a joint statement: "We renew our commitment to the observance of internationally recognized core labor standards. We believe that economic growth and development fostered by increased trade and further trade liberalization contribute to the promotion of these standards." Thus, the official WTO position was "that the WTO and ILO will continue their existing collaboration."

Most of the 135 WTO nations are also ILO members. Within the ILO, international labor standards are subject to direct approval by 174 member nations.[34] The ILO can only encourages voluntary adherence in three ways: 1) defining rights through national adoption of ILO conventions and recommendations; 2) enforcing rights by means of international monitoring and supervision (rather than by trade sanctions); and 3) assisting in implementing measures through technical cooperation and advisory services. The ILO adopts standards with a two-thirds vote, and delegates are obligated to bring an adopted convention recommendation before their domestic legislatures within a year. By ratifying, members agree to modify their standards to comply with the provisions and are required to report annually on compliance.

In the 1950s and 1960s, the majority of UN and ILO members shifted from Europe to developing nations, mainly from Africa and Asia. Many were confronting major socioeconomic problems in dismantling colonialism, and the ILO shifted away from harmonizing standards and toward technical assistance (Rubio 1998). In the 1970s, both more- and less- developed nations struggled with domestic problems of inflation, unemployment, and slow economic growth. Political conflict emerged within the national tripartite delegations as well as among the member nations themselves. Labor delegates have had political and economic incentives to propose labor standards. Over time, this led to an oversupply of conventions, representing the demands of labor groups rather than the preferences of nations themselves, and many other nations refused to ratify them. They viewed regulatory harmonization as unresponsive to changing global and economic conditions. The proliferation of labor standards, despite the increasing heterogeneity of economic development among members, rendered their adoption impractical for many nations, and members began actually to denounce existing mechanisms (Johnson 1998).

By the 1990s, ILO and its members began to confront the overproduction of inflexible and uniform standards. In 1994, the ILO set up a Working Party on the Social Dimension of Globalization, and in a 1997 Declaration, the ILO announced that it would promote only fundamental labor rights. The 1998 ILO Declaration on Fundamental Principles and Rights at Work formally encourages members to adhere to four fundamental principles on—freedom of association and recognition of the right of collective bargaining; the elimination of forced or compulsory labor; the abolition of child labor; and the elimination of employment and occupational discrimination (Coxson 1999). In 1999, ILO also adopted a new fundamental convention to ban the worst forms of child labor. The declaration requires all 174 ILO members, even if they have not ratified the particular conventions, to respect and to promote the core principles. The vote for adoption of the declaration was 85%, with no negative votes, but it was not unanimously supported at the time. Of the nineteen governments that abstained in the voting, two have now ratified conventions that make up fundamental principles and rights (Egypt and Indonesia) and fourteen others supplied follow-up reports under the declaration (ILO 2000).

Many members viewed this as an important agreement on common principles and as a way to reduce political pressure on the WTO to link workers' rights with trade sanctions. Although its impact is hard to assess, the 1998 declaration is only a mechanism to obligate nations to report on "where they are" in relation to these core principles and rights, to set their own baselines against which to measure progress, and to describe efforts within their national labor market regimes to promote and ensure respect for these principles. The 174 ILO members, even if they have not formally ratified the conventions, only have an affirmative obligation to respect and promote the fundamental rights and principles.[35] In terms of follow-up, the overall report rate was 55.7% (ILO 2000). In fact, only six governments reported on progress before the November 1999 deadline. This suggests the difficulties in achieving full respect for the principles and rights (the United States and India with freedom of association; China, Nepal, Sri Lanka, and Vietnam with compulsory labor; Guinea-Bissau and Mexico with abolition of child labor; and Kenya with gender discrimination in employment (ILO 2000). Similar to EU structural funds, technical assistance to developing countries has been characterized as a mechanism to facilitate adoption of higher standards without sacrificing the growth and efficiency gains from trade.

CONCLUSION: NO RACE, BUT A "FLOOR" UNDER COMPETITION

This essay concludes that nation's are not in a race to the bottom or top in labor standards: nation's seek to protect their comparative advantage and mutual gain from trade, but are also responding to the real and perceived distributional concerns with minimum agreements on rules and norms. This essay highlights the varying political responses and impact of one mechanism of globalization—labor agreements—on domestic standards. With to divergent preferences (and underlying heterogeneities in labor market regimes and costs), and decision rules that prevent powerful nations from unilaterally imposing their standards on other countries, and, some form of minimum standards, norms or principles or better enforcement of existing domestic standards has become the consensus outcome across the cases. Thus, the result of globalization is neither a race to the bottom nor a race to the top, but a minimum "floor" of rules under new forms of regional and international competition.

In summary, the EU, the most integrated regional area, harmonizes minimum standards on *specific* labor market issues while allowing collective bargaining and pay determination to remain nationally specific. In another regional areas, NAFTA does not harmonize standards among countries but provides for oversight and enforcement of existing domestic standards. MERCOSUR promotes "core" labor principles according to national legislation and practice as well as collective agreements and conventions while the ASEAN nations agree only to share information and exchange best practices. The WTO does not include a social clause, failure to comply with which would subject members to trade sanctions, but deem ILO voluntary core principles and conventions appropriate.

Standard neoclassical economic conceptions of trade and competition predict that over time the costs of production will equalize across nations. Thus, there is a theoretical expectation for convergence (Berger and Dore 1992). However, actual events have called this conventional economic view into question. Different national labor market regimes appear to be experiencing similar external economic influences but are not necessarily converging. Different political systems are responding in different ways, perhaps resulting in greater, or at least continued, regulatory diversity. The result has been some minimum uniformity on rules and principles in the context of institutional diversity: national political systems continue to determine the nature and character of labor standards. Despite increased integration, nations indeed appear to maintain distinct labor standards if they are willing to bear the costs.

Coordination of minimum rules and norms is attractive as a model for regulatory cooperation because it allows governments to deal with domestic political opposition without suppressing regional and international initiatives toward greater economic openness. These labor agreements serve a purpose for governments, enabling them to maximize the benefits of economic openness, and minimize the political costs (and economic risks) of deeper integration. Minimum standards and principles, and information exchanges and sharing of best practices, have become important means of coordinating and channeling the interactions among diverse labor market regimes (Adnett 1993). This represents a move toward convergence of minimum standards and goals rather than an upward or downward harmonization of standards.

Because of increased competition from low-wage regions, the governments of advanced-economies face adjustments (Agell 2000). As a consequence, many fear, that sooner or later, their governments will have to move toward greater labor market flexibility, relax strict job security laws, abolish the minimum wage, and implement measures that restrict the influence of unions. However, because of greater uncertainty due to globalization, there is increasing evidence that voters might be perfectly willing to pay a higher price for a given labor market or social protection. Economists and political scientists have long suggested that the vulnerability of an open economy provides governments with strong incentives to mitigate economic (and political) risks. Societies seem to demand (and receive) an expanded government role as the price for accepting larger doses of external economic risk (Rodrik 1998). [36] Increased openness may lead to increased institutional involvement in the labor market, thus increasing the demand for labor market and social protection at the very time that it increases the costs of providing them.

This essay concludes that differences in standard of living and real wages between developed and developing nations, which provide much of the aggregate gain from integration, has generated political demands and popular backlash against a race to the bottom outcome. Large discrepancies in labor standards can undermine the legitimacy of free trade and make it harder to maintain domestic consensus on trade policy in advanced economies. Thus, domestic politics might allow the benefits from trade and factor mobility to be fully achieved only if nations at different stages of economic development confront the distributional implications. As the real or perceived level of economic risk that workers face rises, political demands will likely increase, and economic openness could actually lead governments to seek new forms of cooperation on rules and norms that govern working conditions and industrial relations. Rather than a race to the bottom or the top, integration appears to result in an incremental march toward common regional and international minimum rules and norms.

Daniel Gitterman is an Assistant Professor of Public Policy at the University of North Carolina at Chapel Hill.

Notes

1. The process of social dumping can occur by the displacement of high-cost producers by low-cost ones from nations in which compensation costs required by regulation are lower; increasing pressure on firms in high cost nations to relocate, to strengthen their bargaining power, and to exert downward pressure on wages and working conditions; and to pursue low-wage and anti-union strategies (Mosley 1990).

2. Economists investigate market relationships among goods and factors of production within a region, and assume perfect mobility of factor inputs and goods and services. These explanations are positive theories of welfare gains and losses.

3. Import competing and exporting-firms in the high-standard nation may respond by undertaking capital-labor substitution or depending on their market power, by depressing wages. Exporting firms may relocate some of their production to foreign locations with lower standards (Brown, Deardorff, and Stern 1996).

4. Brown, Deardoff, Stern (1996) suggest that a nation's position in international trade, as either a net exporter or net importer of those goods most affected by labor standards, will determine whether they have preferences for high or low standards.

5. Because developed countries tend to specialize in capital-intensive goods, the welfare of workers in labor-intensive industries may increase—even though the welfare of consumers in developed countries will decline if standards are enforced (Krueger 1996; Brown, Deardorff and Stern 1993).

6. As Midford (1993) warns, although the standard three-factor model has explanatory power for less-developed economies, it is often confounded by the complex division of labor found in more developed countries. When an economy becomes more complex, the division of labor becomes finer and large aggregate groups such as labor, land, and capital lose their meaning. Thus, labor cannot be conceived of as homogenous, and changing exposure to trade

will affect the position of some labor differently than others.

7. The complexity of domestic interests and political demands within nations depend on the direct and indirect costs that firms incur in order to employ workers as well as from national regulations that constrain employers' prerogatives in making decisions about compensation and working conditions (Lange 1992).

8. Negative externalities occur when activities in one nation produce consequences that spill over across borders and affect other nations.

9. EU decision-making is as follows: the Commission proposes legislation and the Council of Ministers disposes it. The Parliament has a consultative role. With measures that require unanimity, the Commission formulates legislation and submits to the Council and the European Parliament. The Parliament debates the proposal and will propose amendments via an opinion transmitted to the Commission. The Commission may accept the recommendation before passing it on to the Council. The Council, free to adopt or further amend, must pass it by unanimous vote—giving a single member veto authority.

10. The labor market provisions focused on mobility (articles 48, 52, and 59), training (article 128), and equal opportunity for men and women (article 119). The Treaty also created a European Social Fund (articles 123–128) to make the employment of workers easier, increasing their geographical and occupational mobility within the EC (Teague and Grahl 1989). Article 118 promoted "close cooperation " in matters relating to employment, labor law, and working conditions, vocational training, social security, occupational health and safety, and the right of association and collective bargaining (Lodge 1990).

11. The citizens of Spain and Portugal, admitted to the EC in 1986, fully received these rights in 1993.

12. A 1975 Equal Pay Directive required equal pay for work of equal value and abolished discriminatory clauses in collective agreements; a 1976 Equal Treatment Directive forbade gender discrimination in hiring, vocational training, promotion, and working conditions; a 1978 Social Security Directive required no discrimination against women in terms of contributing to or receiving benefits; a 1978 Collective Redundancies Directive required firms to provide advance notification of mass layoffs; a 1979 Transfers of Undertaking Directive safeguarded employee rights in such layoffs, established an information and consultation procedure, and ensured that workers who, as a result of a closure or merger, would carry the rights and obligations contained in previous contract; and a 1980 Insolvency Directive guaranteed payment of wages and other employee claims in the event of firm insolvency.

13. Employers in the Northern group—Germany, the Netherlands, Belgium, and Denmark—are constrained by rules governing external flexibility, such as their freedom to hire and fire and to employ a wide variety of labor contracts. Employers in the Anglo-Saxon group—the UK and Ireland—have a high degree of external flexibility, with very few constraints on their power to hire and fire and to employ workers on fixed-term or temporary contracts. Employers in the Mediterranean group—France, Italy, Greece, Portugal, and Spain—have neither a high level of external flexibility nor high

internal flexibility (Rhodes 1994).

14. QMV requires a minimum of 54 of the 76 weighted votes cast by representatives in the Council.

15. The EU crafted hybrid directives, combining labor market directives with what were strictly health and safety protections, in order to exert authority under Article 118(A).

16. The Charter set out 47 proposals in 13 chapters, including 17 directives—10 related to worker health and safety (Teague and Grahl 1991).

17. These included: freedom of movement; employment and renumeration; improvement of working and living conditions; social protection; freedom of association and collective bargaining; vocational training; equal treatment for men and women; information, consultation, and participation for workers; health and safety at the workplace; protection of children and adolescents; and the elderly and disabled.

18. The members excluded social security and social protection for workers along with protection of redundant workers, representation and collective defense of workers, and conditions of employment for third-country nationals from QWV.

19. These rights included promotion of employment, improved living and working conditions, proper social protection, dialogue between management and labor, the development of human resources with a view to lasting employment and the combating of exclusion, The Amsterdam Treaty added equality between men and women to the list of Community objectives (Article 2 of the EC Treaty), and a new Article 141 of the Treaty lends greater support to equal treatment of men and women and to equal opportunities, whereas the former Article 119, was confined to issues of equal pay for the two sexes for the same work.

20. The following were excluded: social security and social protection of workers; protection of workers whose employment contract is terminated; representation and collective defense of the interests of workers and employers, including codetermination; conditions of employment for non-EC country nationals legally residing in Community territory; and financial contributions for promotion of employment and job creation.

21. For example, in 1991 the Council adopted a directive on an employer's obligation to inform workers on the conditions applicable to the employment contract or relationship, and directives on fixed-duration or temporary employment relationships. Subsequently, the Council adopted directives on the protection of pregnant women, young people at work, the posting of workers, and the implementation of the framework agreement between the social partners on part-time work. In 1996, the Council adopted a directive on parental leave, which was the first to implement a European-level framework agreement among the Social Partners. In 1997, the Council adopted a directive (97/81/EC) implementing an agreement on part-time work. In 1999, the social partners concluded an agreement on fixed-term contracts (99/70/EC), later amended to cover sectors and activities originally excluded. In 2000, the Council adopted an anti-discrimination directive and a general framework for equal treatment in employment, also aimed at combating discrimination based on religion or belief, disability, age or sexual orientation (2000/78/EC).

22. Guidelines would be translated in National Action Plans for

Employment (NAPs) by members, then analyzed the by the Commission and the Council, and whose results would help reshape the guidelines and prove country-specific recommendations on employment policies.

23. Its provisions are based on the rights and freedoms recognized by the European Convention on Human Rights, the constitutional traditions of the EU Member States, the Council of Europe's Social Charter, the Community Charter of Fundamental Social Rights, and other international conventions to which the EU or its members are parties. See, http://europa.eu.int/comm/justice_home/unit/charte/en/charter02.html.

24. NAFTA was negotiated in two installments: the commercial negotiations (June 1991 to August 1992) and then the supplemental negotiations (February to August 1993).

25. Each partner commits to promote compliance and enforce its labor and employment law by appointing and training inspectors, monitoring compliance and investigating suspected violations, seeking assurance of voluntary compliance, requiring record keeping and reporting, encouraging the establishment of worker-management committees to, providing or encouraging mediation, conciliation, and arbitration services, and initiating proceedings to seek appropriate sanctions or violations (http://www.naalc.org/index.htm).

26. Since January 1994, twenty-four submissions have been filed under NAALC. Sixteen were filed with the U.S. NAO, of which fourteen involved allegations against Mexico, and two against Canada. Five were filed with the Mexican NAO and involved the U.S. Three submissions have been filed in Canada, one against Mexico and two against the U.S. Thirteen of the sixteen submissions filed with the U.S. NAO involved issues of freedom of association; others focus on the illegal use of child labor; on pregnancy-based gender discrimination; on minimum employment standards, on issues of safety and health, on compensation in cases of occupational illnesses and injuries. There have been six Ministerial Implementation Agreements where the trading partners have agreed to consult further on a range of labor and employment issues. For more, see http://www.dol.gov/dol/ilab/public/programs/nao/minagreemt.htm.

27. In a final agreement, the trading partners created domestic entities, the NAOs and National and Governmental Advisory Committees. The NAOs consult and exchange information on labor matters, and each partner has autonomy to determine the functions and powers of its NAO The dispute resolution process is hierarchical, insofar as the lower-level units must respond to those above, and the Ministerial Council possesses ultimate authority. The CLC, the regional entity, divides responsibility between Ministerial Council and the Secretariat. An NAO or a government can trigger ministerial consultation.

28. A Common Market Group (CMG), composed of four permanent members and the ministries of foreign affairs, the economy, and national central bankers, enacts resolutions, intended for incorporation into national law as well. MERCOSUR resembles the EU in its reliance on foundational treaties and protocols for its design and objectives, and institutions and laws to attain those objectives. Decision authority resides with the individual

governments rather than a EU like Commission.

29. See, http://www.mercosur.org.uy/espanol/sinf/varios/sociolaboral.htm.

30. See, www.asesansec.org for full document under "Basic Documents."

31. See, htp://www.aseansec.org/print.asp?file = /function/soc_reco/sreco00.htm).

32. See, Joint Communique, the Fifteenth ASEAN Labor Ministers Meeting, May 2001, Malaysia (www.asesansec.org).

33. Statement by Charlene Barshefsky, Acting U.S. Trade Representative, Ministerial Conference, Singapore, December 9–13, 1996, World Trade WT/MIN (96)/ST/5, December 9, 1996 (96–5176).

34. Membership in the ILO is closely associated with that of the UN. Under the ILO Constitution, the U.S. is one of ten nations of "chief industrial importance" with permanent representation on the Governing Board. The U.S. withdrew its membership in 1978, and rejoined the ILO in 1980 (ILO 1997).

35. The follow-up mechanism is in addition to the supervisory mechanisms established by the ILO constitution for the application of ratified conventions as well as the special Freedom of Association procedure, which already applied to non-ratifying states (ILO 2000; European Commission 2001).

36. For example, Garrett (1998) suggests that a more generous social safety may actually strengthen the ability of governments to adjust to rapidly changing market conditions. Bates, Brock, and Tiefenthaler (1991) report that the greater the social insurance program mounted by a nation, the less likely the government is to block free trade.

References

Addison, John T. and W. Stanley Siebert. 1991. "The Social Charter of the European Community: Evolution and Controversies." *Industrial and Labor Relations Review* 44 (4): 597–625.

———. 1994. "Recent Developments in Social Policy in the New European Union." *Industrial and Labor Relations Review* 48 (1): 5–27.

Adnett, Nick. 1993. "The Social Charter: Unnecessary Regulation or Pre-Requisite for Convergence?" *British Review of Economic Issues* 15 (36): 63–79.

———. 1995. "Social Dumping and European Economic Integration." *Journal of European Social Policy* 1:1–12.

———. 1996. *European Labor Markets: Analysis and Policy.* London: Longman.

Agell, Jonas. 1999. "On the Benefits from Rigid Labor Markets: Norms, Market Failures and Social Insurance." *The Economic Journal* 109 (February): F 143–164.

Alber, Jens and Guy Standing. 2000. "Social Dumping, Catch-up, or

Convergence? Europe in a Comparative Global Context." *Journal of European Social Policy* 10(2): 99–119.

Andersen, Torben M., Niels Haldrup, and Jan Rose Sorensen. 2000. "Labor Market Implications of EU Product Market Integration." *Economic Policy* (April): 107–133.

Baldry, Christopher. 1994. "Convergence in Europe—a Matter of Perspective." *Industrial Relations Journal* 25 (2): 96–109.

Bates, Robert H., Philip Brock, and Jill Tiefenthaler. 1991. "Risk and Trade Regimes: Another Exploration." *International Organization* 45 (1): 1–18.

Bazen, Stephen and Benhayoun, Gilbert. 1992. "Low Pay and Wage Regulation in the European Community." *British Journal of Industrial Relations* 30 (4): 623–638.

Bercussion, Brian and Jan Jacob Van Dijk. 1995. "The Implementation of the Protocol and Agreement on Social Policy of the Treaty on European Union." *International Journal of Comparative Labour Law and Industrial Relations* 10 (1): 3–30.

Bhagwati, Jagdish. 1994. "Policy Perspectives and Future Directions: A View from Academia." In *International Labor Standards and Global Economic Integration: Proceedings of a Symposium.* Washington, D.C.: U.S. Department of Labor, Bureau of International Labor Affairs.

Bierman, Leonard and Rafael Gaely. 1995. "The North American Agreement on Labor Cooperation: A New Frontier in North American Labor Relations." *Connecticut Journal of International Law* 10:533–569.

Black, Ian. 2000. "UK Agrees to Restricted EU Rights Charter." *The Guardian,* October 3.

Brown, Drusilla K., Alan V. Deardorff, and Robert M. Stern. 1996. "International Labor Standards and Trade: A Theoretical Analysis." In Jagdish Bhagwati and Robert E. Hudec, eds., *Fair Trade Harmonization: Prerequisites for Free Trade?* pp. 227–280. Cambridge: MIT Press.

Cameron, Maxwell A. and Brian W. Tomlin. 2000. *The Making of NAFTA: How the Deal was Done.* Ithaca: Cornell University Press.

Commission of the European Communities. 2001. Communication from the Commission to the Council, the European Parliament and the Economic and Social Committee, Promoting Core Labour Standards and Improving Social Governance in the Context of

Globalization. COM (2001) 416 final.

———. 2001. Commission Communication on the Charter of Fundamental Rights of the European Union. COM (2000) 559 final.

———. 2001. Communication from the Commission to the Council, the European Parliament and the Social Committee and The Committee of the Regions, Strengthening the Local Dimension of the European Employment Strategy. COM (2001) 629 final.

———. 2001. Communication from the Commission on the Legal Nature of the Charter of Fundamental Rights of the European Union. COM (2000) 644 final.

———. 2001. Council Recommendation on the Implementation of the Member States' Employment Policies. COM (2000).

Compa, Lance. 1993. "Labor Rights and Labor Standards in International Trade." *Law and Policy in International Business* 25 (1): 165–191.

Cordova, Efren. 1993. "Some Reflections on the Overproduction of International Labor Standards." *Comparative Labor Law Journal* 14 (2): 138–162.

Coxson, Christopher R. 1999. "The 1998 ILO Declaration on Fundamental Principles and Rights at Work: Promoting Labor Law Reforms through the ILO as an Alternative to Imposing Coercive Trade Sanctions." *Dickinson Journal of International Law* 17 (3): 469–504.

de Wet, Erika. 1995. "Labor Standards in the Globalized Economy: The Inclusion of a Social Clause in the GATT/WTO." *Human Rights Quarterly* 17/3 (August): 443–462.

Ehrenberg, Ronald. 1994. *Labor Markets and Integrating National Economies.* Washington, D.C.: Brookings Institution.

Erickson, Christopher and Sarosh Kuruvilla. 1994. "Labor Costs and the Social Dumping Debate in the European Union." *Industrial and Labor Relations Review* 48 (1): 28–47.

Erickson, Christopher L. and Daniel J.B. Mitchell. 1998. "Labor Standards and Trade Agreements: US Experience." *Comparative Labor Law and Policy Journal* 19 (2): 145–183.

European Commission, Directorate-General for Employment, Industrial Relations and Social Affairs. 1999. "Affirming Fundamental Rights in the European Union: Time to Act." Report of the Expert Group on Fundamental Rights.

Falkner, Gerda. 1998. EU Social Policy in the 1990s: Toward a Corporatist Policy Community. London: Routledge.

Financial Times. 2000. "Europe's Rights" (editorial). October 3.

Fletcher, Martin. 2000a. "Britain Fights to Limit European Rights Charter." The Times, September 25.

———. 2000b. "Britain Approves Charter of Rights." The Times, October 3.

Freeman, Richard. 1994. "Comments." In Roland Ehrenberg, ed., Labor Markets and Integrating National Economies. pp. 107–110. Washington, D.C.: Brookings Institution.

Freeman, Richard B. 1995. "Are Your Wages Set in Beijing?" Journal of Economic Perspectives 9 (3): 15–32.

Frieden, Jeffry A. and Ronald Rogowski. 1996. "The Impact of the International Economy on National Politics: An Analytical Overview." In Robert O. Keohane and Helen V. Milner, eds., Internationalization and Domestic Politics. New York: Cambridge University Press.

Friedholm, Greg A. 1999. "The United Kingdom and European Union Labor Policy: Inevitable Participation and the Social Chapter Opportunity." Boston College International and Comparative Law Review XXII (1): 229–248.

Garvey, Jack I. 1997. "AFTA After NAFTA: Regional Trade Blocs and the Propagation of Environmental and Labor Standards." Berkeley Journal of International Law 15 (2): 245–274.

Gatsios, K. and P. Seabright. 1989. "Regulation in the European Community." Oxford Review of Economic Policy 5 (2): 37–60.

Geyer, Robert. R. 2000. Exploring European Social Policy. Cambridge: Polity Press.

Gitterman, Daniel P. 2000. "Competition or Re-regulation: Economic Integration and Labor Market Protection in the European Union." Center for German and European Studies, University of California, Berkeley, Working Paper 2.73 (May).

Grahl, John and Paul Teague. 1992. "Integration Theory and European Labor Markets." British Journal of Industrial Relations 30 (4): 515–527.

Hansson, Gote. 1983. Social Clauses and International Trade. New York: St. Martin's Press.

Hargreaves, Sylvia. 1997. "Social Europe After Maastricht: Is the

United Kingdom Really Opted Out?" *The Journal of Social Welfare and Family Law* 19(1): 1–15.

Hepple, Bob. 1997. "New Approaches to International Labor Regulation." *Industrial Law Journal* 26 (4): 353–366.

International Labor Organization. 1997. *The ILO and Global Change, 1990–1997*. Washington D.C.: Washington Branch Office.

———. 2000. *Working Party on the Social Dimension of the Liberalization of International Trade*. GB.277/WP/SDL/1. Geneva: ILO.

———. 2000. Review of Annual Reports under the Follow-up of the ILO Declaration on Fundamental Principles and Rights at Work. Geneva: ILO.

Johnson, Brian S. 1998. "Ensuring Equality: Pursuing Implementation of the Equal Pay Principle Via the Institutions of the European Union, the North American Agreement on Labor Cooperation, and Corporate Codes of Conduct." *Virginia Journal of International Law* 38: 849–876.

Kluth, Michael F. 1998. *The Political Economy of Social Europe: Understanding Labor Market Integration in the European Union*. New York: St. Martin's.

Krueger, Alan B. 1996. "Observations on International Labor Standards and Trade." NBER Working Paper 5632 (June).

———. 2000. "From Bismarck to Maastricht: The March to European Union." NBER Working Paper 7456 (January).

Lange, Peter. 1992. "The Politics of the Social Dimension." In Alberta Sbragia, ed., *Euro-Politics*. pp. 225–256. Washington, D.C.: Brookings Institution.

———. 1993. "Maastricht and the Social Protocol: Why Did They Do It?" *Politics and Society* 21(1): 5–36.

Lawrence, Robert Z. 1996. *Regionalism, Multilateralism, and Deeper Integration*. Washington, D.C.: Brookings Institution.

Lodge, Julie. 1990. "Social Europe." *Journal of European Integration* 13 (2–3): 135–150.

Makus, Keith E. 1997. "Should Core Labor Standards Be Imposed Through International Trade Policy?" Policy Research Working Paper 1817. The World Bank Development Research Group (August).

Mayer, Frederick W. 1992. "Managing Domestic-Differences in International Negotiations: The Strategic Use of Internal Side-

Payments." *International Organization* 46 (4): 793–818.

Mayer, Frederick. 1998. *Interpreting NAFTA: The Science and Art of Political Analysis.* New York: Columbia University Press.

McGlynn, Clare. 1998. "An Exercise in Futility: The Practical Effects of the Social Policy Opt-Out." *North Ireland Legal Quarterly* 49 (1) (Spring): 60–73.

McGuinness, Michael J. 1994. "The Protection of Labor Rights in North America: a Commentary on the North American Agreement on Labor Cooperation." *Stanford Journal of International Law* 30/2 (Summer): 579–596.

Midford, Paul. 1993. "International Trade and Domestic Politics: Improving on Rogowski's Model of Political Alignments." *International Organization* 47 (4): 535–564.

Moravcsik, Andrew. 1998. *The Choice for Europe.* Ithaca: Cornell University Press.

Mosley, Hugh. 1990. "The Social Dimension of European Integration." *International Labour Review* 129 (2): 147–164.

OECD. 1996. *Trade, Employment and Labour Standards.* Paris: Organisation for Economic Cooperation and Development.

———. 2000. *International Trade and Core Labor Standards.* Paris: Organisation for Economic Cooperation and Development.

Otero, Joaquin. 1995. "The North American Agreement on Labor Cooperation: An Assessment of Its First Year's Implementation." *Columbia Journal of Transnational Law* 33 (3): 637–662.

Pomeroy, Laura Okin. 1996. "The Labor Side Agreement Under the NAFTA: Analysis of Its Failure to Include Strong Enforcement Provisions and Recommendations for Future Labor Agreements Negotiated with Developing Countries." *George Washington Journal of International Law & Economics* 29 (3): 796–801.

Rhodes, Martin. 1991. "The Social Dimension of the Single European Market: National versus Transnational Regulation." *European Journal of Political Research* 19:245–280.

———. 1992. "The Future of the Social Dimension: Labor Market Regulation in Post-1992 Europe." *Journal of Common Market Studies* 30 (1): 23–51.

———. 1993. "The Social Dimension After Maastricht: Setting a New Agenda for the Labor Market." *International Journal of Comparative*

Labor Law and Industrial Relations (Winter): 297–325.

Rice-Oxley, Mark. 1997. "U.K. to Sign on to EU Labor Law Pact: Social Charter Adherence to Boost Business Cost." *The National Law Journal* 19 (43): A9.

Rodrik, Dana. 1996. "Labor Standards in International Trade: Do They Matter and What Do We Do About Them?" In Robert Lawrence et al., *Emerging Agenda for Global Trade: High Stakes for Developing Countries.* pp.35–79. Washington DC: Overseas Development Council Policy Essay (20).

———. 1998. "Why Do More Open Economies Have Bigger Governments?" *Journal of Political Economy* 106 (5): 997–1032.

———. 1999. "Globalization and Labor, or: If Globalization Is a Bowl of Cherries, Why

Are There so Many Glum Faces Around the Table?" In Richard Baldwin et al., *Market Integration, Regionalism, and the Global Economy.* pp.117–150. Cambridge, New York: Cambridge University Press.

Rogowski, Ronald. 1989. *Commerce and Coalitions: How Trade Affects Domestic Political Alignments.* Princeton: Princeton University Press.

Ross, George. 1995. "Assessing the Delors Era and Social Policy." In Stephen Leibfried and Paul Pierson, eds., *European Social Policy.* 357–388. Washington, D.C.: Brookings Institution.

Scharpf, Fritz W. 1997. "Balancing Positive and Negative Integration: The Regulatory Options for Europe." Max Planck Institute for the Study of Societies, MPIFG Working Paper 97/8.

Scharpf, Fritz. 1998. "Negative and Positive Integration in the Political Economy of European Welfare States." In Martin Rhodes and Yves Meny, eds., *The Future of European Welfare,* pp.155–177. New York: St. Martin's.

Silvia, Stephen J. 1991. "The Social Charter of the European Community: A Defeat for European Labor." *Industrial and Labor Relations Review* 44 (4): 626–643.

Spar, Deborah and David B. Yoffie. 2000. "A Race to the Bottom or Governance from the Top? In A. Praakash and J.A. Hart, eds., Coping with Globalization. London: Routledge.

Srinivasan, T. N. 1996. "International Trade and Labor Standards from an Economic Perspective." In Pitou van Dijck and Gerrit Farber, eds,. *Challenges in the New World Trade Organization.* Amsterdam: Kluwer Law International.

Swinnerton, Kenneth A. and Gregory K. Schoepfle. 1994. "Labor Standards in the Context of a Global Economy." *Monthly Labor Review* (September): 52–59.

Teague, Paul and John Grahl. 1989. "European Community Labour Market Policy: Present Scope and Future Direction." *Journal of European Integration* 13 (1): 55–73.

———. 1990. "1992 and the Emergence of a European Industrial Relations Area." *Journal of European Integration* 13 (2–3): 167–183.

———. 1991. "The European Community Social Charter and Labour Market Regulation." *Journal of Public Policy* 11 (2): 207–232.

———. 1992. "Constitution or Regime? The Social Dimension to the 1992 Project." *British Journal of Industrial Relations* 27 (3): 310–329.

Thyygesen, Niels, Yutaka Koasi, and Robert Z. Lawrence. 1996. *Globalization and Trilateral Labor Markets: Evidence and Implications.* New York: The Trilateral Commission.

Ulman, Lloyd, Barry Eichengreen, and William Dickens. 1993. "Labor and an Integrated Europe." In Lloyd Ulman, Barry Eichengreen, and William Dickens, eds., *Labor and an Integrated Europe.* pp.1–12. Washington, D.C.: Brookings Institution.

Van Wezel Stone, Katherine. 1995. "Labor and the Global Economy: Four Approaches to Transnational Labor Regulation." *Michigan Journal of International Law* 16:987–1028.

Williamson, Jeffrey G. "Globalization, Labor Markets, and Policy Backlash in the Past." *Journal of Economic Perspectives* 12 (4): 51–72.

Wood, Adrian. 1995. "How Trade Hurt Unskilled Workers." *Journal of Economic Perspectives* 9 (3): 57–80.

www.ingramcontent.com/pod-product-compliance
Lightning Source LLC
Chambersburg PA
CBHW030810280326
41926CB00085B/161